ACADEMIE DU VIN

· GUIDE TO ·

FRENCH WINES

ACADEMIE DU VIN
· *GUIDE TO* ·
FRENCH WINES

STEVEN SPURRIER

MACMILLAN PUBLISHING COMPANY
New York

MAXWELL MACMILLAN CANADA
Toronto

MAXWELL MACMILLAN INTERNATIONAL
New York Oxford Singapore Sydney

Macmillan Publishing Company
866 Third Avenue
New York, NY 10022

Maxwell Macmillan Canada, Inc.
1200 Eglinton Avenue East, Suite 200
Don Mills, Ontario M3C 3N1

Macmillan Publishing Company is part of the Maxwell Communication Group of Companies.

Library of Congress Catalog Card 91-39405

ISBN 0-02-613262-1

Macmillan books are available at special discounts for bulk purchases for sales promotions, premiums, fund-raising, or educational use. For details, contact:

Special Sales Director
Macmillan Publishing Company
866 Third Avenue
New York, NY 10022

10 9 8 7 6 5 4 3 2 1

Produced by Mandarin Offset Ltd
Printed in Hong Kong

Contents

Wine Regions of France

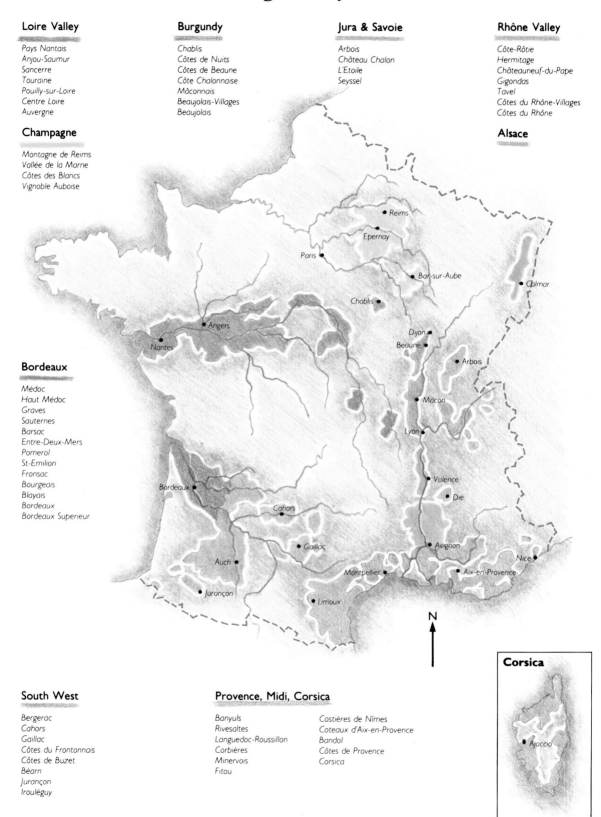

Loire Valley

Pays Nantais
Anjou-Saumur
Sancerre
Touraine
Pouilly-sur-Loire
Centre Loire
Auvergne

Champagne

Montagne de Reims
Vallée de la Marne
Côtes des Blancs
Vignoble Auboise

Burgundy

Chablis
Côtes de Nuits
Côtes de Beaune
Côte Chalonnaise
Mâconnais
Beaujolais-Villages
Beaujolais

Jura & Savoie

Arbois
Château Chalon
L'Etoile
Seyssel

Rhône Valley

Côte-Rôtie
Hermitage
Châteauneuf-du-Pape
Gigondas
Tavel
Côtes du Rhône-Villages
Côtes du Rhône

Alsace

Bordeaux

Médoc
Haut Médoc
Graves
Sauternes
Barsac
Entre-Deux-Mers
Pomerol
St-Emilion
Fronsac
Bourgeais
Blayais
Bordeaux
Bordeaux Supérieur

South West

Bergerac
Cahors
Gaillac
Côtes du Frontonnais
Côtes de Buzet
Béarn
Jurançon
Irouléguy

Provence, Midi, Corsica

Banyuls
Rivesaltes
Languedoc-Roussillon
Corbières
Minervois
Fitou

Costières de Nîmes
Coteaux d'Aix-en-Provence
Bandol
Côtes de Provence
Corsica

N

Corsica

Introduction

Today's wine drinker is living in a Golden Age. Never before – I said this in 1986 for the first edition of this book, and it is even more true in 1991 – have so many good wines been made, and more importantly, made available to the public. Wine is no longer hard to understand and hard to get: it is a part of everyday life. This book is a guide to the vast variety of wines in France.

France is the country with the widest range of fine wines in the world. French, or French-adopted grape varieties are planted in every country which produces wines of quality, and in most cases French wine is used as a benchmark by which wines from other countries are judged.

There are more good wines coming out of France today than ever before. Not just the prestigious names with a reputation to defend, but right across the country, from Strasbourg to Perpignan, each vintage seems to produce a kaleidoscope of styles to match the cornucopia of *appellations*. This is partially due to a succession of fine and plentiful vintages, progress in fighting disease in the vineyards and enormously improved vinification techniques, but even these positive conditions needed the presence of three factors: the increased worldwide interest in and demand for French wines; the strong and constant competition from other countries; and the willingness of the French producers to listen and change. It is the chain reaction resulting from a much wider public interest, which in turn gives growers confidence to invest in land and equipment, thereby improving, even re-inventing their products, which has broadened the base of quality wines and has even saved a few *appellations* from extinction.

The first edition of this book was the result of merging and updating my two previous pocket books: *French Country Wines* and *French Fine Wines*. In the introduction to these books, I described a "country wine" as "one which has certain defined regional characteristics and is not too sophisticated nor expensive", and a "fine wine" more simply as "a wine of quality". This latter definition could cover all wines made in France, provided that they are honestly made and possess individuality and character. In France, as in all other wine regions, good wines are rarely overpriced, yet poor wines always are. Throughout this book I refer, where feasible, to some of the better producers, for their's are the wines most representative of the *appellation*, and which should give the most pleasure.

After more than 25 years working almost exclusively with French wines, my admiration for the vast majority of growers, *cave-coopératives* and merchants, and the wines they produce and sell, is undimmed. I hope that this book will be a useful source of reference to the marvellous and different wines of France.

French Wine in the 1990s

1 Surface under vines

France is the second-largest wine producer in Europe, with a total of almost 1 million hectares under vines. Large as this total may seem, it is 15% less than in 1979, 22% less than in 1970 and under half the area planted in 1962. The basic reason for this is that consumption at home has been falling at a rate for which expanding exports cannot compensate, allied to the general move away from rural areas to the towns by the younger generation. The decrease in land under vines has mainly occurred in regions producing poor-quality wine for mass consumption. Although there were one or two small *appellations* for fine wine which were in danger of extinction this is no longer true, and where replanting has happened, it has been to maintain or increase quality. With the general decrease in land under vines, only the *départements* in the Languedoc-Roussillon are mostly dependent on wine production. The total area of land under vines between 1962 and 1989 is shown in Table 1a; Table 1b gives the breakdown into individual categories of wine in 1989.

TABLE 1a   SURFACE UNDER VINES 1962–1989

Year	AOC	Other	Total Hectares
1962			2,300,000
1965	227,380	1,017,252	1,244,632
1970	243,499	965,306	1,208,805
1980	313,925	803,869	1,117,794
1984	335,400	683,300	1,018,700
1986	374,937	625,837	1,000,774
1989	430,214	516,629	946,843

TABLE 1b   SURFACE UNDER VINES 1989

Categories of Wine	Hectares
AOC	430,214
VDQS	12,559
Vin de Table/Vin de Pays	425,461
Eau de Vie	78,609
Total	946,843

2 Production

While the area of land under vines has fallen, production has remained relatively stable in the last ten years. The size of the crop in proportion to the number of vines planted is determined by the weather: the absence of spring frosts, the need for dry sunny weather at the flowering in June, and not too wet ripening conditions to prevent rot, all these used to be necessary to produce a satisfactory crop. Today, better fertilization, protective measures against frost and improved treatments against disease and rot produce a higher average yield per hectare. The final crop is very variable, however, as can be seen from Table 2. These figures also show the increasing percentage of AOC wines, indicating that while quantity is perhaps falling, quality on the contrary is rising.

TABLE 2a   WINE PRODUCTION 1961–1989 (*million hectolitres*)

Year	AOC	Other	Total
1961	8.02	53.17	61.19
1970	11.46	62.92	74.37
1980	12.91	56.26	69.20
1982	19.84	59.39	79.28
1984	14.02	49.69	63.71
1986	21.17	52.05	73.22
1989	23.02	37.98	61.00

3 Consumption

While total production remains consistent with, and in plentiful years in excess of, total demand, consumption at home has been falling regularly. The French (those under 14 years old are not counted) now drink (only) 83 litres of wine per head per year as opposed to 121 litres in 1969. However, while they are drinking less, it is of better quality (Tables 3a and 3b).

TABLE 3a   FRENCH CONSUMPTION PER HEAD (*in litres*)

Year	AOC	Other	Total
1969	14	107	121
1979	19	84	103
1984	25	66	91
1989	29	54	83

TABLE 3b   WINE CONSUMPTION IN FRANCE (*million hectolitres*)

Year	AOC	Other	Total	% AOC
1970	5.49	40.49	45.98	11.9
1978	7.23	38.52	45.75	15.8
1980	8.70	34.52	43.22	20.1
1982	10.01*	31.54	41.55	24.1
1984	10.92*	28.82	39.74	27.5
1986	11.90	26.33	38.23	31.1
1989	13.08	24.07	37.15	35.2

* = AOC + VDQS = VQPRD

4 Exports

The success story of French wine across the world is evident from the table below. The volume exported has tripled in 20 years, while the percentage of production exported has increased almost four times. As French home consumption continues to fall – and the French themselves are beginning to appreciate wines from other countries – both these export figures will increase further in the next decade.

TABLE 4   WINE EXPORTS 1970–89

Year	Volume (million hectolitres)	% of Total Production
1970	3.81	5.12
1980–1	8.61	12.44
1981–2	8.91	15.63
1982–3	9.45	11.92
1983–4	10.98	17.23
1985–6	13.18	18.00
1988–9	12.70	20.08

5 Landowning in France

As regards production and sales, France has essentially an ancient pattern of landholding, where the vineyards have become so parcellated through inheritance that very many families own very small amounts of land. This is unprofitable and the trend is for greater consolidation, which can be seen by comparing landownership and wine production in 1982 and 1988. In 1982 there were 429,000 families making wine in France, of whom 236,000 regularly sold commercially, the remaining 193,000 keeping almost everything for home consumption. By 1988 these figures had fallen by 157,000 to 272,000 families producing wine, of which 166,000 made a living from it, and 106,000 did not. (This last total represents only 5% of all wine produced in France.) Only 27,800 of these (30,000 in 1982), own more than 10 hectares of vines, but they also own more than 60% of the land under vines. The very large number with less than 5 hectares represents less than 20% of the total area, while those with under 2 hectares count for well under 10%.

That there will be further changes is evident from the fact that 18% of the growers are 65 years old and over, yet an encouraging 11% are under 35. This compares to under 5% for the younger growers in 1982, showing that the younger generation is committed to making wine producing a viable concern. Yet, of all the people who make wine, over one quarter have another job. The rise in importance and quality of the *vins de pays* seems to have arrested the wholesale tearing-up of unprofitable vineyards, but in order to achieve increased benefit, vineyard holdings will have to be made more efficient. The larger the domaine, the more the production of wine predominates, although in the Midi, many producers maintain a secondary activity.

Ownership by négociants is only important in the AOC vineyards and is about 10% overall. In Alsace, négociants own only 3% of the vineyards, in Champagne 12% and in Burgundy and Bordeaux around 7%. It is very small in the south, despite the presence of the Salins du Midi (Listel), Nicolas and Chantovent. Foreign interest is negligible and is concentrated among the very finest *crus*. Négociants, however, commercialize 50% of French wines.

The cooperative movement owns 460,000 hectares (just under 50%). A *cave coopérative* is a group of wine-growers who either cannot, by virtue of the size of their holding, or do not wish to, make their own wine or commercialize it. The *coopérative* therefore buys all the heavy machinery for use on the vines, purchases the grapes from the grower, makes the wine and is responsible for selling it, returning to the grower the money for his grapes and/or a quantity of bottles. The *caves coopératives* produce 50% of French wine: 60% of the *vins de table*, 42% of the AOC and VDQS wines. They are of great importance in the Languedoc-Roussillon, producing 73% of all AOC, VDQS and *vins de pays*. Membership rose from 120,000 in 1939 to 290,000 in 1969 and had fallen to 260,000 in 1981, and further to 210,000 members in 1989.

What for the future? There is a strong resurgence of interest in wine in France at all levels. The blanket of *gros rouge* has been lifted, and everyone has realized that quality pays. The willingness of French wine-drinkers to experiment with different wines has developed only in the last 10 years. Consumers, French and foreign alike, are looking for wines with individual character and regional definition. The AOCs and VDQSs have this, and the *vins de pays* are acquiring it.

One of the aims of this book is to help the consumer find his way through the maze of French wines, as an informed wine-drinker buys well, and supporting the good French winemakers will benefit lovers of wine both in France and abroad.

The Appellation Contrôlée System

The French system of Appellation d'Origine Contrôlée (AOC) is the basis of all controls on wine production in Europe and is now even being accepted and defined in California. It is, quite simply, a system of controls on the origin of the wine, so that the wine in bottle corresponds to the name on the label. If the controls are adhered to (and if they are not, then the wine loses its right to the *appellation*, and may not be called by its name), the wine will correspond to a style or type. This style will be lighter or more intense according to the character of the vintage, more or less "typical", and better or worse according to the quality of viticulture, vinification and ageing, but the type should still be evident. The human element, by far the most important factor in the production of fine wine, cannot be controlled, since a wine producer can search for or disregard quality as he pleases, but the AOC system provides the framework for his efforts.

The Institut National des Appellations d'Origine (INAO) has differentiated between three main types of wine.
  I. Vins d'Appellation d'Origine Contrôlée (AOC)
 II. Vins Délimités de Qualité Supérieure (VDQS)
III. Vins de Pays
There is also a fourth type, Vins de Table Français, from French vines only, often sold under a brand name with no regional origin.

I Vins d'Appellation d'Origine Contrôlée (AOC)

Since the finest wines of France are almost without exception AOCs, it is important to know what actually is controlled. This comes under eight headings.

1. The area of production.
   The land on which vines may be planted to benefit from the *appellation*: vines planted outside the exact region or within the region but on land deemed unsuitable do not conform.

2. Variety of grape.
   In some cases only a single variety is permitted (Volnay, Hermitage), in others, several complementary grapes (Médoc, Châteauneuf-du-Pape), with the proviso that if hybrid grapes are planted anywhere in the vineyard, the *appellation* is completely lost, and if non-permitted *vitis vinifera* grapes are planted in a particular parcel, the *appellation* is forfeited for wines from that parcel. Finally, grapes from newly planted vines may only be used in AOC wine from the *quatrième feuille* or their fourth vintage.

3. Degree of alcohol.
   All AOC wines must have a minimum degree of alcohol and in some cases a maximum. This minimum may be attained by the natural sugar in the grape aided by chaptalization which is strictly controlled to a maximum of 2° in most regions of France and forbidden in the southern Côtes du Rhône and the Midi.

4. Yield per hectare.
   Each *appellation* has a maximum permitted yield per hectare. This is known as the *rendement de base* (basic yield) and is fixed by decree by the INAO. There has been, since the 1970s, a tendency by the INAO to increase these basic yields. Further, the local Syndicats can apply for an augmentation or reduction (never yet applied for) in the basic yield depending on the quality and quantity of the crop. This is known as the *rendement annuel* (yearly yield). On top of this, each *appellation* can apply (but it is refused in the case of Grand Cru wines) for a further increase of up to 20% on the *rendement annuel*, known as the *plafond limite de classement* (PLC). In some cases, AOC Bordeaux for example, these two reclassifications can result in the basic yield being increased by as much as 60%. While this appears dangerously high, it must be added that French vineyards are much more healthy and hence more productive than even ten years ago, yet any producer declaring wine in excess of the *rendement annuel* + PLC will lose the *appellation* for the whole crop.

5. Methods of viticulture.
   Control of the number of vines per hectare, the type of pruning, in some cases the method of

picking (by successive *tries* for Sauternes), and whether or not the grapes may be destalked prior to fermentation.

6. Methods of vinification.

Prohibition of the use of concentrated musts in most *appellations* and of *vinage* (addition of alcohol to the must) in all wines. Acidification and de-acidification are permitted under the control of the local *Station Oenologique*.

7. Analysis and tasting.

Since the 1979 vintage, all AOC wines must be submitted to a tasting panel made up of members of the local Syndicat and representatives of the INAO. Those that do not pass are declassified but may be re-presented. A second declassification is final.

8. Bottling.

Bottling in the region of *appellation* (i.e. if wines are shipped out of the region in bulk, they lose the *appellation*) has been obligatory in Alsace since 1972 and in Champagne since 1919. All AOC *méthode champenoise* wines are fermented in the bottle and thus naturally bottled in the region of origin. It should be noted that the higher *appellations* of Premier and Grand Cru are, with the exception of all the Crus Classés of Bordeaux, based on geographical *climats* in the *appellations*, with stricter controls on yield and alcohol content.

With these controls, the maximum amount of effort is made to maintain quality in French wine. A certain laxity in terms of yield and alcohol content is now being balanced by the obligatory submission of samples for official tastings.

II Vins Délimités de Qualité Supérieure (VDQS)

This group represents the middle ground between the AOCs and the *vins de pays*. The same basic rules apply to the VDQS as to the AOCs, but the range of grape varieties is wider and the degree of alcohol sometimes lower. By contrast, all wines must be submitted to a strict tasting panel to obtain the VDQS "label", without which it is declassified to a *vin de pays* or *vin de table*. In recent years many VDQSs have been elevated to AOC status (Minervois, Coteaux d'Aix-en-Provence) and a few *vins de pays* have risen to join the VDQSs (Coteaux Varois, Fiefs Vendéens).

III Vins de Pays

The *vins de pays* are of increasing importance both to the French economy and to the consumer, so it is worth looking closely at the development of this relatively recent phenomenon (see page 13).

The Cru Classé System

The system of classifying certain *crus*, or growths, to distinguish different levels of potential quality is one that is specifically French. There is also a fundamental difference between the classification of the wines of Bordeaux and those of the rest of France. In Bordeaux, the 1855 classification of the Médoc and Sauternes (including Château Haut-Brion from the Graves), the 1953 and 1959 classifications of Graves, and the 1954 and 1984 classification of Saint-Emilion, are concerned with specific châteaux rather than specific vineyards. Thus, Château Langoa-Barton, a Saint-Julien property, classified 3ème Cru in 1855 (and indeed one of only a handful of châteaux to have remained under the same ownership since this date), would remain a 3ème Cru even if it were to exchange some vines with its neighbours Ducru-Beaucaillou (a 2ème Cru) and Branaire-Ducru (a 4ème Cru). As far as the INAO is concerned, what is classified is the *appellation* Saint-Julien.

In Burgundy the vineyards are classified purely geographically, with no regard to ownership. Thus, the Genevrières vineyard in Meursault is classified Premier Cru, and wine made from this specific plot of land may use the name on the label. If Genevrières and Perrières, another Premier Cru, are blended, the label may state Meursault Premier Cru, but not use the individual names, and if Genevrières is blended with a non-Premier Cru wine, however high in quality, the *cru* status is forfeited.

A further difference between Burgundy and Bordeaux is that between the Premier and Grand Cru in the former, and the various levels of Crus Classés in the latter. In Burgundy, many villages or communes have attached to their name that of their most famous wine (in all cases a Grand Cru), thus, the village of Gevrey added Chambertin to become Gevrey-Chambertin. The Grand Cru "Chambertin" does not need to refer to the village, but the Premier Crus do. In Burgundy, as in Champagne, Grand Cru is the superior *appellation*. In Bordeaux however, the 1855 classification of the Médoc covers five Crus Classés, ranging from Premier through 2ème, 3ème, 4ème and 5ème Crus. To be classified a 5ème Cru Classé, or fifth growth, was to be in the last division of the best sixty-odd wines in Bordeaux at that time. A fifth growth should therefore be viewed as the equal of a Premier Cru in Burgundy – though really no comparison is possible – and on no

account as a wine that is "fifth rate". In any event, prices in Bordeaux and Burgundy follow quality not classification.

With the exception of Champagne (page 225) and Alsace (page 27), the Cru system elsewhere in France is more honorific local usage than an official classification.

Vins de Pays

While all aspects of French viticulture are controlled by decrees from the Minister of Agriculture, the *vins de pays* present such an ever-changing scene that one might think that the *vignerons* were in charge rather than the Government. In a country where the vast majority of *vins d'appellation* have a style and character that have evolved for several generations and are now recognizable and classified, the classification of *vins de pays* is a relatively new part of French wine production. *Vins de pays* came into being officially in 1968, when a decree was passed authorizing certain *vins de table* to indicate the regional origin of the wine. This was designed to inform the consumer and to give him certain guarantees of origin. In 1973, a further decree fixed precisely the conditions of production to which a *vin de pays* must adhere in order to have the right to the appellation: the region, grape varieties, yield, alcohol content, even the level of sulphur dioxide and volatile acidity. Finally, in 1979, these conditions were refined and particular rules were established for individual *vins de pays* in an effort to increase the quality. The aim throughout has been the same as for the most important AOCs and VDQSs, namely that the consumer must be offered a wine with a guarantee of origin which, being easily identifiable, should provide him with an assurance as to the quality of the final product.

The decree of 1973 did away with the Vins d'Appellation d'Origine Simple (AOS), leaving the *vins de pays* as the only category of personalized *vins de table*. There are three basic types of *vin de pays*, corresponding to different geographical interpretations:

1. Vins de Pays Régionaux. These may come from several grouped *départements* as long as they correspond to an accepted style of wine, for example Vin de Pays d'Oc, for the whole of the Languedoc-Roussillon; Vin de Pays du Jardin de la France, for wines from the Loire Valley.

2. Vins de Pays Départementaux. These must carry the name of the *département* where they are produced, for example Vin de Pays du Gard, Vin de Pays de l'Ardèche.

3. Vins de Pays de Zone. These wines may state the name of the individual commune where they are produced, for example Vin de Pays du Val d'Orbieu (Aude), Vins de Pays des Coteaux du Salavès (Gard).

All *vins de pays* fit into one or another of these categories, and it is plain that category (3) can be sold as categories (2) and (1), and category (2) as (1) if it is desirable to do so.

The rules governing the production of *vins de pays* follow the same pattern as for the other *appellations*. First, they must have geographical identity, from a specified region; second, they may only be made from "recommended" grape varieties, of which the list is fixed by decree (these are in most cases the grape varieties used for the more important wines of the region, with the addition of *cépages nobles* if the soil and climate are suitable); third, the yield per hectare must not exceed 80 hl for the Vins de Pays de Zone, 90 hl for the Vins de Pays Départementaux; fourth, the minimum alcohol content must be 9° for the north of France and the Alpes-du-Nord, 9.5° for the South-West, the Rhône Valley and the Alpes-du-Sud, and 10° for the Languedoc-Roussillon, Provence and Corsica; fifth, the level of sulphur dioxide and volatile acidity is strictly controlled and the wine must pass an official tasting before being sold as *vin de pays*.

The volume of *vins de pays* produced is immense, averaging 6.5 million hectolitres a year (760 million bottles), about 15% of the total French production of which 78% is red, 12% rosé and 10% white. *Vins de pays* are produced in 54 *départements*, but are concentrated in the Languedoc-Roussillon region, which represents 75% of the production, with the *département* of the Pyrénées-Orientales alone accounting for 20%. Provence-Côte d'Azur accounts for a further 12% and the Loire Valley for 6%. There are 99 separate Vins de Pays de Zones, to which must be added 41 Vins de Pays Départementaux (*départements* where the name is also that of an *appellation* − Savoie, Jura, Corsica − may not use it for *vin de pays*) and the four Vins de Pays Régionaux, making a total of 144 possible types of *vins de pays*. It should also be remembered that over 10% of the wines presented for classification as *vins de pays* are rejected by the Tasting Commission.

It is not surprising that a large part of this volume is produced by the *caves coopératives*. On a national level, the 1,200 *caves coopératives* in France produce a fraction over half the total of all table wine. For the *vins de pays*, this rises to 64%, against 36% from privately owned *caves*. Many of the Vins de Pays de Zone are produced almost entirely by one *cave coopérative*. With the vast quantity of wine involved, the *coopératives* are now marketing their wine as well as producing it.

While, for the consumer, *vins de pays* would seem to offer an unlimited range of genuine country wines, the French Government is not totally satisfied with their progress. The reason lies in the multiplicity of labels and the, as yet, lack of a defined *image de marque*. On the production side, many *vignerons* consider the *vin de pays* label merely as a stepping-stone to the higher categories of VDQS or even AOC, while the Government wishes to promote *vins de pays* as an *appellation* in its own right. For the consumer, the increasing number of wines available causes confusion. The négociant is often hesitant to purchase a wine with a little-known name, and may prefer to build up a *vin de marque* under their own name. At the same time, the *vignerons* are unwilling to see their wine disappearing into an anonymous "zip-code" product, or even bottled under a négociant's label, and are beginning to bottle their own wine, marketing it direct.

In the midst of this confusion, there are two very encouraging elements. The first is the commitment by the Ministry of Agriculture and the positive reaction from the producers to maintain quality. Wine consumption in France is falling, the noticeable drop being in the consumption of *vin ordinaire*. With higher-quality *vin de pays*, the French are drinking less, but better wine, while export markets are being reconvinced that French wines are good value for money. The second element is the introduction of *cépages nobles* into the production of *vins de pays*. The role played by the grape variety in the taste and style of a wine is as great as that played by the soil and climate. The major *appellations* in France have evolved and refined their varietal base over centuries, and the principles of what varieties should be planted where underlie the whole system of Appellation Contrôlée. For years it had been assumed that wines from the Midi could only be made from *cépages méridionaux*, and only in the last decade have experiments proved that the grapes that make France's finest wines may produce excellent, individual wines outside their region of origin.

Thus, little by little, we are seeing Cabernet Sauvignon, Merlot, Chardonnay and Sauvignon appearing on the labels of *vins de pays*. This development is gathering strong support from *coopératives* as well as from innovative growers. The wines are generally successful, retaining their varietal characteristics and the intrinsic style of the region. There are two main advantages for French viticulture and for the consumer: the name of the grape gives a varietal image to the wine, easier to recognize than a geographical one; and the price is that of a *vin de pays*.

The Vintages of the Last 12 Years

The decade of the 1970s was recognized as being blessed with the best run of good vintages in memory, or at least the fewest poor ones. Much of this is due, of course, to the weather, but the unpredictability of the climate has been lessened in importance by enormous progress in vineyard management and in confident vinification. The "luck" of the 1970s continued, quite without precedent, throughout the 1980s, with a run of successes that makes the 1970s seem almost patchy in comparison. While vintages are always compared to each other and "look-alikes" are found from previous years, each vintage is different at the time of picking, during fermentation and in the way it ages. The following notes of the fine-wine producing regions of France are intended to put some of these differences into perspective. The scale of rating is as follows: 0—9 bad, very poor, poor; 10—11 acceptable; 12—13 quite good; 14—15 good; 16—18 very good; 19—20 exceptional.

Bordeaux—white

(NB the figure for dry wines precedes that for *vins liquoreux*)

1979 Large crop of immediately attractive dry whites and fine *vins liquoreux* with richness and finesse. 15; 16.

1980 Small crop of dry whites lacking in character; also a very difficult year for sweet wines. 12; 13.

1981 Average crop of well-balanced dry wines; sweet wines elegant and concentrated. 16; 16.

1982 Very large crop of supple, dry wines, lacking in acidity and now past their best; the first pickings of *vins liquoreux* were exceptional, the richest since 1959, but early rain ruined most of the vintage. 13; 14.

1983 Good quantity of fine dry wines with balance, elegance and fruit; large (for the Sauternais) volume of exceptionally rich sweet wine, the most impressive for many years. 18; 19.

1984 Good year with crisp, flowery dry wines with well-balanced fruit and acidity. Some *pourriture* in Sauternes produced attractive medium-weight wines. 14; 13.

1985 Very good year for those who picked early to avoid high alcohol but not too early to lose the fruit. The long dry autumn did not allow the *pourriture* to affect the grapes, which nevertheless achieved a high concentration of sugar, unlike the 1976s. 16; 16.

1986 Very good for dry whites, floral and persistent. Exceptional conditions for all sweet wines, perhaps the best in the decade. 17; 19 + .

1987 The dry whites did not suffer too much from this rainy vintage, which produced *pourriture grise* in Sauternes rather than *pourriture noble* after the first successful picking. 15; 13.

1988 A classic vintage, producing firm, elegant wines. Long-lasting dry wines and fine sweet wines with structure and concentration, if not the panache of the 1986s. 18; 18.

1989 The very hot summer produced dry wines with more weight and less acidity than 1988, for early drinking; sweet wines are very rich, unctuous and flamboyant. 17; 19.

1990 Another very hot, dry summer, with the dry wines showing good balance, and the sweet wines great concentration. 18; 19.

Bordeaux—red

1979 Very large crop from a late harvest producing wines with excellent colour, fruit and depth from Saint-Emilion, Pomerol and Graves, a little lighter in the Médoc. 17.

1980 Average crop from a difficult vintage producing light, attractive wines in the 1973 style. Less good in Saint-Emilion and Pomerol, best in Graves. Now past their best. 12.

1981 Good volume of fine, well-balanced wines that have the finesse but not quite the fruit of 1978—9. Excellent Graves. Ready now. 15.

1982 Very large crop of dark-coloured, plummy wines with very great richness and depth of fruit. An extraordinarily impressive vintage, particularly in the Libournais, and in very many cases, the best since 1961, with softer tannins. Begin the better wines in 1990. 19 + .

1983 Large crops of firm, tannic wines, leaner than the 1982s, more irregular in Saint-Emilion/Pomerol than in the Médoc/Graves. Superb in Margaux. 17 + .

1984 A very poor year for the Merlot, leaving the

15

Saint-Emilion and Pomerol wines low in fruit and volume. Much better in the Médoc and Graves, with some attractive early maturing wines and some more concentrated *cuvées* from the Cabernet Sauvignon. 11 (right bank)–13.

1985 An almost unparalleled stretch of sunny, dry weather from August to October produced extremely healthy, very ripe grapes. In contrast to 1984, the Merlot showed a large crop of concentrated, fruity wine. Very successful overall in the Médoc and Graves. Some selection needed in the lesser wines. 18.

1986 A classic tannic vintage, particularly in the Médoc and Graves, where the wines rival those of 1982, 1970 and 1961. More stuffing, more breed than many 1985s. For laying down. 18–19.

1987 A vintage of almost continuous rain, where the Merlot suffered more than the Cabernet. Careful selection produced some attractive wines for drinking while the better wines mature. 14.

1988 A very fine vintage with overall deep colour and fine tannic structure, in the style of 1986. Excellent wines from all *appellations* for long-term keeping. 18–19.

1989 The very hot summer produced rich, fleshy wines, sometimes more flamboyant than even 1982. High natural alcohol levels and concentration, but more open than the 1988s. 18–19.

1990 Another very hot summer, producing wines of richness and concentration, better in Médoc and Graves than Saint-Emilion and Pomerol. 17–19.

Burgundy—white

1979 Large crop and another generally successful vintage, but less depth than the 1978s. 16.

1980 Small crop of uneven wines, some of the Chablis were clean and stylish, but the wines from the Côte d'Or lacked stuffing and balance. 12.

1981 Small crop, with varying quality of Chablis, where the best resemble 1978, but very successful further south, with excellent concentration, acidity and fruit. 16.

1982 Large crop of rich, bouqueted, quite full-bodied wines, a richer version of the 1979s. Very impressive wines for relatively quick drinking due to low acidity. 16.

1983 Wines remarkably high in glycerine and grape sugar, difficult to vinify, but the successful *cuvées* will make very great bottles. 10–18.

1984 Rather firm wines with good fruit and a much better acidity than either 1983 or 1982. 14.

1985 Very sunny weather produced wines with plenty of fruit and body, and with more length than the 1982s. Very stylish wines for medium-term drinking. 18.

1986 Better acidity, less obvious alcohol, and more stylish wines than in 1985. Chablis was magnificent, ready to drink early. The best-balanced vintages of the mid-1980s. 19.

1987 A difficult year that showed good fruit when young, but now shows a slight lack of the ripeness necessary for a great white burgundy. 14–15.

1988 Excellent ripening conditions produced wines with structure and complexity, less stylish than the 1986s, but generally high quality. 18.

1989 A very hot year, producing wines with sometimes more alcohol than acidity in the Côte d'Or, but very successful in Chablis. Lovely wines from the Côte-Chalonnaise. 18–19.

1990 Another hot, dry year, but producing firmer, less "exotic" wines. A very good start to the decade, magnificent in Chablis. 18 + .

Burgundy—red

1979 Large crops of supple, fruity, quick-maturing wines, very attractive and should be drunk now. Better in the Côte de Beaune. 15.

1980 Smallish crop with some of the Côte de Beaune wines lacking colour and fruit, much better in the Côte de Nuits. Drink before the 1978s. 13–16.

1981 Small crop of uneven wines but passable in the southern Côte de Nuits and the northern Côte de Beaune. Should be drunk. 12.

1982 Large crop of wines often lacking colour and balance, only *vignerons* who did not overproduce and carefully selected their vats for bottling, made wine of quality, midway between 1978 and 1979. Should mostly be drunk. 12–16.

1983 Very variable quality due to extraordinarily high sugars and some rot. The successful *cuvées* have a dark colour, with a vigorous fruit and tannin, wines for keeping. Careful selection is needed. 10–17.

1984 Cold weather during the vintage resulted in rather lean wines, lacking a little in colour and fruit, but quite straightforward. 13.

1985 Perfect harvesting conditions produced grapes of a ripeness and healthiness not seen since 1959. Strikingly fruity wines that seemed perfect but may not have the tannin to be long keepers.

Superb in the Beaujolais. 17–18.

1986 Generally a large vintage, swollen by rain at the time of picking, but of good overall quality, with some fine wines made in the Côte de Nuits. Mostly ready to drink. 15.

1987 A difficult year, which has emerged as finer, with more colour and structure than 1986, due to a smaller crop. Higher acidity means they should not be drunk too soon, except for Beaujolais. 16.

1988 An early vintage after three months of hot, dry weather produced wines of deep colour and concentration; limited yields allowed the *terroir* to show through clearly. The finest vintage of the 1980s, for long-term keeping. The Beaujolais *crus* are very fine indeed. 18–19.

1989 The earliest vintage since 1976 produced a large crop with slightly less concentration than 1988, but with a fine, rounded fruit. Drink before the 1988s. Beaujolais *crus* lacked stuffing compared to 1988. 17.

1990 A very hot and very dry year produced another early vintage with grapes in perfect condition and a high proportion of skin to juice, giving the wines a superb colour and great definition. An excellent start to the decade. Less balance in Beaujolais. 18 + .

Alsace

1979 Very large crop of fruity, aromatic wines, some a little too soft. 15.

1980 Very small crop and uneven across the *appellation*. 12–15.

1981 Largish crop, successful throughout *appellation* and in all grape styles. 17.

1982 Enormous crop, with many wines too soft and washed out, but some well-made wines from good vineyards and serious *vignerons*. 14–15.

1983 Average volume of quite exceptional wines, with high sugars and perfect balance. The finest *vendange tardive* wines (and even *sélection des grains nobles*) since 1921, and the best vintage in Alsace since 1959. 19.

1984 Average volume of wines that showed an initial lack of ripeness and were quite over-shadowed by the 1983s. Well-balanced, correct wines for relatively early drinking. 13.

1985 A very dry summer, with almost no rain from July to the end of October, produced concentrated, rich wines, only a little less fine than 1983, and of a reduced quantity. Some excellent *vendange tardive* wines. 18.

1986 A large vintage of well-balanced wines, a little lighter than 1985, but with a stylish fruit and good acidity. 17.

1987 A difficult vintage, saved by good weather towards the end. Riesling more successful than Gewurztraminer, both lacking concentration. 15.

1988 Heavy rain just before the vintage down-graded most of the wines from perfect to very good. Serious growers produced fine, concentrated wines, with some exceptional SGNs made in November. 18.

1989 A very hot year produced an early vintage with high natural alcohol despite a large crop, making fleshy, flavourful wines to rival 1983. The late-picked wines are quite outstanding. 19.

1990 A hot, dry year, with yield lower than 1989 and as much concentration but not quite the richness of fruit. 18.

Anjou/Touraine–white

1979 Large crop, similar to 1978 but a little less class. 14.

1980 Average quantity and quality, light, quick maturing. 12.

1981 Very fine vintage, especially in Vouvray and Montlouis, wines with excellent fruit and balance and more length than the 1978s. 16.

1982 Very large crop, with some very fine *demi-secs* but slight lack of concentration and acidity in the dry wines. 15.

1983 Large crop of well-balanced wines with very good fruit and more structure and acidity than 1982. 16.

1984 Rather a lean year, with the lemony acidity of the Chenin Blanc evident. Average crop. 12.

1985 A very fine year, due to the long sunny harvest, producing aromatic dry wines and the finest *moelleux* since 1976. 18.

1986 A good year, less rich than 1985, giving the ripe fruit a certain crispness. Will age well. 16.

1987 Rain throughout most of the harvest spoilt the already thin chances of a good vintage. 12.

1988 A very good vintage, with both the Sauvignon and Chenin Blanc grapes fully ripe but with good levels of acidity. Some very fine *moelleux*. 17.

1989 An exceptional vintage for all wines made from the Chenin Blanc, a little too rich for the Sauvignon. Quite extraordinary concentration of flavours in the *moelleux* wines, which rival 1947 and 1921. 19–20.

1990 A very hot summer produced wines almost as concentrated as 1989, but without the edge of real greatness. 18–19.

Anjou/Touraine—red

1979 Very large crop of pleasant, fruity wines, now drying out a little. 13.

1980 A cool summer did not bring enough fruit, but better than 1977. 11.

1981 Well-balanced wines with good style, colour and fruit. Should be drunk. 15.

1982 Very large crop, the better wines had the best fruit and colour since 1976, but were not in the same class. 15.

1983 Crop reduced by hail, leaving a deep-coloured, intense wine high in tannin and acidity. Some impressive bottles for laying down. 16.

1984 Similar in style to the whites, being rather lean, light in colour and fruit. All but the best were for early drinking. 12.

1985 Exceptional year, wines packed with colour and dense fruit, the best since 1976, perhaps less tannic but more stylish. Can be drunk or kept. 18.

1986 Very good vintage, but without quite the concentration of the 1985s. Nearing their best. 17.

1987 Heavy rain caused loss of colour and fruit, but improved winemaking saved the vintage from disaster. 13.

1988 A fine, classic vintage in Touraine, with good colour and firm fruit; even better in Saumur and Anjou. 17–18.

1989 An exceptionally hot dry year brought unexpected richness and weight without losing the sense of *terroir*. A quality not seen since 1947; wines that can last 20 years or more. 19–20.

1990 A vintage almost as successful as 1989, with a very high dry extract: concentrated wines for keeping. 18.

Champagne

1979 Large crop of elegant wines, especially successful in the Côte des Blancs. 17.

1980 Very small crop of average quality. Very little was sold as a vintage wine. 11.

1981 Very small crop of good quality. 15.

1982 Very large crop of pleasant wine with quite good acidity and depth. Very good in non-vintage blends, excellent for vintage wine. 18.

1983 Very large crop, better in the Côtes des Blancs, but less good than 1982. 17.

1984 Cold weather during the growing season and the vintage produced a below average crop of lean wines. The Chardonnay, as usual, performed better than the Pinots, being an early ripener. 12.

1985 Perfect conditions during the vintage added to the smaller than average crop of perfect grapes. A fine year that has made a superb vintage. 18+.

1986 A better than average volume, but with an uneven flowering for the Chardonnay and some lack of concentration in the Pinots, but good quality overall. 15.

1987 A rainy summer and harvest produced a large crop of unexceptional wine. 12.

1988 A small crop of high-quality grapes produced wines with concentration and balance, which will make a fine vintage. 17.

1989 An exceptional vintage, with the third highest volume of the decade, but by far the best quality: Chardonnays were uncharacteristically rich, the Pinots perfectly ripe. Will make an outstanding vintage. 20.

1990 A bizarre year, where the crop of Chardonnay was enhanced by a second picking in November. Good quality overall. 17.

Northern Rhône—white

1979 Fine, classic wines with bouquet, flavour, weight and perfect balance. 18.

1980 Very good vintage, with a rich, sweet fruit, but less complete than 1979. 16.

1981 Firm, aromatic wines, more lively but with less roundness than 1980. 15.

1982 Big vintage of extremely rich aromatic wines (extraordinary Condrieu), as rich as the 1976s, but more expressive. 18.

1983 Very successful, not quite so aromatic as 1982. 17.

1984 Floral wines with a firm acidity, attractive but without much weight. 14.

1985 Very hot vintage produced wines naturally high in alcohol which needed careful vinification. The best are excellent. 12–18.

1986 An exceptional vintage with high natural sugars, better balance and breed than even the best 1985s. 19.

1987 Uneven vintage, with highish acidity. 13.

1988 Ripe, with good fruit and balance, but not inspiring, except for Hermitage, which will continue to improve. 16–18.

1989 An exceptional vintage, packed with unctu-ous, aromatic fruit, but with concentration and no flabbiness. Big wines, for keeping. 19.

1990 Almost as rich as 1989, with Condrieu showing more vivacity, and overall a more lively fruit but less concentration. 18.

Northern Rhône—red

1979 Well-made wines with good plummy fruit, overshadowed by the 1978, the Hermitage being the most successful. 17.

1980 Fine, elegant wines with a good Côte-Rôtie and Cornas the most successful. Crozes-Hermitage, Saint-Joseph and Hermitage were fruity, for early drinking. 16.

1981 A difficult year, with much rot, but the best *cuvées* are firmer and have more potential than the 1980s. 8–15.

1982 Very hot weather during the vintage made vinification difficult but produced some very deep-coloured aromatic wines. 16–18.

1983 Very great promise from wines that are more tannic and less fruity than 1978, but even more concentrated. 18–19.

1984 Wines with good colour, but a lightish fruit. Average crop for medium-term drinking. 14.

1985 Exceptionally ripe grapes produced wines with a huge colour and dense fruit. Will rival 1983 as an almost perfect vintage. 18 +.

1986 An average-to-large crop with good colour and weight, but not the ripeness of 1985. Well-made wines for the medium term. 16.

1987 Along with the South-West, the northern Rhône produced some of the most successful red wines in this rainy year, although they are leaner than the 1986s. 15.

1988 An excellent year, below average in quantity, but strong in colour and extract. Very fine wines for laying down. 19.

1989 A hot and arid summer caused irregularities in ripening, producing wines with less concentration than the 1988s, a contrast to other regions in France. 17.

1990 Another very hot summer, but less arid, whose wines fall midway between 1988 and 1989 in quality. 18 +.

Southern Rhône—white

The white wines from the Côtes du Rhône Méridionales should be drunk young, with very, very few exceptions.

Southern Rhône—red

1979 Large crop of smooth wines, full of fruit, less concentrated than 1978 but elegant. 15.

1980 Average crop, with more body and balance than 1979, very good wine. 16.

1981 Very correct wines, a little less fine but longer lasting than 1979 and 1980. 15.

1982 Overripeness of Grenache made most wines unbalanced, too high in alcohol, not enough colour and tannin. Difficult. 10–15.

1983 The *coulure* of the Grenache brought about a wine of complete contrast to 1982, dark-coloured, hard and tannic, very impressive but slow to mature. 17.

1984 A medium crop of firm wines, with the Grenache underproducing. 13.

1985 Very hot vintage produced problems of vinification with some overheated vats. The best wines have a dense colour and fruit, but lack the backbone of the 1983s. 16.

1986 A difficult vintage, but one with deep colour, overall firmness and balance, and more promise than the 1985s. 18.

1987 Very great problems of rot due to rain during the vintage produced many wines lacking colour and clean fruit. 9–13.

1988 A good crop of solid, foursquare wines, with ripe, firm flavours. For the medium term. 17.

1989 Almost drought conditions produced wines with great concentration of colour, fruit and tannin, for long-term ageing. 18 +.

1990 Similar conditions with another range of robust, deep-coloured wines to lay down. 18 +.

Provence, the Midi and the South-West

Vintages in Provence follow very much the pattern of the southern Rhône, except that they do not have the same high percentage of Grenache and do not suffer as much from overripe vintages, such as 1982. White wines and rosés should be drunk as young as possible and very few reds improve past five years.

The Midi follows, in general, the same pattern, but the further west the vineyards are along the coast, the more the wines correspond to the vintages of Bordeaux.

Vintages in the South-West generally correspond to those of Bordeaux, with the exception of 1987, which was very successful in this region.

How to Buy Wines

The traditional way of buying wines has usually been through a specialist wine merchant. The advantages are plain: the merchant knows his wines and tastes regularly enough to know their development and relative merits; his selection will represent a personal choice, and it is as important for the client to know the tastes of his wine merchant as it is for the merchant to know the tastes of his client; a delivery service is usual, and storage of wines and advice on when they should be drunk are all part of this service; finally, almost all wine merchants will take back wines which a client finds unsatisfactory and repurchase surplus wines. The disadvantage is that one pays for this knowledge and service, and the traditional merchant, despite the bargains and special offers, is seldom the cheapest place to buy wines.

This very personal service tends only to exist in owner-run establishments, so if it is impossible to call on the wine merchant, one must buy from his list. An alternative solution, common in Europe, is the chain store. Here, a central office will do the buying for a series of regional, even national outlets, selling from a single list, but with the harder to get wines reserved for the more prestigious sites. The advantage is that the buying will have been done by a team, perhaps equally as knowledgeable as the specialist wine merchant, and with a financial clout that the specialist rarely possesses. Prices will be competitive, usually midway between the specialists and the supermarkets, and the service keen and efficient.

The supermarkets themselves are the newest element in the wine business, who, having only in the last few years changed the habits of the wine-buying public for lesser wines, are now turning their attention to fine wines. Their buying power, the high quality of their buyers, and their wish to attract clients to this new aspect of the business, will make them very competitive on price, particularly for well-known names. Disadvantages are that the range is smaller than that of the specialists and even with excellent storage conditions before sale, the heat and light of a supermarket are not good for wine, although turnover is usually high enough to minimize this problem.

One of the best ways to buy wines is by mail, either from the list of the specialist merchant, or from mail-order wine companies, usually called clubs. Here again, buying is of a high level of expertise, with sufficient volume to get the best prices, the wine lists (the only selling tool available) are interesting and informative and the range of wines very wide, possibly wider than the specialist can afford and the chain store would want to stock. The advantage of buying by mail is that one can compare lists and reflect before placing the order. Most clubs will take back unsatisfactory wine and offer storage facilities.

Perhaps the most concentrated sales of very fine wine are at auction. In Britain, Christie's have led the field since they re-introduced wine auctions in 1966 and, along with Sotheby's and the lesser auction houses, handle tens of millions of pounds per year in wines of all kinds. In France, the volume of fine wine sold at auction has increased dramatically. The range of wines sold at auction, particularly the spread of vintages, is quite extraordinary. Very few of these wines are offered for tasting, but their origin is indicated and the storage conditions and state of each bottle will have been checked before sale. The advantage is that it is an opportunity to purchase wines that have disappeared from wine merchants' lists, or purchase (in quantity) surplus trade stock. The disadvantage is that, apart from the rarest items, the wines are sold in case lots. This fact, along with the growing interest in old and rare fine wines or those which are hard to get, has spawned a new breed of wine shop, specializing in just these wines. The stock is bought at auction or from private cellars, and the personal quality of the shops acts as a further guarantee.

The final, or the first solution is to go direct to the producer. The advantage is in the price (taking into account the expense of getting yourself to the wines, or the wines to you), but many top producers do not sell direct. Moreover, you must rely on your own knowledge and taste, and it is also very difficult to return a wine to a grower once it has left his cellars.

In this book the wines have been given a broad price code, which is set out above. These prices are

20

PRICE CODE

	FF per bottle	FF retail	£ retail	$ retail
A	up to 10	15–20	2.50–3.25	3.75–4.50
B	10–20	20–40	3.25–4.50	4.50–6.75
C	20–30	40–60	4.50–6.50	6.75–10.50
D	30–50	60–100	6.50–10.00	10.50–15.00
E	50–75	100–150	10.00–14.00	15.00–20.00
F	75–100	150–200	14.00–18.00	20.00–30.00
G	100–150	200–300	18.00–27.00	30.00–40.00
H	150–200	300–400	27.00–37.00	40.00–55.00
I	200–300	400–600	37.00–55.00	55.00–75.00
J	300+	600+	55.00+	75.00+

based on those charged by the producer to négociants or importers for the current (1990) vintage. In almost all cases this is a higher price than that charged for previous years, and the retail price for earlier vintages, based on historic cost, may well be lower. With fine wines, where differences in quality are generally related to financial investment or to voluntary limiting of quantity, the range of prices of each *appellation* is very marked. Further, the finer wines tend to be handled by more middlemen than the *petits vins*, so that the producer controls to a lesser extent the price on the retailer's shelves. Finally, the variance in price from vintage to vintage and the speculative element in the fine wine market may cause an unforeseen change in the price charged by the producer, which may have no immediate effect at all on that already in the shops. However, with country wines, apart from some sudden escalations in popularity for a particular region or an individual wine, prices change according to supply and demand and inflation, but the relation between the less expensive and more expensive wines remains fairly constant.

How to Read a Wine Label

Thanks to the rules of Appellation Contrôlée, the label on a bottle of French wine will provide you with full information as to the origin of the product and thereby a good indication as to its taste. The minimum information required is the name of the wine, its *appellation*, the degree of alcohol (not necessary for AOC and VDQS wines until 1990), the contents, and the address of the producer or the bottler if this is not the same person. A vintage date is usual but not obligatory.

If the wine is bottled where it is produced, this will be stated on the label in a manner of different ways: *"Mis en bouteille au Château"* is common for Bordeaux, *"Mis en bouteille au Domaine"* for

Burgundy, *"Mis en bouteille à la Propriété"* is often used for wines that do not come from a specific château or domaine. *"Mis en bouteille dans la région de production"* states that the wine has been bottled within its *appellation* (obligatory for sparkling wines made by the *méthode champenoise* and for the wines of Alsace), usually by a local négociant. *"Mis en bouteille dans nos Caves"* merely states that the bottling has taken place in the cellars of the company or person whose address is on the label. This is often shortened to "meb" followed by the initials of the bottler and his "zip-code" address, thus Pierre Ferraud Vins à Belleville-sur-Sâone would become PF69220 France.

Vin de Pays: Côtes de Pérignan

name of domaine

grape variety, thus this is a 100% Blanc de Blancs

Vin de Pays

mention that it is French wine (not obligatory)

name and address of producer

bottled at the same address

contents

Note: the vintage (not obligatory) will be on the neck label.

DOMAINE
PECH de CELEYRAN
Blanc de Maccabeo
VIN DE PAYS
DES CÔTES DE PÉRIGNAN
VIN DE TABLE FRANÇAIS
Comte de SAINT-EXUPÉRY
11110 SALLES-D'AUDE
Mis en bouteille à la propriété
75 cl
PRODUCE OF FRANCE

VDQS: Gros-Plant du Pays Nantais

bottled on its lees at the domaine

name of wine (also the name of the grape variety)

VDQS

VDQS guarantee label (with its number)

name and address of the domaine (which is only allowed to bottle wine from its own grapes)

contents

Note that the same label can be used for full bottles and half bottles. Since 1983 the obligatory contents are 75 cl and 37.5 cl.

TIRÉ
SUR LIE
A LA
PROPRIÉTÉ
PRODUCE
OF
FRANCE
GROS-PLANT
DU PAYS NANTAIS
Vin Délimité de Qualité Supérieure
BOUT. 73 cl
DEMIE 36 cl
DOMAINE DES DORICES
BOULLAULT & Fils "LA TOUCHE" VALLET (L.A.)
VDQS

AOC: Côtes du Rhône

name of wine

AOC

degree of alcohol

name and address of producer (here it can be seen that this particular wine is bottled at Cornas in the northern Rhône, where Auguste Clape is one of the principal producers)

contents

Note: the vintage will be on the neck label.

PRODUIT DE FRANCE

Côtes du Rhône

APPELLATION COTES-DU-RHONE CONTROLÉE

11,5% vol. MIS EN BOUTEILLE A LA PROPRIÉTÉ 75 cl

A. CLAPE, S.C.E.A. Propriétaire-Viticulteur à CORNAS (Ardèche)

IMP. REYNARD I VALENCE

AOC Pommard (from a négociant)

brand name of the négociant

name of wine

AOC

name and address of négociant where the wine is bottled

contents

Note: the vintage will be on the neck label.

F. Chauvenet

Pommard

Appellation Pommard Contrôlée

Fondée en 1853 à Nuits-St-Georges la Maison F. Chauvenet a élevé pour votre plaisir dans ses caves centenaires ce Vin de France

Product of France

Mis en bouteille par F. CHAUVENET Négociant-Eleveur à Nuits-Saint-Georges (Côte-d'Or) France

75 cl

AOC Pommard Premier Cru (from a grower)

vintage

name of wine

name of 1er cru

AOC

name and address of producer (who can only bottle wine from his own grapes)

domaine bottled

contents

RÉCOLTE 1989

Pommard 1er Cru

Les Grands Epenots

Appellation POMMARD Contrôlée

FRANÇOIS GAUNOUX

Propriétaire à Meursault (Côte-d'Or) France

MIS EN BOUTEILLES AU DOMAINE

PRODUIT DE FRANCE

Château Prieuré-Lichine 4ème Cru Classé
AOC Margaux

name of the château

classified 4ème Cru Classé in 1855 (the mention of the rank of classification is not obligatory)

vintage

AOC

château bottled (the château can only bottle its own wine)

name and address of producer

degree of alcohol

each bottle carries an individual number, a practice at certain châteaux begun by Château Mouton-Rothschild

contents

Château Prieuré-Lichine

GRAND CRU CLASSÉ

1985

MARGAUX

APPELLATION MARGAUX CONTROLEE

MIS EN BOUTEILLE AU CHATEAU

S.A. CHATEAU PRIEURÉ LICHINE PROPRIÉTAIRE A CANTENAC MARGAUX FRANCE

12 ½ vol. Cette bouteille porte le N° 750ml

How to Use this Book

The book is divided into the nine major wine-producing regions of France: Alsace; the eastern vineyards of Jura and Savoie; Burgundy, including Chablis and Beaujolais; the Rhône Valley; Provence, the Midi, Languedoc, Roussillon and Corsica; Bordeaux; the South-West; the Loire Valley; and Champagne. These major regions are divided further into sub-regions, from either the point of view of geography or style, or both, with a short introduction to each. The individual wines are listed, each with a short description, in the following order: AOC, VDQS, *vins de pays*, and are arranged alphabetically.

The listing of alcohol content, yield and grape varieties for many wines may seem repetitive, but this is deliberate as the book is intended as a source of reference for people who may wish to look up just one wine. However, for those seeking more general information, it can be read section by section. The descriptions of what the wines taste like are personal, but should correspond to general opinion.

Each section is introduced with information on the soil, climate and grape varieties planted, which lead to the type of wine made. The various *appellations* are studied (although in Champagne and Alsace there is only one *appellation*), and within these *appellations*, the *climats*, Premiers Crus and Grands Crus. In many instances the actual size and position of the vineyard is given, also the grapes planted and average production, as these factors, particularly the exact geographical situation and make-up of grape varieties, result in subtle differences in flavour. Individual growers and châteaux are singled out if their wines are among the best and most typical of the *appellation*. Much of this selection is classic (one could hardly omit Château Latour or the Domaine de la Romanée-Conti) but the rest is the result of my personal experience.

MEASUREMENT CONVERSION

Measurements of volume and area have been expressed in hectolitres (hl) and hectares (ha):

1 hectolitre = 26.4 US gallons
1 hectare = 2.471 acres

Gazetteer
of
Wine Regions

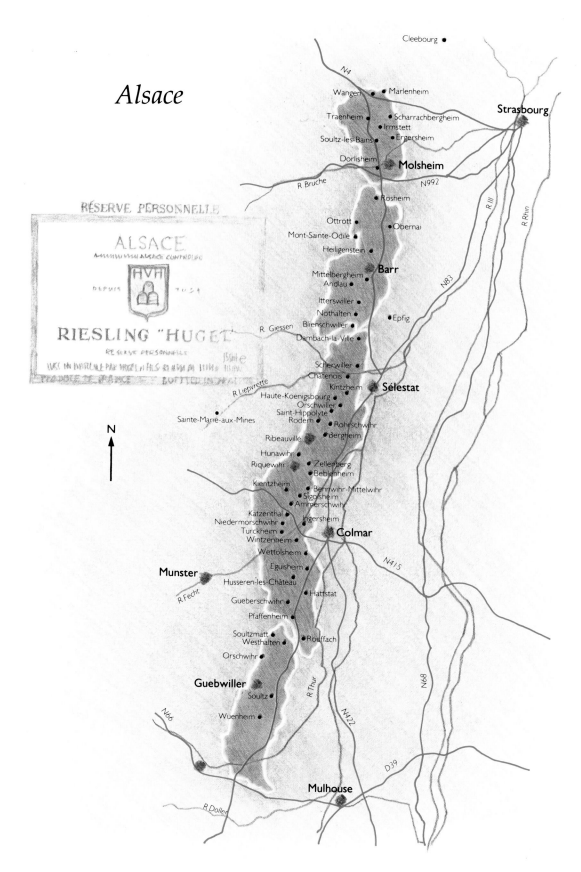

Alsace

RÉSERVE PERSONNELLE

ALSACE
APPELLATION ALSACE CONTROLÉE

HVH

DEPUIS 1639

RIESLING "HUGEL"
RÉSERVE PERSONNELLE

75cl ℮

MISE EN BOUTEILLE PAR HUGEL & FILS A 68340 RIQUEWIHR. HAUT-RHIN.
PRODUCE DE FRANCE — BOTTLED IN FRANCE

N

Cleebourg

N4

Wangen • Marlenheim
Traenheim • Scharrachbergheim
• Irmstett
Soultz-les-Bains • Ergersheim
Dorlisheim • Molsheim
Strasbourg

R Bruche
N992

Rosheim

Ottrott • Obernai
Mont-Sainte-Odile
Heiligenstein
Barr
Mittelbergheim
Andlau
Itterswiller
Nothalten • Epfig
R. Giessen Blienschwiller
Dambach-la-Ville

N83

Scherwiller
Châtenois
Kintzheim • Sélestat
R Liepvrette Haute-Koenigsbourg
Orschwiller
Saint-Hippolyte
Sainte-Marie-aux-Mines Rodern • Rorschwihr
Ribeauville • Bergheim
Hunawihr
Riquewihr • Zellenberg
• Beblenheim
Kientzheim
Bennwihr-Mittelwihr
Sigolsheim
Ammerschwihr
Katzenthal • Ingersheim
Niedermorschwihr
Turckheim • Colmar
Wintzenheim
Wettolsheim
Eguisheim
N415
Munster
Husseren-les-Château
R Fecht Hattstat
Gueberschwihr
Pfaffenheim
Soultzmatt • Rouffach
Westhalten
Orschwihr

Guebwiller
Soultz R Thur
Wuenheim N422

N66

D39

N68

R Doller Mulhouse

Alsace

The vineyards of Alsace occupy the north-eastern corner of France between the Vosges Mountains and the Rhine Valley in the Haut-Rhin and Bas-Rhin *départements*. The mountains protect the 110–kilometre stretch of vines from the wind and rain emanating from the north-west, to the extent that Alsace has one of the driest climates in France, with sunny days lasting long into the autumn. The Bas-Rhin, to the north, is slightly less well protected than the Haut-Rhin, where the wines tend to be correspondingly richer and more intensely aromatic. The types of soil are most varied, with a mix of limestone, clay, silt, sandy-gravel, sandstone and granite running through the vineyards, suiting the different Alsatian grape varieties to a greater or lesser degree. The vines are mostly planted on hillsides facing east and south, at an altitude of 200–450 metres above sea level, with some magnificently accentuated slopes with due-south exposure that give extra ripeness to the grapes to produce *vendange tardive* or even *sélection des grains nobles* wines in good years.

Alsace is a vineyard area with beautiful villages and a family atmosphere that is more marked than anywhere else in France. The Alsatians are intensely proud of their region and its wines. The *caves coopératives*, which represent over half of the production, are of a uniformly high standard. The wines of Alsace, always highly appreciated within France, have not enjoyed their full rewards on the export market until recently. Now, due to consistent and sometimes brilliant quality, good vintages in 1978 and 1981 and excellent vintages, for quantity as well as quality, in 1985, 1986, 1988, 1989, and 1990, they have finally attracted the attention they deserve.

The history of Alsace, a region that has been fought over many times, has caused numerous changes in the volume of the land under vine. From a peak of 30,000 hectares in 1828, a combination of rivalry from other wine regions, rising consumption of beer, and the wars of 1870, 1914 and 1939, ensured that the total had dropped to 7,500 hectares by 1948. Today, Alsace is one of the most prosperous of wine producers, with around 13,000 hectares planted to produce an average of 125 million bottles of wine a year.

The grape varieties permitted in Alsace are the Chasselas (for everyday wines), Sylvaner, Pinot Blanc (also known as Klevner or Clevner), Pinot Noir, Muscat, Gewurztraminer, Pinot Gris (Tokay d'Alsace) and Riesling. In contrast to other wine regions in France, the wines of Alsace are recognized not by their geographical origin, but by their grape variety. The *appellation* Alsace covers the whole of the region with Grand Cru status being given to chosen sites only.

AOC WINES

Alsace

Red, rosé, dry and sweet white wines from 13,000 hectares of vines planted one-third in the northern Bas-Rhin *département* and two-thirds in the Haut-Rhin. The minimum alcohol content must be a natural 8.5° from a maximum yield of 100hl/ha. Despite this yield being the highest in France, it is regularly exceeded and, with the exception of the *vendange tardive* and *sélection des grains nobles* bottlings, Alsace wines almost always need chaptalizing to bring them up to the expected 11°. The style varies according to the type of grape, region (soil, exposition, micro-climate) and vinification. Reds and rosés, obligatorily from the Pinot Noir, are fruity and unpretentious, while the whites have a flowery fruitiness, more or less *sec* according to the varietal and the vintage, but always (except with late-harvested grapes) fermented out to have a dry finish. Since Alsace wines derive their different styles from different grape varieties, these are discussed individually. With few exceptions the wines are best drunk young. Production is nearly 125 million bottles. Price B-C-D.

Alsace Grand Cru

This relatively new *appellation* is limited to white wines only produced from the Riesling, Gewurztraminer, Pinot Gris (Tokay) and Muscat grapes from specific vineyards. The minimum degree of alcohol before chaptalization is 10° for the Muscat and Riesling, 11° for the Gewurztraminer and Pinot Gris, from a low yield for Alsace of 70hl/ha. The label must carry the name of the vineyard, the vintage date and the name of the grape (unblended). An Alsace Grand Cru should always have more structure, body and flavour than a simple Alsace, yet the final character is still determined by the grape variety, soil, siting of the vineyard and vinification. Many producers do not take advantage of the Grand Cru *appellation*, either because they find it too limiting or too confusing, and prefer to differentiate their better wines with such words as *cuvée spéciale*, *cuvée tradition*, *réserve particulière* or *réserve personnelle*. The established Alsace houses of Hugel, Trimbach and Léon Beyer, who have for decades bought grapes for their better *cuvées* from what are now the Grands Crus, follow this practice. Individual domaines with vines in Grand Cru sites — Zind-Humbrecht, Deiss, Ostertag, Josmeyer, J-C Beck, and especially the Cave Coopératives of Eguisheim and Turkheim — have taken full advantage of the new legislation to express the individuality of their wines. For those who believe that it is this individuality, the interrelation between a specific grape variety on a specific soil, rather than

skilful blending, that will provide the future for Alsace wines, the Grands Crus may be viewed in the same way as their Burgundy counterparts. However, since as in Burgundy, it is the site that determines the quality (soil, micro-climate), it is a pity that the other noble grapes — Pinot Blanc, Pinot Noir and Sylvaner — are not allowed to benefit from the exceptional *terroir* of a Grand Cru vineyard. The original list of Grand Crus numbered 26, varying in size from the 2.66 hectare Kantzlerberg to the 75.74 hectare Hengst; a further 22 were accepted in 1986. They are listed below, with the villages they came from, in alphabetical order: Altenberg de Bergbieten (Bergbieten), Altenberg de Bergheim (Bergheim), Altenberg de Wolxheim (Wolxheim), Brand (Turckheim), Eichberg (Eguisheim), Engelberg de Dahlenheim (Dahlenheim), Frankstein (Dambach-la-Ville), Froehn (Zellenberg), Furstentum (Kientzheim), Geisberg (Ribeauvillé), Gloeckelberg (Rodern and Saint-Hippolyte), Goldert (Gueberschwihr), Hatschbourg (Hattstatt and Voegtlinshoffen), Hengst (Wintzenheim), Kanzlerberg (Bergheim), Kastelberg (Andlau), Kessler (Guebwiller), Kirchberg de Barr (Barr), Kirchberg de Ribeauvillé (Ribeauvillé), Kitterlé (Guebwiller), Mambourg (Sigolsheim), Mandelberg (Mittelwihr), Markrain (Bennwihr), Moenchberg (Andlau and Eichhoffen), Muenchberg (Nothalten), Ollwiller (Wuenheim), Osterberg (Ribeauvillé), Pfersigberg (Eguisheim), Pfingstberg (Orschwihr), Praelatenberg (Orschwiller), Rangen (Thann and Vieux-Thann), Rosacker (Hunawihr), Saering (Guebwiller), Schlossberg (Kaysersberg and Kientzheim), Schoenenbourg (Riquewihr), Sommerberg (Niedermorschwihr and Katzenthal), Sonnenglanz (Beblenheim), Spiegel (Bergholtz and Guebwiller), Sporen (Riquewihr), Steinert (Pfaffenheim), Steingrubler (Wettolsheim), Steinklotz (Marlheinem), Vorbourg (Rouffach and Westhalten), Wiebelsberg (Andlau), Wineck-Schlossberg (Katzenthal), Winzenberg (Blienschwiller), Zinnkoepflé (Soultzmatt and Westhalten), Zotzenberg (Mittelbergheim). Price D-E.

Crémant d'Alsace

White and a very little rosé sparkling wine made with Alsatian *vins de base* by the *méthode champenoise*. The Crémant rosé has to be made with wines from the Pinot Noir. The Crémants d'Alsace are good-quality sparkling wines, especially if the *vin de base* is the Pinot Blanc, but they are not yet in the same class as the Crémants which come from the Saône-et-Loire nor the *vins mousseux* from Vouvray. They do represent good value, and production is already over 12 million bottles. Most domaines of any size will make Crémant, but the greater part of the production comes from the cooperatives. Price D.

Vendange Tardive

Wines with an extra intensity due to extra-ripeness of the grapes leading to a higher degree of natural alcohol and a greater concentration of flavour. The name means "late-picked", for usually such ripeness could only be attained by leaving the grapes on the vines until well into November. However, the recent series of hot, dry summers have created *vendange tardive* conditions as early as September. Such wines may be made from any of the noble grapes, but are usually limited to the same as for the Grands Crus: Riesling, Muscat, Gewurztraminer and Pinot Gris. No chaptalization is allowed and the minimum degree of alcohol plus residual sugar must be 12.6° for the Riesling and Muscat, 14° for the Pinot Gris and Gewurztraminer. The naturally aromatic, floral bouquet of the Alsace style is thus intensified, leaving a slight residual sweetness. Only the most conscientious growers make these wines (which must be vintaged and subject to a severe tasting control), and only in good vintages and from the best vineyards. Price F-G.

Sélection des Grains Nobles

Wines resulting from extra-late picking of individual grapes affected by Botrytis (*pourriture noble*), very much in the manner of the greatest châteaux in Sauternes. The sugar in the grapes is concentrated beyond the point of *vendange tardive* by the *pourriture noble* to obtain a minimum of 14.6° potential alcohol for the Riesling and Muscat, 16° for the Gewurztraminer and Pinot Gris. Such wines are made only in exceptional years (1971, 1976, 1983, 1985 and the extraordinary trio of vintages 1988, 1989, 1990), in minuscule quantities. They possess extraordinary intensity and richness, great finesse and a fine acidity coupled with a huge, but totally uncloying natural sweetness which permits the wine to improve over 20 years or more. The wines from Hugel are exceptional, often the only examples of this style, true works of art. The firm of Hugel in Riquewihr were the precursors of this style and such wines remain amongst the finest *vins liquoreux* in the world. The price is very high, but quite justified. Price I-J.

THE ALSATIAN GRAPE VARIETIES

Chasselas

The Chasselas grape is at its best in the AOC Crépy (Savoie) and in Switzerland, where it produces the Fendant and the Dorin wines. In Alsace it makes a light, agreeable wine, low in acidity, to be drunk young "en carafe". Most of the wine goes into the blend known as Zwicker, and Chasselas is almost never seen on a wine label. In 1950, 20% of vineyards were planted with Chasselas, this has regressed to 3% today, in favour of the Sylvaner and the Pinot Blanc. Price B.

Gewurztraminer

The Gewurztraminer grape produces the most typical and popular of the range of Alsatian wines. The colour ranges from pale yellow for the lighter wines to full gold for the splendid *vendange tardive* and *sélection des grains nobles* bottlings, with a heavily perfumed lychee, rosé cashew, slightly spicy aroma and explosive, rather exotic fruit flavours. The lighter wines, with a soft, dry finish, may be drunk young, while the more concentrated *cuvées* need 5–10 years to show their full complexity. They are generally quite full-bodied, but this should never spoil the impression of liveliness and fruit. The Gewurztraminer does well in the heavy limestone-clay soil that is common in Alsace and represents just under 20% of the vineyard area. The best wines are made between Sélestat and Colmar. Two styles of Gewurztraminer exist, one lighter, looking for finesse and able to accompany a meal, the other richer and more heady, which may be drunk on its own.

Klevner or Clevner

These are the Alsatian names for the Pinot Blanc and Auxerrois. The Pinot Blanc is gaining in reputation and is now sold under its own name. The wine has more aroma and body than the Sylvaner and makes very good wine in Pfaffenheim and Westhalten. See Pinot Blanc.

Muscat

Muscat d'Alsace is usually a blend of wine from the Muscat à Petits Grains (the same grape as the Muscat de Frontignan) and the quicker ripening and less fragile Muscat d'Ottonel. Both are extremely aromatic and the richness and body of the former, enhance the lightness and elegance of the latter. The heady, slightly "musky" aroma combines with the pure, grapey taste to make this wine the perfect aperitif. Muscat is a difficult wine to make and although it is much in demand in good years, colder vintages produce a rather thin wine. With rare exceptions, it always finishes dry, which makes a unique contrast between aroma and flavour. Production is a little under 3% of the total crop.

Pinot Blanc – Pinot Auxerrois

The Pinot Blanc and Pinot Auxerrois now represent 18% of the production and are being more and more planted in Alsace, since they are sturdy varietals and the wines are solid and fruity, mid-way in complexity

between Sylvaner and Riesling. The Pinot Auxerrois can be known as Klevner or Clevner and has perhaps an edge of finesse over the Pinot Blanc which is straightforward and reliable. With the typical floral Alsace style, their wines have about the same weight as a Mâcon Blanc. Much of the wine goes into Crémant d'Alsace but Pinot Blanc is a major varietal in its own right.

Pinot Noir

The red grape from Burgundy is often vinified as a rosé, as only in very sunny years is there enough colour in the skins to make a full red wine. However, Alsace has experienced a run of such good vintages in the 1980s, that not only have very good red wines been made, but vignerons have acquired enough confidence to experiment more and more with wood ageing. It is also used to make Crémant d'Alsace rosé and may be vinified *en blanc* to be part of the blend of Crémant d'Alsace. The finer examples are from the north (Cleebourg, Marlenheim, Ottrott and Rodern), yet even at its best it is a fruity, straightforward wine with no great complexity, unless it is treated to a long vinification and expensive ageing in the barrel. Planting has increased to 6% of the Alsace vineyards.

Top: The town of Riquewihr, set among the vineyards with the wooded hills of the Vosges beyond.

Bottom: Riquewihr is typical of the romantic towns and villages of Alsace with their striking half-timbered houses and lovely fountains.

Riesling

Riesling is known as "the king" of the wines of Alsace, although Gewurztraminer is called "the emperor" and Tokay-Pinot Gris "the sultan", and it is without doubt the most elegant of the three. In contrast to the heady richness of the Gewurztraminer and Pinot Gris and the clean grapiness of the Muscat, Riesling is a wine of almost restrained fruit, with a markedly floral bouquet and a firm, clean flavour with a lemony acidity that only adds to its vitality and breed. Lighter *cuvées* are refreshing and can be drunk young, but the *réserve* or Grand Cru wines should be kept for four to five years, and may still be improving ten years after the vintage. Excellent *vendange tardive* wines are made in great years some superlative *sélection des grains nobles* that show the full grandeur of the Riesling grape. The Riesling occupies the finest vineyard sites in Alsace and represents 20% of the vineyard area. The soil on which Riesling provides the best wines is found around Ribeauvillé, Hunawihr and Ammerschwihr, but with proper ripening conditions, good Riesling can be made throughout the region. It is excellent with freshwater fish, white meats and *coq au Riesling*, and remains one of the only dry white wines in France to compare in presence and complexity to the Chardonnays from Burgundy.

Sylvaner

The Sylvaner accounts for just over 20% of the vines in Alsace. It makes a straightforward, light-coloured, refreshing wine with good acidity, different in taste, but fulfilling much the same role as Muscadet from the Loire. Like Muscadet, Sylvaner can also keep a slight *pétillance* if it is bottled very young. It gives of its best in the region of Barr, Rouffach and especially Mittelbergheim, from the Zotzenberg vineyard. It is a wine to drink young.

Pinot Gris (Tokay d'Alsace)

Wines made from the Pinot Gris have habitually been sold under the name of Tokay d'Alsace, but owing to the confusion with the Hungarian Tokay, they must now be sold under the name of *cépage*. The Pinot Gris represents not more than 5% of the vines planted in Alsace and makes a wine that is heavily perfumed, full-bodied and rich on the palate, low in acidity, but basically dry. It does not, however, have the spicy aroma of the Gewurztraminer or the elegant style of the Riesling. Tokay lends itself particularly well to the *vendange tardive* style and, despite its low acidity, will improve for several years in bottle. Wine which is made from the Pinot Gris grape is good with rich pâté, chicken and white meat, or can be drunk on its own, for its appealing broadness of fruit.

Edelzwicker

Edelzwicker is not a grape variety, but a blend of two or more noble grape varieties to which the Chasselas may be added. It is always white and dry, with the typical Alsace flowery aromas, refreshing and easy to drink on its own or with a meal. This wine has superseded the less good Zwicker. Many négociants and cooperatives in Alsace bring out a straightforward "Vin d'Alsace" under a brand name, usually a blend of Chasselas and Sylvaner, which is light and crisp. Price B-C.

THE ROUTE DU VIN

In Alsace the accepted grape varieties may be planted virtually at will, potentially but not actually blurring geographical differences. While the grapes determine the style, the soil determines the character, and throughout the region, certain villages and micro-climates suit certain grapes better than others. The Route du Vin follows the vineyards from north (Bas-Rhin) to south (Haut-Rhin).

It begins at Marlenheim, west of Strasbourg, but there is an enclave of vines at Cleebourg to the north, near the German border, where the *cave coopérative* makes some very good Tokay. The speciality at Marlenheim is Pinot Noir, usually vinified as a rosé (Michel Laugel). Another good Pinot Noir is the Rouge d'Ottrott, produced near Obernai. At Heiligenstein, the finest wines are Klevner and Gewurztraminer (Louis Klipfel, Charles Wantz). Mittelbergheim is known for the Zotzenberg vineyard, with a magnificent southern exposure, where some Tokay and Gewurztraminer is planted (E. Boeckel), and more is being considered, while Sylvaner-Zotzenberg remains probably the finest example of this variety in Alsace (A. Seltz & Fils). Klevner (Clevner or Pinot Blanc) also does well at Mittelbergheim and particularly so at Dambach-la-Ville (Willy Gisselbrecht). At Andlau and Epfig the Pinot Gris is superb (André Ostertag). The Gewürztraminer comes into prominence at Bergheim (Marcel Deiss, Gustave Lorentz), and at Rorschwihr Rolly-Gassmann makes full-bodied wines of an excellent quality. Ribeauvillé is particularly famous for its Riesling (Louis Sipp, Bott Frères and the crisp, long-lasting wines of Trimbach, especially the monopole Clos Ste Hune) and for its elegant, grapey Muscat.

Riquewihr, the most beautiful wine town in Alsace if not in France, has two spectacular vineyards, Schoenenbourg and Sporen, and two of Alsace's finest grower-négociants: Dopff & Irion and Hugel. All the grape varieties grow well on the easy slopes around Riquewihr, especially Riesling. Hugel has deservedly the best reputation possible for their firm, aromatic wines and their speciality of Riesling, Gewurztraminer and Tokay *vendange tardive*. To the south-east, Beblenheim and the neighbouring Mittelwihr are both particularly good for Gewurztraminer and some fine Muscat (Edgard Schaller). The large commune of Sigolsheim has an excellent *cave coopérative*, with vines in the two best sites, Mambourg (Gewurztraminer) and Altenbourg (Riesling) and some rich, spicy Tokay comes from Pierre Sparr. Kientzheim, the centre of the Confrérie Saint-Etienne, harbours the Fürstentum and part of the Schlossberg vineyard, with particularly fine wines from Paul Blanck, while neighbouring Kayserberg shares the Schlossberg vineyard, which is planted almost entirely in Riesling (remarkable wines, with great purity of style from Madame Colette Faller of Domaine Weinbach). The famous Kaefferkopf vineyard at Ammerschwihr produces excellent Gewurztraminer and Riesling (Kuehn), distinctive Pinot Blanc and some fine Muscat. South of Colmar (the centre of the Alsace wine trade), Turckheim is a major wine commune with a good cooperative and very fine wines from the four noble grapes planted in the Brand vineyard.

Further south, Wintzenheim is the home of two of the best family domaines in Alsace, Jos. Meyer and Zind-Humbrecht, who make superb Gewurztraminer from the Hengst vineyard; Wettolshim produces some good Muscat from the Steingrubler vineyard; Eguisheim is known for its cooperative, the largest in Alsace, and for the wines of Léon Beyer; the south-facing slopes at Husserein-les-Châteaux give very good Gewurztraminer and Riesling (Kuentz-Bas) and the Muscat comes into its own again at Voegtlinshoffen (Théo Cattin). At Pfaffenheim, the wines become more full-bodied, richer in style (fine Pinot Blanc and Gewurztraminer from Pierre Frick) and are very unctuous and aromatic at Rouffach (A. & O. Muré). The dry, limestony slopes at Westhalten are suitable for Muscat and Gewurztraminer (Alfred Heim), and the latter also thrives at Orschwihr (Lucien Albrecht, Paul Reinhart). In the very south, Schlumberger dominates at Guebwiller, with over-poweringly fruity Gewurztraminer (Cuvée Christine and Cuvée Anne), and Zind-Humbrecht makes some splendid Riesling from the recently reclaimed Rangen vineyard.

Lorraine

The wines of Lorraine used to be highly esteemed and widely appreciated, but a succession of disastrous vintages for the *vignerons*, wars, the *phylloxera*, general industrialization and the more profitable business of planting plum trees, has reduced the vineyard area to under 1% of the 30,000 hectares of vines in 1890.

VDQS WINES

Côtes de Toul VDQS

Red, dry white, *gris* and rosé wines from 65 hectares of vineyards planted around the city of Toul in the Meurthe-et-Moselle *département*. The vast majority of the production is of *vin gris*, a very pale rosé made almost exclusively from the Gamay. The Pinot Noir and Pinot Meunier are permitted, but are less and less planted. The *vin gris* is very light, with a minimum alcohol content of only 8.5° from a yield of 60hl/ha, with an agreeable fruit and slight acidity that go very well with the local cuisine. The Auxerrois and Pinot Blanc are planted for the whites. The best producers from this region that is beginning to see some replanting are the SCV Laroppe and Claude Vosgien. The production is around 350,000 bottles, which are mostly drunk in the region. Price B.

Vins de Moselle VDQS

Red and dry white wines from what is left of the vineyards in the Moselle *département*. Red wines must be from the Gamay (to a minimum of 30%), the Pinot Noir and Pinot Gris, the whites from the Pinot Blanc, Auxerrois and Sylvaner. They are light, the reds being pale in colour, although there are no rosés. In 1986 the German grape Muller-Thurgau was allowed, its fruity, everyday wines having been so successful in nearby Luxembourg. Good wines come from Mansion-Welferinger and the Château de Vaux. In 1980, 3,600 bottles of red wine were produced and 1,300 bottles of white. Price C.

VINS DE PAYS

VIN DE PAYS DE LA MEUSE

White and *gris* rosé and red wines from a *département* that is more famous for its production of beer than wine. The planting of Chardonnay and Aligoté is being encouraged, alongside the Auxerrois, Pinot Blanc, Pinot Noir and Gamay. The wines are generally light with an attractive fruit and refreshing acidity. Production is increasing and now exceeds 120,000 bottles, 60% white. Price A.

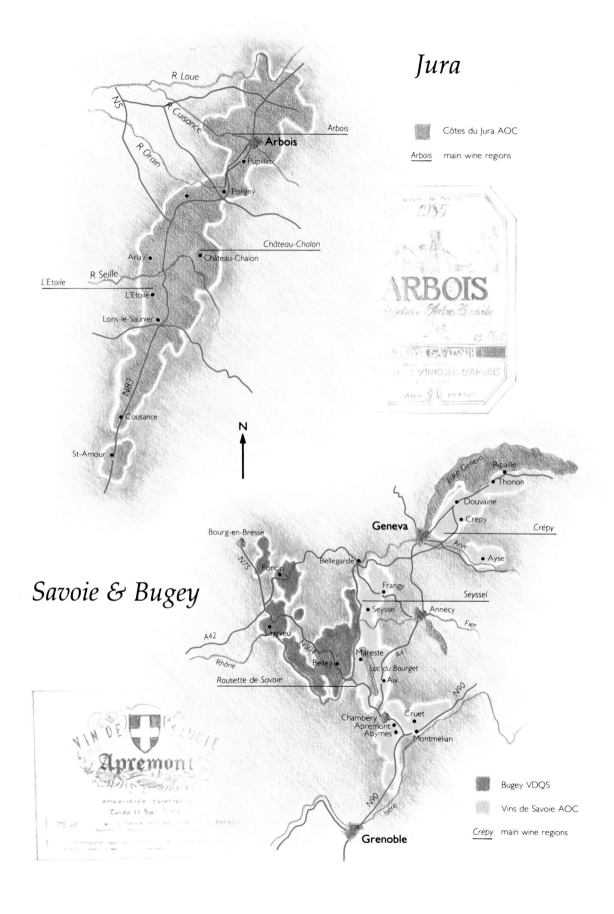

Jura, Savoie & Bugey

The major vineyards of France are well documented and well defined: Burgundy, Bordeaux, Champagne, Alsace, the Rhône and the Loire Valleys. Their grape varieties virtually control the production of fine wines throughout the world and their style is well known. The three regions in this chapter are different, for their wines are mostly drunk in France and their style is not well known. It is, however, distinctive enough to be described as "typical", an adjective that wine tasters are always supposed not to use, as it shows laziness (though to my mind it shows prior knowledge) and does nothing to describe the wine for the uninitiated. These wines are rarely copied by vineyards outside their territory.

The most successful wines are white, including the sparkling wines made by the *méthode champenoise* (a description which soon no region outside Champagne may be allowed to use, replacing it with *méthode traditionelle*), while the reds have more in common, quite naturally, with the neighbouring Beaujolais and Burgundy than with other parts of France. They do not seem to travel well for, partly because they are so delicious and marry so well with the local cuisine, they often seem ill at ease or misunderstood away from home. It is perhaps for this reason that they have retained all their individuality, allowing "minor" grape varieties to express themselves perfectly.

Below: Arbois, in the centre of the Jura.

Jura

The vineyards of the Jura are among the oldest in France and its wines are perhaps the most distinctive. The *appellation* covers 1,400 hectares, all in the Jura *département*, and since the last decade has been in full expansion. The vines are planted on slopes with an incline of between 10% and 40%, at an altitude of 250–470 metres. Exposition is generally south-south-east and the soil is a heavy, multi-coloured clay on a limestone base. The climate is semi-continental, with hard winters, some risk of spring frosts, often heavy rain in summer but with dry, sunny autumns to allow the grapes to ripen. Local *cépages* are much in evidence, with the red and rosé wines coming from the Trousseau, making medium to full deep-coloured, long-lasting wine; the Poulsard, seen only in the Jura, giving a light-coloured wine, often more rosé than red; and the Pinot Noir, lending a light Burgundy fruit. For the whites, the local grape is the Savagnin, which makes very particular full-bodied wines with a sherry-like bouquet, to which some Chardonnay or Pinot Blanc may be added, except in the case of Vin Jaune, which must be made from the Savagnin alone. Chardonnay on its own is becoming more widely grown, although it is less "typically" Jura. There are four main *appellations* in the Jura: Arbois, Château-Chalon, Côtes du Jura and L'Etoile, with a total production of around ten million bottles.

AOC WINES

Arbois

Red, dry white, *gris* and rosé wines from vineyards planted around the town of Arbois in the centre of the Jura wine country. The red wines may be made from Trousseau, Poulsard or Pinot Noir grapes, either alone or blended. The Trousseau makes a medium-coloured, full-bodied *vin-de-garde*, the Poulsard a much lighter wine with great finesse, and is often reserved for rosés, while the Pinot Noir wines much resemble a lighter Côte de Beaune. Rosé d'Arbois is well known for its faded, pale red "onion-skin" colour, the appearance of a rosé with the body of a red wine. White wines are made from the Savagnin, which has a most pronounced slightly sherry-like bouquet – seen in its most exaggerated state in the Vin Jaune style – the Chardonnay or Pinot Blanc. Especially when made with the Savagnin, the whites are full yellow in colour, with a distinctive nutty bouquet, a rich intensity of flavour and completely dry. They are good drunk just on their own, but are at their best with fish or chicken in a cream

sauce, preferably one to which the same wine has been added. Arbois, and the Jura in general, has many domaines that have been in the same hands for many years, and are still managed as well as before, if not better. These include: Rolet Père & Fils, Jacques Forêt, Lucien Aviet, Desiré Petit & Fils, Roger Lornet, Jacques Tissot and A & M Tissot, as well as the Cave Fruitière Vinicole d'Arbois. Production of Arbois wines is limited to 40hl/ha with an alcohol content of 10° for the reds and 10.5° for the whites. Total production is in the region of six million bottles a year, of which 40% is white. The wines are not expensive for this quality but are not cheap either. Price C-D.

Arbois Mousseux

Sparkling wine made by the *méthode champenoise* with wines from the Arbois *appellation*, in the best cases 100% Chardonnay. The genuine sparkling wine from Arbois is of high quality and should not be confused with a cheaper version called *vin fou*. Price low D.

Arbois Pupillin

Red, dry white and rosé wines from the commune of Pupillin, where the soil gives an added intensity of flavour to the wines. Very little seen; the best domaine is Desiré Père & Fils, while the Fruitière Vinicole produces reliable wines. Price low D.

Château-Chalon

The only *appellation* attributed to the different Vins Jaunes produced in the Jura, covering only 25 hectares around Voiteur and Château-Chalon. Despite a legal maximum of 30hl/ha at Château-Chalon (40hl/ha for Vins Jaunes produced elsewhere) the actual production is often declassified due to insufficient ripeness, and the average yield is only 80,000 bottles. Only the Savagnin grape may be used, picked as late as possible, even into December. After fermentation, the wine is racked into oak barrels (*pièces* or *demi-muids*), where it will age with no toppping-up for at least six years. As the level of wine in the barrel descends through evaporation, down to perhaps one-third empty, a *voile* or *flor* of yeast cells forms on the surface of the wine, transforming it, little by little, into a Vin Jaune, a wine of deep yellow colour with a heady, nutty bouquet of great complexity and the flavour of a concentrated fino sherry. After the minimum of six years, during which many casks may have to be discarded since they have not "taken" the *flor* and have followed the rules of oenology to become vinegar, the wine is bottled in the squat high-necked 62cl *clavelins* and may last indefinitely. It is best drunk on its own, or at the end of a meal with an aged gouda cheese, as the pungent flavour of all Vins Jaunes will destroy that of any subsequent wine. Good growers in Château-Chalon are Jean-Marie Courbet, Jean Macle, Marius Perron. Price G.

Côtes du Jura

Red, dry white, *gris* and rosé wines from vineyards in the southern part of the Jura region. Red, *gris* and rosé wines are made from the Poulsard, Trousseau or Pinot Noir, either separately or together, while the whites are from the Savagnin, Chardonnay or Pinot Blanc. Yield is limited to 40hl/ha, not often attained in these hilly vineyards which are susceptible to frost, and the minimum alcohol content is 10° for the reds, *gris* and rosés, 10.5° for the whites. The Côtes du Jura are very much in the style of the Arbois wines, but are considered superior. Good producers include Château d'Arlay, Luc and Sylvie Boilley, Jean Boudry, Château Gréa and the Cave Fruitière Vinicole de Poligny. Production averages around 1.5 million bottles, of which 80% is white. Price C-D.

Côtes du Jura Mousseux

Sparkling wine made by the *méthode champenoise* with wines from the Côtes du Jura *appellation*. The Savagnin grape has too distinctive a flavour, so the grapes used are Chardonnay and Pinot Blanc. Price low D.

L'Etoile

White wines only from 64 hectares of particularly well-situated vineyards just north of Lons-le-Saunier made from the Savagnin, Chardonnay and Poulsard grapes, this last vinified as a white wine. They have more finesse than the wines from Arbois and are much sought after, especially to accompany river-fish in a cream sauce. There is also some excellent sparkling wine with its own *appellation*, L'Etoile Mousseux, and some Vin Jaune and Vin de Paille. Only 300,000 bottles are produced annually. Some of the best coming from Château de l'Etoile and Domaine de Montbourgeau. Price E (G for Vin de Paille and Vin Jaune).

Vin de Paille

A dessert wine of great rarity made under the global *appellations* Arbois or Côtes du Jura, where, after picking, the bunches of grapes are placed on straw mats (*lits de paille*) or suspended from the rafters for a period of three months during which they become raisin-like and very highly concentrated in grape sugar. A very slow fermentation will produce an astoundingly rich, amber-coloured nectar, more like a liqueur than a wine.

Vin de Paille may age for 3–4 years in wood before being bottled in special 37.5cl *pots*, and can be kept almost indefinitely. It is usually drunk on its own and is even supposed to have therapeutic qualities. Top class wines from Domaine Jean-Louis Morel, Rolet Père & Fils, Jacques Tissot. Price F (*le pot*).

Vin Jaune

This is not an *appellation*, but a type of wine made in the Arbois and Jura *appellations*. The word *jaune* comes from the colour the wine acquires through its unique ageing process. The only grape permitted is the Savagnin, and after fermentation, following a very late harvest (the grapes are sometimes picked when snow is on the ground), the wine is racked into oak barrels where it remains on ullage, with no topping-up allowed, for a minimum of six years. The result, which defies the rules of oenology, is a wine of deep yellow colour, with a heady nutty bouquet of great complexity and the flavour of concentrated fino sherry. Having survived this system of ageing, Vin Jaune is virtually indestructible, and may keep for over a hundred years. All Vin Jaune is sold in a special squat bottle called a *clavelin*, containing 62 cl. The best-known Vin Jaune is Château-Chalon which has its own *appellation*. Most good Arbois producers make a Vin Jaune. It is the speciality of Hubert Clavelin et Fils. Price G.

VINS DE PAYS

FRANCHE-COMTE
Red, dry white and rosé wines from vines planted in the *départements* of the Jura and the Haute-Saône. Grapes allowed are the Pinot Noir and Gamay for the reds and rosés, and Chardonnay, Pinot Gris and Auxerrois (Pinot Blanc) for the whites. The white wines are much the best, with a clean fruit and refreshingly crisp finish. Production averages around 350,000 bottles, 55% of white, 25% red, 20% rosé. Price A-B.

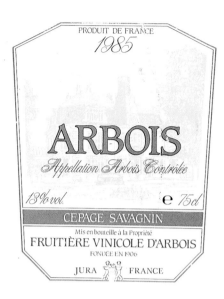

Above: Harvesting Trousseau grapes in the sloping vineyards of the Jura.

Savoie

The Savoie vineyards, currently 1,500 hectares extending over the *départements* of the Savoie, Haute-Savoie and a few communes of the Ain and the Isère, are known principally for their white wine. As with the wines of Alsace, they benefit (or suffer, as the case may be) from a global image of *Vin de Savoie*, and the individual *appellations* sometimes receive less attention. In fact, while the basic style of these wines is light, pale in colour, with a smoky-fruity bouquet and crisp dry finish, there are also some richer white wines made, some delicious reds and rosés and a great deal of sparkling wine. The difference between these wines is evident from the label, which will state either the village or commune the wine comes from, or the grape variety it is made with. Total production is 13 million bottles.

AOC WINES

Vin de Savoie

Red, dry white and rosé wines produced in the *départements* of the Savoie, Haute-Savoie, the Ain and the Isère. The reds and rosés, often called *clairets* in the region, must come from the Mondeuse, Gamay and Pinot Noir, and while 20% white grapes may be added at fermentation, this rarely happens. Wines from the Mondeuse are particularly good, with a deep colour and a smooth fruit flavour. The Pinot Noir and the Gamay make attractive, fruity wines, quite light in colour, that should be drunk young and served cool. The better white wines are made from the local grapes Jacquère and Altesse, which give a particularly Savoie character to the wine, as well as more intensity of flavour. Other white grapes are the Chardonnay, Aligoté and the Chasselas, producing agreeable, crisp, dry wines. They are good as an apéritif, with hors d'oeuvre, fish and chicken, and, of course, a cheese fondue. The reds may be treated like a light burgundy or beaujolais. All wines must have a minimum alcohol content of 9° from a yield of 45hl/ha. Total production ten million bottles, 75% of which is white. Price B-C.

Vin de Savoie + Cru

In 1973, when *Vin de Savoie* became an *appellation*, certain communes or *crus* were singled out to be allowed to add their name to the label, or even sell under the name of the commune, the *appellation* remaining *Vin de Savoie*. Red, dry white and rosé wines are made, as well as some excellent sparkling wine by the *méthode champenoise*. To maintain their superiority

Right: Vineyards below the Col du Granier.

over the plain *Vin de Savoie*, these wines must have a higher minimum alcohol content at 9.5° from a much lower yield of 35hl/ha. The villages with the right to sell wine under their own name are listed alphabetically, with reliable producers in each *cru*: Abymes (Michael Cartier), Apremont (Pierre Boniface), Arbin (an excellent red Mondeuse from Alexis Genoux), Ayse (Patrick and Dominique Belluard), Charpinnat, Chautagne (reds especially from the Cave de Chautagne), Chignin (Jean-Pierre Quénard), Chignin-Bergeron (Raymond Quénard), Cruét (Cave des Vins Fins), Jongieux (Edmond Jacquin), Marignan, Montmélian (best for red wines), Ripaille (Château de Ripaille), and the lesser known Saint-Jean-de-la-Porte, Saint-Jerome-Prieuré and Sainte-Marie-d'Alloix. The white wines are for the most part from the Jacquère, with its slightly smoky character, and are very good indeed. Price C.

Vin de Savoie Ayse Mousseux

Sparkling wine made from grapes grown in the commune of Ayse. The grape varieties must be indigenous: the Gringet, Altesse and up to 30% Roussette d'Ayse. Production is limited to 40hl/ha, as opposed to 45hl/ha for the plain Savoie Mousseux *appellation*. The wines are very elegant and most of the production is consumed locally or in Switzerland or Lyon. Price D.

Vin de Savoie Mousseux

White and a very little rosé wine produced from vines which are grown in the Savoie, by the *méthode champenoise*. The best of these come from the *cru* Ayse, although good wines also come from Chignin, Marignan and Ripaille. Sparkling wines from the Savoie are very pale in colour, often only slightly effervescent, and always dry. There is a large *vin mousseux* industry based in the Savoie that uses wine which is brought from outside the region and, however good these products may be, they have no right to the *appellation*. Price high C-D.

Crépy

Dry white wines, that are faintly sparkling or *pérlant*, from 80 hectares of vines in the Haute-Savoie, to the north-west of Geneva. The wines of Crépy must be made exclusively with the Chasselas grape, known as the Fendant in nearby Switzerland. They have a low alcohol content, 9° minimum, and a high natural acidity which, combined with their hint of sparkle, makes them extremely refreshing. They are more than just a thirst-quencher, however, with a lovely pale golden colour, a hint of violets on the nose, followed by a lively flavour and stylish finish. Due to the acidity, they age well, losing their freshness but becoming more complex.

Crépy is generally sold in a distinctive tall green bottle. Production can attain 800,000 bottles. Price D.

Roussette de Savoie

Dry white wines from the Savoie, Haute-Savoie and a very small part of the Isère *départements*. The grape varieties are the Altesse alone for the *crus*, associated with Chardonnay (called charmingly Petite-Sainte-Marie in the Savoie) to a maximum of 50%, with Mondeuse Blanche for the rest. Minimum alcohol content is 10°, from a low yield of 35hl/ha. Roussette de Savoie is very dry, with good fruit, an attractive acidity and some finesse. Good as an apéritif, with *charcuterie*, fish and poultry. Production is around 600,000 bottles. Price C.

Roussette de Savoie + Cru

Dry white wines grown in the Savoie and Haute-Savoie *départements*, made exclusively from the Altesse grape. The following communes have the right to add their name to that of Roussette de Savoie, or sell under their own name: Frangy, Marestel, Monterminod and Monthoux. These wines, especially those made in the commune of Marestel, have more fruit, flavour and finesse than the Roussette de Savoie *tout court*. An excellent wine is made at Château Monterminod. They are absolutely perfect drunk on the spot with fresh river-fish. Fine wines from Barlet Frères, sold as Marestel. Production is small and very little is exported. Price C.

Seyssel

Dry white wines from 75 hectares in the commune of Seyssel in the Haute-Savoie and the Ain *départements*, the *appellation* being separated by the river Rhône. The vines are planted on south-south-west facing slopes at 200–400 metres, on a chalky limestone soil. The only grape permitted is the Roussette de Seyssel, a local version of the Altesse, with a minimum alcohol content of 10° from a maximum yield of 40hl/ha. Seyssel, which, with Crépy, was for a long time the only AOC in the Savoie, is light and dry, with a distinctive floral bouquet of violets and irises and a beautifully balanced finish. It is delicious as an apéritif, with fish or white meats and the local cheeses. Production is small, around 400,000 bottles, and little of it leaves France. Price C.

Seyssel Mousseux

White sparkling wines made in the Seyssel *appellation* from the Roussette and Chasselas grapes. The wines are wonderfully light, with none of the aggressiveness characteristic of some *vins mousseux*, and most of the 100,000 bottles made a year are drunk locally. Price D.

VINS DE PAYS

BALMES DAUPHINOISES

Red, dry white and rosé wines from the north of the Isère *département*. The wines are similar to the *vins de Savoie*, but a little less distinctive. The reds and rosés (40%) must be made from the Gamay, Pinot Noir and Mondeuse, to which may be added the Syrah, Merlot and the Gamay Teinturiers. In fact, most of the wine is made from the Gamay. The whites (60%), more interesting and excellent *vins de comptoir*, are from the Chardonnay and the Jacquère, with the Aligoté and Pinot Gris admitted. They are light and refreshing. Production about 150,000 bottles. Price A-low B.

COTEAUX DU GRESIVAUDAN

Red, dry white and rosé wines from the Isère and Savoie *départements*. The reds and rosés are from the Gamay and Pinot Noir, the whites from the same varietals as the Vin de Pays des Balmes Dauphinoises, which they very much resemble. Production is 300,000 bottles, 75% red, 15% white, 10% rosé. Price A-low B.

VIN DE PAYS D'ALLOBROGIE

Mostly dry white wine from the Haute-Savoie, Savoie, Isère and the Ain *départements*. Whites come from the Jacquère, and Chardonnay or Chasselas, reds from the Gamay and Mondeuse. Light, refreshing, to be drunk young. Production around 500,000 bottles, 90% white, virtually no rosé. Price A-low B.

Bugey

The wines of the Bugey come from vineyards planted in the Ain *département*, midway between the Beaujolais and the Savoie. Until recently there was a risk that the *appellation*, a VDQS, would die out, but the production, although small, has been growing owing to local demand – and now, thanks to the quality of its wines, international demand. The wines are light and attractive, the reds resembling the wines of the Beaujolais, the whites sometimes those of the Savoie, sometimes those of the Mâconnais, with their own particular *goût de terroir*.

VDQS WINES

Vin du Bugey

Red, dry white and rosé wines from vines planted in the Ain *département*, around the towns of Bellet and Nantua. The reds and rosés must come from the Gamay, Pinot Noir, Poulsard or Mondeuse grapes, with the possibility of adding 20% white grapes. They are light-coloured, fruity and should be drunk young. The white wines are slightly more interesting and individual, being made from the Savoie grapes Altesse, Jacquère and Mondeuse Blanche with some Aligoté and Pinot Gris, there is also a growing, and increasingly dominant, interest in Chardonnay. If a Bugey wine comes entirely from a single grape variety, it will say so on the label. All the wines are light in alcohol, with a minimum of 9° from a yield of 45hl/ha. They are delightful, light, refreshing wines. About two million bottles are produced annually, 60% white. Price B.

Vin du Bugey + Cru

Red, dry white and rosé wines from the *appellation* Bugey, with the right to add the name of the commune to the label, or to sell the wine under the name of the *cru* itself. Five communes have this right: Virieu-le-Grand, Montagnieu, Manicle, Machuraz and Cerdon, but only Montagnieu and Cerdon take advantage of it. The latter is always red or rosé, the former always white. Apart from the *terroir* which distinguishes the wine, the alcohol content must be a little higher at 9.5° minimum, from a lower yield of 40hl/ha. These wines are certainly well worth the small extra expense. The most important producer is Eugène Monin. Price B-C.

Vin du Bugey Mousseux or Pétillant

Dry white sparkling and rosé wine made either by the *méthode champenoise*, or by natural fermentation in the bottle. The latter produces less sparkle, but leaves the wine all its finesse. The wines of Cerdon have their own *appellation* as *vins mousseux* and produce some rosé; the finest sparkling wines come from Montagnieu. Production unfortunately is tiny, what the French call *confidentiel*. Mostly consumed locally, it is a perfect apéritif and very good with Bugey cuisine. Price D.

VINS DE PAYS

VIN DE PAYS DE L'AIN

Very small production, of mostly white wine that otherwise would have the *appellation* Vin de Bugey. None was declared in either 1987 or 1988. Price A.

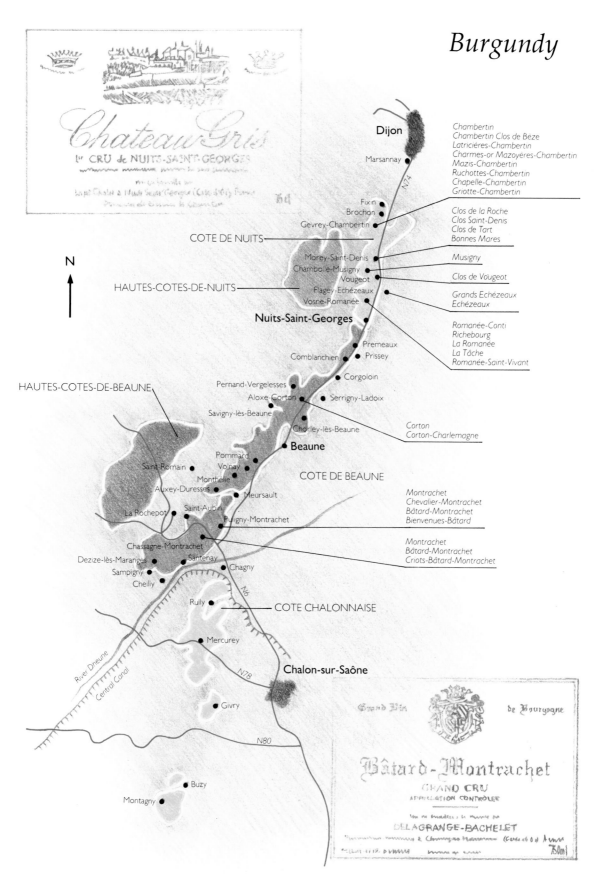

Burgundy

Chambertin
Chambertin Clos de Bèze
Latricières-Chambertin
Charmes-or Mazoyères-Chambertin
Mazis-Chambertin
Ruchottes-Chambertin
Chapelle-Chambertin
Griotte-Chambertin

Clos de la Roche
Clos Saint-Denis
Clos de Tart
Bonnes Mares

Musigny

Clos de Vougeot

Grands Echézeaux
Echézeaux

Romanée-Conti
Richebourg
La Romanée
La Tâche
Romanée-Saint-Vivant

Corton
Corton-Charlemagne

Montrachet
Chevalier-Montrachet
Bâtard-Montrachet
Bienvenues-Bâtard

Montrachet
Bâtard-Montrachet
Criots-Bâtard-Montrachet

Dijon

Marsannay

Fixin
Brochon
Gevrey-Chambertin

COTE DE NUITS

N

Morey-Saint-Denis
Chambolle-Musigny
Vougeot
Flagey-Echézeaux
Vosne-Romanée

HAUTES-COTES-DE-NUITS

Nuits-Saint-Georges

Premeaux
Comblanchien
Prissey

Corgoloin

Pernand-Vergelesses
Aloxe-Corton
Serrigny-Ladoix
Savigny-lès-Beaune

HAUTES-COTES-DE-BEAUNE

Chorley-lès-Beaune

Beaune

COTE DE BEAUNE

Pommard
Saint-Romain
Volnay
Monthélie
Auxey-Duresses
Meursault
Saint-Aubin
La Rochepot
Puligny-Montrachet

Chassagne-Montrachet
Dezize-lès-Maranges
Santenay
Sampigny
Chagny
Cheilly

Rully

COTE CHALONNAISE

Mercurey

River Dheune
Central Canal

Chalon-sur-Saône

Givry

N6
N78
N80

Buzy
Montagny

Château Gris
1er CRU de NUITS-SAINT-GEORGES

Grand Vin   de Bourgogne

Bâtard-Montrachet
GRAND CRU
APPELLATION CONTROLEE

DELAGRANGE-BACHELET

42

Burgundy

The vineyards of Burgundy extend across four *départements* to the south-east of Paris: the Yonne, the Côte d'Or, the Saône-et-Loire and the Rhône. In these *départements* there are five wine regions: Chablis, the Côte d'Or (comprising the Côte de Nuits and the Côte de Beaune), the Côte Chalonnaise, the Mâconnais and the Beaujolais. With the exception of Chablis, only 170 kilometres from Paris, an enclave of vines disconnected from the rest of Burgundy by a distance of 140 kilometres, there are vineyards with little interruption from Dijon to Lyon.

For a region that is covered by a single name, Burgundy's wines are less homogeneous than, say, those of Alsace or Champagne, but less diverse than those from the Loire or the Rhône valleys. The immense variety of *appellations* and *crus* come almost entirely from two red grape varieties, the Pinot Noir and the Gamay, and two white grapes, the Chardonnay and the Aligoté. Of these four, Pinot Noir and Chardonnay produce

Below: All the great red and white wines of Burgundy are aged in wood casks.

the finest wines. Pinot Noir is at its best in the Côte d'Or and the Côte Chalonnaise: further north in the Yonne it ripens well only in good years, while in the Mâconnais and the Beaujolais to the south it makes a dullish wine. Yet in the centre of Burgundy its elegance is unsurpassed and its variety infinite. Chardonnay adapts itself to the different soils and climate to make wines of characteristic style and finesse throughout the Burgundy region. The Gamay plays a minor role in the Côte d'Or and Côte Chalonnaise, and comes into its own on the granite soil of the Beaujolais, while the Aligoté, having no real character except crispness and dryness, behaves in much the same way as the Chardonnay, tasting crisper from the north, more fruity from the south.

From Chablis to Villefranche, these four grapes produce a complete palette of wines – red, white, rosé and sparkling – the difference between one wine and another lying in the soil, the climate and the methods of winemaking.

In complete contrast to the age-old rival for fine wines, Bordeaux, where there are few major *appellations* and many large properties producing a unified wine, Burgundy has a large number of *appellations*, in most cases smaller than a single Cru Classé château, each of them parcellated between many growers. Fine quality wine in any region will result from a combination of the following factors: soil, exposition, age of the vines, yield, vinification, *élevage* and, above all, a special effort on behalf of the producer to make a fine wine. In Burgundy more than anywhere else, with scores of *appellations* split between thousands of

growers, vinified, bottled and sold by either themselves, the *caves coopératives* or the négociants, it is the name of the bottler on the label that counts for as much, if not more, than the *appellation*. For this reason, the names of good growers or négociants are given, their wines being classic examples from each *appellation*.

The idea of a classic wine has become more important with the recent (1982) increase of the permitted minimum yields in Burgundy by between 10 and 25%. The INAO (Institut National des Appellations d'Origine) authorized these increases "in the face of reality", but it is a moot point whether reality lies in modern viticulture being able to produce fine wine in larger quantities than before, or in the easy sale for these wines provided they carry the prestigious name. It is difficult to imagine that a Montrachet will have the same intensity of bouquet and concentration of flavour from vines allowed to produce 40hl/ha (or considerably more) as from the same vines limited to 30hl/ha. This said, there has been a marked movement among both growers and négociants to limit yields, either by severe pruning at the beginning of the year, or by thinning excess bunches of grapes in July and August, or both. The need for the concentration of colour and flavour has since been recognized by the INAO, who have changed tack and are now curbing excessive yields by limiting the PLC (see page 11) to 20%. The great strength of Burgundy lies in the variety of different soils or *terroir*, each giving a different expression to the wine. The "classic" wines in each *appellation* are those that best represent the *terroir*.

REGIONAL OR GENERIC APPELLATIONS

These basic *appellations* can be used throughout the Burgundy region, regardless of where the wine is made, so long as the accepted varietals are used. It is therefore most important for the consumer to see, from the label, where the wine is grown and bottled, as that information will point to the style of the wine. It is plain that a Bourgogne Aligoté or a Crémant de Bourgogne which is bottled in the Chablis region will be a very different wine from one of the same name bottled in the Mâconnais, the difference between them lying in the soil, the climate and possibly even the style of winemaking.

Bourgogne

Red, white and rosé wines from the Burgundy wine region, covering specific areas in the *départements* of the Yonne, Côte d'Or, Saône-et-Loire and Rhône. The reds and rosés must be made from the Pinot Noir and the little known varietals Pinot Beurot and Pinot Liébault, with the exception of wines from the Mâconnais and the Beaujolais, where they may be from the Gamay, and from the Yonne, where the local grapes César and Tressot are permitted. The minimum alcohol content is 10° from a yield of 55hl/ha. Bourgogne from the Pinot

Noir, almost entirely from the Côte d'Or and the Côte Chalonnaise, should have all the qualities of the grape: a lovely cherry-ruby colour, a strawberry fruit aroma, with hints of blackcurrants, raspberries and wild cherries, the fruit carried through into a harmonious finish, neither too heavy, too acidic nor too sweet. The simple *appellation* Bourgogne tends to lack a definition of origin if it is blended from the wines of several communes. If the wine is domaine-bottled however, i.e. by the grower, it will state the origin on the label. A Bourgogne rouge from Philippe Rossignol in Gevrey-Chambertin or a Bourgogne blanc from Guy Roulot in Meursault will have had the same care as these growers' more important wines. Good examples of Bourgogne are very good value, and may be drunk relatively young at two to six years. Poorer examples will be evident from their too thin or too thick colour and lack of fruit and balance. Wines from any one or several of the 10 Beaujolais *crus* (see pages 85–86) may be declassified into Bourgogne, even though the wine is 100% from the Gamay grape. It is unfortunate that some Burgundy négociants use these wines to sell under the *appellation* Bourgogne, generally assumed to be from the Pinot Noir, yet it is still permitted by the INAO. Many Burgundy négociants add "Pinot Noir" to the label of their Bourgognes where this is true, to emphasize that it is 100% from this grape.

White wines are made from the Chardonnay with sometimes some Pinot Blanc and Pinot Beurot, and must have a minimum alcohol content of 10.5° from a yield of 60hl/ha. The vast majority are pure Chardonnay from the Côte d'Or and the Côte Chalonnaise. They have a lovely pale greeny-gold colour, the appley-fruity Chardonnay aroma and a fullish flavour that finishes dry. They are a perfect introduction to the finer white burgundies, and are best drunk with hors d'oeuvres, fish and white meats and the local cheeses. Bourgogne rosé is not common, except in years of over-production like 1982 or 1989, or from growers who regularly produce a *rosé de saignée* (see page 249) to obtain concentration for their red wines. With its salmon-pink colour and delicate Pinot fruit, it is excellent with summer dishes. The *appellation* Bourgogne is usually good value. Production is 1.3 million bottles of white, 13.5 million red and rosé. Price C-low D.

Bourgogne Aligoté

White wine from the Aligoté grape grown throughout the Burgundy region from Chablis to Villefranche-sur-Saône. Chardonnay is tolerated to a maximum of 15%, but the grapes are normally destined for Bourgogne blanc. Minimum alcohol content is 9.5° from a yield of 55hl/ha. Bourgogne Aligoté is always pale in colour, crisp and clean with a dry finish. The style depends on where it is grown, crisper and lighter from around Chablis, for example, fruitier and fuller from Meursault. Always a refreshingly crisp wine, in poor years Aligoté can be severely tart. Delicious and distinctive wines come from the region of Saint-Bris, the Hautes-Côtes de Nuits and Buxy (Côte Chalonnaise). Sometimes referred to as the *Muscadet de la Bourgogne*, Bourgogne Aligoté is generally the least expensive of white burgundies. It is the perfect apéritif, the classic wine to mix with *crème de cassis* to make a Kir, or *vin blanc cassis*, and goes well with hors d'oeuvres and fish. Aligoté should be drunk young and cold. Price high B-C. See Aligoté de Bouzeron, page 78.

Bourgogne Clairet

Rosé wine from the Burgundy region, made with the Pinot Noir. This *appellation* is very seldom seen, the wines being sold under the *appellation* Bourgogne Rosé. Price low C.

Bourgogne Grand Ordinaire

Red, white and rosé wines from the Burgundy region. This *appellation*, also known as Bourgogne Ordinaire, is the lowest on the burgundy scale. Red wines may be made from the Pinot Noir, Gamay, and the César and Tressot if they are from the Yonne. Whites are from the Chardonnay, Pinot Blanc, Aligoté, Melon de Bourgogne (the same grape as the Muscadet), and from the Sacy (Yonne). Minimum alcohol content must be 9.5° for the whites, 9° for reds and rosés, from a yield of 60hl/ha. The wines, mostly red, are unpretentious and fruity, but lack distinction. A few growers still make a BGO, as it is known, for local and Parisian clients. As there is little demand for BGOs, they tend to be genuine and seldom disappointing. It is worth trying when in Burgundy, as very little is exported, but be sure that it is from a recent and good vintage. Production is a little over two million bottles. Price high B-low C.

Bourgogne Passe-Tout-Grains

Red (almost entirely) and rosé wines made principally in the Côte d'Or and the Côte Chalonnaise from a blend of not more than two-thirds Gamay and not less than one-third Pinot Noir. The alcohol content must exceed 9.5°, from a yield of 55hl/ha. The best Passe-Tout-Grains are from the Côte de Beaune and the Côte de Nuits, where the percentage of Pinot is sometimes higher than the legal one-third. In fact, two-thirds of the production comes from the Saône-et-Loire *département*, between Burgundy proper and the Beaujolais. Production is around 7.5 million bottles. The wine is fruity, with good colour, and is in general a very satisfying and slightly lighter alternative to Bourgogne. It should be drunk young, at two to four years, and may be served at cellar temperature. Bourgogne Passe-Tout-Grains is a wine that is well worth looking out for, and it represents good value for money. Price high B-low C.

Bourgogne Rosé

Rosé wines from the Burgundy region made from the Pinot Noir, with the César and Tressot permitted in wines from the Yonne. The minimum alcohol content must be 10°, from a maximum yield of 55hl/ha. The Pinot Noir vinified as a rosé has a pretty salmon-pink colour, a light strawberry-Pinot aroma and a clean, fruity finish. It is at its best the summer after the vintage. Production varies greatly, as growers usually only produce a generic rosé when they have a potential over-production of red wine. Only a very little is exported and therefore it is a wine to drink locally or possibly in Parisian restaurants. Price low C.

Crémant de Bourgogne

White or rosé sparkling wine made from all the accepted Burgundy grapes, by the *méthode champenoise*. While this *appellation*, which has replaced that of Bourgogne Mousseux, covers the whole of Burgundy, the wines are fermented and bottled in their specific regions. Thus a Crémant de Bourgogne from the Yonne will be made from grapes grown in that region, and the same will apply to a Crémant from the Mâconnais. The Crémants de Bourgogne from the Côte Chalonnaise (particularly from Rully) and from the Mâconnais are the best. They have a fine *mousse* and are very elegant. The high proportion of Chardonnay (minimum 30%, sometimes 100%, with the coarser Gamay limited to 20%) makes them a good alternative to the lighter Champagnes. Fine examples come from the Caves de Bailly at Saint-Bris-le-Vineux in the north, André Delorme in Rully, historical home of Burgundy's sparkling wine production, and from the Cave Coopérative at Mâcon-Lugny. They are also superb to drink with cassis in a Kir Royal. The production of Crémant rosé is very small, but that of Crémant blanc is now around three million bottles and it has been in full expansion in recent years. Price C.

Northern Burgundy

The vineyards of Chablis and the Auxerrois are the most northern in Burgundy, being separated from the Côte d'Or by 140 kilometres. The soil is a limestoney-chalk, which gives Chablis more in common with Champagne than with the more clayey soil of central Burgundy. The white wines are crisp and dry, even slightly austere, with good fruit but little of the "fleshiness" of the Chardonnays from further south. The production of reds and rosés having declined considerably, in favour of wines from sunnier climates, has seen an upsurge since the very ripe 1985 vintage and some interesting wines are now available.

Bourgogne Irancy

Red and rosé wine from vineyards to the south-west of Chablis, 15km south of Auxerre. Grapes planted are the Pinot Noir, and the local César and Tressot. The last two grape varieties are in the process of dying out. Wines from Irancy (which have to add Bourgogne to the label) must have a minimum alcohol content of 10°

Above: The vines are carefully pruned to reduce yields and increase the concentration of the wine.

from a yield of 55hl/ha. The wine was well known even in the twelfth century, but the popularity of wines from further south in Burgundy, and then the phylloxera, caused the production to fall to a mere 250,000 bottles today. With the ever-rising prices of red burgundy from the Côte d'Or, the wines of Irancy have been attracting interest. A series of good vintages since 1985 has encouraged growers to bottle more of their wine rather than selling it off in bulk to the négociants. Irancy red has a full, deep colour with a concentrated but slightly rustic fruitiness that softens with age. In poor years, when the Pinot Noir does not ripen fully so far to the north, the rosé is a better bet, fresh and fruity with a pleasant acidity. The finest vineyard is the south-facing Côte de Palotte. Good growers include Léon Bienvenu, Robert Colinot and Lucien Joudelat. Simmonet-Febvre of Chablis has made Irancy his speciality. Price C.

Bourgogne-Coulanges-la-Vineuse

From a village next door to Saint-Bris-le-Vineux, the red wines produced here are made only from the Pinot Noir and are thus classified as Bourgone, to which Coulanges-la-Vineuse may be added on the label. As the demand for country wines increases and prices remain moderate, the production has had some support from Chablis négociants and local restaurants. Price high B-low C.

Bourgogne Saint-Bris

Although Irancy is the best-known wine, four more villages in the region may add their name to the *appellation* Bourgogne. They are Chitry, Coulanges-la-Vineuse, Epineuil and Saint-Bris. The Pinot Noir is the main grape variety, producing red wines a little softer than Irancy. A little rosé is also made from a total of less than 100,000 bottles. As the demand increases, the region is being replanted. Prices should remain very reasonable as these attractive wines are so little known. Price B.

THE CHABLIS APPELLATIONS

This region covers four different *appellations* – Petit Chablis, Chablis, Chablis Premier Cru and Chablis Grand Cru – with a total possible area of 6,834 hectares, of which a little under 2,000 are actually planted. Despite the renown of the Chablis name, the post-war lack of workforce, a weak demand and some poor vintages culminating in the disastrous frost of 1956, saw the region faced with extinction. Replanting began on the finer slopes and has continued to expand rapidly during the last two decades. Although further expansion is possible, the true quality of Chablis comes as much from the limestoney chalk soil, known as Kimmeridgian after the Dorset village of Kimmeridge, as from the Chardonnay grape. One school of thought is in favour of expansion, maintaining that world-wide demand for Chablis is inexhaustible; the other argues that true Chablis is from the chalky soil, and that expansion outside the geological region should be resisted. A run of good, productive vintages in the 1980s have served to enhance the quality image of Chablis in general, giving both the expansionists and the purists further weight to their cause.

Petit Chablis

White wine from the Chardonnay grape from, in principle, 121 hectares of the least favourably exposed vineyards in the Chablis region. Minimum alcohol content is only 9.5°, from a yield of 50hl/ha, which is almost always exceeded. It is light and refreshing, with crisp, clean characteristic Chardonnay fruit. Petit Chablis can be good value, and should be drunk at one to three years. The Cave Coopérative La Chablisienne is one of the major producers. Discussions are under way regarding the replanting of several hundred hectares under this *appellation*, while at the same time changing the name from the slightly derogatory Petit Chablis to Chablis-Hautes-Côtes. The wines should continue to be reasonably priced. Price C.

Chablis

White wine from the Chablis region in the Yonne *département* east of Auxerre. The only grape permitted is the Chardonnay, known locally at the Beaunois. It must have a minimum alcohol content of 10°, from a yield of 50hl/ha, the latter being generally much exceeded. Chablis should be pale yellow with a greeny edge, and should never look too watery or too rich; the bouquet should be flowery, lively, fresh and mouthwatering, the taste crisp, fruity, with a certain structure and a firm finish. Over-production and/or poor vinification leave many of today's Chablis with little or no bouquet, a washed-out taste and a flat finish. It is often better to buy a Petit Chablis or Bourgogne Aligoté at a lower price, or a Chablis Premier Cru at a higher one, but good examples are distinctly delicious. Chablis should be drunk 1–5 years after the vintage. Good producers are Christian Adine, Pascal Bouchard, Jean Durup, the Defaix family, Alain Geoffroy, Michel Laroche, and the Cave Coopérative "La Chablisienne", while reliable local négociants are Pic/Rémon/Regnard, Simmonet-Febvre, J. Moreau and Lamblin & Fils. The Beaune-based house of Joseph Drouhin is now a substantial owner in Chablis, and produces some excellent *cuvées*, as does the Nuits-Saint-Georges-based Labouré-Roi. Total production is now around 10–12 million bottles and is increasing as old vineyards are replaced and new sites cleared. Heavy frosts in early 1985 combined with speculation in white burgundy, temporarily forced prices to very high levels, but high production in the 1989 and 1990 vintages saw Chablis return to a "normal" level, only a little higher than Sancerre or Pouilly-Fumé. Price D.

Chablis Premier Cru

The Premier Cru vineyards surround the town of Chablis on both banks of the river Serein, covering 581 hectares. The best-exposed and generally the finer wines are from the right bank, to the north and east of the town, on either side of the Grands Crus. While there are officially 29 Premiers Crus, since 1967 the different *lieux-dits* have tended to group themselves behind the 12 most famous names. Some of the best known are: **Beugnons**: light, pretty wine that can be drunk early. **Côte de Lechet**: stylish pure Chablis from Domaine Defaix. **Les Forêts**: full-bodied, firm and needs time, with probably the best wine coming from René Dauvissat. **Fourchaume**: round and slightly honeyed, opening up quickly, with good wines from the négociants Drouhin, Laroche, Regnard and Lamblin, and the Cave Coopérative. **Montée de Tonnerre**: lively and firm, with great finesse, almost the quality of a Grand Cru, and can keep well. Especially fine wines are from François and Jean-Marie Raveneau, Maurice Duplessis, Marcel Servin, William Fèvre, Louis Michel and the modern-style Domaine de l'Eglantière. **Montmains**: fruity and supple, quite quick maturing, with very good wine from Louis Pinson. **Monts de Mileu**: well balanced, not too hard, but with the typical flinty Chablis edge; this *cru* is a speciality of Simmonet-Febvre. **Séchets**: firm, elegant, lighter than Les Forêts and also very good from René Dauvissat. **Vaillons**: fruity, straightforward and lasts well; fine wines from the Defaix family, Jean Dauvissat, and the good négociants. Depending on the *lieu-dit* or *climat* (which can be blended and sold simply as Premier Cru), but more on the vintage, vinification and ageing (in wood or in stainless steel), they are best drunk at 2–7 years. Production is approaching six million bottles. A good Premier Cru makes a fine, distinctive bottle of white burgundy. Reasonable value for money. Price E.

Chablis Grand Cru

Planted on the chalky-limestone slopes above the right bank of the river Serein, to the north-east of Chablis, a Grand Cru must have a higher alcohol content (11°) than a Premier Cru, from a lower yield (45hl/ha). There are seven Grands Crus, covering 105 hectares, giving an average yearly yield of 500,000 bottles. They have the weight and structure of the best white burgundies from the Côte de Beaune, but are always a little more reserved. Each of the Grands Crus has its own character and style, which is tempered by the different methods of vinification and ageing, and by the age of the grower's vines. The seven Grands Crus are: **Blanchots** (11.65ha): supple, elegant wines with great persistence of flavour. The wines of François Raveneau, Marcel Servin and Robert Vocoret are particularly good, as well as the Domaine Laroche. **Bougros** (15.85ha): vigorous, bouqueted wines that make up in ageing potential what they perhaps lack in finesse; the most northerly of the Grands Crus. **Les Clos** (25.81ha): the largest of the Grands Crus and the most southern, apart from Blanchots, producing big wines, with a honey-like bouquet, great structure and great length of taste, not really at their best until five years old. The wines from Raveneau, Dauvissat, Maurice Duplessis and William Fèvre are exceptional. An enclave of Les Clos is the excellent vineyard called Le Clos des Hospices, now the monopole of J. Moreau & Fils. **Grenouilles** (9.68ha): fine, but lightish wines with a pronounced floral bouquet, but not quite the quality of Valmur and Vaudésir, the *crus* on either side. "La Chablisienne" is the largest owner. **Preuses** (11.10ha): lovely, almost feminine wines, with great finesse and charm, yet a firm finish. Very fine wines come from Dauvissat, William Fèvre and the négociants Drouhin and Regnard. **Valmur** (13.20ha): highly perfumed wines, with more body than Preuses, but less than Les Clos: a very reputable Grand Cru, and quite quick to mature. **Vaudésir** (16.91ha): generally considered to be the finest of the Grands Crus, Vaudésir may be drunk young, but really needs 4–5 years to develop its potential. Excellent wines come from the Domaine de la Maladière (William Fèvre), Paul Droin, Louis Michel and the better négociants of Chablis and Beaune. The 2.35ha vineyard "La Moutonne" (an honorary Grand Cru) is mostly in Vaudésir. Grand Cru Chablis are expensive but usually worth it. Price F.

VDQS WINES

Sauvignon de Saint-Bris

White wine from the Sauvignon grape, planted around the village of Saint-Bris-le-Vineux, to the south-west of Chablis. The wines are light (9.5° alcohol from a yield of 50hl/ha), crisp and very dry, with the grassy, redcurranty Sauvignon fruit toned down by the chalky soil and northern exposition. Their high acidity makes them a good apéritif, and excellent with shellfish and hors d'oeuvres. Drink very young. This is the only example of Sauvignon grown in Burgundy. Chardonnay is also planted around Saint-Bris and the neighbouring villages of Chitry, Coulanges-la-Vineuse and Irancy, and is sold under the *appellation* Bourgogne. There is also some good Aligoté. Vineyard holdings are small and the growers dedicated to producing quality at reasonable prices. Price high B.

VINS DE PAYS

VIN DE PAYS DE L'YONNE
White wines from the region of Chablis, Irancy, Coulanges-la-Vineuse and Saint-Bris. The grapes may be Chardonnay, Aligoté, Sacy or Sauvignon, with a maximum yield of 80hl/ha and a minimum alcohol content of 9°. Very light, crisp, dry, even rather tart wines, the best from the Chardonnay on its own. Some producers of Chablis (William Fèvre, for example) may choose an over-productive parcel of vines to declassify into *vin de pays*, which usually represents a bargain for the consumer. Price B.

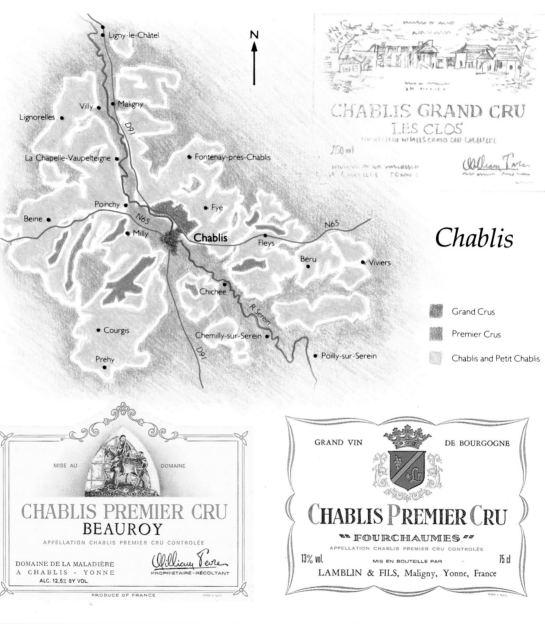

Chablis

Grand Crus
Premier Crus
Chablis and Petit Chablis

CHABLIS GRAND CRU
LES CLOS

MISE AU DOMAINE

CHABLIS PREMIER CRU
BEAUROY

APPELLATION CHABLIS PREMIER CRU CONTROLÉE

DOMAINE DE LA MALADIÈRE
A CHABLIS - YONNE
ALC. 12,5% BY VOL.

PROPRIÉTAIRE-RÉCOLTANT

PRODUCE OF FRANCE

GRAND VIN   DE BOURGOGNE

CHABLIS PREMIER CRU

⸗ FOURCHAUMES ⸗

APPELLATION CHABLIS PREMIER CRU CONTROLÉE

13% vol.   MIS EN BOUTEILLE PAR   75 cl

LAMBLIN & FILS, Maligny, Yonne, France

Château Grenouille G.A.A.

CHABLIS GRAND CRU GRENOUILLE

APPELLATION CHABLIS GRAND CRU CONTROLÉE

GAEC DU DOMAINE DE CHATEAU GRENOUILLE
PROPRIÉTAIRE-VITICULTEUR A CHABLIS - YONNE - FRANCE

13% vol.   PRODUCE OF FRANCE   75 cl e

MIS EN BOUTEILLE A LA PROPRIÉTÉ

La Chablisienne - Chablis - Yonne - France

Domaine Moreau & Fils
SEULS PROPRIÉTAIRES
PRODUCT OF FRANCE
CHABLIS
Clos des Hospices
APPELLATION CHABLIS GRAND CRU LES CLOS CONTROLÉE
MARQUE DÉPOSÉE
DANS LES CLOS

Mis en bouteilles par
J. MOREAU & FILS
à CHABLIS
(Yonne) France   alc.12,5% byvol.   750ml

Central Burgundy

COTE DE NUITS

The Côte de Nuits, the northern part of the Côte d'Or, produces almost exclusively red wines from its 1,300 hectares of vines that run from the outskirts of Dijon to south of Nuits-Saint-Georges. There is a little rosé produced around the village of Marsannay-la-Côte, the most northern commune, while the very rare *cuvées* of white wine come from Morey-Saint-Denis, Musigny, Clos Vougeot and Nuits-Saint-Georges. Together, these account for a little over 1% of the production. The Aligoté and Gamay grapes are planted, particularly in the communes of Gevrey-Chambertin and Morey-Saint-Denis, to make Bourgogne Aligoté and Bourgogne Passe-Tout-Grains – attractive, fruity wines, but with no great character or ageing potential. The finer wines from the Côte de Nuits are made from the Pinot Noir, with a minimum alcohol content of 10.5° from a maximum basic yield of 40hl/ha which is often exceeded. The vines are planted on slopes facing south-south-east, the Côte de Nuits being an archetypical *vignoble de coteaux*, with the best wines coming from vineyards which are situated between 250 and 300 metres above sea level. Above, thinner soil and cooler weather do not always allow the grapes to ripen fully, while below this height the soil is too rich and the wines consequently tend to lack finesse. The soil itself is a slightly stony marl on a base of hard limestone.

Below: a meandering wall separates the Premier Cru vineyards of Lavaux and Clos St-Jacques.

The Côte de Nuits is basically divided into *appellations communales* (Gevrey-Chambertin, Morey-Saint-Denis), Premiers Crus within these *appellations* (Gevrey-Chambertin Clos Saint-Jacques, Morey-Saint-Denis les Sorbés) and Grands Crus (Chambertin, Clos Saint-Denis) that have *appellations* of their own. Below this hierarchy come the *appellations régionales*: Bourgogne Hautes-Côtes de Nuits, Côte de Nuits-Villages. Due to the nature of their particular soil and exposition, each commune has its peculiar character and style, which become more defined among the wines from individual *climats*, and the names of these *climats* or *lieux-dits* may appear on the label, even if they are not Premiers Crus.

Vineyard holdings on the Côte de Nuits are extremely parcellated: with the exception of a few large estates, the small proprietors with less than five hectares dominate, and these holdings are more often than not across several *appellations*. The differences in the site of the actual vines of each grower, their age and the style of winemaking and ageing, are such that as much attention should be paid to the name of the person who bottles the wine, whether grower or négociant, as to the *appellation* of the wine itself.

Bourgogne Hautes-Côtes-de-Nuits

Red, dry white and rosé wines from vineyards outside the *appellations communales* of the Côte de Nuits. Red and rosé wines must be made from the Pinot Noir, whites from the Chardonnay and Pinot Blanc. Minimum alcohol content is 10° for reds and rosés from a yield of 55hl/ha, and 10.5° for the whites from a yield of 60hl/ha. The white wines (only 5% of the *appellation* are bouqueted and firm, really very good. The reds have a fine colour (in good years), good fruit and structure, and are typically slower to mature than the Hautes-Côtes-de-Beaune. They are at their best at four to eight years. Production is around one million bottles a year, greatly increased since the 1970s, and replanting is still continuing. These vineyards have the right to the *appellation* Bourgogne, and may acceed to this category only after being passed by a tasting panel. With current prices in Burgundy, they represent good value. The largest producer is the Cave Coopérative des Hautes-Côtes, whose crisp, flowery whites and wood-aged reds are particularly successful and reasonably priced. Domaines Cornu, Patrick Hudelot and Domaine de Montmain (Bernard Hudelot) are among the best growers. Price C.

Côte de Nuits-Villages

Red and dry white wines from vineyards at both extremes of the Côte de Nuits, covering the communes of Brochon and Fixin in the north and Comblanchien, Corgoloin and Prissey in the south. Production of white is minute, while that of red approaches one million bottles from around 300 hectares of vines. The wines generally have a good colour and firm fruit and in good years are quite robust and can last ten years or more. The *appellation* is principally used by the Nuits-Saint-Georges négociants, such as Labouré-Roi, as a good-value example of wines from the northern Côte d'Or, while fine wines come from the Domaine Gachot-Monot, Huguenot, Quillardet and the "Monopole" Clos de Langres. The best grower's wines are in Brochon and Corgoloin. Price D.

Fixin

Red and a very little white wine from the second most northerly *appellation communale* covering 150 hectares. In the past, much of the wine was sold under the *appellation* Côte de Nuits-Villages, but Fixin has recently acquired a recognition of its own. A typical red Fixin (pronounced Fissin) is deep-coloured and full-bodied, not unlike that which its neighbour, Gevrey-Chambertin, aspires to, but more rustic. In years of heavy production (1973, 1979, 1982) the wine can be light, pretty and fruity, but it generally needs five years to show well and can be very long lived. In common with all wines from the Côte d'Or the Premiers Crus are much finer than the *villages* wines and well worth the extra money. The best Premiers Crus are the Clos de la Perrière (Philippe Joliet) and the Clos du Chapitre (Domaine Gelin et Molin), both *monopoles*. Les Hervelets makes fine, robust wine, while Le Clos Napoléon (Domaine Gelin et Molin, *monopole*) is softer and quicker maturing. Another good domaine is Vincent and Denis Berthaut, who have the best parts of the *lieux-dits*, les Clos, les Arvelets and les Crais. The négociant's wines are usually very sound, making Fixin one of the best value red burgundies. Bruno Clair makes an interesting and delicious Fixin blanc from the Pinot Blanc. Total production is nearly 500,000 bottles. Price D-E.

Marsannay

Red and rosé wines from the communes of Marsannay-la-Côte and Couchey, whose vines are being progressively surrounded by the suburbs of Dijon. Until 1986, only red and rosé wines were made in this commune and were sold as Bourgogne Rouge/Rosé de Marsannay. Proud of the high quality of the Marsannay wines, the growers lobbied for communal *appellation* status, which was awarded in 1986. White wine may only be made from the Chardonnay and Pinot Blanc showing a minimum of 11° from a low yield of 40hl/ha, and the tradition of allowing up to 15% of these grapes to the Pinot Noir when making red wine has been maintained, but is seldom used. The best-known wine is the rosé, with its light salmon-pink colour from a very short maceration, and delicate strawberry-like bouquet backed up by the habitual firmness of wines from the Côte de Nuits. Along with Tavel, Palette and Bandol from the South, and the very rare Rosé des Riceys, Marsannay rosé is considered one of the best rosés in France, and one of the very few to stand up well to food more usually associated with red wines. It is best drunk young, at 1–3 years, before it loses its fruit. Average production is 250,000 bottles, including the Rouge de Marsannay, which is quickly gaining a reputation of its own. Marsannay rouge is a firm, fruity wine in the style of the Côte de Nuits-Villages, sometimes a little hard-edged when young, but lasting well. The best-known grower in Marsannay is the Domaine Clair-Daü (who invented the Rosé de Marsannay with the 1919 vintage), which is now owned by the négociant Louis Jadot. Some of the Domaine's vineyards have passed to Bruno Clair, grandson of the Rosé's inventor, who is now making some of the best wine of the new *appellation*, with an exceptionally fine white. Other good growers include Charles Quillardet and Hugue-not Père & Fils. The wines from Marsannay still represent good value. Price D.

GEVREY-CHAMBERTIN

Gevrey-Chambertin

Red wine only from the largest commune in the Côte de Nuits, with a total of almost 500 hectares under vine, including 60 in Premiers Crus and 90 in Grands Crus. Red wines are only produced from the Pinot Noir grape, showing 10.5° or more from a basic yield of 40hl/ha. The diversity of the *terroir*, running from Brochon to Morey-Saint-Denis, with much of the *villages* wine coming from the plain on either side of the main Dijon-Beaune road, allied to the very different styles of vinification, makes it difficult to describe a Gevrey-Chambertin. They should be firm wines, with a good deep colour for a Pinot Noir, a bouquet of fruit and spice and a long, velvety finish. In good years, and from good growers or négociants, they are, but many wines are either too light, as a result of over-production and/or too short vinification, or too alcoholic, from over-chaptalization. All of the major domaines have holdings in Premier Cru vineyards, and while it is usually worth paying the extra money, the simple *villages* wines receive the same care from these producers as do the Premiers and Grands Crus wines. Among the growers that can be relied on are: Alain Burget, Bruno Clair, Domaine Geoffroy, Domaine des Varoilles, Domaine Tortochot, René and Philippe Leclerc, Philippe Marchand, Henri Rebourseau, Joseph Roty, Armand Rousseau and Louis Trapet. Production of plain Gevrey-Chambertin is very large at 1.2 million

bottles a year – more even than that of Beaune, whose vineyards cover a greater area – and there is more wine available for the négocians than in smaller *appellations* such as Vosne-Romanée or Volnay. J. H. Faiveley, with considerable vineyards in the *appellation*, produces fine, sturdy wines, and Leroy, Joseph Drouhin and Louis Jadot are also good. Gevrey-Chambertin is a popular name and perhaps due to severe criticism following a range of feeble, over-produced wines from the 1982 vintage, quality has been improving overall, and price reflects this, so careful selection is most important. Price F.

Gevrey-Chambertin Premier Cru

Gevrey-Chambertin possesses 25 Premiers Crus, from over 60 hectares, the best being on the slopes behind the village, and going north towards Brochon. Here, as at Gevrey-Chambertin, only red wine is produced and quality is much more evident than in the plain *villages* wines, the 15–30% increase in price being definitely worth it. The most famous is the Clos Saint-Jacques, owned almost 50% by the Domaine Rousseau, which thinks so highly of the wine that it is priced higher than the Grands Crus with the exception of Chambertin and Chambertin Clos de Bèze. Les Lavaux-Saint-Jacques and Les Cazetiers are very fine, while Les Varoilles (*monopole* of the Domaine Les Varoilles) has great class, although not perhaps the lasting velvety elegance of the Clos Saint-Jacques. La Combe-aux-Moines is another well-known *cru*, with lovely meaty wines from J. H. Faiveley, and down at the southern end of the *appellation*, on the edge of Morey-Saint-Denis, lies Les Combottes, whose wines are especially fine from Domaine Dujac. A few proprietors and most négo-ciants sell a Gevrey-Chambertin Premier Cru, usually a blend of more than one vineyard. The house of Leroy offers a particularly impressive range of wines which are intended for keeping. In light vintages, the Premiers Crus are attractive at 3–4 years, while the better vintages need 6–7 years to open up and are at their best at 10–15 years. Production averages 240,000 bottles. Price mostly G.

The Grands Crus of Gevrey-Chambertin

Gevrey-Chambertin possesses eight Grands Crus, more than any other commune in Burgundy, and produces about a quarter of all Grand Cru red burgundy. Minimum alcohol content must be 11.5°, as opposed to 11° for the Premiers Crus and 10.5° for the *villages* wines, from a yield of 35–7hl/ha. All the Grands Crus are from vineyards south of the village, on the middle of the *coteaux*.

Chambertin

One of the best-known wines of France and certainly the most famous red wine from Burgundy, Chambertin (and Chambertin Clos de Bèze) has all the qualities of a great wine: clarity and depth of colour, striking yet often delicate bouquet, intensity of flavour, and finesse and harmony in the lingering aftertaste. Chambertin is a big wine, yet should never be heavy in the way that a Corton may be and a Châteauneuf-du-Pape should be, and which takes several years to develop the sought-after elegant, velvety character. Fifteen growers own the 13 hectares of Chambertin, to which must be added the very many négociants who have to have a Chambertin on their list. Of the growers, very fine wines come from Camus, Domaine Jacques Prieur (now controlled by négociant Antonin Rodet), Rebourseau, Rousseau, Tortochot and Trapet, while the négociants, Drouhin, Jaboulet-Verchère, Jadot, Leroy and Latour are very good. Chambertin from a good vintage should be kept at least six years, and is at its best at 12–20 years, while exceptional vintages can last half a century. Production at 35hl/ha is generally no more than 60,000 bottles. Price H-I.

Below: Wines ageing in the cellars of Moillard at Nuits-St-Georges.

Chambertin Clos de Bèze

Chambertin Clos de Bèze occupies 15 hectares on the same *coteaux* as, and adjacent to, Chambertin, going north towards the village. The wines may be sold as Chambertin, but the name of the Clos is usually added to distinguish it from Le Chambertin. While possessing the same blend of solidity and finesse, warmth and flavour and elegant finish, the Clos de Bèze is thought to have the edge for stylishness and length. (Charles Rousseau, who has vines in both *crus*, serves the Clos de Bèze before Chambertin at a tasting, as he thinks the former more "lacy" and the latter more powerful.) The largest holding is that of Damoy, and the wines of Clair-Daü, Drouhin, Faiveley, Gelin and Rousseau are superb. The keeping qualities are as for Chambertin, while the quantity produced at 35hl/ha maximum is slightly less, despite the higher acreage. Price H-I.

Chapelle-Chambertin

Extremely fine wine, although less vigorous than Chambertin, from a 5.4-hectare vineyard just south of the Clos de Bèze. What Chapelle-Chambertin lacks in weight, it makes up for in delicacy. The best-known producers are Damoy, Drouhin-Laroze and Trapet. Production is 25,000 bottles. Price G-H.

Charmes-Chambertin

The largest of the Grands Crus, with 31.6 hectares of vines just south of Le Chambertin, producing fine, supple red wine, generally very good, but occasionally not up to Grand Cru quality. The *appellation* includes 19 hectares previously (and still) classified as Mazoyères-Chambertin, a name which all growers except Monsieur Camus have forsaken in favour of the more attractive-sounding Charmes. Among the best domaines are Camus, Rebourseau, Roty, Rousseau, Taupenot and Tortochot, while the size of the *appellation* also allows the négociants to produce some successful *cuvées*. Good vintages can be drunk at between 6 and 12 years of age. Production is about 150,000 bottles. Price G.

Griotte-Chambertin

The third-smallest of the Grands Crus in size, after Ruchottes- and Chapelle-Chambertin, with 5.48 hectares, yet the smallest in production, averaging hardly 10,000 bottles from a permitted yield of 37hl/ha. The wine has a beautiful deep velvety colour and seems to have more depth and personality than its neighbour Chapelle-Chambertin. Growers, all of them making superb wine, include Pernot, Roty and Thomas-Bassot (with 1.75ha), while among the négociants, Drouhin is one of the few to propose a Griotte-Chambertin. Price H.

Latricières-Chambertin

The vineyard of Latricières covers 6.94 hectares, being the southern continuation of the Chambertin vineyard, above Mazoyères-Chambertin and north of the Premier Cru Les Combottes. In style, it is reckoned to be the nearest thing to Chambertin, yet lacking the grandeur and longevity of its neighbour. Latricières is certainly a more "masculine" wine than Charmes, Chapelle or Mazis-Chambertin, at its best at 10–15 years. The domaines Camus and Rémy produce a meaty, old-fashioned wine for keeping, while Drouhin-Laroze and Trapet make lighter wines with great finesse. Madame Bize-Leroy has recently purchased part of the vines from the Domaine Rémy and will no doubt make the most splendid Latricières, (and a little Chambertin), whose quality will justify its price. Faiveley is a major proprietor (1.5ha). Average production, from 37hl/ha, 35,000 bottles. Price H.

Mazis-Chambertin

This 12.59-hectare Grand Cru is the continuation of the Chambertin Clos de Bèze vineyard north towards the village of Gevrey-Chambertin. Mazis, or Mazy, has the most finesse of the second group of Grands Crus,

Chambertin and Clos de Bèze apart, and perfect balance. It matures relatively early and may be drunk at 6–12 years. Principal owners are Camus, Rebourseau, Roty, Rousseau, Thomas-Bassot (3ha), Tortochot and Faiveley. The most famous and most expensive Mazis-Chambertin is the Cuvée Madeleine Colignon of the Hospices de Beaune. Production averages 50,000 bottles. Price H.

Mazoyères-Chambertin

See Charmes-Chambertin, above left.

Ruchottes-Chambertin

The smallest of the Grands Crus with 3.10 hectares of vines situated higher up the slopes from Mazis-Chambertin. Ruchottes-Chambertin is rich and delicate at the same time, with a firmer edge than Mazis and longer-lasting. The principal owner is the Domaine Rousseau, with a one-hectare *monopole* – the Clos des Ruchottes – with Thomas-Bassot possessing 0.75 hectare. Domaine G. Roumier, based in Chambolle-Musigny, makes a magnificent Ruchottes. Average production 14,000 bottles. Price H.

MOREY-SAINT-DENIS

Red and a very little white wine produced from 109 hectares of *villages* and Premier Cru and 40 hectares of Grand Cru vines. The commune of Morey-Saint-Denis is situated between those of Gevrey-Chambertin and Chambolle-Musigny, and it is only in the last ten years that the wines have made a name for themselves and come to sell at prices similar to other communes in the Côte de Nuits. In fact, the over-all quality of the *villages* wine at Morey-Saint-Denis is more reliable than at Gevrey-Chambertin and even Vosne-Romanée.

Morey-Saint-Denis

The red wines have a good, full colour, an intense bouquet with a certain animal-like *rôti* overlaying the Pinot fruit, and a smooth but firm finish: perfect wines for laying down. In good vintages, they must not be drunk for at least six years. The white wine, mostly from the Premier Cru Les Monts Luisants planted with the same strain of Pinot Noir as discovered by Henri Gouges in Nuits-Saint-Georges, and owned by the Domaine Ponsot, is rich and full with certain Meursault characteristics. Production varies between 2 and 5,000 bottles. Good growers for red Morey-Saint-Denis *villages* include domaines Dujac, Bryczek, Groffier, Magnien, Ponsot, Taupenot, Tortochot and Truchot-Martin, while many other fine domaines make only Premier or Grand Cru wine. Less expensive than Gevrey-Chambertin, Vosne-Romanée or Chambolle-Musigny; wines worth looking out for. Average production, including Premiers Crus, 400,000 bottles. Price F.

Morey-Saint-Denis Premier Cru

Although there are 25 Premiers Crus in Morey-Saint-Denis, they tend to be overshadowed by the five Grands Crus in the same commune. The high quality of the *villages* wine also means that it is not necessary to buy a Premier Cru, and the actual names of the *crus* themselves are less well known. Perhaps the best are Le Clos de Ormes (Georges Lignier), Les Sorbés (Truchot-Martin), Les Clos Sorbés (Bryczek), Les Sorbets (Bernard Serveau), Les Fremières, Les Charmes (Pierre Amiot) and Le Clos de la Bussière, a *monopole* of the Domaine Georges Roumier. These robust velvety wines are at their best at 8–12 years. Price G.

The Grands Crus of Morey-Saint-Denis

These are situated on the same latitude as the Grands Crus of Gevrey-Chambertin, perfectly exposed on the slopes back from the village. The maximum yield is 35hl/ha, with a minimum alcohol content of 11.5°, while the actual content is nearer 13°. Since only the Clos Saint-Denis carries the name of the commune, the remaining four tend to be less closely associated with their village than are the Grands Crus from other communes in the Côte de Nuits, especially since two of them are *monopoles*.

Bonnes-Mares

Only 1.84 hectares of the 15.54-hectare Bonnes-Mares vineyard are in Morey-Saint-Denis, the remainder coming from the commune of Chambolle-Musigny. Most of the vineyard is owned by the Domaine Clair-Daü, who make a fine, aromatic, powerful wine that requires long ageing in order to be at its best. Domaine Roumier has a few rows of vines here, but the vast majority of its holding is situated in Chambolle. See page 57. Price H-I.

Clos des Lambrays

Although the label always stated "Grand Cru Classé", this was merely the opinion of the last owner, Mme Cosson, and the 8-hectare vineyard only obtained official Grand Cru status in 1981. This used to be one of the finest wines from the Côte d'Or, due partly to the superb exposition on the higher slopes above the village and partly to the great age of the vines, many of which were ungrafted. Erratic vinification led to some disappointments, and following the death of Mme Cosson the vineyard was sold in the late 1970s to the Saïer brothers, and considerable replanting has been instigated. This *cru* is beginning to return to its former glory. Price H-I.

Clos de la Roche

With 15.34 hectares, this is the largest Grand Cru of the commune, and is generally accepted to be the finest. Situated in the north of the *appellation*, with only the Premier Cru, Les Combettes, in Gevrey separating it from Latricières-Chambertin, Clos de la Roche is a powerful wine with great depth and elegance. The top-soil is poor and thinly laid over a solid bed of limestone, and the vines have to put down long roots to flourish. While the intense fruit of the bouquet shows quite early, the wine is really at its best from 8–15 years. Superlative wines comes from Rousseau, Dujac, Ponsot, Lignier and Rémy. Production around 70,000 bottles. Price H.

Clos Saint-Denis

Directly south of the Clos de la Roche, the 6.56-hectare Clos Saint-Denis has seen its name added to that of Morey in the way that Chambertin and

Musigny have been added to Gevrey and Chambolle. The wine is lighter and perhaps more subtle than Clos de la Roche, but more reticent and less intense, almost untypical of the commune. Its elegance and harmony allow it to be drunk at 6–10 years. The domaines Dujac and Lignier are the largest proprietors and Domaine Bertagna has a half hectare. Production is now about 25,000 bottles. Always slightly less expensive than Clos de la Roche. Price H.

Clos de Tart

A 7.22-hectare *monopole* of Ets. Mommessin of Mâcon, the Clos de Tart is a walled-in vineyard situated between the Clos des Lambrays and Les Bonnes Mares, on the edge of the village of Morey. It does not possess the richness of Clos de la Roche, but is perhaps more intense than Clos Saint-Denis, with all the velvety firmness of the best wines from the Côte de Nuits. The fact that the Clos de Tart is a *monopole* allows for more control from the vines to the bottling line, and the Morey-Chambolle character of the wine is confirmed with each successive vintage. It is a long-lasting wine, at its best at 8–15 years. Production varies, averaging 30,000 bottles. Price H.

CHAMBOLLE-MUSIGNY

Red and a very little white wine only (from the Grand Cru Musigny), coming from 173 hectares of *villages* and Premier Cru vines. The soil is more chalky and less clayey than in other parts of the Côte de Nuits, and the wines of Chambolle are correspondingly more marked in finesse than weight.

Chambolle-Musigny

Red wines only, made from Pinot Noir. Maximum yield is now 40hl/ha, in common with the other *appellation communales* of the Côte d'Or, but is generally exceeded; minimum alcohol content is 10.5° (always exceeded). The charm, elegance and "femininity" of these wines means that they are often compared to those from the Côte de Beaune, particularly to Volnay. They should not be too light, and the underlying firmness of the Côte de Nuits backs up their delicacy and gives them a deliciously harmonious fruit and texture. These extremely attractive wines are at their best between 5–10 years. Domaines making fine, stylish wines include Bernard Amiot, Jean Brunet, Jean Grivot, Alain Hudelot, Daniel Moine, Drouhin-Laroze, Ponsot, Marchard de Gramont and Roumier. Some other wines are often too heavy or alcoholic. Total production, including the Premiers Crus, averages around 900,000 bottles. Price F, some G.

Chambolle-Musigny Premier Cru

Of the 19 Premiers Crus in Chambolle-Musigny, the best are Les Amoureuses and Les Charmes. Les Amoureuses, situated just below Le Musigny and next to Les Petits Vougeots, is one of the most sought-after wines in Burgundy. The colour is much deeper than a Chambolle *villages*, the fruit more concentrated on the bouquet (raspberries, cherries, violets), and the taste more forceful and striking. The finest examples come from the Domaine de Vogüé and the domaines Georges Roumier, Daniel Moine and Robert Groffier. Les Charmes, situated in the middle of the *appellation* below the village, is very fine but lacks the reputation of Les Amoureuses. Excellent wines from domaines Clerget, Grivelet (also in Amoureuses), Paul Hudelot and Servelle-Tachot. J-F Mugnier has recently retaken most of the family domaine of the Château de Chambolle, and makes a superb Les Fuées. The *appellation* Chambolle-Musigny is in such demand that, Les Amoureuses and Les Charmes excepted, most growers do not put the name of the *climat* on the label, nor do the négociants, whose wine is generally a blend of more than one Premier Cru. An exception of note is Les Chabiots from Bernard Serveau. These wines are at their best at 6–12 years, much more for great vintages. Expensive but the best wines are worth it. Price G-H.

The Grands Crus of Chambolle-Musigny

Bonnes Mares

Of a total 15.54 hectares of this Grand Cru, 13.7 are in the northern part of the commune Chambolle-Musigny. While Bonnes Mares has the charm and femininity that is typical of the wines of Chambolle, they have a richness, depth and power that surpasses even Les Amoureuses. Compared to the velvety finesse of le Musigny, Bonnes Mares is almost tannic, and certainly has a greater capacity for ageing. A great Bonnes-Mares is Burgundy at its best, on a par with the wines of Chambertin, Musigny and Corton, and will be perfect at 15–20 years but can last longer. The wines from de Vogüé, Drouhin-Laroze, Dujac, Groffier, J-F Mugnier, Domaine Naigeon and Roumier are superlative, as are the *cuvées* from Bouchard Père & Fils, Drouhin and Jadot. Average production, including the 1.84 hectares in the commune of Morey-Saint-Denis, totals 60,000 bottles. Bonnes-Mares is certainly a collector's wine. Price H-I.

Musigny

The Musigny vineyards cover 10.65 hectares, of which 0.30 hectares are planted in Chardonnay and constitute the *monopole* of Musigny blanc, owned by the Domaine de Vogüé. The permitted yield is 5hl/ha higher, at 40hl/ha (similar to the Grands Crus blancs of the Côte de Beaune), than for Le Musigny or Bonnes-Mares, but the actual production is rarely more than 100 cases of 12 bottles. While it is not in the same class as the finer Grands Crus of Puligny and Chassagne-Montrachet, Le Musigny blanc, with its lovely greeny-gold colour, firm texture and exquisite aftertaste of almonds, is respected for more than just its rarity. Red Musigny is almost without equal in Burgundy. Its perfect colour and delicate, silky, velvety flavour allow it to be compared to Château Margaux, as Chambertin might be compared to Château Latour. It is elegance personified: almost impossible to imagine a wine more fine. The Domaine de Vogüé possesses seven hectares, and with a combination of old vines, low yields, skilful vinification and rigorous selection at the time of bottling, produces the finest wine of the commune. Faiveley, Joseph Drouhin, J-F Mugnier and the Domaine Jacques Prieur are important growers, while impeccable wines come from Roumier, Jadot and Leroy. A fine Musigny needs 10–12 years to develop and can last more than 20. Production is about 40,000 bottles. Very rare and very expensive. Price I.

VOUGEOT

Red and white wine of which Grand Cru Clos de Vougeot is by far the most prestigious, covering 65 hectares of the commune.

Vougeot

The *villages* and Premier Cru vines cover only slightly more than 12 hectares, producing an average of 60,000 bottles of red and 9,000 bottles of white wine. The white (with a high permitted yield of 45hl/ha) comes from the Clos Blanc de Vougeot, a *monopole* of L'Héritier Guyot, making fine, well-balanced wine which, despite a firm acidity, is slightly reminiscent of a Meursault. The red, mostly seen under the Premier Cru *climats* of Clos de la Perrière (*monopole* of Les Ets. Bertagna), Les Petits Vougeots and Les Cras, is a middle-of-the-road Côte de Nuits but without great personality or finesse. Price G.

Clos de Vougeot

The walled-in Clos de Vougeot comprises the same amount of land under vines as it did when the Clos was created in the late 14th century: 50.22 hectares, now divided between 77 proprietors, of whom about one-third only make between two and three *pièces* (of 215 litres) a year. This is an insufficient volume to vinify a red wine with great success, with the result that the grapes from these tiny parcels of vines tend to be vinified with other *appellations* and separated after fermentation, or simply do not have the depth and personality of a Grand Cru. Of the larger holdings, those from the top of the slope provide unquestionably the finest wines, while those from the more clayey, less well-drained soil at the bottom of the slope next to the *route nationale* give wines that are sometimes disappointing. The middle section provides fine-quality wines, and throughout the Clos, vinification counts for almost as much as, and sometimes more than, situation. (This is true throughout the Burgundy region.) A well-made Clos de Vougeot should have a fine ruby colour, a slightly reticent, floral bouquet with firmness and length of flavour. It is good between 7 and 15 years. Most négociants offer a Clos de Vougeot for prestige reasons, while only Champy Père & Fils of Beaune and J. H. Faiveley have large holdings. Grower's names to look out for: Arnoux, Drouhin-Laroze, Confuron, Jayer, Engel, Grivot, Rebourseau, Gros, Lamarche, Méo-Camuzet, Château de la Tour, Mugneret and recently Leroy, who purchased the holdings of Domaine Charles Noëllat. Average production, from a permitted yield of 35hl/ha, nearly 200,000 bottles. Price H.

Château du Clos de Vougeot – Les Chevaliers de Tastevin

The Confrérie des Chevaliers de Tastevin are owners of the Château du Clos de Vougeot, where they hold their banquets and receptions as well as the tastings to discern which burgundy wines shall be *tasteviné*, and therefore have the right to be sold with the label of the Confrérie. The Chevaliers de Tastevin organization is known the world over, born out of the necessity (in the 1930s) to sell burgundy wines.

VOSNE-ROMANEE

Red wines only from the commune south of Vougeot and north of Nuits-Saint-Georges. Vineyards surrounding the villages of Flagey-Echézeaux and Vosne-Romanée cover an area of 240 hectares, of which 48 are in Premier Cru and 66 in Grand Cru. It is the concentration of seven Grands Crus, harbouring the two most illustrious and expensive wines in Burgundy – La Romanée-Conti and La Tâche – that has given Vosne-Romanée the reputation of being *la perle du milieu* of the Côte de Nuits.

Right: Harvest time at Domaine de la Romanée-Conti's Grand Cru vineyards, Clos des Echézeaux.

Vosne-Romanée

In style, the wines of Vosne are firmer than those of Chambolle-Musigny, lighter than Gevrey-Chambertin, less concentrated but more elegant than Nuits-Saint-Georges. They should combine all the desirable qualities of fine burgundy, with a delicate but well-defined bouquet, a stylish, velvety depth of flavour and lingering but firm finish. Such wines, however, are more easily found in the Premiers and Grands Crus than in Vosne-Romanée *tout court*. Notable exceptions are from domaines Jacky Confuron-Contidot, Jean Gros, Gros Frère et Soeur, the Jayer family, Méo-Camuzet, Mongeard-Mugneret, Mugneret-Gibourg and the négociants Faiveley and especially Leroy, following Madame Bize-Leroy's purchase of the Charles Noëllat estate, which is based in Vosne-Romanée. These are racy, elegant wines, at their best after 7–12 years. They are not cheap, but the quality should be there. Average production is 700,000 bottles, including the Premiers Crus. Price high F-G.

Vosne-Romanée Premier Cru

Vosne-Romanée possesses nine Premiers Crus, all admirably situated on either side of or above the Grands Crus. In the north of the commune, lying between Echézeaux, Richebourg and Romanée-Saint-Vivant, are Les Beaumonts, Les Brûlées and Les Suchots. In the hands of good *vignerons*-vinifiers, these wines can be exceptional, and fine examples are Les Brûlées (René Engel and Henri Jayer), Les Beaumonts (Jean Grivot and Leroy) and Les Suchots (Henri Lamarche, Mongeard-Mugneret, René Mugneret, Manière-Noirot, Confuron and Jayer). To the south lie the rather richer, less fiery Les Malconsorts (excellent wines from Moillard-Grivot and the Clos Frantin) and the beautifully made Clos des Réas, the *monopole* of Jean and François Gros. Of the four remaining, Les Gaudichots has been largely absorbed by La Tâche, and Les Chaumes, Les Reignots and Les Petits Monts are seldom seen under their own name. For the négociants, Joseph Drouhin regularly produces some excellent Beaumonts. A Premier Cru should be drunk at 8–15 years depending on the vintage. Fairly expensive. Price G-low H.

The Grands Crus of Vosne-Romanée

There are eight Grands Crus, of which two – Echézeaux and Grands Echézeaux – belong in the commune of Flagey-Echézeaux, but as the village does not have an *appellation*, perhaps because it is on the "wrong" (east) side of the *route nationale*, they come under the auspices of Vosne-Romanée. Minimum alcohol content is 11.5°, but is usually around 13°, from a maximum yield of 35hl/ha. The six Grands Crus above the village of Vosne – La Grande Rue, La Tâche, Richebourg, La Romanée, La Romanée-Conti and La Romanée-Saint-Vivant – are dominated by the holdings of the Domaine de la Romanée-Conti.

Echézeaux

Wines from this large vineyard (30.08ha) are often sold under the declassification Vosne-Romanée Premier Cru, which, lacking some concentration and length, they are nearer to in quality than the other Grands Crus. They do not, however, fetch Grand Cru prices. Good wines are made by the domaines Dujac, Engel, Jayer, Mongeard-Mugneret, René Mugneret, Louis Gouroux, Faiveley and the Domaine de la Romanée-Conti. Average production 120,000 bottles. Fairly expensive. Price G-H.

Grands Echézeaux

A nine-hectare vineyard adjoining the best parts of the Clos de Vougeot, producing wines with a rich ruby colour and fine bouquet. They are firm and velvety on the palate, in flavour not unlike a good Pomerol. The wines from the Domaine de la Romanée-Conti are outstanding, those of Joseph Drouhin, Engel and Mongeard-Mugneret very good. They need ten years to show well, and age superbly. Production is some 37,000 bottles. Price H-I (Domaine de la Romanée-Conti).

La Grand Rue

This 1.5-hectare *monopole* of the Domaine Lamarche is a strip of vines sandwiched between La Romanée-Conti and La Tâche. Geographically, therefore, it should have been a Grand Cru before 1990, when it was upgraded from a Premier Cru. Whatever the soil may give, the actual vinification does not produce a wine that can compare with its direct neighbours. Potentially, it is a wine of very great class. Price H.

Richebourg

An eight-hectare vineyard producing the richest, most voluptuous and overpowering wine of all the Grands Crus, with deep colour, an explosive floral-spicy bouquet, great warmth and generous concentration of flavour, and a sturdy, velvet finish. Young, it is a little massive, and should be drunk at 12–20 years, more for great vintages. The two Gros families, Charles Noëllat, Henri Jayer, Liger-Belair & Fils from Nuits-Saint-Georges and Charles Viénot from the commune of Prémeaux, all make excellent wine; that of the Domaine de la Romanée-Conti is exceptional. Production around 30,000 bottles. Very expensive. Price I.

La Romanée

La Romanée is the smallest *appellation contrôlée* in France, covering only 0.84 hectares just above La Romanée-Conti. It is the *monopole* of the Liger-Belair family and the wine is currently distributed by Bouchard Père & Fils of Beaune. In spite of its name and exceptional situation, it did not in the 1970s and early 1980s, show the extraordinary class of La Tâche or La Romanée-Conti and was rather hard and inelegant. Bouchard are determined to restore its reputation. Production is under 4,000 bottles. Price high I.

La Romanée-Conti

This 1.8–hectare *monopole* of the Domaine de la Romanée-Conti (DRC) is without doubt the most prestigious red burgundy and probably the most sought-after red wine in the world. The vines are perfectly sited above the village of Vosne-Romanée, flanked by Romanée-Saint-Vivant and Richebourg to the north and La Grand Rue and La Tâche to the south, but even this does not explain the extraordinary elegance, purity of tone, complexity and sheer class of the wine. Pre-war, and even wartime vintages from ungrafted vines are unforgettable, and the recent vintages, with grapes from vines over 30 years old, and impeccable vinification, have again proved the unique-ness of La Romanée-Conti. It is always the last wine in comparative tastings of DRC wines, and follows the rich splendour of Le Richebourg and the satiny finesse of La Tâche with confidence. Ten years after the vintage is the earliest one should open a bottle of Romanée-Conti; it is better at 15 and may last twice as long. Average production 7,500 bottles. Price J + .

Romanée-Saint-Vivant

A 9.54-hectare vineyard just above the village of Vosne and below the vines of Richebourg. Over half is owned by the Domaine Marey-Monge, but the vineyards are looked after by and the wine made at the Domaine de la Romanée-Conti. The co-owner of the Domaine de la Romanée-Conti, Madame Bize-Leroy, purchased the Domaine Charles Noëllat in 1988, and her first vintage from this 1.5-hectare site was exceptional. Louis Latour owns the one-hectare Les Quatre Journaux and Moillard has a small parcel. The wines should have perfect balance: initial lightness with great finesse, breeding and length. Should be drunk from 8–15 years. Production 30,000 bottles. Price I-J.

La Tâche

Separated from La Romanée-Conti by the narrow strip of vines known as La Grande Rue, La Tâche covers 6.06 hectares and is a *monopole* of the Domaine de la Romanée-Conti. Some tasters, fortunate enough to have drunk both, prefer la Tâche to La Romanée-Conti. The colour is always beautiful, the bouquet subtle and entrancing, the taste silky and seductive with a totally satisfying finish. La Tâche shows itself earlier than La Romanée-Conti, and in light years may be more attractive. It is perfection at 10–20 years, will last longer. Production is around 24,000 bottles. Price J.

NUITS-SAINT-GEORGES

Nuits-Saint-Georges is the most southern *appellation* in the Côte de Nuits, covering 375 hectares in Nuits-Saint-Georges and Prémeaux, producing red and a very limited amount of the white wine. Nuits-Saint-Georges possesses no Grands Crus, but has the largest number of Premiers Crus in Burgundy (38).

Nuits-Saint-Georges

Red wines from the Pinot Noir limited to 40hl/ha (plus the PLC) and a tiny quantity of white wine from the Chardonnay or Pinot Blanc, limited to 45hl/ha. Despite their world-wide reputation, the red wines of Nuits-Saint-Georges have often been a disappointment, although efforts to improve quality are now having the desired effect. This is partly due to the popularity of the name, which allows the poorer *cuvées* to sell at high prices, but also to the slow-maturing nature of the wine, which makes it hard and ungracious if drunk too young. A good Nuits-Saint-Georges is a sturdy, serious wine, lacking the finesse and charm of Cham-bolle-Musigny, the stylishness of Vosne-Romanée and the vibrancy of Morey-Saint-Denis, and needs ten years to begin to show well. Many other fine burgundies with the fruity (blackcurrants, strawberries, raspberries, cherries), youthful Pinot Noir aroma, are agreeable when young, but not Nuits-Saint-Georges, and in this respect they are like a Saint-Estèphe or Pauillac in comparison to the smoother Médocs. Once mature, their deep mahogany-red colour reveals a concentrated, complex bouquet of dried fruits with great warmth and length of flavour. As the vines leave the commune of Prémeaux, they lose the right to the *appellation* Nuits-Saint-Georges, and the villages of Prissey, Comblanchien (more famous for its marble quarries) and Corgoloin produce Côte de Nuits-Villages. All the good domaines in Nuits-Saint-Georges own vines in the Premiers Crus, and it is generally worth paying the extra money for these. The Nuits-based négociants — Faiveley, Labouré-Roi, Moillard, Chauvenet — generally succeed in producing fine wines that fit their reputation and that of their commune. Average production is 1.5 million bottles of red, not more than 4,000 of white. Price F.

Nuits-Saint-Georges Premier Cru

The Premiers Crus of Nuits-Saint-Georges cover the whole length of the *appellation*, from just south of Vosne-Romanée to just past Prémeaux, in a narrow stretch of vines planted right up to the tree-line. Those vineyards nearer to Vosne-Romanée have some of the finesse and style of this commune, while the most typical wines are from the south of the town to just north of Prémeaux. The commune of Prémeaux itself produces only Premier Cru wines, slightly softer than their neighbours, but with great finesse. From north of Nuits-Saint-Georges comes Les Boudots, the next-door vineyard to Les Malconsorts in Vosne, with fine, elegant wines from Jean Grivot and Mongeard-Mugneret; Les Chaignots produces excellent wine from the middle of the slope (Maurice Chevillon and

Above: The traditional "pannier" or basket used during the vintage in Burgundy. Nowadays plastic containers are more common.

Alain Michelot), Les Cras and Les Argillats are also well thought of. From south of the town come the finest wines, some up to Grand Cru standard. Les Saint-Georges is generally recognized to produce the most intensely flavoured, long-lived wines from its 7.5 hectares, with exemplary bottles from the domaines Robert and Maurice Chevillon, Auguste and Lucien Chicotot, Henri Remoriquet, Henri Gouges, L. Audidier and P. Missery. Just above Les Saint-Georges, Les Vaucrains (6ha) produces deep-coloured, mouth-filling wines with great class, especially from the domaines Gouges and Audidier, and from Jean Chauvenet, Jean Confuron and Alain Michelot. Progressing north

1986
VOSNE~ROMANÉE
AUX REIGNOTS

APPELLATION VOSNE·ROMANÉE PREMIER CRU CONTROLÉE

RÉCOLTE DU DOMAINE
DE LA S.C.I. DU CHATEAU DE VOSNE·ROMANÉE
PROPRIÉTÉ DE LA FAMILLE DE M. LE COMTE LIGER·BELAIR

ÉLEVÉ ET MIS EN BOUTEILLE PAR LA MAISON
BOUCHARD PÈRE & FILS
NÉGOCIANT AU CHATEAU, BEAUNE, COTE·D'OR, FRANCE

PRODUIT DE FRANCE

towards Nuits, Les Cailles — largely owned by Morin Père & Fils — produces rich, smooth wines; Les Perrières robust, long-lived reds as well as the exceptional La Perrière white from the Domaine Gouges, an unctuous, splendidly fruity greeny-gold-coloured wine from an albino clone of the Pinot Noir; Les Porrets (including the *monopole* Clos des Porrets-Saint-Georges of Henri Gouges), Les Pruliers (Gouges and Chevillon) and Les Hauts Pruliers (Machard de Gramont) are typically Nuits in needing ten years at least to show the complexity and fruit behind their hard exterior. It is a great pity that too many of the Premiers Crus are drunk long before they are at their best. One of the specialities of the négociant Leroy is bottling the Premiers Crus, each with the character of their particular *climat* intact, and releasing them only when they are fully mature. They are expensive, but a revelation. From the commune of Prémeaux come some very fine wines, many of them well known owing to their being *monopoles* of the local négociants: Clos de la Maréchale (9.6ha, Faiveley), Clos de Forêts-Saint-Georges and Clos de l'Arlot (7ha, and 4ha), the latter producing a little white wine, Clos des Corvées (5ha, Domaine Général Gouachon), Aux Perdrix (Bernard Mugneret-Gouachon) and Clos des Corvées-Paget (Charles Viénot). These wines may be drunk at 10–15 years, while those from nearer to Nuits (not forgetting the four-hectare Château Gris of Lupé Cholet) may last further ten years or more. Quite expensive, but the better wines are worth it. Price G.

Les Hospices de Nuits

The foundation of the Hospices de Nuits dates from 1692, but the first public auction of wine was not held until 1962. The date is the Sunday before Palm Sunday, and the wines certainly show better after spending the winter in barrel than they would on the third Sunday in November, the date on which the Hospices de Beaune auction takes place. All the wines, from a total of about ten hectares of vines, are first growths. Price H.

Left: The wooded hills west of Nuits-St-Georges partly shield the vineyards from the rain-bearing winds.

COTE DE BEAUNE

The Côte de Beaune vineyards, the natural continuation of the Côte de Nuits, and the southern part of the Côte d'Or, commence at Ladoix and end 26 kilometres further south at Santenay near Chagny, covering over 2,900 hectares, an area more than twice that of the Côte de Nuits. Vines are planted on the right (west) side of the RN74 right up to a height of 400 metres, with the accompanying risks of spring frost, while, with some few exceptions, wines from the left of the main road may only take the *appellation* Bourgogne. The rocky, limestone-based terrain is covered in part with a deep layer of dark-coloured soil, suitable for full-bodied red wines, and in other parts with a lightish marl, best for fine white wines. A higher proportion of chalk gives wines of more finesse than body, such as the lighter *crus* of Beaune and Savigny, while a more stony, clayey soil is found at Pommard and Volnay. The exposition of the vineyards is from north-east to south-west, and it is this diversity of exposition allied to the nuances of soil and elevation that give the wines of each commune their different character. In contrast to the Côte de Nuits, a high proportion of the wines produced on the Côte de Beaune are white, and these are in several cases superior to the red wines from communes where both are produced. Some communes (Pommard, Volnay) produce exclusively red wines and some *appellations* (Corton-Charlemagne, Montrachet) exclusively white wine. Apart from the Aligoté and Gamay grapes, for the minor but pleasant wines Bourgogne-Aligoté and Bourgogne Passe-Tout-Grains, Pinot Noir is planted for red wines, and Chardonnay and a very little Pinot Blanc for the whites. The very rare white wines from the Côte de Nuits hardly bear comparison with those from the Côte de Beaune, whose whites are justifiably world famous. Red wines from the Côte de Beaune are for the most part rounder, more supple and softer than those from the Côte de Nuits.

Bourgogne Hautes-Côtes-de-Beaune

Red, dry white and rosé wines from vineyards outside (and, as the name implies, higher in elevation than) the *appellation* Côte de Beaune. Reds and rosés are from the Pinot Noir grape, whites from the Chardonnay and Pinot Blanc. The wines must have a minimum alcohol content of 10°, from a maximum yield of 50hl/ha. This relatively new *appellation* produces red wines with good colour, fruit and personality that are less complex and velvety than the more expensive wines from the Côte de Beaune *appellation*. There has been much replanting of vines and the growers are very serious. A large part of the production is handled by the excellent

Cave Coopérative des Hautes-Côtes, on the Route de Pommard, while growers of note include Claude Cornu, Jean Jolliet, Château de Mandelot, Marcilly Père & Fils and Denis Carré at Meloisy. These wines, as with those of the Hautes-Côtes-de-Nuits, have the right to the straight *appellation* Bourgogne, and may only use the Hautes-Côtes label after an official tasting. Production is around two million bottles of which 98% is red. Good value for money especially in fine vintages; quality is improving year by year. Price C.

Côte de Beaune-Villages

Red wine only, from Pinot Noir grapes planted in 16 communes in the Côte d'Or and parts of the Saône-et-Loire, with a minimum alcohol content of 10.5° (almost always exceeded) from a maximum yield of 40hl/ha. The rules are different from those controlling Côtes de Nuits-Villages, for while the latter is a distinct, separate *appellation* the following *appellations* may, and often do, sell their wine under the Côte de Beaune-Villages label, and this is obligatory if wines from two or more *appellations* are blended: Auxey-Duresses, Blagny, Chassagne-Montrachet, Cheilly-lès-Maranges, Chorey-lès-Beaune, Dézize-lès-Maranges, Ladoix, Meursault, Monthélie, Pernand-Vergelesses, Puligny-Montrachet, Saint-Aubin, Saint-Romain, Sampigny-lès-Maranges, Santenay, and Savigny-lès-Beaune. The wine should naturally have all the qualities of a fine *appellation communale*: an attractive ruby colour and distinctively Pinot bouquet and flavour. Depending on the vintage, they are at their best between three and eight years. Many négociants show a reliable Côte de Beaune-Villages, while if the wine is domaine-bottled from a grower, the address on the label will indicate the origin. Production varies not only with the size of the vintage, but also according to the decision of the grower or négociant to use the individual *appellation* or not. With the creation in 1989 (retroactive to the wines from 1988) of the new *appellation* Maranges (see page 77), and the emergence of *appellations* such as Chorey-lès-Beaune and Ladoix-Serrigny, the Côtes de Beaune-Villages label is mostly reserved by growers and négociants for their export markets. Average production is around one million bottles. Price D.

Chorey-lès-Beaune

Red wine (although the *appellation* does allow for white but only a few barrels are made each year) from a 121–hectare *appellation* almost entirely planted on the plain to the east of the RN74. While most of the wine is sold under the Côte de Beaune-Villages label, the efforts of local growers including the domaines Charles Allexant, Jacques Germain, Goud de Beaupuis, Maurice Martin and especially Tollot-Beaut, have produced wines consistently fine enough to have given Chorey-lès-Beaune its own reputation. They have an attractive, lively fruit with a round, supple finish. Of the négociants, Drouhin has a particularly good Chorey. Best at 4–8 years. Average production 600,000 bottles. Very good value. Price high D, low E.

Ladoix

Mostly red, with a very little white wine, from Ladoix-Serrigny, the most northern commune of the Côte de Beaune on the border of the Côte de Nuits. In the commune of Ladoix-Serrigny, 120ha are classified AOC Ladoix, 14ha Ladoix Premier Cru, 11ha Aloxe-Corton Premier Cru and 22ha Corton, Corton-Charlemagne or Corton blanc. In the past, the red wines, possessing much of the power of the Côtes de Nuits with the roundness of the Côtes de Beaune, were sold as Aloxe-Corton, and are now often seen under the Côtes de Beaune-Villages label. To complicate matters further, although the *appellation* is Ladoix, it frequently appears as the more recognizable Ladoix-Côte de Beaune. The Premiers Crus, of which the best are Les Maréchaudes, La Toppe au Vert and Les Lolières, still carry the *appellation* Aloxe-Corton, while the best part of the vineyard, Le Rognet and Les Vergennes, are classified Grand Cru Corton. This leaves around 300,000 bottles of red and 15,000 of white *villages* wine, with some excellent *cuvées* from domaines Cachat, Capitain, Chevalier and Nudant. The red Ladoix is firm, fruity, rather acidic when young and long-lasting, while the white is deliciously clean yet also quite firm. Generally good value for money. Price E.

ALOXE-CORTON

The commune of Aloxe-Corton produces its own *villages* wine, some fine Premiers Crus, but is known above all for the Grand Cru vineyards Corton and Corton-Charlemagne, which it shares with the communes of Ladoix-Serrigny and Pernand-Vergelesses.

Aloxe-Corton

Almost entirely red wine, (with only 3,000 or so bottles of white from the Chardonnay or Pinot Blanc), made from the Pinot Noir. The communal rules of 40hl/ha and a minimum degree of 10.5 apply and are generally exceeded in both cases by the tolerated 20%. Although situated in the Côte de Beaune, the wines of Aloxe have much in common with those of the Côte de Nuits, with a deep colour and solid, even rough, fruit that needs some years to soften. They are well known through the local négociants, Louis Latour and La Reine Pedauque, while particularly fine examples come from the domaines Denis Boussey, Antonin Guyon, Prince de Mérode, Daniel Senard, Tollot-Beaut and Michel Voarick. They are at their best at 6–12 years after the vintage. The reputation of Louis Latour obliges him to produce a fine, meaty wine. Drouhin and Jadot are, as usual, very good. Despite their solidity, Aloxe-Corton wines mature quite quickly and are at their best at 5–10 years, and are generally not too expensive. Production, including the Premiers Crus, is around 650,000 bottles. Price F.

Aloxe-Corton Premier Cru

Whether from the commune of Ladoix-Serrigny or Aloxe-Corton, the Premiers Crus are situated at the beginning of the slope, between the *villages* wines nearer the plain and the Grands Crus higher up. The wines, particularly those from Les Vazolières, Les Fournières, Les Maréchaudes and Les Paulands, are more intense yet with more finesse than Aloxe-Corton *simple*, and last longer. Unlike the commune of Gevrey-Chambertin, where some Premiers Crus may easily rival the lesser Grands Crus, these wines approach, but do not rival, the red wines of Corton. Domaines Cachat-Ocquidant and André Nudant are names to look out for. Price G.

Corton

The Grands Crus of Corton, producing red wine, cover nearly 120 hectares in the communes of Ladoix-Serrigny and Aloxe-Corton. If the wine comes from one of the *climats* with Grand Cru status (Bressandes, Clos du Roi, etc), the name of the *climat* is generally added after Corton. The hillside vineyards of Corton are perhaps the most impressive of the Côte de Beaune. At the top, just under the Corton woods, is **Le Corton**, which gives severe, straightforward wines, finally maturing with great style; the high incidence of limestone suits the Chardonnay grape, which produces an elegant, firm white wine, with a little less richness than Corton-Charlemagne. The major proprietors in Le Corton are Bouchard Père & Fils and Domaine Bonneau de Martray. Directly below Le Corton are the three best-known Grands Crus: **Le Clos du Roi**, producing deep-coloured, richly textured wines, especially fine from the domaines Chandon de Briailles, Dubreuil-Fontaine, Prince de Mérode, Baron Thénard, Michel Voarick and Daniel Senard; **Les Renardes**, perhaps (as the name suggests) rather more animal and aggressive, with superb long-lasting wines from the late Michel Gaunoux; and **Les Bressandes**, beautifully balanced

CHOREY-LES-BEAUNE

Appellation Chorey-les-Beaune Contrôlée

DOMAINE
GOUD DE BEAUPUIS
Chorey-les-Beaune (Côte-d'Or)
Mis en bouteille à la propriété

75 cl   12,5% Vol

Savigny-Serpentières
APPELLATION SAVIGNY-LES-BEAUNE 1er CRU CONTROLÉE

Mis en bouteille à la propriété par
Domaine Pierre Guillemot 75 cl
Viticulteurs à Savigny-les-Beaune (Côte-d'Or)
12,5% Vol.   Produit de France

wines of great finesse but still with the power of Corton, with excellent *cuvées* from Chandon de Briailles, Tollot-Beaut, Laleure-Piot, Pierre Poisot and Max Quénot. Of the other Grands Crus, **Les Pougets** is lighter, almost a feminine Corton (Louis Jadot owns 2.5ha here), and Le Prince de Mérode (Domaine de Serrigny) makes a splendidly meaty wine from the upper part of **Les Maréchaudes**. **Les Languettes** (Domaine Voarick), **Les Grèves** (Tollot-Beaut), **La Vigne au Saint** (Domaine Belland, Louis Latour), **Les Perrières**, **Le Rognet** (Domaine Chevalier) and the *monopole* **Clos des Meix** of Daniel Senard all combine the richness and style of a typical Corton. The *monopole* Clos de Vergennes from Domaine Cachat-Ocquidant in Ladoix-Serrigny, is vibrant and powerful. The largest owner in Corton is the Domaine Louis Latour, with 16 hectares of various *climats*, as well as the 2.75-hectare *monopole* Clos de la Vigne au Saint. The wine is vinified at Château de Grancey and sold as Château de Corton-Grancey, an honorary Grand Cru. Special mention should be made of the Cortons sold by La Maison Leroy, that carry the individual names of the Grand Cru *climats*, and are rarely surpassed in quality and ageing potential by any other wines throughout the Côte d'Or. The red wines of Corton seem to combine the splendid structure of the Côte de Nuits with the supple elegance of the Côte de Beaune. They should on no

account be drunk young, being at their best only after being allowed to age for ten or many more years. Average production, from a maximum yield of 35hl/ha, totals 350,000 bottles of red wine, 5,000 of white. Expensive but rarely over-priced. Price H-I.

Corton Blanc

Very small amount of white wine from the communes of Ladoix-Serrigny and Aloxe-Corton, not to be confused with Corton-Charlemagne. The finest wine is the Corton-Vergennes, bequeathed to the Hospices de Beaune by Paul Chanson in 1975, which is planted in Pinot Blanc, not Chardonnay. The Domaine Chandon de Briailles makes a very fine Corton blanc from the Bressandes vineyard, planted half in Chardonnay, half in Pinot Blanc. With the demand for and price of white Corton exceeding red, some producers with lighter soil at the top of the slope are replacing Pinot Noir with Chardonnay. Production may increase but Corton blanc will always be expensive. Price H.

Corton-Charlemagne

White wines only from vines planted on the higher, south-west facing slopes of the communes of Aloxe-Corton and Pernand-Vergelesses. Corton-Charlemagne is sometimes placed alongside Le Montrachet as the finest expression of white burgundy. While its rich, nutty wines have perhaps more in common with those of Meursault than with the floral wines of the Montrachet family, the grandiose structure and extraordinarily long life places the best in the category of works of art. It should never be drunk young, since the colour (changing from butter-coloured yellow to a rich gold), the bouquet (a mixture of Chardonnay fruit, almonds, cinnamon, honey and oak) and the flavour (high in natural acidity despite being also, at 13–14°, quite rich in alcohol) need at least two years in bottle to harmonize, and may improve for ten years or more. Quite spectacular wines come from Bonneau de Martray, the largest owner in the *appellation* with nine hectares in a single block on the Corton hill above Pernand-Vergelesses. Other fine growers include Roland Rapet, André Thiély, Laleure-Piot, Dubreuil-Fontaine and Jean François Coche-Dury. The négociants, whether they own vines here or not, seem to reserve some of their best efforts for Corton-Charlemagne: Louis Latour (with almost 9ha), Bouchard Père et Fils (3ha), Joseph Drouhin, Louis Jadot, Olivier Leflaive are all superb. The Hospices de Beaune possesses a highly prized parcel of 1.4ha, the Cuvée François de Salins. The old *appellation* "Charlemagne", to which the Aligoté grape was admitted, was discontinued in 1948, but a few growers still produce a magnificent Bourgogne-Aligoté. Production rarely exceeds 150,000 bottles. Very expensive. Price I-J.

Pernand-Vergelesses

Red and white wines from 190 hectares between Aloxe-Corton and Savigny-lès-Beaune. The reds, most of which are now sold under the *appellation* Pernand-Vergelesses rather than Côte de Beaune-Villages, are a little hard when young, firmer than those of Savigny, less velvety than those of Beaune, but age well, and the simple *villages* wine is one of the best values on the Côte d'Or. The Premier Cru Ile de Vergelesses produces without doubt wines with the most finesse, length and harmony of the commune, with excellent examples coming from the domaines Chandon de Briailles, Dubreuil-Fontaine and Laleure-Piot, while Les Vergelesses and Les Fichots (domaines Thiély and Doudet-Naudin) produce full-bodied, long-lasting wines. The *villages* wines need 4–5 years and the Premiers Crus 6–8 years. Les Caradeaux, just below the Corton-Charlemagne vines from the commune, produces a fine, none-too-soft white wine, a speciality of Chanson Père & Fils and Louis Jadot of Beaune. The whites are firm, with mouth-watering acidity, excellent mid-way in a meal, between the fine Aligoté made in the village and the exceptional Corton-Charlemagne. Production is around 300,000 bottles of red wine, 50,000 of white. Quality has greatly improved during the 1980s due to the efforts of local growers, particularly those who own Grand Cru vines. Price E.

Above: The vineyards of the Côte d'Or commune of Pernand-Vergelesses with the backdrop of the Bois de Corton.

SAVIGNY-LES-BEAUNE

Red and a little white wine from nearly 400 hectares in the commune of Savigny, surrounded by the vines of Pernand-Vergelesses, Aloxe-Corton and Beaune. The *villages* wines are generally attractive, elegantly light, and while they have the advantage of being able to be enjoyed young, they do not have the quality and intensity of the Premiers Crus. The white Savigny-lès-Beaune is stylish and elegant, with a little less depth than the Pernand blanc, one of the finest examples coming from the Vergelesses vineyard of the Domaine Louis Jacob. Producers to look for are Simon Bize (who makes excellent red and white Bourgogne from nearby vines), Maurice Ecart and Jean-Marc Pavelot. Production of red Savigny is the third largest on the Côte de Beaune after Beaune and Pommard, averaging approximately 1.2 million bottles, with only about 45,000 bottles of white. They both represent good value for money. Price low E.

Savigny-lès-Beaune Premier Cru

The finer wines of Savigny are of two different styles: the slopes on the Pernand-Vergelesses side of the *appellation* produce wines with a firm backbone that develop a silky texture and floral bouquet with age. The best Premiers Crus *climats* are Les Clous, Les Serpentières (domaines Louis Ecard-Guyot and Pierre Guillemot), Les Guettes (domaines Pavelot, rather heavy wines from Doudet-Naudin and Henri de Villamont), Les Lavières (deep coloured, fleshy wines, especially from Pierre Bitouzet, Chandon de Briailles and Tollot-Beaut) and Aux Vergelesses (the most delicate and bouqueted, with lovely wines from Simon Bize & Fils and Lucien Jacob); the slopes to the south, near to Beaune, with a more gravelly, less clayey soil, produce wines that are rounder and more complete and open up earlier than those from the other side. The best known are Les Marconnets, almost Beaune in style, Les Dominodes (solid, meaty wines, especially from Clair-Daü), Les Jarrons (Ecard-Guyot, Valentin-Bouchotte), and the more delicate Les Rouvrettes. With its proximity to Beaune, it is not surprising that the local négociants have considerable holdings in Savigny, and the elegant, old-fashioned wines of Chanson (Les Marconnets, Les Dominodes), the richer Les Lavières from Bouchard Père & Fils, and the long-lasting *cuvées* from Leroy are good examples. A fine Premier Cru from Savigny has a wonderfully scented aroma with a suave elegance on the palate, sometimes likened to Vosne-Romanée. They begin to be at their best after six years. Not cheap but very good. Price E-low F.

Côte de Beaune

A tiny (16ha) *appellation* producing red and white wine from the hills above Beaune. Maurice Jolliette, who purchased the Domaine de Pierre Blanches on the death of Paul Chanson in 1973, makes a full-bodied red. Other growers are Jean Allexant, Domaine Cauvard, Marchard de Gramont and Voirot. These wines resemble those of Beaune, but lack the elegance. Production is 100,000 bottles. Price low E.

BEAUNE

The vineyards of Beaune cover 538 hectares running for two kilometres to the north and south of the town. Beaune is thus the largest commune in the Côte d'Or, although the quantity of wine produced is exceeded by Gevrey-Chambertin from a smaller acreage. Beaune is the centre of the Burgundy wine trade where most well-known négociants have a base. It is also home to the Hôtel Dieu, for whose charity the famous Hospices de Beaune auction is held every November.

Beaune

Although 95% of the production is red, (from the Pinot Noir, with a basic yield of 40hl/ha and minimum 10.5° alcohol), there is a little white wine made from the Chardonnay, (45hl/ha, 11° alcohol). With the vineyards linking the northern Côte de Beaune – Aloxe Corton, Pernand-Vergelesses and Savigny – and those to the south – Pommard, Volnay – the red *villages* wines of Beaune have had some difficulty in creating a distinctive image for themselves, despite uniformly good colour, straightforward Pinot fruit and harmonious finish. As a result, although the town of Beaune is the centre of the Burgundy wine trade and despite the undisputed quality of wines produced from its vineyards, Beaune sells for less than Volnay or Pommard. Perhaps the size of the vineyards, however well exposed, which are owned largely by the town's négociants, offers such a range of Premiers Crus and different "house styles" as to lead to confusion. Most of the vines in the commune are classified Premier Cru, so the simple *appellation* Beaune is not common, but good wines are to be had from the domaines Bernard Delagrange, Michel Gaunoux and Thévenin-Monthélie as well as some négociants. This *appellation* must not be confused with Côte de Beaune (left), nor with Côte de Beaune-Villages see page 64). May be drunk from 4–8 years after the vintage. Production, including Premiers Crus – Beaune produces no Grands Crus – is 1.8 million bottles of red, 130,000 of white. Price E.

Beaune Premier Cru

The style of the many Premiers Crus of Beaune are (allowing for the variations in the "house styles" of the négociants), like those of Savigny, different between the north and the south of the vineyard. To the north they are firm and complete, with a velvety finish, wines of great breed and distinction that are excellent at ten years and may last 20. The best known, from the borders with Savigny to the RN470, are: Les Marconnets (classically elegant wines from Chanson, classically robust wines from Bouchard Père & Fils); Le Clos du Roi (perhaps the finest of all, from Tollot-Beaut, Robert Ampeau, Chanson, Louis Jadot, Louis Latour); the robust Les Perrières (Louis Latour); the lighter Clos des Fèves (Chanson); Les Cent Vignes (fleshy, fruity wines from domaines Duchet, Albert Morot and Besancenot-Mathouillet); Les Bressandes (velvety-soft, harmonious wines from Duchet, Albert Morot, Jaffelin, Louis Jadot); the extremely fine Les Grèves (Tollot-Beaut, Jean Darviot, Besancenot-Mathouillet, not forgetting the four-hectare *monopole* of Bouchard Père & Fils, La Vigne de L'Enfant Jésus); Les Teurons (harmonious and aromatic, lovely elegant wines from Jacques Germain, more full-bodied from Domaine Rossignol-Trapet, Bouchard Père & Fils and Louis Jadot); and Les

Cras (including the *monopole* Le Clos de la Féguine of Domaine Jacques Prieur). South of the RN470, going towards Pommard and Volnay, the wines are just as elegant, but softer and quicker maturing. The well-known *crus* include: La Montée Rouge (firm, lightish, Gaston Boisseaux, Léon Violland); Le Clos de la Mousse, *monopole* of Bouchard Père & Fils; Les Champimonts (Chanson, Coron Père & Fils); Les Avaux (Champy, Jaffelin, Patriarche); Les Aigrots; Les Vignes Franches (Louis Latour, and the very fine Clos des Ursules, *monopole* of Louis Jadot); Le Clos des Mouches, best known for the exceptionally stylish wines, both red and white, from Joseph Drouhin and rustic ones from Domaine Garandet; Les Boucherottes (Louis Jadot) and, just on the edge of Pommard, Les Epenottes (domaines Parent, Mussy). Mention should also be made of Bouchard Père & Fils' red and white Beaune du Château, a blend of several Premiers Crus, and many fine wines from Leroy and Remoissenet. This panoply of Premiers Crus provides a large enough range to satisfy any lover of fine burgundy. For the quality, they are in general not over-priced. Price high F, low G.

Les Hospices de Beaune

The Hôtel-Dieu in Beaune was founded in the middle of the 15th century by Nicolas Rolin, chancellor to the Duchy of Burgundy, and his wife, Guigone de Salins. Since its inception, Les Hospices de Beaune, as it is more popularly known, has received legacies of all kinds, the most famous and profitable being the parcels of vines bequeathed to the Hospices, the produce of which is sold on the third Sunday in November at the largest (in financial terms) charity sale in the world. Today, Les Hospices possesses 55 hectares of Premier and Grand Cru vines, of which 1.5 are in the Côte de Nuits. They comprise of 25 *cuvées* of red and ten of white wine, sold under the following *appellations*, followed by the names of the benefactors and the vineyards:

RED WINES

Mazis-Chambertin, Cuvée Madeleine Collignon: Mazis-Chambertin 1.5ha.
Corton, Cuvée Charlotte Dumay: Renardes 2ha, Les Bressandes 1ha, Clos du Roi 0.5ha.
Corton, Cuvée Docteur Peste: Bressandes 1ha, Chaumes & Voirosses 1ha, Clos du Roi 0.5ha, Fiètre 0.4ha, Les Grèves 0.1ha.
Pernand-Vergelesses, Cuvée Rameau-Lamarosse: Les Basses Vergelesses 0.6ha.
Savigny-lès-Beaune, Cuvée Forneret: Les Vergelesses 1ha, Aux Gravains 0.66ha.
Savigny-lès-Beaune, Cuvée Fouquerand: Basses Vergelesses 1ha, Les Talmettes 0.66ha, Aux Gravains 0.33ha, Aux Serpentières 0.14ha.

Savigny-lès-Beaune, Cuvée Arthur Girard: Les Peuillets 1ha, Les Marconnets 0.8ha.
Beaune, Cuvée Nicolas Rolin: Les Cents Vignes 1.5ha, Les Grèves 0.8ha, En Genêt 0.4ha.
Beaune, Cuvée Guigone de Salins: Les Bressandes 1ha, En Sebrey 0.8ha, Champs Pimont 0.6ha.
Beaune, Cuvée Clos des Avaux: Les Avaux 2ha.
Beaune, Cuvée Brunet: Les Teurons 0.88ha, Les Bressandes 0.66ha, La Mignotte 0.5ha, Les Cents Vignes 0.33ha.
Beaune, Cuvée Maurice Drouhin: Les Avaux 0.8ha, Les Broucherottes 0.4ha, Champs Pimont 0.6ha, Les Grèves 0.4ha.
Beaune, Cuvée Hugues et Louis Bétault: Les Grèves 0.88ha, La Mignotte 0.5ha, Les Aigrots 0.4ha, Les Sizies 0.33ha, Les Vignes Franches 0.2ha.
Beaune, Cuvée Rousseau-Deslands: Les Cents Vignes 1ha, Les Montrevenots 0.66ha, La Mignotte 0.4ha, Les Avaux 0.33ha.
Beaune, Cuvée Dames Hospitalières: Les Bressandes 1ha, La Mignotte 0.66ha, Les Teurons 0.5ha, Les Grèves 0.33ha.
Beaune, Cuvée Cyrot Chaudron: 1ha.
Pommard, Cuvée Cyrot Chaudron: 2.9ha.
Pommard, Dames de la Charité: Les Epenots 0.4ha, Les Rugiens 0.33ha, Les Noizons 0.33ha, La Refène 0.33ha, Les Combes Dessus 0.2ha.
Pommard, Cuvée Billardet: Petits-Epenots 0.66ha, Les Noizons 0.5ha, Les Arvelets 0.4ha, Les Rugiens 0.33ha.
Volnay, Cuvée Blondeau: Champans 0.6ha, Taille-Pieds 0.6ha, Ronceret 0.33ha, En l'Ormeau 0.2ha.
Volnay, Cuvée Général Muteau: Volnay le Village 0.8ha, Carelle sous la Chapelle 0.33ha, Cailleret Dessus 0.2ha, Frémiet 0.2ha, Taille-Pieds 0.2ha.
Volnay-Santenots, Cuvée Jehan de Massol: Les Santenots 1.5ha.
Volnay, Cuvée Gauvain: Les Santenots 1.5ha, Les Pitures 0.33ha.
Monthélie, Cuvée Lebelin: Les Duresses 0.88ha.
Auxey-Duresses, Cuvée Boillot: Les Duresses 0.75ha.

WHITE WINES

Bâtard-Montrachet, Cuvée de Flandres 0.3ha.
Corton-Charlemagne, Cuvée François de Salins: Corton-Charlemagne 0.25ha.
Corton-Vergennes, Cuvée Paul Chanson: Corton-Vergennes 0.25ha.
Meursault-Genevrières, Cuvée Baudot: Les Genevrières Dessus 0.2ha, Les Genevrières Dessous 0.4ha.
Meursault-Genevrières, Cuvée Philippe Le Bon: Les Genevrières Dessus 0.2ha, Les Genevrières Dessous 0.4ha.
Meursault-Charmes, Cuvée de Bahèzre de Lanlay: Les Charmes Dessus 0.5ha, Les Charmes Dessous 0.4ha.

Meursault-Charmes, Cuvée Albert Grivault: Les Charmes Dessus 0.5ha.
Meursault, Cuvée Jehan Humblot: Le Poruzot 0.6ha, Grands Charrons 0.1ha.
Meursault, Cuvée Loppin: Les Criots 0.6ha.
Meursault, Cuvée Goureau: Le Poruzot 0.33ha, Les Pitures 0.33ha, Les Cras 0.2ha.

Following much criticism for unreliable winemaking and great variation in the quality even between different barrels of the same *cuvée*, a modern *cuverie* has been installed at the back of the Hôtel-Dieu. All the wines are lodged in new oak barrels, and in plentiful years like 1982 and 1985, a pre-selection is made so that the least successful barrels are not presented at auction. Wines made from vines under eight years old are now no longer admitted to the sale. In 1988 André Porcheret, the winemaker who had been appointed in 1982 to improve the quality of the Hospices wines, (which he indeed did), was hired by Madame Bize-Leroy to oversee the winemaking at her new estate in Vosne-Romanée. In 1989 and 1990, the red wines have lacked the depth and colour and intensity of flavour that make for great burgundy. The Hospices de Beaune delivers its own distinctive labels to each purchaser, carrying with them the prestige that partially justifies the high price of these wines. Price H-I-J.

Below: Les Hospices de Beaune annual auction takes place at the market hall across the road from the Hospices.

POMMARD

Pommard

Red wine from 340 hectares of vines situated between Beaune in the north and Volnay in the south. Pommard has a reputation for being full-bodied to the point of heaviness, the old-fashioned idea of a tyical burgundy, but the vines being where they are, between Beaune and Volnay, it is nothing of the sort. The wines from the bottom of the slopes, between the RN73 and RN74, do tend to be full and tannic, but those higher up have a firmness and elegance that is never heavy. The popularity of the name has made Pommard a fixture on the wine lists of most négociants, and many of these are lacking in fruit, over-chaptalized, or plain dull and, as such, are over-priced. As is usual in Burgundy, while there are some good *villages* wines, the real quality and value are to be found in the Premiers Crus. Production of Pommard, Premiers Crus included, is the second largest on the Côte de Beaune and the total averages around 1.4 million bottles. Quite expensive. Price F.

Pommard Premier Cru

There are no Grands Crus in Pommard, but Les Rugiens (and particularly Les Rugiens-Bas) and Les Epenots are certainly of Grand Cru quality. They are very different in style: Les Rugiens, with its reddish, ferruginous soil, produces sumptuous, deep-coloured wines with the weight of a Corton and the elegance of a Volnay. The domaines Mme de Courcel and Jules Guillemard are very fine, but are eclipsed by the Rugiens of domaines Michel Gaunoux, Hubert de Montille and Billard-Gonnet which represent burgundy at its best. Les Epenots is softer, with a rich, heady bouquet and velvet finish that is sometimes compared to a Musigny. Les Grands Epenots of Michel Gaunoux is exceptional, and excellent wines come from domaines Parent, Mme de Courcel, Jean Monnier and Pothier-Rieusset. On the Beaune border lies the Clos de Epeneaux, *monopole* of Le Comte Armand, not in fact a Premier Cru, but making rich, velvety wines of excellent quality from a high proportion of old vines. On the other side of the road is the 20–hectare *monopole* Le Château de Pommard, whose wines are finer than the exposition of the vines (all planted on the plain) would suggest. Other fine Premiers Crus are Les Pézerolles (de Montille), Les Chaponnières (Parent), Les Arvelets (Gaunoux), Les Jarollières (light, elegant wines from Domaine de la Pousse d'Or), Le Clos de la Commaraine (*monopole* of Jabolet-Vercherre), Le Clos Blanc (Roger Clerget), Le Clos du Verger (Pothier-Rieusset), Le Clos Saint-Jean (Domaine Lahaye), Les Bertins (Labouré Roi), Les Argillières (Domaine Lejeune) and Les Frémiers, on the Pommard/Volnay border (Coste-

Above: Topping up the casks to avoid oxidation at the Domaine Leflaive in Puligny-Montrachet.

Caumartin). Of the négociants, Louis Latour has a *cuverie* in the village, Drouhin of Beaune and Ropiteau of Meursault have some fine *cuvées*, and the firmness, intensity and ageing potential of the better Premiers Crus are very well seen in the wines of Leroy. A good Pommard needs ten years to open up and is better at 15 or more. Expensive. Price G.

VOLNAY

Volnay

Red wine from 215 hectares of vines on easy slopes overlooking the Saône Valley. They are considered the most lissom, bouqueted, expressive wines of the Côte de Beaune and are often compared with Chambolle-Musigny. The style is more homogeneous than in any other commune in Burgundy, with the words "graceful, elegant, smooth, harmonious" applying to both *villages* and Premiers Crus. A Volnay *tout court* may be drunk at 4–5 years, when its violet bouquet begins to expand

and will improve for a few years more. During the 1980s, particularly since 1985, a drive for quality through lower yields, cleaner cellars, longer and better vinification, has been evident both at grower and négociant level. The commune of Volnay has always had a handful of domaines – d'Angerville, de Montille, Pousse d'Or, Lafarge – who set the tone for quality even during the slapdash 1970s. As a result, the standard of *villages* Volnays has always been reliable. Production, including Premiers Crus, around one million bottles. Expensive, but less than Pommard. Price F.

Volnay Premier Cru

The Premiers Crus of Volnay are neatly arranged on either side of the RN73, with the woods above and the *villages* wines below. The vineyards above the road, with a higher proportion of limestone in the soil, tend to produce lighter, quicker maturing wines than those from the more iron-based soil below. Of the higher vineyards, the largest is Le Clos des Chênes, with fine, elegant wines from Antonin Guyon, Michel Lafarge and Louis Glantenay; continuing north, Les Taille Pieds (domaines d'Angerville, de Montille), produces wines that are more complete. Around the village of Volnay, there are four *monopoles* in Premier Cru: Les Clos du Verseuil (Domaine Clerget), the delicious Clos d'Audignac, the spectacularly stylish and elegant Clos de la Bousse d'Or (both Domaine de la Pousse d'Or) and the fiery, even tannic Clos de Ducs (Domaine d'Angerville); after these last two, Les Angles (Henri Boillot) and Les Frémiets (Bouchard Père & Fils, a large owner in Volnay) tend to suffer by comparison. Below the road, descending towards Meursault, the most famous vineyard is Les Caillerets, perhaps the most typical Volnay, allying a certain firmness to lacy elegance: Le Clos des 60 Ouvrées *monopole* Domaine de la Pousse d'Or (an *ouvrée* is historically the amount of vines one worker could work in one day, officially it is 4 acres and 28 *centiares*, in this case a Clos of 0.2568ha), is sometimes the best wine in Volnay and may last 20 years, the simple Caillerets from the same Domaine has a fine bouquet of violets, while wines from d'Angerville, Jean Clerget and Bouchard Père & Fils are excellent. In the commune of Meursault lies Les Santenots which, if planted with Pinot Noir, has the right to the *appellation* Volnay-Santenots (Domaine Potinet-Ampeau and superb Santenot-du-Mileu from Domaine des Comtes Lafon). Les Champans is well situated, with classic, harmonious wines from d'Angerville, de Montille and Lafon (some of the finest Volnays currently made), while the other Premiers Crus planted towards Pommard – La Carelle sous la Chapelle, En l'Ormeau, Les Mitans, Les Brouillards – are less complex. Many *vignerons* have the same surname (Rossignol, Clerget, Glantenay), all make good wine. Volnay Premier Cru is excellent 6–12 years after vintage. Price G.

Monthélie

Mostly red, with a little white wine, produced from 100 hectares west of Volnay and north of Meursault. The reds are said to have the finesse of a Volnay and the power of a Pommard, which is generally true, albeit in a minor key. The finest wine in the *appellation* comes from the Château de Monthélie, where le Comte Eric de Suremain makes a deep-coloured, long-lasting wine (especially his *tête-de-cuvée* from very old vines). The Premier Cru Les Champs-Fulliots, a continuation of Les Caillerets from the commune of Volnay, makes a rounded, fruity, harmonious wine (domaines Boussey, Ropiteau-Mignon), while that of Les Duresses, from the other side of the commune, above Auxey-Duresses, is elegant but lighter. The white wine is fruity and agreeable and should be drunk young. Other good domaines with vines in Monthélie are Thévenin-Monthélie, Deschamps, Maurice Bourgeois, Monthélie-Douhairet, Paul Garaudet and Potinet-Ampeau, Parent and Roulot, and reliable négociants are Chanson, Leroy and Ropiteau, Monthélie can be drunk at 3–6 years, but the better *cuvées* age well. Average production 48,000 bottles of red, 9,000 of white. Not expensive and good value. Price E.

Auxey-Duresses

Red and white wine from 150 hectares on the northwest side of Meursault, just below Monthélie. The whites, coming from the Meursault side, do indeed resemble a minor Meursault, lively and stylish with a hint of nuttiness, but are best drunk young, at 2–3 years. The reds, despite a fine colour and a raspberry/cassis aroma, are leaner than those from Monthélie and often lack fruit in poor years. There are two Premiers Crus of note: Le Val, with fine wines from Jean Prunier, Gérard Creusefond and Bernard Roy; and Les Duresses, again good from Bernard Roy and especially so from Jean-Pierre Diconne and Ropiteau-Mignon. The white Auxey from the Duc de Magenta is crisp and elegant and many growers from Meursault (Ampeau, Roulot) have vines here. The local négociant, La Maison Leory, makes a Meursault-style red of very high quality. Much of the wine of Auxey is still bought by the Beaune négociants to make up their *cuvées* of Bourgogne blanc or Côte de Beaune-Villages. Production is around 500,000 bottles of red, 160,000 of white. Not very expensive and good value. Price E.

Saint-Romain

Red and white wine from 140 hectares in the hills above Meursault and Auxey-Duresses. Although geographically in the Hautes-Côtes de Beaune, it is classified as a Côte de Beaune, yet is the only commune to have no Premiers Crus. The whites are fine, with good, sometimes too much, acidity, which allows them to improve with age. Saint-Romain, due to its elevated situation, suffers more than other communes from frost, resulting in reduced yields and less prosperity for the *vignerons*. In comparison to its equals in quality – Monthélie, Auxey-Duresses – the village has a run-down, almost deserted air. The major négociants have not shown much interest in these wines, leaving the field open for smaller companies like Jaffelin and Olivier Leflaive, whose white Saint-Romains are models of Bourgogne blanc. The reds have good colour, a cherry flavour, are rather rustic and perhaps lack charm, but age well. Good domaines are Fernand Bazenet, Henri Buisson, Denis Carré, Alain Gras, and René Thévenin-Monthélie. Production is around 200,000 bottles of red, 160,000 of white. Good value, especially the whites. Price low E.

MEURSAULT

Meursault

Mainly white, with a very little red wine from 417 hectares of vines grouped around the town of Meursault, between Volnay and Puligny-Montrachet. The red wines are, naturally, found on the borders of Volnay, and the Premier Cru Les Santenots, if planted in Pinot Noir, is sold under the *appellation* Volnay-Santenots (see page 72). There is also some excellent red wine from high up on the Puligny border at Blagny, and this also has its own *appellation* (below). Meursault rouge is full with good soft fruit, and has some of the qualities of the better-known Côte de Beaune. The best wines are from the Clos de Mazeray of Domaine Jacques Prieur, Clos la Baronne (Labouré-Roi) and those of Ropiteau Frères. The make-up of the soil and sub-soil, however, is perfect for the Chardonnay, and Meursault is white burgundy at its most characteristic. Colour can vary from a pale, sometimes greeny yellow to a full gold, the bouquet is rich, fruity, with buttery, nutty, spicy overtones leading into a full, complex flavour and dry finish. The finest wines, as usual, come from the Premier Cru vineyards, but the *villages* wines of Meursault are generally typical of the *appellation* and of good quality. Some of the *climats* around the town are often of Premier Cru quality, notably Le Clos de la Barre, Les Casse-Têtes, Les Narvaux, Les Tillets, Les Luchets and Les Tessons. Superb wines are made by the domaines Coche-Dury, Guy Roulot, Eric Boussey, Boyer-Martenot, Michelot-Buisson, Joseph and Pierre Matrot. The major négociants pride themselves on their *cuvées* of Meursault, many now made from grapes bought in and vinified in-house rather than from wine bought in barrel. Wines of this quality are not cheap, but large production and overall high standard, mean

that they are not excessively expensive. Wines like these are at their best 3–5 years after the vintage. Production is around 2.5 million bottles of white, including Premiers Crus, 100,000 of red. Price F.

Meursault Premier Cru

The finest Premiers Crus come from a band of vineyards running south from the town towards Puligny-Montrachet. North, on the Volnay borders, lie Les Santenots, where the Marquis d'Angerville makes a full-bodied Meursault-Santenots, Les Cras and Les Petures. On the Puligny border at Blagny, the wines are firmer and tougher and sell under the *appellation* Meursault-Blagny (below). Of the six Premiers Crus south of the town, Les Perrières is reckoned to have the most distinction, both in its subtle bouquet and great length of flavour. The style of even a single *cru* varies according to the age of the vines, vinification and ageing, but there are few disappointing Perrières, and superb wines are to be found from the domaines Robert Ampeau, Comte Lafon, Michelot-Buisson, Guy Roulot, Coche-Dury and Pierre Morey. (Morey's superb Perrières, Genevrières and Charmes, as well as some lovely village Meursault, come from vines belonging to the Domaine des Comte Lafon, which will revert to Lafon from the 1990 vintage. Pierre Morey is now the *régisseur* at Domaine Laflaive in Puligny-Montrachet.) Les Genevrières is perhaps more intense than Les Perrières, and is often preferred by the local *vignerons* for its typical Meursault aroma of hazelnuts. Excellent wines from Lafon, Michelot-Buisson, François Jobard, Pierre Morey and Ropiteau-Mignon. Les Charmes is the largest of the Premiers Crus, with the higher part of the vineyard – Les Charmes Dessus as opposed to Les Charmes Dessous – making the finer wine. Charmes is richer than Les Perrières or Les Genevrières, but with a little less style and keeps less well. Excellent wines again from Lafon, Michelot-Buisson and François Jobard, as well as André Brunet, Pierre Matrot and René Monnier. Les Poruzots, the smallest of the Premiers Crus with only four hectares, is more lively than Les Charmes, less rich, but with great finesse. Fine wines from Ropiteau-Mignon and domaines J.P. Gauffroy, Roux and René Manuel. Les Bouchères resembles Les Poruzots but is less subtle, with good examples from Charles Alexant, Jaffelin, Ropiteau-Mignon and Domaine René Manuel. Finally, La Goutte d'Or, just above the town, is round and full-bodied, a mouth-filling wine that sometimes lacks acidity, but is particularly good from Lafon, Ropiteau-Mignon and François Gaunoux. The size of the commune permits négociants to choose some fine *cuvées*, both *villages* and Premiers Crus can be had from Drouhin, Jadot, Latour and Leroy. Premiers Crus need three years to begin showing at their best, and are splendid 5–8 years after vintage. Expensive but very fine. Price G.

Blagny

White and red wine from vineyards just above the Premier Cru Les Perrières in the commune of Meursault, with vines both in Meursault and Puligny-Montrachet. White wine from certain *climats* near Meursault may be sold as Meursault Premier Cru, and from vines near Puligny as Puligny-Montrachet. Red wine must carry the *appellation* Blagny. The best white is Meursault-Blagny, a Premier Cru in its own right, which actually more resembles a Puligny than a Meursault with lively acidity and firm elegant fruit, especially fine from Domaine Matrot. The red has a good colour and, particularly if it comes from the Premier Cru La Pièce sous le Bois (Domaine Matrot, Robert Ampeau), has a certain harshness and *goût de terroir* that becomes very marked in more tannic vintages like 1976. In lighter vintages (1979, 1980, 1986), or if the vines are planted in the commune of Puligny-Montrachet (lovely, lightish wines from Domaine Leflaive), Blagny rouge may be drunk at 3–4 years, otherwise it needs twice this time to soften up. The young négociant firm Olivier Leflaive Frères sells some delicious red Blagny. These wines are not well-known but reliable and good value. Price E.

PULIGNY-MONTRACHET

The commune of Puligny shares, although it has the larger portion, with the commune of Chassagne the fabled Grands Crus of the Montrachet family. The fame of the Montrachet name has made the reputation of the *village* wine, yet it is not always as reliable as either Meursault or Chassagne-Montrachet.

Puligny-Montrachet

White and a very small quantity of red wine from 234 hectares of vines to the south of Meursault and to the north of Chassagne-Montrachet. The red wine can be sold as Côte de Beaune-Villages, but owing to its relative scarcity and the renown of the Puligny name, it is more often seen under the Puligny-Montrachet-Côte de Beaune *appellation*. It is fruity and quite soft, and may be drunk at 3–6 years (Domaine Henri Clerc). The white wine represents over 95% of the production and 100% of the reputation. It is paler in colour and lighter in style than Meursault, less rich, being both more flowery and more steely at the same time. It is more elegant than Meursault, more diffident or less aggressive, but some poorer examples lack concentration and flavour. The commune of Puligny harbours four Grands Crus and 11 Premiers Crus, all on beautifully exposed slopes above the village, which produce some of the finest white wine in Burgundy. A simple *villages* wine should be drunk 2–4 years after the vintage, but in good years from careful producers they may last longer. There is fierce competition for grapes and for wine in barrel among the négociants, and preference should be given to those with long connections with the commune: Drouhin, Jadot, Latour, Chartron and Trebuchet, Olivier Leflaive Frères. Total production is now around 1.3 million bottles of white, 50,000 of red. Expensive. Price E (red), F-low G (white).

Puligny-Montrachet Premier Cru

The Premier Cru vineyards of Puligny continue from those of Meursault (Les Charmes and Les Perrières) and run into the Grands Crus of Le Montrachet, Bâtard- and Chevalier-Montrachet on the border of the commune of Chassagne. Up near Blagny, Le Hameau de Blagny (Comtesse de Montlivaut) and Les Chalumeaux (domaines Matrot, Pascal) are fresh, lively and firm, with a certain *goût de terroir*; below Les Chalumeaux, Le Champ-Canet (Domaine Etienne Sauzet) and La Garenne (extremely fine Clos de la Garenne, *monopole* of the Duc de Magenta) produce lightish, perfectly balanced wines with an aroma of hazelnuts; Les Combettes (the continuation of Les Charmes Dessus in Meursault) makes a bigger wine, stylish and complex with a certain richness (domaines Leflaive, Sauzet,

Ampeau, Henri Clerc, Robert Carillon); Les Referts is similar to Les Combettes, with less intensity (domaines Carillon, Sauzet); Les Folatières produces wines combining body and finesse, with some of the length of a Grand Cru (Domaine Jean Chartron, Gérard Chavy, Henri Clerc, René Monnier, Joseph Drouhin); just below Les Folatières, Les Clavoillons has a lovely bouquet of dog-roses, great breeding and a firm finish (quite superb wines from Leflaive, the principal owner in this *cru*); Les Pucelles is known for its suppleness and elegance, classic Puligny at its best (domaines Leflaive and Chartron); Le Cailleret, whose vines are separated by a footpath from Le Montrachet, produces wines which, with Les Pucelles, are the finest in the village, firm, perfectly balanced, requiring 4–5 years to show well (Pierre Amiot, Domaine Jean Chartron and Domaine Dupard Aîné, whose *monopole* Les Clos du Cailleret is sold by Drouhin). Puligny-Montrachet Premier Cru is much sought after by Burgundy's négociants, with fine examples from Drouhin, Latour, Jadot and Antonin Rodet. They may be drunk young to appreciate the flowery aroma and purity of style, but can be kept 7–8 years. Expensive. Price G-H.

Above: The town of Puligny-Montrachet beyond the entrance to Clos de la Pucelle.

The Grands Crus of Puligny-Montrachet

Bâtard-Montrachet

In common with Le Montrachet, the 11.83-hectare vineyard of Bâtard-Montrachet is situated in both the communes of Puligny and Chassagne. The vines are planted directly below those of Le Montrachet, and the wine has great richness and intensity of flavour, without perhaps the unique elegant concentration and suavity of Montrachet. A Bâtard-Montrachet is generally a wine of some weight (over 13° alcohol), and can in some cases lack acidity, but good examples have a fine golden colour, an assertive, nutty, toasty bouquet, mouth-filling fruit and the complexity and harmony of a *grand vin*. Excellent wines come from Leflaive, Pierre Morey, Etienne Sauzet, Domaine Poirier, Michel Nielon, Claude Ramonet, Ramonet-Prudhon, Bachelet-Ramonet and Blain-Gagnard. Drink 5–10 years after vintage. Production around 50,000 bottles. Price H-I.

Bienvenues-Bâtard-Montrachet

Extremely fine wine from a vineyard of only 2.3 hectares situated entirely in Puligny below Le Montrachet, between Bâtard-Montrachet and Puligny-Montrachet Les Pucelles. It is lighter than Bâtard-Montrachet, but supremely elegant, and thanks to the superb vinification of the two best-known growers – domaines Leflaive and Ramonet-Prudhon – is seldom disappointing. At its best at 4–7 years. Average production is about 12,000 bottles. Price I.

Chevalier-Montrachet

A 7.14-hectare parcel of vines directly above Le Montrachet, entirely in the commune of Puligny, producing wines second only to Le Montrachet itself. Chevalier-Montrachet is a wine of great floral finesse and distinction, so finely structured, despite 13–14° of alcohol, and with such persistence of flavour that it is not easily forgotten. Quite superb wines come from the Domaine Leflaive, Domaine Jean Chartron (the two largest owners in this *cru*), and Bouchard Père & Fils, Louis Latour and Louis Jadot, who share between them the Demoiselles vineyard. These wines are magnificent at 5–10 years but can last much longer. Production, which is low for the size of the *cru*, is less than 25,000 bottles. Very expensive. Price high I.

Le Montrachet

The wine made from this 7.49-hectare vineyard (4ha in Puligny, 3.49 in Chassagne) is generally accepted to be the finest dry white wine in France. The soil, poor and stony with a high limestone content, is particularly well suited to the Chardonnay grape; the exposition is exceptional, on gently sloping south-facing *coteaux*, the drainage perfect. Many vineyards benefit from almost perfect growing conditions, yet do not produce wines with the almost mythical reputation of Le Montrachet. It combines the richness of a Bâtard with the finesse of a Chevalier and has an intense, floral aroma with a mixture of honey and almonds on the palate. It is a wine with a great concentration and richness of fruit that nevertheless finishes dry. The largest parcel of vines (2ha in Puligny) belongs to the Marquis de Laguiche, whose impressive wine is made and commercialized by Joseph Drouhin; Baron Thénard has 1.89 hectares on the Chassagne side, producing a meaty, greeny-gold-coloured wine. The Montrachet of Bouchard Père & Fils, just over one hectare in Puligny, is spectacular, and that of the Domaine de la Romanée-Conti extraordinarily suave, complex and long lived. The domaines Jacques Prieur, Comte Lafon and René Fleurot have possessed vines in Le Montrachet for many years, while relatively new owners, making only 300 bottles or so, include Ramonet-Prudhon and Delagrange-Bachelet. Since Montrachet costs more than twice as much as Chevalier-Montrachet, its value for money is often questioned. The best wines need at least five years in bottle to show the complexity behind the power. Production is seldom more than 30,000 bottles. Price J+.

CHASSAGNE-MONTRACHET

The commune of Chassagne, which like Puligny has added Montrachet to its name, forms the southern limit to top-quality white wine in the Côte d'Or. The wines, both red and white, have a firmness and richness of flavour that contrasts with the overall finesse of those from Puligny.

Chassagne-Montrachet

Red and white wines from the second most southern commune on the Côte de Beaune, situated south of Puligny and north of Santenay. Chassagne is a large commune, with 356 hectares permitted for the *appellation*, but some of the land is still planted in Gamay and Aligoté. Even though the name Montrachet suggests that the finest wines from the commune are white, red is still produced in more volume, and the quality of Chassagne-Montrachet rouge is often very high. Even the simple *villages* wines have a good colour and firm, generous fruit, with more in common with wines from Aloxe-Corton or Nuits-Saint-Georges than with their neighbours Volnay or Santenay. The whites have a lovely greeny-gold colour, are a little less stylish than those from Puligny, but have a good natural fruit and acidity and are seldom disappointing. Chassagne harbours some very important domaines, most of which have been parcellated and re-formed through inheritance or marriage, and the following names are much in evidence on the wine labels: Ramonet, Bachelet, Delagrange, Gagnard, Deléger and Morey. Chassagne possesses three Grands Crus for white wine only, and many Premiers Crus for both red and white. Total production is one million bottles of red and 800,000 of white. Red not expensive, white quite expensive, but less than Puligny. Price E (red), F (white).

Chassagne-Montrachet Premier Cru

The white wines vary in style according to the situation of the vineyards. At the highest elevation, La Grande Montagne, Le Virondot and La Romanée give lightish but firm wines with a certain flintiness (domaines Bachelet-Ramonet, Marc Morey); a little lower, Les Caillerets has great length and finesse (especially good chez Blain-Gagnard, a domaine that has inherited over half of the vines of Edmond Delagrange, and fine wines from Pierre Amiot, Marc Colin, Jean-Noël Gagnard and Albert Morey); Les Ruchottes and Les Grandes Ruchottes are extremely elegant, even delicate for a Chassagne, with superb wines from Marcel Moreau, Ramonet-Prudhon, Bachelet-Ramonet and André Ramonet; wines from Le Morgeot are more complete, with a more intense bouquet and great depth and complexity (Ramonet-Prudhon, André Ramonet, Claude Ramonet, Delagrange-Bachelet, Roger Berland's Clos Pitois, Blain-Gagnard, Jean-Noël Gagnard, Marquis de Laguiche, and the Abbaye de Morgeot of the Duc de Magenta); Les Chevenottes, turning towards Saint-Aubin, gives a very aromatic, honeyed, softer wine (Raoul Clerget, Marcel Moreau). A fine Chassagne Premier Cru blanc is at its best from 4–8 years after the vintage. The reds, which constitute the biggest wines of the southern part of the Côte de Beaune, have a good deep colour, a spicy aroma and a plummy, rather rough flavour that needs time in which to soften up. The best wines come from Le Clos de la Boudriotte (Ramonet-Prudhon, Claude Ramonet, Bachelet-Ramonet) and the Clos Saint-Jean (Ramonet, Bachelet, Paul Pillot). The Clos de la Chapelle of the Duc de Magenta and the Clos Pitois of Joseph Belland are very fine, with definite Chassagne character, and good red wines come from the Morgeot vineyards of Blain-Gagnard, Alphonse Pillot, Marquis de Laguiche, Fleurot-Larose and Prieur-Brunet. These wines are best at 8–12 years after the vintage. Expensive. Price F (red), G (white).

The Grands Crus of Chassagne-Montrachet

Bâtard-Montrachet

See page 75.

Criots-Bâtard-Montrachet

The smallest (1.6ha) of the white Grands Crus of the Côte de Beaune lies entirely in Chassagne. The only domaines concentrating on Criots are Blain-Gagnard, who have inherited the vines of Edmond Delagrange, and Joseph Belland, who own 0.64ha. The wines are less fat than Bâtard-Montrachet with a more discreet elegance and the firm, persistent flavour of a *grand vin*. 7,000 very fine bottles are produced. Expensive. Price H.

Le Montrachet

See page 75.

Saint-Aubin

Red and white wines from 120 hectares of vines planted entirely *en côteaux* up behind Chassagne- and Puligny-Montrachet. The white has great finesse, with a refreshing acidity and slightly nutty finish. It can be drunk very young, but is best at 3–4 years. The Premiers Crus Les Frionnes and Les Murgers-des-Dents-de-Chien are particularly fine. The reds have a lovely cherry-ruby colour and good fruit, and may be drunk at 3–5 years. A good Saint-Aubin is often the equal of a Meursault or a Chassagne-Montrachet, and better value for money. The most important producer is grower-négociant Raoul Clerget, and other excellent wines comes from domaines Jean Lamy, René Lamy-Pillot, Roux and Colin and Gérard Thomas. The smaller négociants like Jaffelin, Chartron & Trebuchet and Olivier Leflaive Frères show equally fine *cuvées*. Average production is 300,000 bottles of red, 150,000 of white. Price E.

SANTENAY

Almost entirely red wine from the most southern commune in the Côte de Beaune, covering 380 hectares, not all in production. The white wines are quite sturdy with a certain acidity, more resembling a Pernand-Vergelesses than, say, a Meursault. The reds, particularly those near to Chassagne-Montrachet, have a good colour, lively, fruity bouquet and firm, robust flavour. They have none of the soft charm of the wines of Volnay or Beaune and are more in the style of Pommard, needing several years to open up. However, their broadness of flavour balances the tannin and they can be enjoyed young with not-too-delicate food. The wines of Santenay are still not well known, and the wines from good growers – Vincent Girardin, Jacques Girardin, Domaine des Hautes-Cornières, Adrien Belland, Lequin-Roussot – and carefully selected *négociants-cuvées* (in particular those from Santenay-based Prosper Maufoux) are good value. Santenay in a light vintage may be drunk at 4–5 years, with the better wines needing twice the length of time. Production of red wine is large, totalling over 1.5 million bottles, with 25,000 bottles of white. Price E.

Santenay Premier Cru

The finest wines of the commune come from the Premiers Crus near to Chassagne-Montrachet: Les Gravières combines sturdiness and elegance (Domaine de la Pousse d'Or, Domaine des Hautes Cornières, Domaine Jessiaume, Philippe Mestre, Louis Clair and a rare and excellent white Gravières from Jaffelin of Beaune) and the enclave Clos de Tavannes is still more complete and satisfying (Domaine de la Pousse d'Or, Louis Clair); La Comme is generally lighter, with a more expressive, floral bouquet (Philippe Mestre, Louis Clair), with more vigorous, meaty wines from Joseph Belland and the Domaine Lequin-Roussot; Le Beauregard is similarly fruity and firm (Joseph Belland); Le Passe-Temps, near the village, gives firm, straightforward wines (Domaine Lequin-Roussot, René Fleurot) and above the village, La Maladière is lighter, supple, quicker to mature (Domaine Prieur-Brunet). Les Clos Rousseau, divided into Le Petit and Les Grand Clos, always has a firm depth of fruit (Domaine de la Buissière, Claude Nouveau). These are not the finest wines of the Côte d'Or, but they are very satisfying and good value for money. Price F.

Maranges

Red and a very little white wine from the newest *appellation* in Burgundy, applicable from the 1988 vintage. This regroups the villages of Dézize-lès-Maranges (the most tannic reds), Cheilly-lès-Maranges and Sampigny-lès-Maranges all at the southern end of the Côte de Beaune, whose wine was previously sold as Côte de Beaune-Villages. Because the name is virtually unknown, the *vignerons* hardly dare to bottle a poor wine, and firm, fruity examples can be found from Vincent Girardin, Maurice Charleux, Bernard Bachelet and Claude Nouveau. Domaine Chevrot makes the best white wine. Of the négociants, Jaffelin has begun using the new *appellation*, and others will follow. Very good-value wines for quite early drinking. Price high D.

THE COTE CHALONNAISE

The Côte Chalonnaise is the continuation of the vineyards of the Côte d'Or into the *département* of the Saône-et-Loire. The area covers 24 kilometres running along the RN481 from Chagny in the north of Saint-Vallérin in the south, but vines are planted less regularly here than in the Côte de Nuits and Côte de Beaune, keeping to the best south-facing slopes and alternating with fruit-growing, grazing and other forms of culture. Wines benefiting from the *appellations communales* (Givry, Mercurey, Montagny, Rully) must be from the Pinot Noir for the reds and rosés, and the Chardonnay for the whites, although the Pinot Blanc is still permitted. The Gamay is heavily planted for Bourgogne Passe-Tout-Grains or Bourgogne Grand Ordinaire (now little seen), and the Aligoté succeeds so well around the village of Bouzeron that a new *appellation* has recently been created: Bourgogne Aligoté de Bouzeron. Although Montagny produces only white wines, the reds are dominant in the region, led by those of Mercurey, to the extent that the Côte Chalonnaise was sometimes known as *"la région de Mercurey"*. With high demand for burgundies causing a notable rise in their price, more interest has been focused on the Côte Chalonnaise, and improved vinification techniques and attention to quality have been the positive result. Red wines produced outside the *appellations communales* are sold as Bourgogne, and to distinguish these wines from others in the Burgundy region from Chablis to the Beaujolais, a demand was submitted to the INAO for the creation of an *appellation* Bourgogne Côte Chalonnaise for Pinot Noir and Chardonnay wines of superior quality. This was accepted by a decree of March 1990, retroactive to the 1989 vintage. The Côte Chalonnaise also produces some of the finest *cuvées* of Crémant de Bourgogne.

Bourgogne-Côte-Chalonnaise

Red wines from the Pinot Noir (minimum 10° alcohol from a yield of 55hl/ha) and white wines from the Chardonnay (10.5° and 60hl/ha) that can be produced throughout the region, but which are subject to a severe offical tasting before being granted access to this new *appellation*. The red wines have a fine cherry colour, a lively, fruity aroma and pure Pinot flavour. Depending on the site of the vineyard, but more particularly on the age of the vines and the style of winemaking, they can be drunk at 2–5 years; the more intense *cuvées* can last longer. The whites have a distinctive panache, with none of the rich nuttiness of a Meursault, but more firmness than a Mâcon blanc. The

creation of this *appellation* will force the older *appellations* to underline their individuality and stylistic differences. This is an exciting development, for the Côte-Chalonnaise has always produced fine red and white burgundy. Less expensive than Cru Beaujolais, excellent value for money. Price C–low D.

Bourgogne Aligoté de Bouzeron

The particular limestone-clayey soil from this tiny village on the outskirts of Chagny gives the Aligoté grape a character and stylishness that is not found elsewhere in Burgundy. Lobbying from the major proprietors, Bouchard Père & Fils and Aubert and Pamela de Villaine, persuaded the INAO to create this new *appellation* in 1979. Expensive for an Aligoté but worth it, especially from de Villaine. Bouchard Père & Fils' wines from L'Ancien Domaine Carnot are good, as are those from Domaine Chanzy. Price C-D.

Givry

Red and white wines from 120 hectares of vines in the middle of the Côte Chalonnaise. Historically, the wines of Givry were more renowned than those of Mercurey, but today this is no longer true. The white wine is attractive, with a fresh acidity and firm fruit, but quite light and should be drunk young. The reds are similar to those of Mercurey, being a little lighter, a little smoother, but lacking Mercurey's definition and depth. They are quite drinkable 2–3 years after the vintage and very good at 5–6. There are no Premiers Crus at Givry, but some well-known *climats*, including Le Clos Salomon (du Gardin), Le Cellier aux Moines (Baron Thénard, Domaine Joblot), and Le Clos Saint-Pierre (Baron Thénard). Reliable wines come also from Gérard Mouton, Madame Steinmeyer, Domaine Ragot and Domaine Desvignes. Current production averages a little more than 500,000 bottles of red wine, 65,000 bottles of white. Inexpensive for burgundy. Price D.

Mercurey

Red and white wines from the most prestigious commune in the Côte Chalonnaise. Over 600 hectares are in production, 95% for red wines. The small quantity of white is interesting, but less successful than Rully, owing to a high acidity, but the wine goes well with the local cuisine. Good examples are from the Château de Chamirey, Michel Juillot, Bouchard Aîné, and Faiveley. The red, which used to be grouped with the wines of the Côte de Beaune before the laws of *appellation contrôlée*, is a rather old-fashioned wine, usually quite deep in colour, with fruity, briary aromas and a firm, sinewy impression on the palate, with none of the easy charm of some of the softer wines from the Pinot Noir. They are concentrated and rather tannic when young, and are at their best at 5–10 years. In light years, or as a result of over-production, the wines can be disappointingly pale and thin. Growers making excellent wine include Hugues and Yves de Suremain, Michel Juillot, Yves de Launay, Roland Brintet, Chanzy Frères, Domaine Jeannin-Naltet, Emile Voarick and the grower-négociants J. Faiveley, while wines from François Protheau and Rodet are reliable. There are five Premiers Crus of which the best is Le Clos du Roy; some *lieux-dits* that are not Premiers Crus are almost as good: Clos des Barraults and Clos Tonnerre (*monopole*) of Michel Juillot, and the Sazenay, Clos Voyen and Clos l'Evêque of Domaine de Suremain. The *vignerons* in Mercurey have grouped together to form La Confrérie des Disciples de la Chante Flûte, which blind-tastes wines of the region, much in the manner of the Chevaliers de Tastevin, and awards a special label to the wines that have been *chante-flûtés*. Production of red wine is now over three million bottles with 130,000 of white. Still reasonably priced. Price E.

Montagny

White wine only from the most southerly *appellation* of the Côte-Chalonnaise. Where the wines of Rully tend to resemble those of the Côte de Beaune, those of Montagny are more in the style of the Mâconnais. They are stylish and fruity, with a lovely Chardonnay flavour and finish. Most are delicious young, and the better wines improve for 3–4 years in bottle, acquiring complexity and a nutty character. Although there are some excellent *climats*, such as Les Monts Cuchots of Mme Steinmeyer, the *appellation* Premier Cru is awarded to all wines which have more than 11.5° alcohol, the only example of this sort of legislation in Burgundy. Fine wines come from Domaine Arnoux, Bernard Michel, Mme Steinmeyer, Domaine Martial de Laboulaye, the Cave Coopérative at Buxy and Louis Latour. There is a project to increase substantially the *appellation*, which should further enhance the reputation of the white wines of the Côte Chalonnaise. Production is increasing as the vineyards are replanted and is now around 480,000 bottles. Price D.

Below: Chardonnay grapes arriving at the Cave Coopérative at Buxy.

Rully

Red and white wines from the communes of Rully and Chagny. The white is better known, the limestone-based soil allowing the Chardonnay to produce a stylish wine with a fresh sappy fruit and great length of flavour, the equal of many more prestigious wines from the Côte de Beaune. The well-exposed Premiers Crus are very fine, and excellent wines come from domaines de Suremain in Monthélie, René Brelière, Paul and Henri Jacqueson, Ninot-Rigaud, de la Folie, Belleville and Chanzy. Some Rully whites are full in style, resembling a Meursault (de Suremain), while others are lighter, with more acidity and panache (Domaine de la Folie). The reds tend to be lighter than those of the Côte de Beaune (Delorme), but in good years have a striking ruby colour, a strawberry-blackcurranty aroma and a firm, fruity finish. The whites may be drunk as soon as they are in bottle, but a good natural acidity allows them to improve for 3–4 years more. The reds can be drunk 2–3 years after the vintage and improve with age. Production is increasing as new planting takes place, and currently averages 500,000 bottles of each red and white wine. The Beaune négociants, on the lookout for good value wines, have shown a growing interest in Rully, with Drouhin and Jaffelin producing excellent wines. Faiveley is an important owner in Rully; Antonin Rodet have recently bought control of the vines of the Château de Rully; and Chartron and Trebuchet, Oliver Leflaive Frères and the local négociants André Delorme are to be recommended. Price D.

The Mâconnais and Beaujolais

THE MACONNAIS

The vineyards of the Mâconnais continue Burgundy's descent through the Saône-et-Loire *département* towards Lyon. 6,000 hectares are in production, with 67.5% in Chardonnay including a little Pinot Blanc and Aligoté, the rest being planted in Gamay (25%) and Pinot Noir (7.5%), this last showing a recent slight increase against the Gamay. The white wines are unquestionably finer than the reds, for the Chardonnay thrives on the high limestone content of the granite-based soil and world demand for white wine has encouraged growers to replant with this varietal. The most widely produced are Mâcon blanc and Mâcon-Villages, fruity, pure Chardonnay wines with some body and a refreshing acidity. The finest come from the villages between Tournus and Mâcon (all the vines are on the right bank of the river Saône): Clessé, Lugny and Viré. Further south, opposite and below Mâcon, are the vineyards of Saint-Véran and Pouilly-Fuissé. The reds – Bourgogne rouge, Bourgogne Passe-Tout-Grains and Mâcon rouge – are pleasant, fruity, everyday wines, completely outclassed by the burgundies in the north and the Beaujolais in the south. The Mâconnais *cave coopératives* also produce some of the best Crémant de Bourgogne in Burgundy.

Mâcon (Blanc) or Pinot-Chardonnay-Mâcon

White wine from the Mâconnais, made from the Chardonnay grape, with the Pinot Blanc permitted, but playing a smaller and smaller role. The wine must have a minimum alcohol content of 10°, from a maximum basic yield of 60hl/ha. Mâcon blanc is the lightest of the white Mâconnais wines, pale primrose yellow, clean, fresh and fruity with an attractive acidity. It should be drunk within two years of the vintage with hors d'oeuvres, *charcuterie*, fish or poultry, or just on its own, served cold. Good value. Price high B-low C.

Mâcon (Blanc) Supérieur

Dry white wine from the Mâconnais, similar in every way to Mâcon blanc, except that the wine must have a degree more alcohol at 11°, hence more body and fruit. This *appellation* is being superseded by the better-sounding Mâcon-Villages. Good value in plentiful years. Production is over 1.5 million bottles. Price C.

Right: Well-tended vineyards of Chardonnay in the Mâconnais.

Mâcon (Rouge or Rosé)

Red and rosé wines from the Mâconnais. The grapes used are the Gamay, Pinot Noir with Pinot Gris permitted but seldom seen, and the wines must have a minimum of 9° alcohol from a yield of 60hl/ha. They are attractive, fruity, everyday wines, usually light in colour, without too much body and flavour and are best drunk on the spot. Every now and then there is a *cuvée* from old vines that has more intensity and body, particularly from the village of Pierreclos (Domaines Guffeyns, des Bruyères). Production is 340,000 bottles. Price B, D for the special *cuvées*.

Mâcon Supérieur Rouge (or Rosé)

Red and rosé wines from the Mâconnais, with one degree more alcohol than Mâcon rouge. Red Mâcon may be made either from the Gamay or the Pinot Noir – if it is a mix of these two grapes it must be of a minimum of one-third Pinot Noir, and is called Bourgogne Passe-Tout-Grains – and the wine tends to resemble either a Beaujolais or a rather rustic Bourgogne. The wines have a deep cherry colour, a good deal of fruit, but are never very smooth. They are best drunk with food, *charcuterie*, poultry, red meats and cheese at 1–4 years after the vintage. Mâcon rosés have a pretty violety-pink colour and should be drunk young, while still fresh, served cold. Even the reds may be served cool. Annual production is around eight million bottles. Since the neighbouring Beaujolais are much more popular, Mâcon rouge is often ignored, and is usually good value. Although Bordeaux Supérieur, known locally as Bordeaux Sup, is recognized as being definitively better than just Bordeaux, Mâcon Supérior seems to lack this esteem, and most growers prefer to use the plain Mâcon *appellation*. Price B-low C.

Mâcon-Villages or Mâcon–followed by the name of the commune

Dry white wine from the Mâconnais with rules as for Mâcon Supérieur. Mâcon-Villages is the most commercialized of the white Mâcons and represents 11 million of the 14 million bottles produced annually. It is a classic Chardonnay type: pale yellow, with flowery appley aromas, a strikingly fruity taste and enough body to enhance the flavour without making the wine too serious. A good Mâcon-Villages should have a refreshing acidity, perfect for drinking on its own, or with food, preferably *charcuterie* and river-fish. The name of any of 43 communes may be added to the word Mâcon to replace Villages (which is generally a blend of more than one commune) if the wine is from that village alone. The best known are: Charnay (Manciat-Poncet), Clessé (Jean Thévenet), Fuissé (Jean-Paul Thibert), Igé (Francis Fichet), Loché (Domaine Saint-Philibert), Lugny (Cave Coopérative), Péronne (Domaine Rousset), Prissé (Cave de Prissé), Viré (Cave des Vignerons, André Bonhomme) and Uchizy (Jean-Paul Talmard). 80 percent of the production is handled by the *caves coopératives*, of which Lugny and Viré are the largest and the best. The local négociants from Beaune are equally proud of their selections, almost 100% from the *coopératives*, and Louis Latour's Mâcon-Lugny is a well-known example. Although the style of Mâcon-Villages is a little less complex than a Bourgogne blanc from the Côte d'Or or the Côte Chalonnaise, these wines may be "declassified" into Bourgogne blanc – a legality which does neither of their images any favours, and confuses the consumer. Except in years when the quantity of wine made is much reduced by weather conditions and short supply pushes prices up, Mâcon-Villages is very good value. Price C.

Pouilly-Fuissé

White wines grown in the five communes of Fuissé, Pouilly, Solutré, Chaintré and Vergisson to the west of Mâcon. Wines made at Loché should be called Pouilly-Loché, but may take the name of the next-door village, Vinzelles, whose own wines are usually better, but not as full-bodied as Pouilly-Fuissé itself. Pouilly-Fuissé is without doubt the finest wine of the Mâconnais: when young, it has a straw-yellow colour, sometimes with greeny tints, a heady, floral bouquet and all the sappy fruit of the Chardonnay grape; if left to mature, its class is underlined by a richness and complexity of taste, while keeping its youthful freshness, that recalls some fine wines from the Côte de Beaune. Château Fuissé (Domaine Vincent) is the most remarkable wine of the *appellation*, extraordinarily rich and long-lived, the result of a combination of old vines, late picking, long fermentation in a high proportion of new oak barrels and severe selection before bottling. Other very fine wines come from Mme Féret, André Forest, Maurice Luquet, Joseph Corsin, Roger Lassarat, Guffeyns-Heynen and Roger Cordier. There are many other fine *vignerons* in the *appellation*, but international demand is such that a very high proportion of the crop is bought and bottled by négociants (Drouhin, Loron, Duboeuf, Rodet, Latour). While Mâcon blanc and Saint-Véran may be drunk young, at 1–2 years, Pouilly-Fuissé needs 3–5 years to show at its best. Despite a production of 5.5 million bottles, the popularity of the name ensures that prices remain high, over twice the price of a Mâcon-Villages, and even higher when the American market is feeling bullish. Price low E.

Pouilly-Loché

The same style of dry white wine as Pouilly-Fuissé,

from the commune of Loché. They do not match the quality of Pouilly-Fuissé, but are less expensive. Only 150,000 bottles are produced a year, dominated by Les Caves des Grands Crus Blancs, and are mostly drunk on the spot or bought by a French clientele. Price is nearer to a Mâcon-Villages than a Pouilly-Fuissé, quality usually the other way round. Price C-low D.

Pouilly-Vinzelles

Dry white wine similar to Pouilly-Loché, from the commune of Vinzelles and part of Loché. The next best thing to Pouilly-Fuissé. Better known than Pouilly-Loché, with an average production of 270,000 bottles. Price C-low D.

Saint-Véran

White wines made from the Chardonnay grape planted in eight communes surrounding Fuissé: Saint-Véran, Chanes, Chasselas, Davayé, Leynes, Prissé, Saint-Amour and Solutré. Before receiving its own *appellation* in 1971, these wines were sold as either Beaujolais blanc or Mâcon-Villages. They have a lovely pale yellow colour, more vivacity and fruit than a Mâcon blanc, without the richness and depth of a Pouilly-Fuissé. The finest wines come from Leynes (domaines Duperron, Chagny, du Colombier) and Davayé (Grégoire, Corsin and the Lycée Agricole). Domaine Vincent in Fuissé produces a superb Saint-Véran, and Georges Duboeuf is one of the most reliable négociants. The permitted yield has recently been increased from 45 to 55hl/ha, more than Pouilly-Fuissé, less than Mâcon-Villages, but quality is still high. About two million bottles are produced. Although now well-known for quality, the Saint-Véran wines are only a little more expensive than the better Mâcon blancs, and so are good value for money and age well. Price high C.

THE BEAUJOLAIS

The Beaujolais is the most southerly vineyard area in Burgundy, running for over 50 kilometres down the right-hand side of the RN6, from just below Mâcon to just above Lyon. The area covers 22,000 hectares, mostly in the Rhône *département*, producing nearly 150 million bottles of wine, and may be divided qualitatively into the Haut-Beaujolais in the north, with a clayey-sandy top-soil on a schistous-granite base, from which come all the Beaujolais *crus* and Beaujolais-Villages, and the Bas-Beaujolais (or Beaujolais-Bâtard) to the south, with a more limestone-clayey soil, producing Beaujolais *tout court* and most of the Beaujolais Primeur. The only grape variety permitted for Beaujolais rouge and rosé is the Gamay, already seen in other parts of Burgundy as an element (two-thirds maximum, with one-third minimum Pinot Noir) in Bourgogne Passe-Tout-Grains. The Gamay is particularly successful, due in part to its predilection for a granite-based soil, but also to the local style of *macération carbonique* vinification, whereby the bunches of grapes arrive in the fermentation vats uncrushed and whole, and the usually short fermentation takes place inside the grape itself. The light, fruity Primeur, which used to be released on 15 November, a date now changed to the third Thursday in the month, is a quaffing wine, to be drunk very young. Beaujolais *tout court* should be drunk in the year following the vintage, and Beaujolais-Villages at 1–2 years. Although they are not fine wines there are some good Beaujolais-Villages from individual growers or conscientious négociants. In the very north of the region some excellent Beaujolais blanc is still made (despite the introduction of the *appellation* Saint-Véran) from the Chardonnay, producing a fresh, mouth-wateringly fruity wine, with more verve than a Mâcon blanc. Only the ten Beaujolais *crus* (with the recent addition of Regnié) are capable of producing wines of distinction, and in some cases with a potential for ageing, yet even here differences in style can be lost in the interests of quick commercialization. They have a maximum permitted yield of 48hl/ha (as against 55hl/ha for Beaujolais *tout court* and 50hl/ha for Beaujolais-Villages), but this is almost always exceeded, and, thanks to the PLC (see page 11), an average of 20% more is permitted each year. The minimum alcohol content is 10°, 11° if a vineyard or *climat* is specified, but in practice the natural degree of alcohol is raised by chaptalization to 12–12.5°. Production is around 170 million bottles of red wine (just half of which is sold as Beaujolais Nouveau), 1.3 million of white and very little rosé.

Mâcconnais and Beaujolais

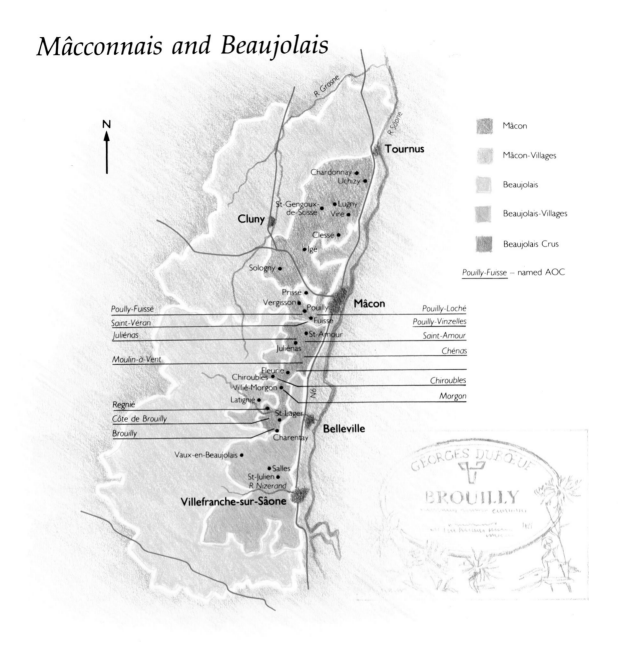

N

Mâcon

Mâcon-Villages

Beaujolais

Beaujolais-Villages

Beaujolais Crus

Pouilly-Fuisse – named AOC

R. Grosne

R. Saône

Tournus

Chardonnay

Uchizy

St-Gengoux-
de-Scisse

Lugny

Viré

Cluny

Clessé

Igé

Sologny

Prissé

Vergisson

Pouilly

Mâcon

Pouilly-Loché

Poully-Fuissé

Saint-Véran

Juliénas

Moulin-à-Vent

Fuissé

Pouilly-Vinzelles

St-Amour

Saint-Amour

Juliénas

Chénas

Fleurie

Chiroubles

Villié-Morgon

Latignié

Chiroubles

Morgon

N6

Regnié

Côte de Brouilly

Brouilly

St-Lager

Charentay

Belleville

Vaux-en-Beaujolais

Salles

St-Julien

R. Nizerand

Villefranche-sur-Sâone

GEORGES DUBŒUF

BROUILLY

Beaujolais

Red, dry white and rosé wines from vineyards in the Saône-et-Loire *département* south of Mâcon and the Rhône *département* north of Lyon. The reds and rosés are from the Gamay grape, the whites from the Chardonnay. Pinot Noir, Pinot Gris and Aligoté grapes are permitted in theory, but in fact are not used for Beaujolais. Reds and rosés must have a minimum alcohol content of 9°, whites of 9.5° from a yield of 50hl/ha (almost always exceeded). The wines are light,

fruity, quaffable, the perfect *vin de carafe*. Over 90% of the *appellation* is red, a little under half of all Beaujolais produced, and should always be drunk under one year old, served cool. Beaujolais, especially the Beaujolais Nouveau that is released for sale on the third Thursday in November, only a few weeks after the vintage, should have a pretty violety-red colour, an attractive grapey nose and a fresh fruity taste. It is a delicious, cheerful wine, but too often has its personality smothered by over-chaptalization. A true Beaujolais, with just a touch of *terroir*, is difficult to beat. Price B.

Beaujolais Supérieur

Red, dry white and rosé wines conforming to the same rules of Beaujolais, with a higher minimum alcohol content of 10°. White wines represent under 5% of the two million or so bottles declared annually, and the production of rosé is insignificant. This is an old-fashioned *appellation*, not seen outside France. The wines very much resemble Beaujolais *tout court*, but may be kept a little longer. Price high B.

Beaujolais-Villages

Red, dry white and rosé wines from the Gamay and Chardonnay grapes grown on 5,600 hectares in the northern part of the Beaujolais region. Production of white is minute, much of what is made being sold under the Saint-Véran *appellation*, although Beaujolais blanc is worth looking out for. Rosé tends to be drunk up locally. The red Villages wines are fruity, charming, and can be quite full-bodied, while losing nothing of their quaffability. In terms of quality, they are only slightly less good than the *crus*, and represent the best value for money in the Beaujolais. Apart from the communes whose production may go into the ten *crus* (see below), the villages that regularly make the best wine are: Saint-Etienne-de-Ouillières, Saint-Jean-d'Ardières, Saint-Georges-de-Reneins, Lantignié and Leynes. Local négociants with a reputation to maintain – Duboeuf, Ferraud, Loron, Beaudet, Tête, Pasquier-Desvignes and many others – will show several good *cuvées* of Beaujolais-Villages throughout the year, releasing the firmer wines later in the season. Drink preferably in the first year after the vintage, although good vintages keep longer. Price high B, low C.

THE BEAUJOLAIS CRUS

The northern part of the Beaujolais region, previously known as the Haut-Beaujolais, is possessed of ten *crus*, each of which may sell under its own name.

Brouilly

The most southern and the largest of the ten *crus*, with 1,200 hectares on the lower slopes of Le Mont Brouilly. The wine has a violety red colour and soft grapey charm, and except in vintages with some tannin – 1976, 1985, 1988 – it should be drunk at 1–2 years. Many growers make a Beaujolais-Villages as well as a

Brouilly. The best wines come from the communes of Odenas (Domaine Rolland, Château de la Chaize and Domaine Crêt des Garanches), Saint-Lager and Cercié (Jean-Paul Ruet). Production is over eight million bottles which gives the négociants a wide choice. Popularity has pushed the price of Brouilly to 50% more than the best Beaujolais-Villages. Price C.

Chénas

The smallest *cru*, with 260 hectares between Moulin-à-Vent and Saint-Amour. The wine is dark-coloured, full-bodied, without perhaps the fruit of Juliénas or the class of Moulin-à-Vent, but very satisfying. It has a generous texture and a distinctively floral aroma (peonies), and can be drunk the year after the vintage, but keeps remarkably well. The *cave coopérative* vinifies 45% of the *appellation*, while excellent wines come from Jean Benon, Pierre Perrachon and Domaine Robin. Production averages 1.5 million bottles. Although Chénas is not the cheapest of the *crus*, it is the most underrated. In the recent run of good vintages 1988, 1989, 1990, Chénas has shown it is almost the equal of its close neighbour Moulin-à-Vent. Price high C-low D.

Chiroubles

The fourth-smallest *cru*, with 350 hectares on high 350–400-metre slopes situated north-west of Morgon and south-west of Fleurie, producing lightish, racy wines with a very flowery bouquet and firm finish. Chiroubles is the most *primeur* of the *crus*, and should be drunk young to capture the charm. Georges Duboeuf sells an award-winning *cuvée*; the best domaine is probably that of Georges Passot, or of Georges Boulon. Production is 2.3 million bottles. Chiroubles is very fashionable in France and Switzerland and regularly sells out early at a high price. Price D.

Côte-de-Brouilly

As the name implies, Côte-de-Brouilly occupies 290 hectares on the higher slopes of Le Mont Brouilly, surrounded by the *appellation* Brouilly. The schistous soil and the higher elevation result in a wine with a deeper colour than Brouilly, more vigorous and slower to open up. It also shares the commune of Odenas with Brouilly (Château Thivin, Domaine de Chavanne), and some excellent *cuvées* are to be found from négociants Georges Duboeuf and Pierre Ferraud. Côte-de-Brouilly has a distinctive aroma of violets and acquires great finesse after 2–3 years. Having the second smallest production of the *crus*, with just over two million bottles, Côte-de-Brouilly is only fractionally more expensive than Brouilly, despite its better breeding. Price high C.

Fleurie

Producing perhaps the best-balanced and most sophisticated wines of the ten Beaujolais *crus*, the *appellation* Fleurie covers 800 hectares on a fine granite-based terrain. With its deep colour, floral bouquet of roses and irises, silky texture and harmonious finish, Fleurie is known as "the Queen of the Beaujolais". The wines are quite firm, but are best drunk 1–3 years after the vintage. The best *climats* are La Chapelle des Bois, La Madone, Les Garands, Le Point du Jour, Les Viviers and Les Quatre Vents. The nearer the vines get to Moulin-a-Vent, the more assertive it becomes. Fine wines come from Paul Bernard, Michel Chignard, Clos des Garands and Domaine des Quatre Vents. Production averages 5.5 million bottles. Fleurie since the late 1980s has been the most expensive of the *crus*. Price D.

Juliénas

The vines of Juliénas cover 580 hectares to the north-west of Chénas and Saint-Amour, producing deep, purple-coloured, exciting wines with a striking bouquet of raspberries and peaches. Juliénas may be supple and fruity or big and chewy, with a depth of fruit that makes them attractive the summer after the vintage, but that should keep them improving for 2–3 years more. The best wines come from the slopes around the village, where there is a very good Coopérative La Cave des Grands Vins, which vinifies 30% of the *appellation*. Other excellent *cuvées* come from the Evantail des Vignerons group (Domaine André Pelletier), Thierry Descombes and the négociant Pierre Ferraud. Juliénas is only a little more expensive than Brouilly, which makes it excellent value. Production is over four million bottles. Price low D.

Morgon

The second largest of the *crus*, with 1,030 hectares in the commune of Villié-Morgon, Morgon is also the most generous, meaty and robust. It has a deep garnet colour and an aroma of wild cherries when young that develops into a kirsch-like bouquet with age. Morgon ages well – the *vignerons* say "il morgonne", as they say of a good Mâcon-Villages "il pouillotte" – the better *cuvées* surviving to take on a burgundy-like flavour after half a dozen years in the cellar. The wines coming from vineyards situated around the village of Villié-Morgon, particularly the *climats* Le Py (René Savoye), Le Clachet (Georges Brun) and Les Charmes, are the finest. The *coopérative*, Le Caveau de Villié-Morgan, produces delicious wines, and other good domaines include Domaine Descombes (Duboeuf), de la Chanaise, Jambon and Louis-Claude Desvignes. Prices are reasonable, on the level of Juliénas. Production is just over seven million bottles. Price low D.

Moulin-à-Vent

The most prestigious of the *crus*, Moulin-à-Vent covers 670 hectares of vines in the communes of Romanèche-Thorins and Chénas. The granite-based soil has a high magnesium content which imparts to the wines an intensity of bouquet (violets) and depth of flavour that seems to combine the best elements of the finer *crus* with an added touch of class. They are so stylish that they can be drunk young, for the rich, velvety fruit, but their real fame comes from bottles which are 5–10 years old and even more. If Moulin-à-Vent is known as "the Burgundy of the Beaujolais", it is not through copying the wines which come from the Côte d'Or, but through the intrinsic quality that, in ageing, begins to resemble the *grandes appellations* from further north. The finest wines come from Romanèche-Thorins (Robert Diochon, Georges Duboeuf), in particular the *climats* Les Thorins (superb wine from Château des Jacques) and Le Moulin-à-Vent. 1988, 1989 and 1990 have all allowed this *cru* to show its real quality as the "King of the Beaujolais". Production around 4.5 million bottles. The most expensive of the *crus*, alongside Fleurie, but generally worth it. Price D.

Regnié

The newest of the *crus*, created with the 1988 vintage as a result of ten years of lobbying by the *vignerons* of Regnié and Durette. The latter village could have been classified partly in Morgon and partly in Brouilly in 1936, but at the same time preferred to remain *le premier des Villages*. Regnié has much of the violety vivacity and damson-like fruit of Juliénas, if a little lighter. Prior to achieving AOC status, a few serious négociants sold these wines as Beaujolais-Regnié, Appellation Beaujolais-Villages Contrôlée, to show the origin. Top producers are Paul Cinquin (Domaine des Braves), Domaine de la Ronce and Jacques Trichard. This new *cru* covers 600 hectares. It is the least expensive of the *crus*, about 25% more than a Villages. Price low C.

Saint-Amour

Saint-Amour is the most northerly of the *crus*, with 295 hectares of vines situated entirely in the Saône-et-Loire *département*. The soil has more clay than the granite-based soil to the south, but less limestone than in the Mâconnais. The wine is fruity and straightforward, softer than the next-door Juliénas, less intense than Moulin-à-Vent, with a lively peach-like aroma and open fruit that may be appreciated quite young. Despite the popularity of the name and its relatively high price, Saint-Amour is the least well-defined of the *crus*. Georges Spay and Guy Patissier are the best known producers. Production nearly two million bottles. Price D.

REGIONAL APPELLATIONS

Coteaux du Lyonnais

Red, dry white and rosé wines from vineyards to the south of Villefranche-sur-Saône and around Lyon in the Rhône *département*. The reds and rosés, over 95% of the production, are from the Gamay, producing a wine like Beaujolais, a little less lively, but with a genuine *goût de terroir*. The whites can be from the Chardonnay, Aligoté and Melon de Bourgogne, and are crisp, fruity and dry. Coteaux du Lyonnais moved from VDQS to AOC status in 1984, and the double benefit of this and the good vintages of the late 1980s has given the wines more than just a local reputation. The Cave Coopérative de Sain-Bel vinifies 70% of the crop for light, easy drinking. More serious, very good value wines come from Domaine Sainte-Agathe, Bernard Fayolle and François Descottes. The region had 13,500 hectares under vines in 1836, now has 200 planted from a total envisageable of 350 hectares. Not at all expensive and worth looking out for. Price B.

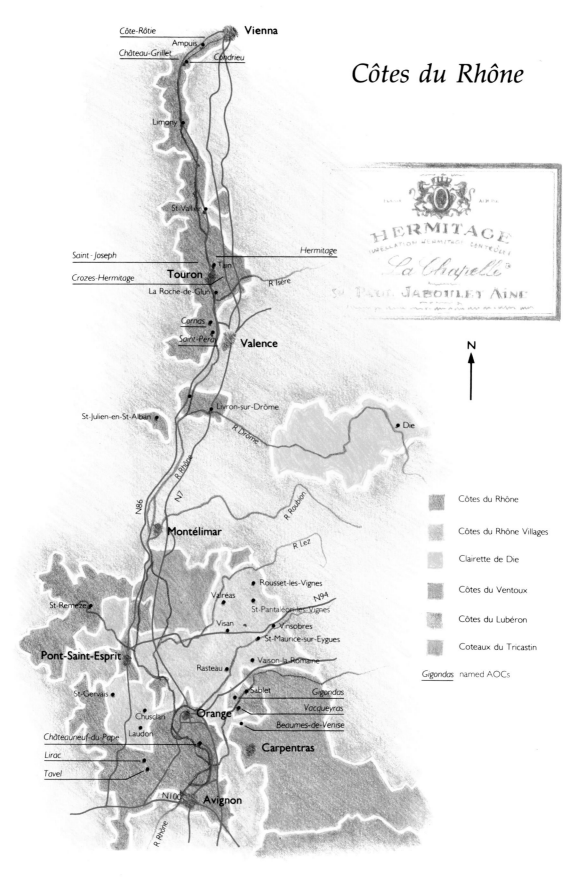

Côte-Rôtie
Vienna
Ampuis
Château-Grillet
Condrieu

Limony

St-Vallier

Hermitage
Saint-Joseph
Tain
Crozes-Hermitage
Touron
R Isère
La Roche-de-Glun

Cornas
Saint-Péray
Valence

Livron-sur-Drôme
St-Julien-en-St-Alban
Die
R Drôme

R Rhône
N86
N7

Montélimar
R Lez

Rousset-les-Vignes
Valréas
N94
St-Pantaléon-les-Vignes
Visan
St-Remèze
Vinsobres
St-Maurice-sur-Eygues
Vaison-la-Romaine
Rasteau

Pont-Saint-Esprit
St-Gervais
Sablet
Gigondas
Chusclan
Orange
Vacqueyras
Beaumes-de-Venise
Châteauneuf-du-Pape
Laudon
Carpentras
Lirac
Tavel
N100
Avignon

R Rhône

Côtes du Rhône

HERMITAGE
APPELLATION HERMITAGE CONTRÔLÉE
La Chapelle
SUR PAUL JABOULET AÎNE

N

Côtes du Rhône

Côtes du Rhône Villages

Clairette de Die

Côtes du Ventoux

Côtes du Lubéron

Coteaux du Tricastin

Gigondas named AOCs

The Rhône Valley

The vineyards of the Côtes du Rhône follow the Rhône river from the Roman city of Vienne, just south of Lyon, for 200 kilometres to Avignon. In common with the Loire Valley, this region offers the most diverse selection possible of different types of wine: clean, dry whites, rich aromatic whites, heady rosés (some of the best in France), light, medium and full-bodied reds, sparkling wines and even some *vins doux naturels*. If there is a theme, it is perhaps the presence of aromatic fruit and a certain fleshiness of flavour. Even the driest white wines have a sunniness about them, yet although the sun is ever-present, Rhône wines each have their defined character and do not suffer from the uniformity of style often found in wines from hot climates.

The vineyards cover 61,800 hectares and are neatly divided into two regions: the Côtes du Rhône Septentrionales in the north and the Côtes du Rhône Méridionales, with 60,000 hectares to itself, in the south. There are also some interesting wines (but no major *appellations*) produced between the two and to the south-east. A wide variety of grape varieties are admitted, with the Syrah totally dominating the northern red wines and the Grenache dominating the south. The Syrah produces wines with a dark, purple robe, a plummy-spicy flavour and firm finish; the Grenache has big colour and body, but can be overripe and soft, needing the balance offered by the Cinsaut, which gives a sappy leanness, and the Mourvèdre for structure and ageing potential. The small production of white wines comes from the Roussanne and Marsanne grapes in the north,

to which the Clairette, Grenache blanc and Bourboulenc are added in the south. Despite grape varieties with such intensity of flavour, the soil still dominates and the difference between the *appellations* is apparent. Good winemaking is showing a firm trend towards elegance, without losing depth, and away from massiveness.

Vineyard planting between the north and south is quite different: vines in the north tend to be planted on steeply terraced, difficult to work vineyards; those from the south are mostly to be found on the dry, arid plains.

The Rhône tends to be thought of as a red wine region in the same way as the Loire is considered white-wine country. This exclusiveness is more true of the Rhône, where white and rosés account for less than 10% of the *appellations*. With two notable exceptions, Condrieu (and Château Grillet) and Hermitage from the north, the Rhône does not produce white wine to rival the great wines from Alsace, Burgundy and the Loire. The most interesting white from the southern Rhône is actually not a table wine at all, but a *vin doux naturel*, the Muscat de Beaumes-de-Venise. Throughout the last decade, all Rhône wines have been gaining in popularity. This is due partly to wine-drinkers moving away from the more classic names, but more so to the efforts of the growers, *caves coopératives* and négociants to improve the quality and retain the individuality of their wines. The hoardings along the *autoroute du sud* still announce "Côtes du Rhône, Vins du Soleil". They are much more than that.

Côtes du Rhône

Red, dry white and rosé wines from grapes planted on both sides of the Rhône Valley, from Vienne in the north to Avignon in the south, covering 40,800 hectares in the *départements* of the Rhône, Loire, Drôme, Ardèche, Gard and the Vaucluse. The *appellation* covers 80% of all wines produced in the Rhône Valley. The red wines and the small quantity of rosés are made from a minimum of 70% *cépages nobles*: Grenache, Syrah, Mourvèdre and Cinsaut, with the addition of the lesser-known Counoise, Muscardin, Vaccarèse, Terret Noir and Camarèse, and a maximum of 30% Carignan, the high-producing grape from the Midi.

For all wine bearing the Côtes du Rhône *appellation*, minimum alcohol content must be 11°, from a yield of 50 hl/ha. White wines must be made from the Clairette, Roussanne, Marsanne, Grenache Blanc and Bourboulenc grapes, with a little Ugni Blanc. These are generally pleasant and fruity, yet all but the best lack acidity, and should definitely be drunk up in the year after the vintage, before they lose their freshness. They go well with the local food and climate. Rosés are often too high in alcohol to be really refreshing, and should always be drunk young and cold. Even the red Côtes du Rhône *génériques* are best drunk at 1 to 3 years, and in hot weather should be served cool to lower the impression of alcohol and to enhance the fruit. Average production is about 200 million bottles of red and rosé, 3 million bottles of white. Most of this is produced by *caves coopératives*, correct wines but too often uninspiring, generally sold to négociants for bottling under their own brands. Domaine bottled wines, particularly those in heavy burgundy bottles with restrained labels, are much more interesting, with some very good surprises and modest prices. Price B.

Côtes du Rhône-Villages

Red, dry white and rosé wines from 16 specific communes in the Vaucluse, Gard and southern Drôme *départements*. All Côtes du Rhône-Villages come from the southern part of the valley and are discussed on page 102.

The Northern Rhône Valley

The vineyards of the Côtes du Rhône Septentrionales cover a 65-kilometre stretch running from Vienne to Valence, with the finest wines coming from well-exposed terraced vineyards overlooking the river. The latitude, close to the 45° parallel, offers a near-perfect climate for the vine. The soil is granite-based, exceptionally hard and costly to work, but allowing the *cépages* Syrah, Marsanne, Roussanne and Viognier to produce wines of an intensity of bouquet and flavour rarely rivalled elsewhere in France. Vines planted on the higher-yielding, more sandy soils of the plain produce wines of much less interest.

AOC WINES

Château Grillet

The smallest single *appellation contrôlée* (if one does not count the Burgundian Grand Cru *appellations* of La Romanée, La Romanée-Conti, Bienvenues- and Criots-Bâtard-Montrachet), covering three hectares in the communes of Vérin and Saint-Michel-sur-Rhône. It is the *monopole* of the Neyret-Gachet family. The wine is white, from the same grape as Condrieu, the Viognier, planted on south-facing terraced slopes high above the right bank of the Rhône. Château Grillet spends 18 months in small oak casks before being bottled in the distinctive brown 70 cl *flûtes*, making a wine of similar aromatic intensity and richness to Condrieu, but perhaps closer-knit. It is best drunk at 3–6 years and does not improve past 10 even in very good vintages. Production is rarely more than 10,000 bottles, which makes the wine an expensive collector's item. Price H.

Condrieu

White wine, grown on the right bank of the Rhône in the communes of Condrieu, Vérin, Saint Michel-sur-Rhône and Limony. The *appellation* covers 200 hectares, yet only 60 are planted, with a further 5 to 10 coming into production in the next 10 years. Fruit-growing, the proximity to Lyon for secondary homes, and the unpredictability of the Viognier grape, are the main reasons for the decline in production, which risked total extinction in the 1950s. The single grape planted, the Viognier, finds the perfect site in the fine, loose top-soil of rocky terraces carved out from the slopes above the Rhône, and, experimental planting apart, flourishes nowhere else in France. It is therefore the smallest produced *cépage noble* in the country, making Condrieu one of France's rarest *appellations*. The wine is pale golden in colour, with an intense, floral, ripe-fruit aroma (violets and irises, dominated by the scent of peaches and apricots), spicy, glyceriny and quite full-bodied on the palate but finishing dry. Some growers used to make a sweet Condrieu by stopping the fermentation, but this is no longer practised. Great years 1978, 1985, 1988 and 1989 however, can produce wines with a little residual sugar. The wine is usually bottled early in the year following the vintage, and may be drunk immediately, but it is best at 1–3 years, before the extraordinary aromatic qualities fade. The largest producer is Georges Vernay, with several *cuvées*, the best being his Coteaux de Vernon. Other good growers are Dumazet, Paul Multier (Château du Rozay), André Dezormeaux and Delas, who are replanting, while Marcel Guigal who now vinifies almost half this crop, always makes a superbly sophisticated and seductive wine. The yield is limited to 40 hl/ha, but the Viognier is capricious, and the actual yield, which used to average only 17 hl/ha, is now just above 30. Production is 250,000 bottles. Expensive but worth it for the good wines. Price F-G.

Cornas

Red wine only from 80 hectares of Syrah grapes planted on the right bank of the Rhône, opposite Valence. The wine of Cornas is Syrah personified: very deep, nearly black in colour, with a rich, heady aroma of concentrated fruit (blackcurrants, raspberries, violets), finishing with a vigorous, mouthfilling flavour. The *appellation's* unique micro-climate and exposition, sheltered from the Mistral, produces grapes of a more consistent ripeness than elsewhere in the northern Rhône, and the wine is correspondingly dark-coloured, full-bodied, rough at first, but never heavy. Lighter *cuvées* can be made from vines nearer the plain, from the more sandy soil near Saint-Péray, or from shorter vatting during fermentation, and may be drunk at 3–4 years. A classic Cornas should be drunk at 6–10 years and from a great year can last 15–20. The finest are made by Auguste Clape, with excellent wines from Guy de Barjac, Marcel Juge, Jean Lionner, Robert Michel, Alain Voge and the négociants Delas and Paul Jaboulet Aîné. Cornas is an *appellation* that was declining for many years and is now in full expansion due to the effort of the established growers and the interest that their sons are taking. Production is always below the permitted 40 hl/ha, about 400,000 bottles. Cornas has become comparatively expensive. Price D-E.

Côte-Rôtie

The most northern *appellation* of the Rhône Valley, with 140 hectares of vines planted on steeply terraced, south-west facing slopes on the right bank of the river centred around Ampuis. Only red wine is made, principally from the Syrah, although up to 20% of Viognier grapes may be added during fermentation to produce a lighter, more aromatic wine. In fact, Viognier represents only 5% of the *appellation* and is to be found mostly in the Côte Blonde and above Condrieu. The Syrah, planted on the narrow terraces with inclines of more than 40%, has to be trained specially by the Guyot method, which allows the vine to climb up the support stakes to achieve maximum exposure. The stakes are cumbersome and the planting is close together and disorganized, so no machinery can be used in these vineyards, which are the most labour-intensive in France. Vines are now planted on the plateau above the slopes, which is easier to work, but tends to produce thinner wines, lacking the velvety intensity of a true Côte-Rôtie. A classic Côte-Rôtie has a dark purple colour when young, ageing to a deep mahogany, a markedly floral, spicy bouquet and a rich, suave, complex flavour and a lingering finish. The finer wines undergo a slow fermentation to extract colour and body and spend 2, sometimes 3, years in cask, *pièces*, *demi-muids* or *foudres*, before bottling. Lighter vintages need 3–4 years more in bottle to open up fully, while bigger wines need 7–8, and can last up to 20 years. While most Côte-Rôties are a blend of grapes or wines from different parts of the *appellation*, the finest come from the middle, the Côte Brune and Côte Blonde. The heavier, clayey soil of the Côte Brune produces wines with immense colour, vigorous and concentrated, that require long ageing, perfect examples being the wines of Gentaz-Dervieux or Guigal's La Landonne. The lighter, more limestony soil of the Côte Blonde produces wines that are full-bodied but more gentle, with a scent of violets and a smooth finish, and that are ready to drink earlier. The finest and most typical example is again from Guigal, La Mouline, which is a synthesis of richness, intensity and finesse: it is Musigny or Château Lafite to the Chambertin or Château Latour of La Landonne. Wines from the Coteaux de Verenay in the north tend to be deep coloured and tannic, with excellent examples from Emile Champet and Albert Dervieux-Thaize, while those from the Coteaux de Tupic, just above Condrieu in the south, are lighter, but fine and elegant, especially if some Viognier is used (Georges Vernay). Other fine producers are Georges and Robert Jasmin, Marius Gentaz-Dervieux, René Rostaing, Pierre and Gilles Barge, Bernard Burgaud, and Edmond Duclaux. Of the négociants, Vidal-Fleury at Ampuis were taken over by the next-door neighbour Guigal in 1985, but continue to produce wine from their considerable holdings under their own label. Their finest vineyard, La Turque, is now owned by Marcel Guigal and will form a fine trio with La Landonne and La Mouline. Jaboulet, Guigal and Chapoutier make excellent wine from the Côte Brune and Côte Blonde combined. Production is almost 650,000 bottles. Expensive, but rarely disappointing. Price F, G for special *cuvées*.

Crozes-Hermitage

Red and white wine from the largest *appellation* in northern Rhône, covering 1,000 hectares on the left bank of the Rhône, north and south of Tain-l'Hermitage. The style of wine, especially the red, which represents 90% of the crop, varies considerably. While production is expanding on the plain, where total mechanization is possible and the wines are pleasantly fruity but with no great depth, certain better-sited parts of the *appellation* provide wines of very high quality: the hillside vineyard and sandy soil at Mercurol is particularly suited to white grapes; at Gervans, the terraced, south-facing vineyards produce a wine of great solidity and character from a granite-based soil; at Les Sept Chemins, south of Tain, the stony, well exposed vineyard produces firm, stylish wines, perhaps the best in the *appellation*. Made from the Marsanne (dominant) and Roussanne grapes, the white Crozes is a pale yellow, racily fruity wine with an acacia-like aroma. Many producers prefer it not to undergo malolactic fermentation, to preserve the acidity (Jaboulet, Jules Fayolle, Jean-Louis Pradelle). These wines are best drunk young, while the wine of Albert Desmeure spends over a year in cask, and takes on the richness and complexity of an Hermitage. With few exceptions (Domaine de Thalabert from Jaboulet, Alain Graillot), a red Crozes-Hermitage cannot be compared to an Hermitage, although it comes from the same grape, the Syrah. The colour should be full, purple-red when young, with an aroma of raspberries and blackcurrants, a pleasantly fruity flavour and some Syrah firmness in the finish. Rather old-fashioned wines come from Albert Bégot and Raymond Rouré, more fruity *cuvées* from the Cave des Clairmonts, Tardy et Ange, Robert Michelas and the *cave coopérative*, and the négociants Chapoutier, Delas, Jaboulet and Vidal Fleury are always reliable. Alain Graillot, only recently established, is making superbly rich wine. The lesser vintages can be drunk at 2–3 years, while the more serious wines need 5–8 years to develop. Production, at 45 hl/ha, is 4.6 million bottles of red and 570,000 of white. Price C-D.

Hermitage

Red and white wines from 140 hectares of vines planted on the left bank of the Rhône around the town of Tain-l'Hermitage. The red is made from the Syrah, to which up to 15% Marsanne may be added during fermentation, although in practice the white grapes are rarely used and never exceed 5%. The white is made from the Marsanne and the Roussanne, although the latter has seen a decline owing to its low yield and fragility. The vines are planted on terraces, not quite so steep as at Côte-Rôtie, where the granite-based, flinty soil has the same heat-retaining qualities and is equally

Above: Terraced vineyards of the appellation Hermitage *rising steeply behind the town of Tain-l'Hermitage.*

as hard to work. The slopes are less abrupt towards the east and the soil more sandy, producing a wine that is lighter and less intense. Throughout the Hermitage vineyards particular *lieux-dits* or *mas* are recognized as producing wines of different styles, although their names rarely appear on the label, most Hermitage wines being a blend of wines from several *mas*. White Hermitage is generally pale straw or golden in colour, with a pronounced aroma of apricots and dried fruit, a rich unctuosity on the palate, but a dry finish. Full-bodied wines, able to improve for 5–10 years, come from Gérard Chave, Chapoutier, Sorrel, Guigal; a crisper, but oaky style is that of Jaboulet's Le Chevalier de Sterimberg; and very attractive elegant wines come from Jean-Louis Grippat, Albert Desmeure and Domaine de l'Hermite. The red Hermitage should have a huge colour (deep purple, almost black when bottled, maturing to a rich mahogany with ruby glints), a pronounced aroma of blackcurrants and spices and an assured intensity of flavour. Vinification lasts two

weeks or more to extract colour, fruit and tannin, followed by at least 12 months in *pièces* or *foudres* to produce one of the greatest wines in France. In good vintages it should be drunk at 10–20 years and even in lesser vintages between 5 and 10. The finest wines, delicately scented yet plummy and intense, come from the *mas* Le Méal, at the heart of the *appellation* with superbly exposed vines (Henri Sorrel, Domaine de l'Hermite); Les Béssards produces tough, meaty wines, too hard when young, but with great structure; Le Greffieux produces rounder, more aromatic wines (B. Faurie), while those from Le Beaume and Le Peléat are deep-coloured, less intense, with great finesse. It is rare to find an Hermitage from a single *mas*, and the blending of complimentary wines from several *mas* is considered superior. Very successful *cuvées* come from

Jaboulet (La Chapelle), Chapoutier (La Sizeranne), Guigal and especially from Gérard Chave of Mauves. Despite being a dark-coloured 'manly' wine, red Hermitage should never be clumsy or heavy. The minimum alcohol content is 10°, but a fine Hermitage is usually between 12° and 13°. The allowed yield of 40 hl/ha is almost never attained from the Syrah. Production is now 450,000 bottles of red, 150,000 of white. Expensive, but one of the great wines of France. Price high F-G.

Saint-Joseph

Red and white wines from a very parcellated 65 kilometre stretch of vineyards covering 360 hectares and running from just south of Condrieu to just north of Cornas on the right bank of the river Rhône in the Ardèche *département*. Grapes permitted are the Syrah for the reds, and the Roussanne (now very seldom planted) and the Marsanne for the whites. The vines in the northern part of the *appellation* are mainly planted on the easier, lower part of the slopes, making a pleasant, fruity wine for relatively early drinking (2–3 years), much of it vinified at the *cave coopérative* at Saint-Désirat-Champagne. Much better wine comes from Saint-Jean-de-Muzols, where Raymond Trollat makes a fresh, lively white with an aroma of peaches and a sturdy, raspberry-scented red from vines facing those of Hermitage. At Tournon, the wines are bigger and the acidity in the whites and the tannin in the reds allows them to keep well for 5–6 years. Excellent *cuvées* come from Jean-Louis Grippat (the best white of the *appellation*), Bernard Gripa, Alain Graillot and Chapoutier. Further south, around the village of Mauves, the heart of Saint-Joseph, the reds have a lovely purple colour and a striking raspberry-blackcurrant aroma when young, having more immediate fruit than Cornas or Hermitage, but maintaining the firm backbone from the Syrah. Very little white wine is made here, but superb reds come from domaines Chave, Coursodon, Gonon and Marsanne. Approaching Cornas, the wines are stronger and rougher and require long ageing. Production, from a maximum yield of 40 hl/ha, almost never achieved, is approaching two million bottles, with 15% white. Not expensive in comparison with other wines from the North. Price D.

Saint-Péray

The last of the vineyards in the northern Côtes du Rhône, situated directly opposite Valence; the 80 hectares of Saint-Péray are planted with Marsanne and Roussanne (only 20%) grapes, to make a lively, aromatic white, of which much is sold as a *méthode champenoise* sparkling wine. The climate, the grape varieties and the sandy, stony, clay-based soil give a certain roundness to the wine, but it retains the high natural acidity that is essential for a successful sparkling wine. A fine Saint-Péray has more body but perhaps less finesse than champagne, with a lovely pale gold colour, a bouquet of violets and a lively, grapey taste. Its reputation is mostly local, where it is principally drunk as an aperitif. The still wine is usually made solely with the Marsanne, although Jean-François Chaboud makes a separate *cuvée* from the low-yielding and fragile Roussanne. This pale-straw-coloured, fruity, quite assertive wine should be drunk young, at 2–3 years, but can continue to develop for 7–8. Good producers are Jean-François Chaboud, Pierre Darona, René Milliand, Auguste Clape, Marcel Juge, Alain Voge, the local cooperative and the négociants Verilhac and Delas. Production, from 45 hl/ha, is almost 400,000 bottles, 70% *méthode champenoise*. Price D.

The Centre of the Rhône Valley

Between the easily defined areas of the Côtes du Rhône Septentrionales and Méridionales lie vineyards covering the *départements* of the Drôme and the Ardèche. There has been much replanting in this middle area, particularly of the Tricastin *appellation* between Montélimar and Bollène, but the main form of agriculture remains fruit-growing. Apart from the *appellations* cited below, there is some soft, fruity Côtes du Rhône, made south of Valence around La Voulte-sur-Rhône on the right bank and Livron-sur-Drôme on the left. The finest is known as Brézème, whose 100% Syrah is worthy of a good Crozes-Hermitage.

AOC WINES

Châtillon-en-Diois

Red, dry white and rosé wines from vineyards on the left bank of the Rhône in the Drôme *département* south and east of Die. Reds and rosés must be from a minimum of 75% Gamay and a maximum of 25% Syrah and Pinot Noir. They are light in alcohol, with an average of 11° from a maximum yield of 50 hl/ha, quite light in colour and body, fruity and should be drunk young. The whites, about 10% of the *appellation,* are from the Burgundy grapes Chardonnay and Aligoté; they are light and lively for wines of this region. Almost all the production of 240,000 bottles comes from the *caves coopératives.* Although inexpensive, the quality is really not much better than a good *vin de pays.* Price B.

Clairette de Die

Dry and *demi-sec* sparkling wine from 1,000 hectares around Die on both banks of the river Drôme, to the west of Valence. The region of Die has for centuries been celebrated specifically for its sparkling wines, which were already protected by an edict of 1380 which forbade the use of "foreign" grapes. Grape varieties now planted are the Clairette and the Muscat à Petits Grains. The still wines, made exclusively from the Clairette, are crisp and lively, but the emphasis is on the sparkling wine. For this, two methods are used: the *méthode champenoise,* using wines principally from the Clairette, and sold as Clairette de Die brut, and the *méthode dioise* (or *méthode rurale,* similar to the *méthode gaillaçoise,* page 249), dealing with wines generally with at least 50% Muscat, and sold as Clairette de Die *demi-sec* or *Tradition.* The latter wine is much superior with a less aggressive sparkle and the bouquet of the Muscat completely preserved. Clairette de Die Mousseux is best drunk young, on its own or with desserts, and served very cold. The *cave coopérative* produces three-quarters of the annual 7 million bottles, the Cuvée Tradition being the best. Among the few growers, Georges Raspail makes a superb demi-sec with 80% Muscat and a fine Brut. Inexpensive. Price B-C.

Coteaux du Tricastin

Red, dry white and rosé wines from vineyards to the east of the Rhône, between Montélimar and Bollène in the Drôme *département.* Tricastin has been the fastest-growing vineyard in the Côtes du Rhône, receiving VDQS status in 1964 from nothing ten years before and full *appellation* status ten years later. The grapes planted are the classic Rhône varieties, with about 50–60% Grenache, 20% Syrah, the rest being made up of Cinsaut, Mourvèdre and Carignan. The better reds resemble the deep-coloured, soft fruity Côtes du Rhônes from the south, with a satisfying spiciness and liveliness from the Syrah. The rosés are pleasant, and the small quantity of white (all consumed on the spot) is full and flavourful. Minimum alcohol content is 11°, from a yield of 50 hl/ha. Vines now cover almost 2,000 hectares – the whole of the Côte de Beaune counts only for 2,800 – and the 13 million bottle production keeps prices low. Those from the Domaine de Grangeneuve are among the best. Price B.

VDQS WINES

Côtes du Vivarais

Red, dry white and rosé wines from 739 hectares of vineyards on the west bank of the Rhône, in the Ardèche and northern Gard *départements,* above Pont-Saint-Esprit. Grapes planted are the same as for the Côtes du Rhône *génériques,* with the Gamay admitted. Chardonnay, Merlot and Cabernet Sauvignon are also planted, but may not use the *appellation.* The production of white is tiny, under 1% of the total of almost 3 million bottles. The reds and rosés are fruity and easy to drink, perhaps lighter and more lively than the Côtes du Rhône. They are perfect wines to drink when on holiday in the Ardèche. Very good value. Price B.

Haut-Comtat

Red and rosé wines from at least 50% Grenache, planted to the east of the Rhône, around Nyons in the Drôme *département.* These solid, well-made wines are not seen any more, as they now mostly sell under the Côtes du Rhône-Villages *appellation* from the villages of Saint-Pantaléon-les-Vignes and Rousset (see page 102). Price B.

VINS DE PAYS

See page 105.

Below: Rolling vineyards surround the town of Châteauneuf-du-Pape.

The Southern Rhône Valley

The Côtes du Rhône Méridionales occupy land on either side of the Rhône, between Pont-Saint-Esprit and Avignon, stretching across the *départements* of the southern Drôme, the Vaucluse and the Gard. The vines, covering an area 60 kilometres wide and up to 80 kilometres long, are basically planted on the plain. The soil is also quite unique, being very arid and covered with round stones to the extent that, especially in Châteauneuf-du-Pape, it hardly looks like soil at all. The grape varieties planted in the southern region are the same as throughout the Rhône Valley (page 89), with the Grenache heavily dominant, and although the "mix" of grape varieties is wide, the differences in style between the various villages come mostly from the soil and exposition of the vineyards. The vast majority of the wines produced are red, with white wines repre-

Above: Mature vines in a Châteauneuf-du-Pape vineyard are carefully pruned to maximize exposure to the sun.

senting under 2% of the crop. Most of the Côtes du Rhône *génériques* and all the Côtes du Rhône-Villages come from the south. The largest single unit of production is the *caves coopératives* whose name and that of the village will appear on the label, but the proportion of growers bottling their own wine is increasing as varietal selection and improved vinification have their effect. This change has been particularly evident in the search for elegance and fruit rather than alcohol in the red wines and rosés, and for freshness in the whites.

AOC WINES

Châteauneuf-du-Pape

Red and white wines from the largest *appellation* in the Côtes du Rhône, covering 3,100 hectares north of Avignon, across the communes of Châteauneuf-du-Pape, Orange, Corthézon, Bédarrides and Sorgues. Although the wines of Châteauneuf are known the world over and are recognized as the foremost wines from the southern Rhône, quality has been variable, and only recently has a concerted effort been made by growers and négociants alike to ensure they reflect the quality of their reputation. Whereas many *appellations* in France are restricted to a single grape variety, the red wine of Châteauneuf-du-Pape may be made up of one or all of 13 grape varieties. This, combined with the differences in aspect of the vineyards – from the typical "Châteauneuf" expanse of large, smooth stones, that covers completely the clayey soil beneath, to the gravelly, sandy soil of Château Rayas – gives widely varying styles of wine.

In order of importance of planting, the 13 grape varieties are: Grenache (noir and blanc), Syrah, Mourvèdre, Cinsaut, Clairette (blanc), Bourboulenc (blanc), Roussanne (blanc), Picpoul (blanc), Counoise, Terret Noir, Vaccarèse, Muscardin and Picardan (blanc). The Grenache is planted to over 80%, a proportion considered by the better growers to be quite excessive; nine-tenths of the 500 growers in the *appellation* have less than six varieties planted; and only two domaines, Château de Beaucastel and Domaine de Mont-Redon, have the full 13.

While the Grenache dominates the *cuvées* of Châteauneuf, each *cépage* has particular characteristics that play their part: Grenache: body, fruitiness, high alcohol, glyceriny "fat", good colour but oxidizes rather quickly; Syrah: dark colour, spiciness, fruit and backbone; Mourvèdre: colour depth, complexity and long-lasting firmness; Cinsaut: leanness and elegance, a foil of the Grenache; Counoise: colour, firm backbone, spicy fruit (much favoured by Châteaux Fortia and Beaucastel); Vaccarèse: solidity, durability; the white grapes, fermented with the red, add freshness and delicacy of bouquet, but they are being used more and more on their own for the white Châteauneuf-du-Pape.

The minimum alcohol content in Châteauneuf is the highest in France at 12.5°, and many of the Grenache-dominated *cuvées* are nearer 14°. Chaptalization is forbidden, but would not be necessary in any case since the stones covering most of the vineyards act as night-storage heaters to compound the effect of the naturally sunny climate to produce high grape sugars. Yield is limited to 35 hl/ha, which is low in itself, but considering the low density of plantation in the *appellation* (3,000 vines per hectare as opposed to 8–

10,000 in Bordeaux) the maximum yield per vine plant is relatively high, leading to further variation in quality. A particularity of Châteauneuf-du-Pape (and Gigondas) is that between 5 and 15% of the production must be declassified and may only be sold as *vin ordinaire*. This is known as *le rapé*, and is an effective incitement to maintaining quality.

A fine Châteauneuf-du-Pape rouge is a majestic wine, with a deep ruby colour, with floral, fruity, spicy, even herby aromas, and a rich, mouth-filling, warm flavour. It is a big, even massive wine, but one that should always have an edge of finesse and a well-balanced finish. They may be drunk earlier than wines from the northern Rhône, at 3–4 years, but wines from the better domaines benefit from longer ageing and may still be good at 10–20 years. Vinification has changed much in recent years and some of the most modern equipment and sophisticated cellars are to be found in the area. Of the many fine domaines the following may be singled out: Château de Beaucastel (one of the most forward-looking but influentially conservative growers, making complex wines for long ageing), Domaine du Vieux Télégraphe (superb vinification, big plummy wines), Domaine Font de Michelle, Château Fortia (both classic wines), Château Rayas (now back on form after the death of Louis Reynaud in 1978). The reputation of these has the edge over the very good wines from Chante Perdrix, Château la Nerte, Clos de l'Oratoire des Papes, Clos des Papes, Domaine des Cabrières, Domaine de la Gardine, Les Clefs d'Or, and Domaine de Mont-Redon. Quicker-maturing wines, no less interesting, are made by the Domaine de Beaurenard, Château de Fines Roches, Domaine de Nalys, Domaine de la Solitude and Roger Sabon. In Châteauneuf itself, there are two *caveaux*, Caves Reflets, and Prestige et Tradition, that group a number of smaller proprietors, all making reliable wine. Around 30% of the production is domaine-bottled, bearing the coat-of-arms of the popes of Avignon embossed above the label. Of the négociants, Bérard, Brotte, Chapoutier, Guigal, Jaboulet and Vidal Fleury regularly produce some fine *cuvées*.

There is growing interest in Châteauneuf-du-Pape blanc, which now represents 3% of the production. The Grenache Blanc and Clairette produce sunny, aromatic wines that do not go through malolactic fermentation in order to preserve their acidity and freshness. The Bouboulenc and Roussanne have more character and body and may be aged. Stylish, racy white wines are the speciality of domaines Nalys, Mont-Redon, Père-Caboche, Font-de-Michelle and Bérard, while bigger wines come from Fortia and Vieux Télégraphe. At Château de Beaucastel two white wines are made: a floral but firm blend of the white grapes and an exceptional barrel-fermented 100% Roussanne from very old vines, whose flavour (and price) place it outside the norm. Generally, however, the whites are best drunk young, while the flowery freshness hides the basic high level of alcohol and lack of acidity. Production is around 14 million bottles. Prices are reasonable for the quality, even for the top wines. Price D-low E.

Gigondas

Red and rosé wines from 1,200 hectares planted at the foot of the Dentelles de Montmirail to the east of Orange in the Vaucluse *département*. A little white wine is produced which must take the *appellation* Côtes du Rhône, not Gigondas. The soil is made up of a heavy clay on the high ground just below the Dentelles, producing lightish wines for the *appellation*; a more stony, less clayey mix on the middle slopes, producing full-bodied, well-balanced wines, and the sandy, stony vineyards on the plain, producing rich, deep-coloured wines with a pronounced *goût de terroir*. Many growers believe that the most typical Gigondas is a judicious blend of wines from these three sectors. Grenache is planted to a maximum of 80%, with a minimum of 20% Syrah, Mourvèdre and Cinsaut for firmness and finesse, the balance, being made up, if necessary, with minor grape varieties such as the Clairette, now very little planted. Many growers would like to see the proportion of Grenache increased, for its quality here is exceptional. A red Gigondas is a big, sturdy wine, with a magnificent, deep, almost black colour, a powerful, briary, spicy bouquet and a rich, tannic taste. With a minimum of 12.5° alcohol from a yield of 35 hl/ha, it has the same weight as a Châteauneuf, and is even a little firmer. Gigondas may be drunk 3–4 years after the vintage, with its plummy, Christmas-pudding-like fruit matching the tannin, but really needs 5–8 years to develop complexity, and can last 15–20 years. The rosé, made from a maximum of 60% Grenache and a minimum of 15% Cinsaut, is a very heady wine with the same weight as the red but not the richness of flavour, neither does it have the raciness and fruit of a Tavel. Gigondas is a village totally devoted to wine and there are many first-class domaines: Les Pallières, Domaine Saint-Gayan, Château Raspail, Domaine Raspail-Ay, Domaine les Gouberts, Château de Montmirail, Domaine de Longue-Toque, Domaine de la Mavette, Domaine l'Oustaou Fauquet, Domaine de Piaugier, and Château du Trignon. The *cave coopérative* is reliable, but not in the same class as the aforementioned growers, and the local négociants Amadieu and Pascal also produce some good wines, as do Jaboulet and Guigal from the northern Rhône. Total production is 5 million bottles. Price mid-way between Côtes du Rhône-Villages and Châteauneuf-du-Pape, representing good value for the quality. Price low D.

Lirac

Red, rosé and a very small quantity of white wine from 660 hectares of vines planted just north of Tavel across the Rhône from Châteauneuf-du-Pape in the Gard *département*. The reds and rosés come from the main Rhône grapes, Grenache (minimum 40%), a high proportion of Cinsaut, Syrah and Mourvèdre. Clairette is the principal white grape, the others being Bourboulenc, Picpoul, the very rare Calitor, and Maccabeo. Although the rosé is equally as fine as Tavel, though with less vinosity and depth, production is decreasing in favour of red and white (now already 4%), the last being the lightest, most aromatic white in the southern Rhône, rivalled only by the wines from just further north at Laudun. The red is lighter and more restrained than the other two major *appellations*, Châteauneuf-du-Pape and Gigondas, lacking their weight and warmth, yet has a subdued ruby colour and a spicy elegance; it repays keeping for 4–5 years. Although the wines of Lirac are gaining in reputation, they lack a recognisable style. Some are big, almost earthy, made for long-keeping (Château d'Aquéria, Domaine Les Queyrades), some are less rich, with the Cinsaut's elegance (Château Saint-Roch, Château de Segriés, Domaine Maby, Domaine du Devoy), some show wines packed with ripe, spicy fruit (Jean-Claude Assémat, Domaine de la Mordorée), and some are just up-grade Côtes du Rhônes. As a result, Lirac is an *appellation* that is relatively underpriced. Production is around 2.5 million bottles. Price B-low C.

Tavel

Rosé wine from 850 hectares planted to the north-west of Avignon in the Gard *département*. Tavel is the major *appellation* in the Gard and the most important rosé in France. The major grape varieties are the Grenache, to a maximum of 60%, and the Cinsaut, to a minimum of 15%. Ancillary white grapes are permitted, to add freshness (Bourboulenc, Picpoul, Clairette), as are red grapes (Syrah, Mourvèdre), to add depth and colour, but Tavel is basically a Grenache (fruitiness, body) Cinsaut (liveliness, acidity) wine. The soil is stony, with a clay base which gives the wine a robustness typical of the southern Côtes du Rhône. While some domaines still age their wine in wood to bring out an "onion-skin" Tavel of some complexity but little freshness, the best wines have a pretty violetty-pink colour, a spicy, floral aroma and a fruity, firm finish. Since they have the weight of a red wine, and in hot years (1989, 1990), their alcohol content can exceed 14° naturally – not really suitable for quaffing – Tavel is a rosé that may be drunk throughout the meal, even with red meat. It should be drunk in the year following the vintage, and can hold for a year or two more but gain nothing. The *cave coopérative* produces 55% of the crop and is very

Above: The imposing Château des Fines Roches.

Left: The layer of smooth stones covering the Châteauneuf-du-Pape vineyards absorbs the sun's heat during the day and radiates it at night to continue the ripening process.

reliable, while perhaps more individual wines come from the following domaines: Domaine de la Mordorée, Château de Trinquevedel, Domaine de la Genestière, Domaine du Vieux Moulin, Domaine de la Forcadière, Château d'Aquéria and the wood-aged Château de Manissy. Production is almost 5 million bottles. Prices are reasonable, with the best *cuvées* only a little more than the others. Price C.

Vacqueyras

Situated between Gigondas and Beaumes-de-Venise, Vacqueyras has a reputation second to none for excellent Côtes du Rhône-Villages wines. This has now been recognised and from the 1989 vintage the 1,300 hectares from this commune now benefit from their own *appellation*. The wines are always very deep in colour with a concentrated spicy bouquet and a powerful velvety impression on the palate. They should be kept 3 to 4 years before drinking and will last 10 years or more. A good Vacqueyras is almost as impressive as a Gigondas or a Châteauneuf-du-Pape and, having been the most expensive of the Villages, it is now the least expensive, along with the undervalued Lirac, of the grander *appellations*. It offers excellent value for money. Vacqueyras has more growers bottling their own wine than any other village, and the choice is wide, the best being: Domaine la Fourmone (Roger Combe), Domaine Clos des Cazaux, Le Clos du Caveau, Domaine des Lambertins, Château de Montmirail, Château des Roques, Domaine de Montuac, Domaine Le Sang des Cailloux and rich warming wines from the négociants Pascal and Jaboulet. Price C.

Côtes du Rhône-Villages

Red, dry white and rosé wines from 16 specific communes in the Vaucluse, Gard and southern Drôme départements. Red and rosé wines that may add 'Villages' (or the name of the individual commune) to the simple *appellation* Côtes du Rhône must have a minimum of 12.5° alcohol from a yield of 35 hl/ha as opposed to 50 for the *génériques*. To improve the quality further, the proportion of Grenache for the red wines is limited to a maximum of 65%, that of Carignan to 10%, and the *cépages nobles* Syrah, Cinsaut and Mourvèdre must represent at least 25%. The Villages generally have a deeper colour than the *génériques* with pronounced aromas of blackcurrants or violets, they are often rather rough when young, but develop and improve with age. White wines, a tiny proportion in Villages, being mostly sold under the higher production Côtes du Rhône *appellation*, must use the Clairette, Roussanne or Bourboulenc grapes to a minimum of 80%, and must have 12° minimum alcohol. If they are well made, with sufficient acidity, they are delightful as an aperitif or throughout a meal. The rosés, usually from a Grenache-Cinsaut blend, are fruity and quite weighty, with enough alcohol to support ageing, but at their best drunk young.

The Côtes du Rhône-Villages represent some of the best value for money in France today. About 15 million bottles are produced annually. More than two dozen communes are under review for extending the range of Côtes du Rhône-Villages, but as yet only 16 communes are accepted (17 before the admission of Vacqueyras to single AOC status in 1989). Price high B-C.

Beaumes-de-Venise

Situated south-east of Vacqueyras and Gigondas, this village is better known for its *vin doux naturel*. The red wines are spicy and well made, with good deep colour. Owing to the confusion with the VDN (see page 136), many growers use the simple Côtes du Rhône *appellation*. Good properties are Château Redortier, Guy Jullien, Domaine du Cassan, Château des Applanats and Domaine de Coyeux.

Cairanne

One of the larger villages, in the centre of the vine-growing area to the east of the Rhône in the Vaucluse *département*, and one of the best. Most of the production comes from the clayey soils and is soft and rounded with a full colour. Vines planted on the stonier soil (*garrigue*) produce a wine incredibly deep in colour, with a rich, spicy bouquet, and masses of fruit with a tannic finish that means it should be kept. Most of the wine comes from the *cave coopérative*, which also makes

a little white, to be drunk young, a full rosé and even some light *primeur* red. A fine wine from Cairanne is at its best at 2 years after the vintage and can last 10. Excellent robust wines from Domaines Rabasse-Charavin, Château de l'Ameillaud, Delubac, Brusset, Berthet-Rayne, du Banvin, du Grand-Jas as well as the special *cuvées* from the *cave coopérative*.

Chusclan

Chusclan is situated between Pont-Saint-Esprit and Laudun, to the west of the Rhône in the Gard *département*. Once more famous for its rosé (it shares the same soil as Tavel), the majority of the wine is now red, fruity and attractive, and can be drunk young. The rosé, from the Grenache and the Cinsaut, is extremely well made and is at its best the year after the vintage. Almost all the wine is made in four *caves coopératives*, of which the largest is the Cave du Chusclan.

Laudun

Situated midway between Chusclan and Lirac, Laudun makes the best white wines of the Côtes du Rhône-Villages. It is pale in colour, with a flowery bouquet from the Clairette grape and, for the southern Rhône, very good acidity. The rosés are good, but not as fine as those of Chusclan, and the reds have a good deep colour and a certain spiciness. The best wines come from Domaines Pélaquié, Estournel and Rousseau, the Caves des Quatre Chemins and the Cave des Vignerons de Laudun.

Rasteau

An important village, 20 kilometres north and east of Orange, to the east of Cairanne. The soil is the stony *garrigue* from which come the best wines of Cairanne. The most famous wine is the Rasteau VDN (see page 136), but it represents under a third of the production of table wine. The red Rasteau is a big wine, very like Cairanne; the whites and rosés are quite pleasant, but there are better wines elsewhere. The reds, among the best Villages, should be kept for a year or two. Top growers include Bressy-Masson (Domaine de la Grangeneuve), Domaine de la Soumade, Maurice Charavin, Emile Charavin, Francis Vache and Roger Meffre from Gigondas, while the Caves des Vignerons de Rasteau is also very reliable.

Roaix

The village of Roaix lies to the east of Rasteau, near the Ouvèze tributary of the Rhône. The wine, which is mostly red, has slightly less colour and body than Cairanne or Rasteau, but is of good quality, ready for drinking at 1 to 3 years after the vintage. Most of the wine is made at the Cave Coopérative de Roaix-Séguret, but a grower who bottles his own wine is Florimond Lambert.

Rochegude

The wine, all red, from Rochegude, comes from vines planted on the plain about 8 kilometres from the *autoroute* exit at Bollène, bounded by Suze-la-Rousse and Sainte-Cécile-les-Vignes. It has a deep plummy colour and a fruity softness and is very good at 1 to 3 years. Almost all the wine comes from the local *coopérative*.

Rousset

The most northern of the wine-producing villages, in the Drôme *département*, above Saint-Pantéléon-Les-Vignes, with whose wine it is linked by the *cave coopérative*, which accounts for most of the production. Production is small and the wines are lighter than those from the Vaucluse *département*, but quite fruity.

Sablet

Sablet is situated between Séguret and Gigondas, making wine that mostly lacks the rich weightiness of Gigondas, but has a smoothness that sets it apart from the solid, spicy Cairanne. Well-made wines with firm fruit, but easy to drink. Leading growers are Jean Marc Autran (Domaine de Piaugier) and Christian Bonfils (Domaine du Boissan), but other fine wines come from Paul Roumanille, René Bernard, Domaine de Verquière and Domaine du Parandou.

Saint-Gervais

The most westerly of the villages, south of Pont-Saint-Esprit, in the Gard *département*. The red wines have more elegance than some from the Vaucluse, with good colour and blackcurranty fruit, but they are generally less dense than those from Laudun or Chusclan. The whites, although not as famous as those of Laudun, are excellent. By far the best grower is Guy Steinmaier (Domaine Sainte-Anne) who is making some superb white from the Viognier, and a rich Mourvèdre-based red. Les Frères Pailhon as well as the *cave coopérative* make good wine.

Saint-Maurice-sur-Eygues

Situated on a limestony soil between the much better-known villages Vinsobres and Visan, to the east of the Rhône in the Vaucluse *département*, the wines from Saint-Maurice-sur-Eygues, mostly red and mostly from the *cave coopérative*, are of good average quality.

Saint-Pantéléon-les-Vignes

The second most northern of the wine-producing communes, next to Rousset. These two village wines are made together in the *cave coopérative*. They are typically fruity and can be drunk quite young.

Séguret

Next door to Roaix, with whom it shares a *cave coopérative*, and a kilometre or so north of Sablet. The wines from Séguret have a deep colour, good fruit and are quite robust. They should be drunk at 2 to 4 years. Excellent wines come from Nadine Latour (Domaine de Cabasse), Domaine Garancière and Domaine du Sommier. The perched village of Séguret is one of the prettiest in France, and the reputation of its wine, as fine as that from Sablet, suffers in comparison.

Valréas

Situated to the east of the Rhône, to the north of Visan and the west of Vinsobres, Valréas is one of the 4 villages that make up the 'Enclave des Papes', a Papal enclave of the Vaucluse in the *département* of the Drôme. The size of the vineyard is impressive, totalling over 1,400 hectares. The red wines, which have a dark velvety colour, are big but not heavy and are generally of very high quality. They are at their best at 3 to 5 years. A little rosé is produced, clean and dry, and pleasant to drink young. Very good wines come from Romain Bouchard, René Sinard (Domaine des Grands-Devers), Domaine de la Prévosse, and Domaine de la Fuzière.

Vinsobres

One of the most eastern of the villages, making a large amount of Côtes du Rhône *génériques*, and a full-bodied, meaty Villages. It is good, but often lacks the depth and character of the villages further south. Three good bottlers are Domaine les Aussellons, Domaine le Deurre and Domaine du Moulin.

Visan

Situated to the north-east of Orange, in the centre of the 'Enclave des Papes', Visan makes a wine full in colour and flavour, but equally full in alcohol. In good years they are well worth waiting for. Some good white wine is made for early drinking. The Coopérative des Coteaux de Visan is one of the largest, controlling 2,500 hectares, and also one of the best of the southern Côtes du Rhône, making top quality white, rosé and red wines, while Domaine de la Cantharide and le Clos du Père Clement are exceptionally good. Some good white wine is made but for early drinking.

103

Côtes du Ventoux

Red, dry white and rosé wines from a vast spread of 6,400 hectares of vines running haphazardly from the foot of the Mont Ventoux in the Vaucluse *département* to the edge of the Luberon in the Alpes-de-Haute-Provence. Grape varieties are the same as for the Côtes du Rhône (page 89) and the minimum alcohol content and maximum yield are the same at 11° and 50 hl/ha. The majority of the production of 30 million bottles used to be vinified as a very light red wine, known as a *vin de café*, but the tendency now is to get more colour and body from the fermentation, and to approach the Côtes du Rhône in style. The white wines are hardly seen outside the area, the rosés are pleasant and fruity, but it is the reds that are worth looking for. This region has been the object of some speculative investment, although not to the extent of the Côtes de Luberon. The Domaine wines (Domaine des Anges, Château Valcombe, Domaine de la Verrerie) are more interesting, although more expensive than those of the *caves-coopératives*. Jean-Pierre Perrin's brand, 'La Vieille Ferme', remains the best value for money. In general these are very attractive wines, fruity and *gouléyant* – which a Côtes du Rhône rarely is – to be drunk at 1–3 years. Price B.

Côtes du Lubéron

Red, dry white and rosé wines far to the east of Avignon, on the right bank of the Durance river in the Vaucluse *département*. This is one of the newest AOCs, having been upgraded from VDQS in 1988. This is hardly surprising, since the grape varieties, alcoholic content and minimum yield are the same as for Côtes du Rhône *génériques*, and the wines were at one time sold as Côtes du Rhône. The white wines are light,

Left: The arid, stony vineyards of Beaumes-de-Venise, from which the Muscat grape produces a nectar-like wine.

clean and very attractive when young, the rosés have a pretty colour and go very well with the local cuisine, or with summer meals; the reds are more like the Côtes du Ventoux than Côtes du Rhône in style, with an attractive ruby colour and a soft, ripe, fruity finish. They are at their best young, not older than 3 years. In addition to the highly respected Château de Mille – the oldest property in the Luberon, once owned by the Pope Clement V – Château de l'Isolette and Château La Canorgue, newly created domaines include Val Joanis, Château La Sable and Clos Murabeau. The wines from the vast *cave coopérative*, Les Celliers de Marrenon, are not in this class. For this region, the whites are beginning to attract attention. Still not too expensive. Price B.

VINS DE PAYS

There are so many different local wines produced in the Rhône Valley, particularly in the south, that there does not seem room for more wines or more vineyards. In fact, the *vins de pays* are either wines grown outside the accepted Rhône Valley *appellation*, but still geographically attached to the Rhône Valley region, or wines produced from grape varieties not usually associated with wines from this area. Few of them are expensive. Prices are generally A.

Vins de Pays Départmentaux

VIN DE PAYS DE L'ARDECHE

Red, dry white and rosé wines which are similar in style to the Vins de Pays des Coteaux de l'Ardèche, which represent over 95% of the total production. A group of producers at Ruoms and the *cave coopérative* at Saint-Désirat-Champagne produce most of the annual 35,000 bottles.

VIN DE PAYS DE LA DROME

Red, dry white and rosé wines from the northern part of the *département* on the east bank of the Rhône. The principal grape for the reds is the Syrah with some Grenache and Cinsaut, the wines resembling a light, spicy Crozes-Hermitage or Coteaux du Tricastin. The whites, mainly from the Clairette, are light and aromatic. Production is at over 4 million bottles and is mostly from the *coopératives* at Saint-Donat and Tulette.

VIN DE PAYS DU VAUCLUSE

Red, dry white and rosé wines from vineyards mostly in the south of the *département* in the Lubéron region. Large production of mostly (70%) soft red wines made from the Grenache and Cinsaut grapes, in the style of a light Côtes du Rhône. Rosés and white wines each represent 15% of the total 18 million bottles whose biggest producer is the *coopérative* at La Tour d'Aigues. Most of the Côtes du Rhône-Villages in the Vaucluse produce some *vin de pays* from wines not allowed in the *appellation*.

COLLINES RHODANIENNES

Red, dry white and rosé wines from the northern part of the Rhône Valley, stretching across the *départements* of the Rhône, the Isère, the Loire, the Ardèche and the Drôme. The principal red grapes are the Syrah and Gamay, with a little Pinot Noir permitted in the Loire, and Merlot and Cabernet Franc in the Isère. The whites are from the local Marsanne and Roussanne with Aligoté and Chardonnay and Jacquère admitted, making them a bit crisper than is usual for a white from the Rhône Valley. Production is 25 million bottles, 95% red, and will double in a few years.

COMTE DE GRIGNAN

Red, dry white and rosé wines for the southern part of the Drôme *département* to the east of the Rhône. The usual Rhône grape varieties are planted, with some Pinot Noir and Gamay admitted for the reds and rosé and some Chardonnay for the whites. Almost the entire production of 2 million bottles is red, resembling a lighter Côtes du Rhône. The major producer is the Cellier des Dauphins at Tulette, the largest négociant/*coopérative* in the whole region, commercialising over 40 million bottles a year, and the comparatively tiny, but better, Vignerons Ardéchois.

COTEAUX DE L'ARDECHE

Red (90%), dry white (3%) and rosé (7%) wines from a large wine-growing area south of Privas, covering the southern part of the Ardèche *département* down to the edge of the Gard. Apart from the local grapes, Syrah, Grenache and Cinsaut, the principal red grapes are Cabernet Sauvignon, Gamay, Pinot Noir and Merlot. Of these, the Syrah, Cabernet Sauvignon and Gamay are very successful as single grape varieties, and offer some of the best-value wine in France. The whites, made with a little Chardonnay, Aligoté, Sauvignon and Ugni Blanc as well as the local grapes, are well made, light and refreshing, and will provide much of the increase in production from 20 million to 30 million bottles. Apart from Les Vignerons Ardéchois, La Cevenne Ardéchoise is highly recommended for excellent *vins de cépage*. A good grower is Domaine du Colombier.

COTEAUX DES BARONNIES

Red (95%), dry white and rosé wines from the extreme south-east of the Drôme *département*. Principal red grapes planted are Cinsaut, Grenache, Carignan, while Gamay, Merlot and Cabernet Sauvignon are being introduced to make attractive, fruity, wines from relatively high-altitude vineyards. The whites are from the usual Rhône varietals, plus Aligoté and Chardonnay. The Vins de Pays des Coteaux de Baronnies must have a higher alcohol content than most other *vins de pays*, 10.5° for the whites, 11° for the reds, which makes them a little more serious and full-bodied in style. Much of the 2.5 million bottles comes from *coopératives* at Nyons, Vinsobres and Vaison-la-Romaine.

PRINCIPAUTE D'ORANGE

Reds and a very little rosé from the communes of Bollène, Orange, Vaison-la-Romaine and Valréas in the Vaucluse *département*. The principal Côtes du Rhône grape varieties are used, and the wines resemble lighter versions of *appellation contrôlée* wines from this area. *Coopératives*, the most important being at Sainte-Cecile-les-Vignes, represent 95% of the current 1.8 million bottles.

Provence, the Midi and Corsica

This vast area extends in an almost unbroken sea of vineyards along the full length of the Mediterranean coast of France. In recent years it has been referred to as the "California of France", and there are indeed certain similarities. The region is incredibly large and varied but, thought of as a whole, the sun is omnipresent, and the rules of *appellation* are perhaps less strict than in other parts of France. Perhaps because of this, but to a greater extent because of the historically low quality of the wines in general and the resulting unprofitability of wine-growing in the south, the Provence-Languedoc region has become the centre for modern and experimental winemaking and innovative changes in the accepted types of grapes that may be planted. The emergence of the Midi as a producer of good wine is one of the most exciting factors in the current French wine scene.

The vineyards of Provence, Languedoc and Roussillon are some of the oldest in France, having been planted by the Romans. Their wines were well known and of such good quality that they rivalled those of Rome. Two thousand years later, the Midi was best-known for *gros rouge* and over-alcoholic rosés which only rivalled each other in unpleasantness. Since the 1960s, however, there have been many changes, and much investment, and this dedication to quality rather than quantity is having its effect.

From east to west, the vineyards of the south of France are split into five major regions: (1) Côtes de Provence, Coteaux d'Aix-en-Provence, Coteaux des Baux-en-Provence and older *appellations* in the Alpes-Maritimes, the Var and Bouches-du-Rhône *départements*; (2) Costières de Nîmes from the Gard; (3) Coteaux du Languedoc from the Hérault; (4) Corbières and Minervois from the Aude; and (5) Côtes-du-Roussillon from the Pyrénées-Orientales. These are wines of all colours and strengths made from a myriad of grape varieties, the dominant one still being the Carignan. In addition to the immense quantity of AOCs, VDQSs and *vins de pays*, two of the best VDNs in France come from this area, they are Muscat de Frontignan and Banyuls. Neither must the wines of Corsica, legally a part of France, be forgotten.

Throughout this region, *cépages nobles* — Cabernet Sauvignon and Merlot from Bordeaux, Sauvignon from the Loire, Chardonnay from Burgundy, Syrah and even Viognier from the Rhône, and Mourvèdre from Bandol — are being planted with great success. The styles, even the names, of the wines are constantly changing. For most wine-drinkers, the future for everyday wines from France lies along the Mediterranean coastline.

Provence, The Midi and Corsica

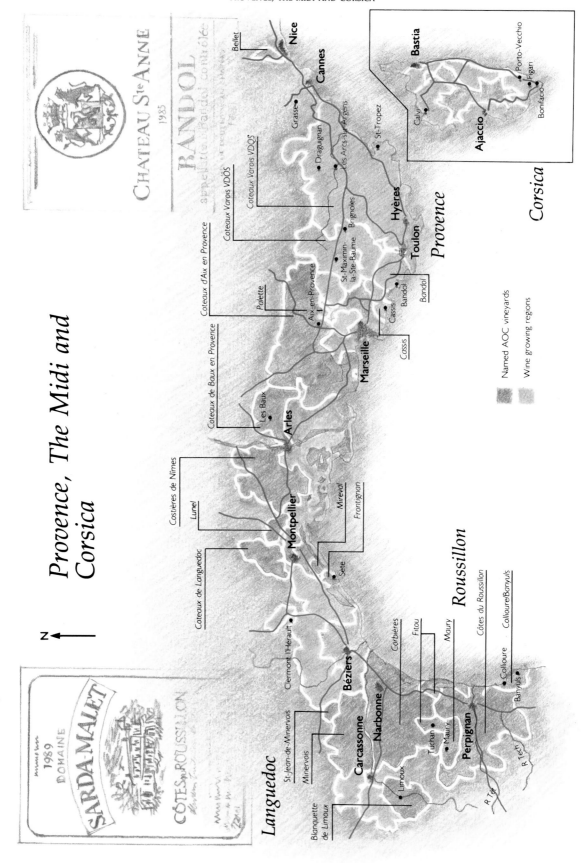

N

Corsica

Bastia
Calvi
Ajaccio
Porto-Vecchio
Figari
Bonifacio

Provence

Bellet
Nice
Cannes
Grasse
Draguignan
Les Arcs-sur-Argens
Coteaux Varois VDQS
Coteaux Varois VDQS
St-Tropez
Hyères
Brignoles
Toulon
Coteaux d'Aix en Provence
St-Maximin-la-Ste-Baume
Palette
Aix-en-Provence
Bandol
Bandol
Cassis
Cassis
Marseille
Coteaux de Baux en Provence
Les Baux
Arles

Languedoc

Costières de Nîmes
Lunel
Mireval
Frontignan
Montpellier
Coteaux de Languedoc
Sete
Clermont l'Hérault
St-Jean-de-Minervois
Minervois
Béziers
Carcassonne
Narbonne
Limoux
Blanquette de Limoux

Roussillon

Corbières
Fitou
Maury
Côtes du Roussillon
Tuchan
Maury
Colliore/Banyuls
Colliore
Perpignan
Banyuls
R Têt
R Tech
R Têt

Named AOC vineyards

Wine growing regions

CHATEAU Ste ANNE
1985
BANDOL
appellation Bandol contrôlée

SARDA-MALET
1989
DOMAINE
CÔTES du ROUSSILLON

Provence

(The *départements* of the Alpes-Maritimes, Basses-Alpes, Hautes-Alpes, Bouches-du-Rhône and the Var)

Provence is one of the oldest wine-growing regions in France, with vines being planted over 2,500 years ago. Globally famous for its rosé, seldom its best wine, this south-east corner of France harbours some of the finest, most interesting and most individual reds and whites. In the face of massive volumes of dull bottles produced by the *caves coopératives*, Provence has emerged as a quality region due, its soil and climate apart, to two factors: the determination of established growers to maintain at all costs their regionality, and the arrival of outsiders determined to break with tradition. Surprisingly the result has proved a recipe for success.

Above: A hard-pruned Bandol vineyard close to the village of La Cadière-d'Azur.

AOC WINES

Bandol

Red, white and rosé wines from a possible 1,200 hectares of vines (although only one-half is planted) between Toulon and La Ciotat in the Var *département*. The white wine must come from a minimum of 60% local varietals (Bourboulenc, Clairette and Ugni Blanc), with a 40% maximum of Sauvignon. The local grapes impart a fruity floweriness while the Sauvignon adds an edge of acidity, and the wine should be drunk young. The rosé, which cannot be sold until eight months after the vintage, has a lively colour, sometimes with a touch of orange, a spicy flavour from the Mourvèdre and Grenache, and a firm finish. The red is the only style with real character and potential. It is made with a minimum of 50% Mourvèdre, with the balance of Grenache and Cinsaut and up to 20% of other grapes Syrah, Carignan, or the local Tibouren which makes a heady rosé, may be added during fermentation. The key to quality is the Mourvèdre, which completes the richness of the Grenache and the leanness of the Cinsaut, giving a deep, velvety colour, a firm, vibrant fruit and great structure. By law, Bandol must spend 18 months in cask (usually in large *foudres*) before bottling, and needs the same amount of time to show its quality. Properly made, with a yield not exceeding 40 hl/ha, Bandol has none of the weightiness of a Châteauneuf-du-Pape or a Gigondas, and can age like a Médoc: good vintages from domaines like Tempier (the most fervent supporter of Mourvèdre), La Laidière, Château Pradeaux, Château des Baumelles, Ott and Pibarnon are at their best at 8–12 years. Other good producers – Château de Vannières, Moulin des Costes, Domaine de Frégate, Domaine la Galandin, Domaine de la Bastide Blanche – make wines to drink at 3–5 years. Production is three million bottles of red and rosé, 150,000 of white, and would easily be more had not the Bandol growers demanded that the INAO remove their right to excessive production under the PLC. The wines of Bandol have become fashionable and only the Cave Coopérative La Roque remains relatively inexpensive. Price D-E.

Bellet

Red, white and rosé wines from a very small *appellation* whose vines are planted on terraces above the city of Nice in the Alpes-Maritimes. Due to the altitude of the vines at around 300 metres and the proximity of the Alps, the climate is cooler than on the plains of the Côte d'Azur, and the wine has a delicacy and finesse uncharacteristic of Provence. The *encépagement* is particular to Bellet: Braquet (Brachetto from Italy), Folle Noire (Fuella Nera), Cinsaut and a little Grenache for the reds and rosés, Rolle, Roussanne, Clairette, Bourboulenc and Chardonnay for the whites. The red has a fine deep colour, firm briary fruit and a touch of acidity that benefits from keeping; the rosés are delicate and firm at the same time and the whites, perhaps the most interesting of all, have a pale straw colour, a striking aroma of wild flowers and a firm, dry flavour with the weight of a white burgundy. The two principal producers are the Château de Crémat and the Château de Bellet. Production is 100,000 bottles of red and rosé, only 40,000 of white. Price, as much for rarity as for quality, E-F.

Cassis

Red, dry white and rosé wines from around the port of Cassis, in the Bouches-du-Rhône. This small *appellation*, with only 180 hectares under vines, is known particularly for its white wine. Made principally from the Clairette, Ugni Blanc, Marsanne and Sauvignon, with a little Doucillon (Grenache Blanc) and Pascal Blanc, Cassis is dry, but without acidity, and should be pale yellow in colour, with even a little saltiness on the palate. It should be drunk young and is perfect with *bouillabaisse* and all Mediterranean fish. The minimum alcohol content of 11° gives it enough body and the low yield for Provence of 40 hl/ha prevents over-production. Reds and rosés, representing half the 700,000 bottles produced annually, are from the typical red varietals: Grenache, Cinsaut, Mourvèdre and Carignan. The rosés are light and fresh, the reds often a little dull. There is much local demand, especially for the white; well-known producers are Domaine de la Ferme Blanche, Domaine Calliol and Clos Sainte-Magdeleine. Prices are high for Provence. Price D.

Coteaux d'Aix-en-Provence

Red, dry white and rosé wines from 3,000 hectares of vineyards to the south and east of Aix-en-Provence in the Bouches-du-Rhône *département*, including a little of the Var. The reds and rosés come from the classic Mediterranean grape varieties: Grenache, Cinsaut, Mourvèdre, Counoise, Carignan, with the addition of Cabernet Sauvignon, now admitted to a maximum of 60%. This gives the red wines an intense colour and a blackcurranty-cedary bouquet that is unusual in the wines of Provence. The domaine that once made a great success with the Cabernet Sauvignon is Château Vignelaure, the creation of Georges Brunet, who resuscitated Château La Lagune in the Médoc. Brunet sold in 1986 and the quality declined noticeably, but Vignelaure has now been brought by the owners of Domaine de Galoupet near Hyères. While Brunet's experiments drew attention to Coteaux d'Aix, the trend now is to reaffirm the quality of the local varieties. The red wines have more in common with the better Côtes de Provence to the south than with Côtes du Rhône to the north. All have good colour and a firm, spicy fruit for drinking at 3–5 years. The most established domaines have a *cuvée speciale* with either more intensity, a touch of new wood, or both, pitched at rivalling the wines of the Médoc in price if not in style. The rosés are light and pretty, especially the "Rosé d'une nuit", a very pale rosé that has drawn only a little colour from the skins. Even with the same alcoholic degree (11°) and yield (50 hl/ha) as Provence, the Coteaux d'Aix wines seem lighter. Whites are made from the Grenache Blanc, Sémillon, Ugni Blanc and a growing proportion of Sauvignon. They should be pale yellow, with good fruit and just a hint of the sun, and no real acidity, so must be drunk young. They are very good with hors d'oeuvres and fish. Coteaux d'Aix passed into AOC status with the 1985 vintage and the wines now fetching a price equal to that of Côtes de Provence. There are many good producers, including Château de Beaupré, Château la Coste, Château de Beaulieu, Château de Calissanne, Jean Salen and Château du Seuil. Production is about 14 million bottles, of which only 5% is white. Price C (D for special cuvées).

Coteaux des Baux-en-Provence

Red, dry white and rosé wines from the region of Saint-Rémy-de-Provence, Fontvieille and Les Baux-de-Provence. These wines achieved AOC status alongside those of Coteaux d'Aix-en-Provence, under which *appellation* they are now grouped. Although there are many similarities, the basic grape varieties – Grenache, Cinsaut, Syrah, Mourvèdre and more or less Cabernet Sauvignon according to taste – being the same, the Coteaux des Baux wines tend to be more meaty and warm. The outstanding wine here is Domaine de Trévallon, with Cabernet dominant. Opposite in style is the Rhône-like Mas de Gourgonnier. Other good domaines are Les Terres Blanches and Mas de la Dame. Rosé accounts for about 10% of the production, white wine is hardly made. Prices, Trévallon apart, are reasonable, but Trévallon is worth the difference. Price C-D.

Côtes de Provence

Red, dry white and rosé wines from vineyards covering 18,000 hectares, principally in the Var *département*. Côtes de Provence wines were granted full *appellation* status in 1977, as a result of an improvement in quality and further improvement to come. The most popular wines are still the rosés, but the real progress has been among the red and white wines. The whites, representing only 10% of the production, are made from the Clairette, Rolle, Ugni Blanc, Sémillon and the local Vermentino grape, with some Sauvignon used to add acidity. If the grapes are picked before they are too ripe, the wines are pale in colour, with a floral bouquet and a soft, fruity finish. They must be drunk as young as possible, since they soon lose their freshness, although some may be kept. Red wines are made from a minimum of 70% of the following grape varieties: Grenache, Cinsaut, Mourvèdre and Carignan, of which Carignan must progressively be reduced to a maximum of 40%. Added to these local grapes are the Cabernet Sauvignon from Bordeaux and the Syrah from the Rhône, both of which bring nuances of flavour and depth. The "old-style" Côtes de Provence red will be a Carignan-Grenache wine, probably sold in one of the fanciful Provençal bottles, and will be full-bodied, warm and fruity. The "new-style" wine, made by a growing number of *vignerons*, will have a proportion of non-Provençal varietals in its make-up, and will probably be sold in a Bordeaux bottle under the name of a domaine or a château. These are the best wines from Provence. The minimum alcohol content of 11° is easily attained given the amount of sun in the region, but the maximum yield of 50 hl/ha is seldom exceeded, especially by those growers looking for quality. Rosés are still the mainstay of the production, being made fruitier and fresher to be enjoyed young and cold.

There are three main wine-growing areas in Provence, although there are vines almost everywhere: the coastal vineyards from Sainte-Maxime to well past Toulon; the central plains, south of the *autoroute* from Vidauban to Brignoles; and the vineyards north of the *autoroute* on the slopes around les Arcs and Draguignan. The further north the vineyards are planted, the less full-bodied the wines. Côtes de Provence wines are perfect with the Provençal cuisine: *salade niçoise*, fish or meat cooked with herbs over a grill, all sorts of spicy dishes. The whites and rosés should be drunk cold, and the red wines are at their best chilled if drunk on a hot day. While the vintage plays more of a role in Provence than some more northern wine-growers would like one to believe, with few exceptions the red wines should be drunk at 2–4 years. Total production is around 90 million bottles. There are some very good wines to be found. Styles of winemaking are so different that some recommended producers are simply listed in alphabetical order: Domaine de l'Aumérade, Château Barbeyr-

olles, Domaine de la Bernarde (superb white and rosé), Commanderie de Peyrassol, Domaine de la Croix (rather old-fashioned, long wood-ageing), Domaine des Féraud, Château Ferrey-Lacombe (from the Bouches-du-Rhône; spectacular wines in very recent vintages), Domaine de Galoupet (one of the original ten Crus Classés of the region), Château Grand'Boise, Domaine de Marchandise (high in Mourvèdre), Château Minuty (the best wine from near Saint-Tropez), Château Réal Martin (reds made for ageing), Domaine de Rimauresq, Domaine de Saint-Baillon (superb rosé), the rare Clos Saint Joseph, situated above Nice but included in this *appellation*, Domaine Sainte-Roseline (another Cru Classé, old style, but high class), and the Maitres Vignerons de Saint-Tropez. With the vast improvement in quality, necessitating financial and physical investment, only the ordinary Côtes de Provence wines are cheap. The others sell for what they are worth, and remain reasonably priced. Price C.

Palette

Red, white and rosé wines from a tiny *appellation* due south of Aix-en-Provence in the Bouches-du-Rhône. The particularity lies in the soil, derived from the geological formation known as the *Calcaire de Langesse*, which is quite different from the neighbouring Côtes du Rhône and Côtes de Provence. The grapes, principally Clairette, Grenache Blanc and Ugni Blanc for the whites and Mourvèdre, Grenache and Cinsaut for the reds and rosés, are all local, but acquire a firmness, even austerity, on the limestony soil that necessitates and repays ageing. As a result, the rosés sometimes lack the freshness of a Tavel, the reds have more of the leanness of a Bordeaux than the "fat" of a Côtes du Rhône and the whites have a subtlety and vigour that is reminiscent of a Graves. The principal producer is Château Simone. Château Crémade is a new producer. Output is about 60,000 bottles of red and rosé, 25,000 bottles of white. Price low E.

VDQS WINES

Coteaux de Pierrevert

Red, rosé and dry white wines from around 400 hectares in the *département* of the Alpes-de-Haute-Provence north-east of the Côtes du Luberon. One of the highest vineyards in France, producing mostly rosé from the classic Provençal grape varieties Grenache, Cinsaut and Carignan, quite pale in colour, fresh and lively. The whites, from Clairette, Picpoul, Ugni Blanc, Roussanne and Marsanne, are very like white Côtes du Rhône. Not much seen outside the region. Production 2.4 million. Price B.

Château Simone

Coteaux Varois

Red, dry white and rosé wines from vineyards planted across the Var *département*. Les Vins de Pays du Coteaux Varois represented, before being upgraded to VDQS, the second largest volume of *vins de pays* in the Midi (after the Coteaux de Peyriac), with a production of almost 30 million bottles. The grapes are largely the same as for the Côtes de Provence: Grenache, Cinsaut, Mourvèdre and a high proportion of Carignan for the reds and rosés; Ugni Blanc, Clairette, Grenache Blanc and Malvoisie for the whites. The red grapes may also include some Alicante and Aramon, varieties not admitted for the AOC Provence. Parallel to these classic, deep-coloured, rather rustic reds, are the wines made from Cabernet Sauvignon and Syrah, with more personality and intensity of flavour, but less obviously Provence. The white wines tend to lack acidity and should be drunk very young. There has been much improvement, more at the private estate level than at that of the *caves coopératives*, in the wines of the Coteaux Varois, with the result that they have been elevated to VDQS status since 1985. Extremely good wines come from the Domaine du Déffends, Domaine de Fontainbleau, Domaine de Garbelle and the *Cuvée Spéciale* Cabernet Sauvignon from the Domaine Saint-Jean. Price B.

VINS DE PAYS

The *vins de pays* from the *départements* of the Bouches-du-Rhône and the Var follow the same trend as elsewhere in France: they are generally wines made from the same grapes as the neighbouring AOCs or VDQSs, but in different proportions and with a lower degree of alcohol, or planted just outside the delimited region; alternatively, the recent experimental planting of *cépages nobles* produces wines which do not fit into the *appellation* and which must therefore be sold as *vins de pays*. None of them are expensive and winemaking

has improved to make them a risk worth taking. This region contains four Vins de Pays Départementaux and six Vins de Pays de Zone. Price A – low B.

Vins de Pays Départementaux

VIN DE PAYS DES ALPES-DE-HAUTE-PROVENCE
Red, dry white and rosé wines from vineyards in the Durance Valley, the same region as the VDQS Coteaux de Pierrevert. Grenache, Cinsaut and Carignan are the principal grapes for the reds (70%) and rosés (30%). Hardly any white is made. Production of 120,000 bottles of lively, fruity, relatively light wine of which the two *caves coopératives* at Manosque and Pierrevert produce 80%. Claude Dieudonné of Domaine de Régusse is the best grower.

VIN DE PAYS DES ALPES-MARITIMES
Red, white and rosé wines from vineyards on the west side of the *département* near Mougins. Similar to, but lighter than, the Vin de Pays du Var. Very small production of 190,000 bottles, 70% red, 30% rosé.

VIN DE PAYS DES BOUCHES-DU-RHONE
Red, white and rosé produced throughout the *département*, but concentrated to the south of Aix-en-Provence (60%), and the Carmargue (30%). Red wines account for 80–85%, with rosés just over 10% and whites having increased to over 5%. The main grapes are Grenache, Cinsaut, Carignan, and the better wines, like the Mas de Rey near Arles, resemble a Côtes de Provence or a Coteaux d'Aix. Chardonnay and Merlot have been planted with successful results from the Domaine de l'Ille Saint-Pierre. Total production in 1983 was 15 million bottles but by 1989 was nudging 30 million.

VIN DE PAYS DU VAR
Red, white and rosé wines from vineyards in the northern part of the *département*. There is a large production of everyday wines, but they are less interesting than the Coteaux Varois, which has now moved to VDQS status. The reds (now down to 55%) are standard, and the rosés (40%) and whites (5%) are improving in freshness. Production is 25 million bottles, 80% produced by *caves coopératives*.

Vins de Pays de Zone

ARGENS
Red, dry white and rosé wines from vineyards around La Motte and Draguignan in the centre-west of the Var. The wines are very similar to the Coteaux Varois, perhaps a little lighter owing to the higher elevation of the vineyards. In 1988 production was 1.5 million bottles, with rosé exceeding red for the first time, and white representing 6%.

MAURES

Red, dry white and rosé wines from a large area in the south-east of the Var, including Saint-Raphaël, les Arcs, Saint-Tropez and Hyères. Total production in 1988 was 11 million bottles, 50% red, 44% rosé and 6% white, confirming the trend in Provence Vin de Pays away from red wine dominance. In general, the same grapes are used as for Côtes de Provence, with a high proportion of Carignan.

MONT CAUME

Red, white and rosé wines from the Mediterranean coast of the Var, around Bandol. The grape varieties are Grenache, Cinsaut, Mourvèdre and Carignan, producing deep-coloured, full-bodied red wines (55%) and very good rosés (40%), and white (only 5%) from Ugni Blanc and Clairette. Reliable *caves coopératives* account for 90% of the production of two million bottles.

PETITE CRAU

Red, dry white and rosé wines from the region of Saint-Rémy-en-Provence in the north of the Bouches-du-Rhône *département*. The reds (75%) and rosés (20%) are made from the Grenache, Cinsaut, Syrah, Mourvèdre and Carignan, with the addition of Cabernet Sauvignon. Whites (5%) are made from the Clairette, Ugni Blanc, Grenache Blanc and Sauvignon. The reds resemble the Coteaux des Baux-en-Provence with a little less body, the rosés are clean, fruity and refreshing and the whites, soft and aromatic. The *cave coopérative* at Noves accounts for 60% of the current production of 850,000 bottles.

SABLES DU GOLFE DU LION

Red, dry white, *gris* and rosé wines from vines planted on the sand-dunes in the Golfe du Lion, stretching across the *départements* of the Bouches-du-Rhône, the Gard and the Hérault. This is a large area, and one where there is much experimentation with new grape varieties and ultra-modern methods of vinification. The principal grape varieties used for the reds, rosés and *gris* are Cabernet Sauvignon, Cabernet Franc, Cinsaut, Grenache, Carignan, Syrah and Merlot. The red wines have a good colour and are attractively low in alcohol,

Below: Vineyards in Provence — one of the oldest wine-growing regions in France.

generally around 10.5°. The single *cépage* wines are very successful, notably the Cabernet Sauvignon. The rosés are pale and delicious, the *gris* only faintly coloured, and there is even some *gris de gris* made exclusively from the Grenache Gris and Carignan Gris. The white wines are probably some of the best *vins de pays* from the Midi. The principal grapes are the Ugni Blanc, Clairette, Sauvignon, Carignan Blanc and Mus-cat, with the Rhône Valley varietals allowed up to 30%, and some Chardonnay now planted. The whites and *gris* may use *"sur lie"* (reserved almost exclusively to Muscadet) if they are bottled off their first fermentation lees after only one winter *en cuve*. With the exception of the reds, these wines should be drunk very young. The production of around 20 million bottles is of 30% red, 60% rosé and *gris*, and 10% white.

The Gard

The Roman province of the Gard produces wines that link those of the southern Rhône to those of the Midi, while being a little less robust than either. The Gard is a region less fashionable than eastern Provence and consequently, whereas Provence has seen a vast influx of new money in the last two decades, the majority of big domaines in the Gard have changed hands through inheritance. Alongside the continuity has been seen a process of slow experimentation, a determination to re-define and improve the style of wines produced, particularly in the new *appellation* Costières de Nîmes.

AOC WINES

Clairette de Bellegarde

Dry white wine from 50 hectares in the commune of Bellegarde between Nîmes and Arles. The only grape permitted is the Clairette and the wine must have a minimum of 11.5° alcohol from a yield of 45 hl/ha. The Clairette is a grape variety seen only in the Côtes du Rhône and the south of France, where it makes a wine with a pale golden colour, a lovely floral aroma of honeysuckle and violets, with soft fruit and low acidity. It must be drunk very young, served cold but not iced and is one of the rare wines to go well with asparagus. For a dry white wine, Clairette de Bellegarde is the opposite in style to the crisp, lemony Loire whites from the Chenin Blanc. There are fine examples from Domaine de l'Amarine and Domaine Saint-Louis-la-Perdrix. Production is quite small, under 300,000 bottles. Price B.

Costières de Nîmes

Red, dry white and rosé wines from a vast region of almost 25,000 hectares from Nîmes almost to Mont-pellier, of which half are under vines and 3,500 are producing wine under this new *appellation*. Created in 1989, Costières de Nîmes replaces the *appellation* Costières du Gard, thus ending the confusion between these wines and the Vins de Pays du Gard, and encouraging further the improvements already evi-dent. The vineyards very much resemble the southern Côtes du Rhône, basically flat, with an arid, sandy soil covered with stones. The red wines are made from the Carignan (to a maximum of 50%, decreasing to 40% and much less in the better domaines), Cinsaut, Mourvèdre, Grenache, Syrah (from the northern Rhône), and the minor grapes Counoise and Terret Noir. The colour is generally an attractive deep red, and the taste has a typically Mediterranean spiciness and fruit, with some of the roundness of the Côtes du Rhône. They should be drunk at 1 to 3 years. The rosés have just the right balance between fruit and alcohol and make lovely quaffing wines to be drunk within the year after the vintage. There is a little white wine made, only 5% of the 25 million bottles produced – but this is increasing due to replanting and more careful vinifica-tion – from the Clairette, Bourboulenc, Maccabeo and Ugni Blanc. If the grapes are picked early, the whites are light and attractive, with a refreshing clean, soft finish. A great deal of Costières de Nîmes is still sold in bulk by the *coopératives* for bottling by négociants, and is very good value for money, there are also more and more domaines bottling their own wine with very satisfactory results. Among these are: Domaine de l'Amarine (floral whites, reds for long ageing), Château Paul Blanc, Domaines Devèze and Mourier from the Camfrancq family, Château de Campuget, Château Roubaud, (the first domaine to bottle in the region), and Château de la Tuilerie, owned by Chantal Comte, whose avant-garde labels match the stylishness of her wines. Price B-low C.

VINS DE PAYS

Vins de Pays Départementaux

VIN DE PAYS DU GARD
Red, dry white and rosé wines from vines planted throughout the Gard *département*. The principal grapes used for the reds and rosés are Carignan (usually up to 50%), Cinsaut, Grenache, Mourvèdre and Syrah. The secondary grapes from Provence, the Rhône and the Languedoc are permitted to a maximum of 30%, and the *cépages nobles* from Bordeaux, Cabernet Sauvignon and Merlot are being planted with great success. If a wine is made exclusively from one of these, it will say so on the label. The white wines are made from the Clairette, Ugni Blanc, Bourboulenc and Grenache Blanc, with some experimental plantings of Sauvignon and Chardonnay. All these grape varieties are permitted in the Vins de Pays de Zone, described below. The red wines have a good colour, a straightforward fruitiness and a pleasantly warm finish. They are good up to three years old and have had some success *"en primeur"*. The rosés are some of the best from the Midi, fruity and not too heavy, while the whites are improving as modern methods of vinification are adopted. Production varies between 50 and 60 million bottles, 80% red, 20% rosé and white. Price A.

Vins de Pays de Zone

COTEAUX CEVENOLS
Red, dry white and rosé wines from the north of the Gard *département* around Saint-Christol-les-Alès. These wines have a little less alcohol and a bit more acidity than those which come from the coast, and have perhaps more in common with the Vins de Pays de l'Ardèche. Production, 60% red, 30% rosé and 10% white from traditional grape varieties, is 700,000 bottles.

COTEAUX DE CEZE
Red, dry white and rosé wines from the north-eastern part of the Gard *département*, around Bagnols-sur-Cèze and up to the right bank of the Rhône. From this area come the Côtes du Rhône-Villages-Chusclan, Lirac and Tavel, and the wines more resemble the lighter Côtes du Rhône than the Vins de Pays du Gard from further south. Very little white is made, and the production of 800,000 bottles is three-quarters red to one-quarter rosé, made mostly by *caves coopératives*.

COTEAUX FLAVIENS
Red, dry white and rosé wines from vineyards planted south of Nîmes, running along the Rhône-Sète canal. The name comes from the Roman Emperor Flavius, and the wines resemble a light Côtes du Rhône, with delightful rosés and some successful whites from the Grenache and Ugni Blanc. Production of four million bottles, 70% red, 25% rosé, 5% white.

COTEAUX DU PONT-DU-GARD
Red, dry white and rosé wines from the Pont-du-Gard region west of Avignon and north-west of Nîmes. Grapes planted are the traditional Carignan, Grenache and Cinsaut, with a little Syrah. Production is quite large, around five million bottles of wine mid-way in style between the lighter Côtes du Rhône and the Costières de Nîmes. The rosés are particularly successful and the quantity of white is increasing.

COTEAUX DU SALAVES
Red, dry white and rosé wines from the vineyards lying to the east of Nîmes and south of Alès. The wines, which are mostly red (80%) and rosé, are in the same style as the Vins de Pays du Gard, with a firm character due to a lower yield per hectare (70 hl), and the addition of Merlot and Cabernet grapes from the South-West. Production 1.5 million bottles, mostly coming from the *cave coopérative* at Quissac.

COTES DU VIDOURLE
Red and rosé wines from vines planted in a small region to the west of Nîmes on the way to Montpellier. The wines are typically Midi in style, very much resembling the Costières de Nîmes *appellation*. Production, 80% red, 20% rosé from around two million bottles.

MONT BOUQUET
Red and rosé wines from the north of the Gard *département*, just south of the Coteaux Cévenols. In style, the wines resemble the lighter Côtes du Rhône and the Vins de Pays de l'Ardèche. Production of 3.5 million bottles, almost entirely red, is largely controlled by L'Union des Coopératives at Nîmes.

SABLES DU GOLFE DU LION
See page 113.

SERRE DE COIRAN
Red, dry white and rosé wines from vineyards to the south of Alès and south-east of Nîmes. This is the same country as Costières de Nîmes and the wines are very similar. Since the new *appellation* Costières du Nîmes is in full evolution, production has dropped from over one million bottles to under 500,000. In 1987, no white wine was presented for the *agrément*, yet over 300,000 bottles were in 1988.

UZEGE
Red, dry white and rosé wines from the region of Uzès, due north of Nîmes. Similar to those of the Costières de Nîmes, but a little lighter. Production of 1.5 million bottles, 70% red, 20% rosé, 10% white.

VAUNAGE

Almost exclusively red and rosé wines from a small region to the north-west of Nîmes. The Vins de Pays de la Vaunage rosés represent the best wines from this region. Tiny production of less than 150,000 bottles.

Below: Vineyards outside the town of Aigues-Mortes.

VISTRENQUE

Almost exclusively red wines from vines planted in a small region in the centre of the *département* around Nîmes. The wines are light and easy to drink. Production is the smallest of all the *vins de pays* in the Gard *département*, at 100,000 bottles, but there is room for expansion to ten times this figure.

The Hérault

The Hérault is one of the most densely planted wine regions in France, producing a high proportion of the country's *vin de table*. The majority of these are without interest, and serious attention is now being paid to the hillside vineyards of the Coteaux du Languedoc, whose wines show an intensity of ripe fruit, a certain robustness and a definite *goût de terroir*. The improvement in grape selection and vinification continue to have a positive effect on quality.

AOC WINES

Clairette du Languedoc

Dry and semi-sweet white wines exclusively from the Clairette grape grown in 11 specific communes around Aspiran and Cabrières in the middle of the *département*. The Clairette produces a heavier, more alcoholic wine in the rich soil of the Languedoc than at Bellegarde or Die, from a low yield of 35 hl/ha. It is richer in colour, almost golden, with a full aromatic flavour but a dry finish. Much of the Clairette du Languedoc is not sold as table wine, but is used as a base for high-quality French vermouths. If the grapes are picked late, and the wine reaches 14° alcohol, it is aged for three years and, having acquired a heady, almost maderized taste like a light *vin doux naturel*, it may be sold as Clairette du Languedoc Rancio. Generally too heavy, with the exception of the lively wines of Château Saint André, to go well with food, Clairette du Languedoc is drunk on its own or with appetizers. Very little of the potential 1.2 million bottles is exported. Price B-C.

Coteaux du Languedoc

Red and rosé wines from a vast plantation of 14,000 hectares of vines right across the Hérault, even touching the Gard and the Aude (La Clape and Quatourze). They must be made from at least 80% of the accepted Mediterranean grape varieties – Carignan (to a maximum of 50%), Cinsaut, Grenache, Counoise, Mourvèdre, Syrah and Terret Noir – and must have a minimum alcohol content of at least 11°. The red wines have a fine deep colour and are satisfyingly full-bodied without being heavy. They can be equally as good as the Costières de Nîmes, if more robust. Rosés are pretty to look at, straightforwardly fruity, and go well with the local food. White wines do not have the right to the *appellation*. Constant progress in winemaking is helping to rebuild the reputation of wines from this area,

resulting in the upgrading from VDQS to AOC in 1985. In general, the quality is very reliable and special mention should be made of some growers making markedly superior wines: Prieuré de Saint-Jean de Bébian, Château Saint-Ferréol, Château Carrion-Nizas, Mas du Daumas Gassac, Abbaye de Valmagne, Château Labglade, Mas Jullien, Château la Condamine-Bertrand. Production 40 million bottles. Price B-C.

Within the region, there are 11 communes (excluding the Picpoul de Pintet, producing only white wine) that have the right to use their own name on the label while remaining a part of the global Coteaux du Languedoc *appellation*. These communes are set out below.

Cabrières

Mainly rosé wines from vines planted on steep, schistous slopes outside the town of Béziers not far from Faugères. They must be made from a maximum of 50% Carignan and a minimum of 45% Cinsaut, the rest coming from the Grenache. Minimum alcohol content is 11° from a yield of 50 hl/ha, but the terraced vineyards rarely achieve this quantity. Cabrières rosé is fine and lively, with a subtle floral aroma and a quite full-bodied flavour. It is without doubt the best rosé produced in the Languedoc, typified by that of the Cave de Cabrières. Production is about 750,000 bottles. Price B.

Coteaux de la Méjanelle

Red wines, with a minute production of dry white, from east of Montpellier. The grape varieties are the Carignan, Cinsaut and Grenache, producing a wine that is dark coloured, rich and tannic, one of the few wines from the Languedoc that repays keeping. The leading producer is Henri de Colbert of the Château de Fal_gergues, who has added Mourvèdre, Syrah, Cabernet Sauvignon and Merlot to the established varietals, thus producing some *vins de pays* as well. Price B.

Coteaux de Saint-Christol

Red wine from vines grown on chalky-clayey soil in the region of Saint-Christol, east of Montpellier. The classic Languedoc grape varieties, Carignan, Cinsaut and Grenache, allied to the Syrah and Mourvèdre, produce a wine that is fruity and spicy. Production is about 800,000 bottles, mostly from the *cave coopérative*; there are also some good domaine-bottled wines from Martin Pierrat. Price A-B.

Coteaux de Verargues

Red and rosé wines from hillside vineyards around Lunel, north-east of Montpellier. Of the usual Mediterranean grape varieties, Carignan is permitted up to 50%, but is giving way to more planting of Grenache and Cinsaut, while the *cépage ordinaire*, the Aramon, is still admitted up to 15%. The wines, with 11° minimum alcohol from a yield of 50 hl/ha (often exceeded), are classic Coteaux du Languedoc: full, fruity, sunny wines, uncomplicated and easy to drink, with all the qualities and sometimes the faults of *les vins du Midi*. Jean-Philippe Servière (Château du Grès-St Paul) is showing how good they can be. Production is almost two million bottles. Price A-B.

La Clape

Red, dry white and rosé wines from vineyards covering 1,000 hectares on the edge of the Corbières *appellation*, between Narbonne and the Mediterranean in the Aude *département*. Reds and rosés may be made entirely from the Carignan grape, but more usually two-thirds Carignan and one-third Grenache, Cinsaut and Terret Noir. They are deep-coloured, well-built wines that age well, especially if they are the old-fashioned Carignan style. The chalk-based soil, rare in the Midi, gives the rosés an unexpected lightness and fruit. The whites, from the Clairette, Picpoul and Bourboulenc grapes, come in two styles: the light, flowery soft wines from the Clairette, and the richer, more golden wines from the Bourboulenc (known locally as Malvoisie), a most interesting wine with finesse and character. The minimum alcohol content for all La Clape wines is 11°, from a yield of 50 hl/ha. They have a high reputation locally, and are beginning to be exported. Top proprietors are Château Pech-Celeyran, Château Pech-Redon and Château Moujan, with very polished wines from Château la Roquette-sur-Mer and more old-fashioned ones from Jean Ségura at Domaine de Rivière-le-Haut. Production is over three million bottles, about 10% white. Price B-C.

Montpeyroux

Red and rosé wines from the schistous soil of the hills to the north of Béziers. The red, made from the classic Languedoc mix of 50% Carignan and the rest Grenache, Cinsaut and Syrah, is a surprisingly good, solid, deep-coloured wine with unexpected roundness. The rosés are typically fruity and must be drunk cold. Production: almost two million bottles mostly from the Cave Coopérative de Montpeyroux. This is the most northerly vineyard in the Midi. Price A-B.

Picpoul de Pinet

Dry white wine from vines planted back from the coast, between Sète and Béziers. The wine must come from the Picpoul, to a minimum of 70%, and blended with the Clairette and Terret Blanc to reach an alcohol content of 11.5°, from the normal yield in the Midi of 50 hl/ha. Picpoul de Pinet is fragrant and fruity, dry but without acidity. It is absolutely perfect on the spot, with the local Bouzigues oysters. Fortunately, the local demand for the million or so bottles is high, as it does not taste as well outside its own region. The *cave coopérative* is the largest producer, Domaine de Gaujal and Domaine de la Grangette reliable growers. Price B.

Pic-Saint-Loup

Red, dry white and rosé wines from vineyards to the north-east of Montpellier. Production of white is minuscule, about 5,000 bottles, mostly from the Clairette and experimental varieties. The reds and rosés are typical Coteaux du Languedoc in style, but lighter than most due to much of the wine being made by the *macération carbonique* process, with a freshness that makes them attractive young. Production is around three million bottles. The classic style is altogether more robust and warming. Price A-B.

Quatourze

Red, dry white and rosé wines from the region of Narbonne in the Aude at the western edge of the *appellation*. The production is almost all red, from the accepted Mediterranean grapes Carignan, Cinsaut, Grenache, Mourvèdre and Terret Noir, grown on a stony plateau that gives a dark-coloured, rich, powerful wine. Much of this wine was, and still is, used as *vins médecins*, to bolster up rather lighter *cuvées* of other wines. They are much fuller than the minimum alcohol content of 11°, and will age well. Quatourze is a big, old-fashioned wine, good with roast meat or game, well exemplified by wine from the Château Notre-Dame de Quatourze. Production 1.2 million bottles. Price A-B.

Saint-Drézery

Red wine only from the commune of Saint-Drézery near Saint-Christol, outside Montpellier. These are typical "Midi" wines, high in Carignan, deep coloured and fruity, often only a little better than the Frenchman's everyday table wine. The minimum alcohol content is 11°, as for all the Coteaux du Languedoc, and the yield of 50 hl/ha is almost always exceeded. Small production. Very inexpensive. Price A.

Saint-Georges d'Orques

Red wine and a little rosé from vineyards which lie to the west of Montpellier. The grapes planted are Carignan to 50%, Cinsaut to a minimum of 35% and Grenache between 100% and 40%. These give the wine a deep colour and a lot of body, the high proportion of Cinsaut bringing finesse. These are wines which can improve with age and are very much appreciated in the region. Production totals about 2.5 million bottles, mostly from the local *coopératives*. The best grower is the Château de l'Engarran. Price A-B.

Saint-Saturnin

Red and rosé wines made from the classic Languedoc grapes of Carignan (usually 50%), Grenache, Cinsaut and Syrah. Minimum alcohol content is 11°, from the accepted maximum yield of 50 hl/ha. Saint-Saturnin red has a fine ruby colour and is solid and generous, a good everyday wine from the Midi. Production is two million bottles, entirely from the *cave coopérative*. Price A-B.

Faugères

Red and dry white wines from the vineyards of seven communes to the north of Béziers. The white wine is made from the Clairette, but its production is insignificant. The red is made principally from the Carignan grape, with Cinsaut and Grenache in increasing proportions. As with all the Coteaux du Languedoc wines, Faugères must have a minimum alcohol content of 11° from a yield of 50 hl/ha. It is a robust, ripe, meaty wine, a good example of wines from Languedoc and very popular in the region. Like its neighbour Saint-Chinian, Faugères was awarded *appellation* status in 1982, three years before the Coteaux du Languedoc. Fine examples come from Gilbert Alquier & Fils, Domaine du Fraisse, Château des Estanilles, Domaine de Rogue (owned by the President of the *appellation*, M. Rogue), and Château Haut-Fabrèges. Production is quite large at six million bottles. Price A-B.

Saint-Chinian

Red wine only from vines planted on stony slopes above the Mediterranean in the Béziers region. Saint-Chinian is the largest *appellation* of the Languedoc, with a production of 12 million bottles. Great improvements have been made in planting, with the Carignan grape, permitted at up to 50%, giving way to Grenache, Cinsaut, Syrah and Mourvèdre. The clayey, limestone soil gives wines of character and solidity, while in the northern part of the *appellation* the presence of schist produces more finesse. Neither are too heavy, seldom more than one degree higher than the minimum 11°,

and may be drunk at 1–3 years after the vintage. The excellent Cave Coopérative Les Coteaux du Rieux-Berlou, the acknowledged leader in the *appellation*, probably in the whole *département*, produces a series of interesting wines of which Cuvée Prestige is the best. Very good growers are the Château de Coujan, Château Casals-Viel, Domaine Guiraud-Boyer and Domaine de Jougla. Inexpensive. Price A-B.

VINS DE PAYS

Red, dry white, *gris* and rosé wines from vines planted throughout the *département*. In 1982 the Hérault produced over 200 million bottles of *vins de pays*, a quantity exceeding even that of the Aude. The range of grape varieties allowed is large: for the reds and rosés the most planted grape is the Carignan, which gives a wine with a fine ruby colour and good body. It is rather hard and common when used on its own, and is limited for AOC and VDQS wines to a maximum of 50% of the *encépagement*. The proportion allowed is much higher for *vins de pays*, as is the yield (80 hl/ha as opposed to 50 hl/ha), but the Carignan on its own is particularly successful if vinified by the *macération carbonique* process. If the grape is used to 100%, it will say so on the label. Other major red grape varieties for reds and rosés are the Grenache for body and colour, Cinsaut for finesse, especially in the rosés, and a little Mourvèdre and Syrah, both deep-coloured, but low-yielding grapes. The *cépages nobles* from Bordeaux, Cabernet Sauvignon and Merlot, are being planted more and more although their presence is still hardly significant in terms of over-all production, they are very useful as a blender grape to add another facet to the "Midi" character of the wines from the south, and are particularly interesting on their own. Minor grapes such as the Aramon, Alicante, Terret Noir and Counoise are still in evidence. The white wines, a very small percentage compared to reds and rosés, are made from the Ugni Blanc and Clairette grapes for the most part, with Picpoul, Marsanne, Maccabeo, Bourboulenc, Grenache Blanc and Muscat. The Sauvignon grape is making progress, as it can flourish in a hot climate, while keeping its natural acidity. Some very good white wines are being developed with modern methods of vinification. Price generally A.

Vins de Pays Départementaux

VIN DE PAYS DE L'HERAULT
Red, dry white, gris and rosé wines from local and imported grape varieties, as described above. Declared production in 1988 was 150 million bottles, 87% red, 7.5% rosé and 5.5% white. The percentage of rosé and white is on the increase.

Vins de Pays de Zone

There are 28 different Vins de Pays de Zone in the Hérault, some producing over 10 million bottles, the Vin de Pays des Collines de la Moure for example, and others, such as the Haute Vallée de l'Orb, producing as little as 60,000. Generally similar to Coteaux du Languedoc in style, with a full colour and good fruit; straightforward, everyday wines. However, new grape varieties and modern vinification, combined with a realization on behalf of the producers, who are mostly *caves coopératives*, that quality pays, has moved the brand image of these wines up from *gros rouge*, to wines that are well worth drinking. The range of wine in the Hérault is so large and in constant flux that it is impossible to assess each Vin de Pays de Zone as one can the different *appellations*, so they are listed here alphabetically with the minimum information given for each. All very inexpensive. Price A.

ARDAILHOU

Mostly red and a little rosé wine from the very south of the *département*, first declared *vins de pays* in 1982. 1988 production was 18 million bottles, 60% red, 30% rosé, 10% white.

BENOVIE

Red, dry white and rosé wines produced to the north-east of the region of the Coteaux du Languedoc *appellation,* from vines planted around Saint-Christol and Saint-Drézery. Production 1.5 million bottles with 75% red, 20% rosé and 5% white wine.

BERANGE

Small production of red, white and rosé wines from the Lunel region, better known for its VDN Muscat de Lunel. Production 900,000 bottles. 85% red, 10% rosé, 5% white, mostly from the *coopérative* at Castries.

BESSAN

Red, dry white and rosé wines from the commune of Bessan north of Agde and south of Pézenas, in the centre of the *département*, not far from the coast. Production around one million bottles, 60% rosé, 25% white, 15% red.

CASSAN

Mostly red, with rosé and white wines from the north of Pézenas in the centre of the *département*. Production of around one million bottles is dominated by the *coopérative* at Roujan.

CAUX

Red, dry white and rosé wines from vines planted throughout the region of Béziers, south-east of the VDQS Cabrières. The production is two million bottles and the wines are generally good, with the rosé being

the best known, representing 60% of the *appellation*, of which a good example is the Domaine de Salletes.

CESSENON

Red and rosé wines from vines planted in the commune of Cessenon, between the AOCs, Faugères and Saint-Chinian. Total production of 800,000 bottles, mostly red, and mostly from the Cave Coopérative de Cessenon. This used to be much larger at four million, but 75% of the old production now goes into the *appellation*.

COLLINES DE LA MOURE

Red, dry white and rosé wines from vineyards planted from Montpellier to Frontignan, in the hills just back from the coast. Very large production (12 million bottles, 80% red, 15% rosé, 5% white) of everyday wines, with some interesting individual domaines.

COTEAUX DE BESSILLES

Red, white and rosé wines from the Picpoul de Pinet region. The wines from local grapes are as to be expected, but wines of great interest come from the Domaine's Saint-Martin-de-la-Garrigue: with Chardonnay, Merlot, Cabernet Sauvingon. Production is 1.5 million bottles, 70% red, 20% rosé, 10% white.

COTEAUX D'ENSERUNE

Red and rosé wines from the region to the west of Béziers. Production of two million bottles of everyday wines, 85% red, 10% rosé, 5% white.

COTEAUX DE FONTCAUDE

Red and rosé wines from vineyards planted to the west of Béziers. A lower than usual yield of 70 hl/ha and their situation south-east of Saint-Chinian help to give these wines some character. Production two million bottles, 85% red, 10% rosé, 5% white.

COTEAUX DE LAURENS

Red, dry white and rosé wines from just south of the AOC Faugères. Production is quite large, around 2.5 million bottles (85% red) and the wine is above average for a *vins de pays*. Some interesting wines are made by the *macération carbonique* method of vinification. Virtually no white wine is declared.

COTEAUX DE LIBRON

Red, dry white and rosé wines from vineyards following the river Libron, to the north of Béziers. A very large production of six million bottles of fairly meaty red wines (80%), with some influence from the grape varieties of the South-West.

COTEAUX DE MURVIEL

Red, dry white (only 2%) and rosé wines from vineyards which are planted in the area to the north-

west of Béziers, on the left bank of the river Orb. Quite a large annual production of five million bottles (85% red). One of the best producers is Château Coujan.

COTEAUX DE PEYRIAC
Red and rosé wines from the Minervois region mostly in the Aude *département*. See page 124.

COTEAUX DU SALAGOU
Red and rosé wines from the north of the *département* in the region of Saint-Saturnin. The reds are well worth drinking, being deep-coloured and full-bodied. These provide 80% of the total production of 750,000 bottles.

Above: Vineyards on the shores of Lac de Salagou in the Herault.

COTES DE BRIAN
Red and rosé wines from the south-west of the *département*, including vines planted at Saint-Jean-de-Minervois. Large production of five million bottles of mostly red wines, with a high proportion of Carginan, some sold *"en primeur"*.

COTES DE CERESSOU
Red, dry white and rosé wines from the region of Cabrières, in the centre of the *département*. Production of only 600,000 bottles of good rosés and full-bodied

reds, with 15% whites from the Ugni Blanc, Clairette and Terrets Blanc and Gris. Most of the four million bottles produced in 1982 are now worthy of the Cabrières *appellation*.

COTES DU THAU
Red, dry white and rosé wines from the south of the *département*, near the vineyards of Picpoul de Pinet, planted a short distance from the coast. Large production of white wine from the Picpoul and the Terret Blanc, representing 40% of the six million bottle total.

COTES DE THONGUE
Red, dry white and rosé wines from vineyards in the southern centre of the *département*, north-east of Béziers. Production is large (five million bottles, 70% red, 25% rosé, 5% white) and there has been some interesting planting of Syrah, Merlot and Cabernet Sauvignon. One of the better *vins de pays*, with several fine individual domaines: Domaine de la Serre, Domaine de l'Arjolle, Domaine Deshenrys.

GORGES DE L'HERAULT
Red, dry white and rosé wines from well-situated vineyards inland to the west of Montpellier. Production 800,000 bottles, 80% red, 10% rosé, 10% white.

HAUTE VALLEE DE L'ORB
Small production of red, white and rosé wines from vineyards planted in the Orb Valley, to the north-west of the *département*. Only 60,000 bottles were declared in 1988, compared to 600,000 in 1987.

MONT BAUDILE AND MONTPEYROUX
Red, dry white and rosé wines from vineyards planted throughout the same region as the VDQS Coteaux du Languedoc Saint-Saturnin. Quite large production (1.5 million bottles) of solidly built wines, mostly red and rosé.

MONTS DE LA GRAGE
Red (mostly) and rosé wines from the region of Saint-Chinian. Very little wine is produced, as the *appellation* Saint-Chinian is preferred when possible. 1988 produced 165,000 bottles, 96% red.

PEZENAS
Red, dry white and rosé wines from vineyards planted in the commune of Pézenas in the middle of the *département* between Montpellier and Béziers. Quite good wines, 80% red, the rest equally good rosé and white, totalling 750,000 bottles.

SABLES DU GOLFE DU LION
See page 113.

VAL DE MONTFERRAND
Red, dry white and rosé wines from vineyards planted in the north-eastern corner of the *département*, north of Montpellier, near Pic-Saint-Loup and Saint-Drézery. Large production (four million bottles) of mostly red wines, full-bodied in the same style as the Coteaux du Languedoc, and 10% white wines based on the Ugni Blanc.

VICOMTE D'AUMELAS
Red, dry white and rosé wines from well-placed vineyards west of the VDQS Cabrières. Quite large production of five million bottles of good wine, with the usual high proportion of red (70%), 15% rosé and 15% white. Domaine Puech is a good producer.

The Aude

The wines of the Aude are almost exclusively red, full-bodied and deep-coloured, typified by Corbières, Fitou and Minervois. Although the production is still largely of everyday wines, there has been much experimentation with grape varieties other than the habitual Carignan and Grenache. As in the adjoining *départements* of the Midi, this has taken two directions for red and rosé wines: the Syrah, Cinsaut and encouragingly the Mourvèdre from the Rhône valley and Provence, and Cabernet Sauvignon and Merlot from Bordeaux. Outside investment has permitted old and new domaines to produce *cuvées* aged in new oak, common practice in the Médoc, but unheard of a decade ago in the Aude. A certain smoothness and polish is appearing, which seems at odds with the rugged landscape. For the whites, the Chardonnay has been transplanted from Burgundy, slightly diminished and softened by the sun, but still recognisable. White wines from the local grapes, if well made, remain more interesting.

AOC WINES

Blanquette de Limoux

Sparkling white wines from vines planted in the region of Limoux, south of Carcassonne. The name "Blanquette" comes from the white dust that covers the underside of the leaves of the Mauzac Blanc grape from which the wine is made. The Mauzac must be planted to a minimum of 80%, the balance being made up by the Chenin and Chardonnay, the still wine has a minimum of 9.5° alcohol from a maximum yield of 50 hl/ha, from which not more than 100 litres of juice may be extracted from 150 kilograms of grapes. It is made sparkling by either the *méthode rurale* or the *méthode champenoise*, keeping the distinctive bouquet of the Mauzac with a soft, fruity flavour and dry finish. Blanquette de Limoux is excellent as an apéritif, or with fish or chicken dishes. Provided the proportion of Mauzac is respected in the vineyard, different *cuvées* may be made of over 50% Chardonnay, with all the finesse this implies, or alternatively 100% Mauzac, more for local consumption. The *cave coopérative*, under its most popular brand "Aimery", is responsible for much of the eight million bottles sold annually, but very good producers include: Domaine Laurens (who also make Champagne), Georges and Roger Antech, Domaine Collin and Domaine de Fourn. Quality is in general very high, and Blanquette de Limoux is seeing a justified vogue and expansion. Price C.

Corbières

Red, dry, white and rosé wines from a vast expanse of vineyards covering 23,000 hectares, planted between the Languedoc and Roussillon regions, to the southeast of Carcassonne. The reds and rosés must come from the classic Mediterranean grape varieties, Carignan, Cinsaut, Grenache, Mourvèdre, Terret Noir, Picpoul (a white grape) and Syrah, to a minimum of 90%. Minimum alcohol content is 11° from a yield, often exceeded, but not for the better wines, of 50 hl/ha. Very little rosé is made, for the reds are much better, solid wines, with a deep, rich colour, a concentrated fruit aroma and a big, meaty flavour. At their best, Corbières can rival any wine from the Mediterranean except Bandol and Palette, and many from the South-West. At their worst, they are heavy, common wines not worthy of the *appellation*. For such a vast production, about 90 million bottles (90% red, 10% white and rosé), the proportion of good to bad is high. They may be drunk young, one year after the vintage, while the better wines improve for several years more. Red Corbières is extremely versatile, and goes well with any meat-based dish, it stands up to spicy food and is excellent with cheese. The white is made principally from the Clairette and Malvoisie (or Bourboulenc) grapes. They are attractive, light wines, with a fragrant bouquet and dry, fruity finish, very rarely seen ouside the region. Corbières can be found at many price levels, and is often an outstanding bargain. The *appellation* is divided into four regions: Corbières-Maritimes, Corbières-Centrales, Corbières-Hautes and Alaric-Corbières. Characteristics are specific to each, but it is more important to look for the name of the producer than for the sub-region. There are some very good *cave coopératives* at Ribaute, Lézignan-Corbières, Mont-Tauch and Côtes d'Alaric. Top class domaines include: Domaine du Révérend (a new venture of Peter Sichel of Château Palmer), Domaine de Villemajou, Château Etang des Colombes, Château de Lastours, Château Vaugelas, Château de Caraguilhes for reds, superb rosés from Château la Voulte-Gasparets and Château Surbéry-Cartier, and fine whites from Château Hélène and Château Pech-Latt. Price B-C.

Corbières Supérieurs

Red and dry white wines from the same region as Corbières, with a higher minimum alcohol content of 12° from a lower yield of 40 hl/ha. To avoid confusion, this *appellation* is reserved for white wines. With the exception of Bordeaux, the addition of Supérieur is not seen to be an advantage, and wines are very seldom sold under this *appellation*. Price B-C.

Fitou

Red wine only from 1,000 hectares of coastal vineyards at the edge of the Aude *département*, on the border of the Pyrénées-Orientales. Fitou has the particularity of being the oldest *appellation* in the Midi (1948) and of being made from a minimum of 60% Carignan, at a time when many growers are replacing this grape with the more supple Grenache and Cinsaut. While the other 40% may be made from these two, with the addition of Mourvèdre and Syrah, the Carignan imposes on the wines of Fitou its very deep, dark ruby colour, rough, tannic fruit and powerful, concentrated flavour. The best wine comes from the vines planted on limestony slopes well inland. As is usual for the Midi, most of the wine is made in *cave coopératives* of which Les Producteurs Réunis at Narbonne and the Cave de Mont-Tauch (an excellent 60% Carginan-40% Grenache *cuvée* called Château de Segure) are the best. Of the growers, the best known, longest aged, most extraordinary and most expensive wines come from Château des Nouvelles, but other good wines are made by Paul Colomer, Alain Castex and the Domaine de Fenals. A classic Fitou has to have at least 12° alcohol and must spend 18 months in wood before bottling, and is at its best between 4 and 6 years after the vintage, one of the rare wines from the Midi that age

makes the wines from Minervois agreeable young, while good examples can age as well as the better wines from Corbières. The vast proportion of the production of 30 million bottles comes from *caves coopératives* as is normal in the Midi, and nearly all of it is red. The tiny amount of white, under 3%, is made from the Grenache Blanc, Bourboulenc (known as the Malvoisie in this region), Maccabeo, Picpoul and Terret Blanc, non-local varieties being excluded. Rosé is also rare, but good examples of both come from Domaine Maris. As a whole, the growers in the Minervois are energetic and have been successful in getting their wines better known, profiting from *appellation* status that was awarded in 1984. Very good wines are made by the following domaines: in the Hérault, Château de Gourgazaud, Domaine Sainte-Eulalie (both smooth, rich and spicy) and Domaine Maris; in the Aude, Château de Paraza, Château de Blomac, incredibly concentrated reds from Daniel Domergue, elegant and polished from Château Villerambert-Julien, classic from Château Fabas and Château du Donjon. Apart from the wines aged "à la Bordelaise" in new wood, the wines of Minervois are reasonably priced. Also produced in this region is the excellent Muscat de Saint-Jean-de-Minervois (see page 136). Price B.

Vin Noble du Minervois

Sweet white wine, not to be confused with the red Minervois, made from the Muscat, Malvoisie, Grenache and Maccabeo grapes. The grapes are harvested very late, and their natural concentration brings them easily to the legal minimum of 13°, with some residual sugar left in the wine. Hardly any is now made. Price C.

VDQS WINES

Cabardès

Red and rosé wines (also known under the *appellation* "Côtes du Cabardès et de l'Orbiel") from over 2,200 hectares of vines grown on the southern slopes of the Montagne Noire, west of the Minervois, north of Carcassonne. Principal grapes are the Carignan, Cinsaut, Grenache, Mourvèdre and Syrah, with the Carignan allowed to a maximum of only 30%. Also permitted are varieties from the South-West, such as the Cabernet Sauvignon, Cot, Fer and Merlot. As for the wines of Languedoc and Corbières, the minimum alcohol content is 11°, from a yield of 50 hl/ha. The rosés are pleasant, fruity, everyday wines, the reds firm and lively, a little more interesting, particularly if they are drunk on the spot. The finest wines are from Château Rivals, with a rosé of great finesse and a

well. It is particularly good with *daubes* and game. The production is large, around 12 million bottles; it is relatively expensive for the Midi as a whole, but the better wines are worth it. Many growers, and, of course, the *coopératives*, also produce a Muscat-en-Lunel, a Vin Doux Naturel (see page 135). Price B-C.

Minervois

Red, white and rosé wines from a large vineyard area (18,000 hectares of which 5,000 are in the *appellation*), north-west of Narbonne and north-east of Carcassonne, straddling the *départements* of the Aude and the Hérault. The wine is made principally from the Carignan (usually over 50%), the Grenache, Syrah and the Cinsaut grape varieties, with a minimum alcohol content of 11° from a yield of 50 hl/ha. The region is surrounded by mountains, and the hot, dry climate ripens the *cépages méridionaux* to produce a wine with deep crimson colour, a spicy, concentrated bouquet and a firm velvety finish. The concentration of fruit plummily fruity red; and Château de Pennautier, whose red wine can be aged. The *coopérative* at Pézenas also has some good *cuvées*. The style of these wines is already veering towards that of the South-West (see pages 187–201). Production is around 1.2 million bottles. Not expensive. Price B.

Côtes de la Malepère

Red and rosé wines from the region of Carcassonne. The Côtes de la Malepère wines were elevated to VDQS status in 1982, quite justified by the quality of the wines from selected low-yielding grape varieties. The reds must come principally from the Merlot, Cot and Cinsaut, none of which may represent more than 60% of the total, and from the Cabernet Sauvignon, Cabernet Franc, Grenache and Syrah, these last four

limited to 30%. The wines have a good colour and are quite elegant, showing the influence of the grapes from South-West and the exclusion of Carignan from *appellation*. The Cave de Razès produces some extremely good reds under the names Domaine de Cazes (light and fruity), Domaine de Fournerey and the Cabernet Sauvignon dominated Domaine de Beauséjour. Château de Malviés and Château de Routier are fine private producers. The rosés come from the Grenache and Cinsaut, the classic rosé mix seen in Tavel, with juice from other grapes allowed at up to 30%. They are pleasant, fruity, with a certain body. With production at 1.5 million bottles, this is an inexpensive *appellation* to look out for. Price A-B.

Below: Vineyards of La Clape – the Coteaux du Languedoc region hills between Narbonne and the sea.

VINS DE PAYS

Visually, the *départements* of the Hérault and the Aude resemble a sea of vines, wine being by far the major economic resource of the Midi. Although a proportion still goes for distillation, and a further quantity remains resolutely *ordinaire*, the quality of *vins de pays* increases year by year.

Vins de Pays Régionaux

VIN DE PAYS D'OC
Red, dry white and rosé wines from vines planted throughout the Midi but mostly in the *départements* of the Hérault, Aude and Pyrénées-Orientales. This is the regional grouping under which all *vins de pays* in the Midi may sell, comparable to the Jardin de la France in the Loire and the Comté Tolosan in the South-West. Most producers, however, prefer the more closely defined *appellation* of a Vins de Pays Départemental or a Vins de Pays de Zone. The basic grape varieties are the Carignan and Grenache, which comprise the reds and rosés that represent most of the production. In 1988, 48 million bottles were declared from a bumper crop. 70% red, 15% rosé, 15% white. Unpretentious table wines and very inexpensive. Price A.

Vins de Pays Départementaux

VIN DE PAYS DE L'AUDE
Red, dry white and rosé wines produced throughout the *département*. In 1988, 160 million bottles were produced under this label, 93% red, 5% rosé and 2% white. The major grape variety for the reds and rosés is the Carignan, followed by the Grenache, Cinsaut, Mourvèdre, Terret Noir, and Alicante from the south, and in second line the Cabernet Sauvignon, Cabernet Franc, Merlot and Cot from the South-West. In style, many of the wines are mid-way between that of the Midi and that of the South-West, depending on which grapes are planted. White wines, a small part of the total production, are principally made from the Clairette, Ugni Blanc, Bourboulenc, Maccabeo, Carignan Blanc and Grenache Blanc, and to a lesser degree the Muscat à Petits Grains, Mauzac, Roussanne, Picpoul, Baroque and the *cépages nobles*, Sauvignon, Sémillon, Chardonnay and Chenin Blanc. As in the neighbouring Hérault and Pyrénées-Orientales, wines from the Aude are undergoing, none too soon, a process of improvement and change. Much credit can go to two large Paris-based companies: Nicolas and Chantovent. Their far-sighted investment in vineyards, up-to-date equipment and long-term contracts with the *caves coopératives*, created a basis for upgrading the French *vin de table* in the eyes of the consumer and the producer. Examples of this are the excellent single-

varietal wines, with the name of the grape stated on the label. Very inexpensive. Price A.

Vins de Pays de Zone

COTEAUX DE LA CABRERISSE
Red and rosé wines from vineyards in the Corbières region. Both Midi and South-West grapes are planted to make solid, deep-coloured wines, with a little sold "*en primeur*". Production two million bottles, 97% red.

COTEAUX DE LA CITE DE CARCASSONNE
Red and rosé wines from the south of Carcassonne, touching the northern Corbières vineyards. The Bordelais grapes, especially the Merlot, do well here, producing deep-coloured, soft, fruity wines. Production four to five million bottles, 95% red.

COTEAUX DE LEZIGNANAIS
Mainly red wines from the region of Lézignan, one of the better vineyards in the *département*. Only 1% of white and rosé is produced from the total of 3.5 million bottles of meaty, Corbières-style wine, mostly sold by the Union des Coopératives de Lézignan.

COTEAUX DE MIRAMONT
Red and rosé wines from south-east of Carcassonne below Minervois. Large production of eight million bottles, mostly red; fruity wines in the Minervois style.

COTEAUX DE NARBONNE
Red (almost 100%), dry white and rosé wines from the region of Narbonne, made mostly from the Carignan grape. The wines are good everyday reds, but not very exciting. Production two million bottles.

COTEAUX DE PEYRIAC
Red, dry white and rosé wines from a large area in the Minervois region, touching the Hérault. The reds have a fine ruby colour and more character than many other *vins de pays*. Very large production of nearly 35 million bottles, 85% red, 14% rosé, with 1% white.

COTEAUX DE TERMENES
Red, dry white and rosé wines from well-placed elevated vineyards situated in the centre of the *département*. Very much like Corbières wines in style and, when the law permits, the wines are sold under the Corbières label. Possible production just over one million bottles, but none was declared in 1987, and only 25,000 bottles in 1988, all red.

COTEAUX DU LITTORAL AUDOIS
Red, dry white and rosé wines from vineyards on the western coastal edge of the *département*, in the same region as the AOC wines of Fitou. Mostly red (98%), deep-coloured and quite full-bodied, with a tiny

production of white from the Grenache Blanc and Maccabeo. Total production three million bottles. The yield is low for a *vins de pays* at 70 hl/ha.

COTES DE LASTOURS
Red, dry white and rosé wines from the region of Val d'Orbieu and Cabardès north of Carcassonne. One million bottles of well-made wines with a leaning to the South-West rather than Midi style. Production in 1988 was 1.5 million bottles, 86% red, 10% rosé, 4% white.

COTES DE PERIGNAN
Red, dry white and rosé wines from the same region as the VDQS wines of La Clape. The whites and reds are light and fruity, the rosés (11%) rather heady. Production two million bottles.

COTES DE PROUILLE
Red, dry white and rosé wines from vineyards planted in the west of the *département*. The Midi grape varieties still dominate, but much replanting has been done with grapes from the South-West. Production of 70,000, down from 900,000 in 1982, due to the upgrading of the quality to VDQS Côtes de Malpère.

CUCUGNAN
Red and rosé wines from the vineyards situated on the borders of the Pyrénées-Orientales *département*. Full-bodied wines almost entirely red, with a sunny Midi flavour. Production 700,000 bottles.

HAUTE VALLEE DE L'AUDE
Red, dry white and rosé wines from the west of the *département* in the Limoux region. The southern grapes are not permitted, and the reds and rosés are made soley from the Cabernet Sauvignon, Cabernet Franc, Cot and Merlot, with the addition of Cinsaut for the rosés. The whites are from the Mauzac with sometimes some Chenin Blanc, Sémillon, Chardonnay and Terret Gris. The elevation of the vineyards and the grapes planted make these wines very interesting and quite different from the full-bodied rather weighty style of wines from the Carignan and Grenache grapes. This is a fine *vin de pays*, especially for white wines, 1988 production was 8.5 million bottles, 75% white.

HAUTRIVE EN PAYS DE L'AUDE
Red, dry white and rosé wines from a large vineyard area up from the coast to the west of Narbonne. All the grapes that are admitted for the Vin de Pays de l'Aude may be planted. Large production (three million bottles, 96% red), with quality varying according to the grapes planted and the methods of vinification. The style resembles that of Corbières.

HAUTS DE BADENS
Red and rosé wines from the commune of Badens south of the Minervois. Pleasant everyday wines. Small production of 300,000 bottles which may be expanded. 98% red.

TORGAN
Red and rosé wines from the south-west corner of the *département*, to the north of the Corbières vineyards. Production three million bottles, all red.

VAL DE CESSE
Red, dry white and rosé wines from vineyards north of Narbonne on the borders of the Hérault. Large production, three million bottles, of mostly red wine of excellent colour and style. One of the better *vins de pays* in the Aude.

VAL DE DAGNE
Red, dry white and rosé wines from vineyards planted in the middle of the *départment*, south-east of Carcassonne. The whites, principally from the Clairette, are clean and fruity, the reds full-bodied and earthy, with an influence from the South-West grape varieties. Production in 1988 1.3 million bottles, with only 26,000 white and no rosé.

VAL D'ORBIEU
Red, dry white and rosé wines from vineyards situated in the east of the *département*, surrounded by Corbières and Corbières Supérieures. These are some of the best and most typical *vins de pays* in the Midi, deep-coloured, full of fruit and sun, yet well made and not too heavy. Some of the most innovative private *caves* are to be found in this area. Production is 5.5 million bottles, about 95% red and 4% rosé with only 1% white.

VALLEE DE PARADIS
Red and rosé wines from vineyards situated near the Pyrénées-Atlantiques border, just back from the Mediterranean coast. The wines, despite their enticing name, resemble a simpler, lighter style of Corbières. Production 4.5 million bottles, almost exclusively red.

The Pyrénées-Orientales

This is the hottest and driest *appellation* in France, and the wines reflect this in their full colour and big taste. Côtes du Roussillon is the best *appellation*, as good as anything from the Mediterranean coast. Despite the many improvements and changes that are to be seen throughout the Midi, it is perhaps the Roussillon that is the most exciting *appellation* of all. Tradition has been broken with, returned to and enhanced to an extent unimaginable 20 years ago. And if one needed further proof of this renaissance, one has only to look at the superb quality of the Vin Doux Naturels now being produced (see page 135).

AOC WINES

Banyuls VDN

See page 135.

Collioure

Red wine only from steeply terraced vineyards planted in the same region as Banyuls, near the Spanish border. Grenache is the dominant grape, to a minimum of 60%, with Mourvèdre, Cinsaut and a very little Carignan. Collioure, with its splendid deep velvety colour, is a rich heady wine with great personality. The lighter *cuvées* can be drunk young, still rather rough and tannic, while the more concentrated wines from low-yielding older vines can last five to ten years. Only the most dedicated growers, of which Dr Andre Parcé of the Domaine du Mas Blanc is the prime example, produced Collioure 20 years ago. Parcé's wines are low in Grenache, which he uses for his Banyuls, and high in low-yielding Mourvèdre and Syrah. The result can be compared to the Châteauneuf-du-Pape of Château de Beaucastel. Dr Parcé is the Grand Old Man of Collioure/Banyuls, and through his influence, these wines are now served in some of the best restaurants in France. Other growers include Les Clos de Pauilles, the Domaine de la Rectoire, Domaine de Villa Rose and the fine Cave Coopérative Cellier des Templiers. Production 250,000 bottles, not cheap, but interesting. Price C-D.

Left: Vineyards of the Abbaye du Marcevol, with the Pic du Canigou, landmark of the Languedoc-Roussillon, in the background.

Côtes du Roussillon

Red, dry white and rosé wines from the old French province of Roussillon spreading from Perpignan to the Pyrenees. These are the most southern vineyards in France, with vines planted both on the hillsides and on the plain. Reds and rosés must come from Carignan to a maximum of 70%, Cinsaut, Grenache, Mourvèdre and a few minor varieties. Along with the Coteaux du Languedoc, Corbières and Minervois, Côtes du Roussillon wines are slowly escaping from the reputation of being *le gros rouge qui tâche*. The reds, mostly made by *caves coopératives*, have a deep ruby colour, a soft, spicy bouquet and a firm, plummy finish. A few *cuvées* are vinified by carbonic maceration, allowing the wines to be drunk *en primeur*, but most Côtes du Roussillon is drunk at 1 to 3 years. The rosés have a striking colour and good fruit. Minimum alcohol content is 11.5°, from a yield of 50 hl/ha, but the wines are naturally full-bodied, owing to the long sunny days. The whites come principally from the Maccabeo with Grenache Blanc admitted, which makes a pale golden-colour, soft, fragrant wine with very little acidity. If the grapes are not left to get too ripe, Côtes du Roussillon blanc is attractive and refreshing and must be drunk young. Across the Midi improvements in planting and vinification have been extraordinary, and fine wines are being made. Good examples are from: Domaine André et Bernard Cazes (a solidly implanted but forward-looking domaine, whose wines are first class in all colours, including the VDNs), Domaine Sarda-Malet (equally as impressive), Château de Jau, Domaine Jaubert-Noury, Château de Corneilla, Domaine Saint-Luc, Domaine Pierre d'Aspres, Domaine de la Rourède. The *coopératives* are also aiming for quality, especially Les Vignerons de Baixas, Les Vignerons Catalans (with a lively Taichat Reserve white), and Les Vignerons de Terrassous. Production is around 25 million bottles, 90% red. Inexpensive and rewarding. Price B.

Côtes du Roussillon-Villages

Red wines only from the most favourable parts of the Roussillon region, around the valley of the river Agly. The wines must have an alcohol content of at least 12°, from a yield of 45 hl/ha, and are deeper in colour, spicy, concentrated and velvety. They age beautifully. The best wines come from the communes of Caramany and Latour-de-France, they are much sought after and travel well. The villages of Rasiguères, Lesquerde, Cassagnes and Planèz also produce fine wine. Only a little more in price than the Côtes du Roussillon, so

Above: The Pyrenees rise majestically above the autumn vineyards of Roussillon.

"Villages" on the label is well worth looking for. Many of the innovative growers – Domaine Cazes, Sarda-Malet, Château de Jau – make exellent Villages, but owing to the low price obtained, have concentrated some of their efforts to great effect on making *vins de pays* from "foreign" grape varieties. The largest range of Villages is to be found from the *caves coopératives*, notably Les Celliers Saint Jacques, Le Cellier des Capitelles, Les Vignerons Catalans and the Caves at Agly, Latour-de-France and Lesquerde. About five million bottles are produced, none of them expensive. Price B.

Maury

See page 136.

Muscat de Rivesaltes

See page 136.

Rivesaltes

See page 137.

VINS DE PAYS

Vins de Pays Départementaux

VIN DE PAYS DES PYRENEES-ORIENTALES

Red, dry white and rosé wines from vineyards throughout the *département*. Total production in 1988 was 21 million bottles, split into 92.5% red, 4.5% rosé, and 3% white. The reds and rosés are made with a high proportion of Carignan (often over 75%), Cinsaut, Grenache and a little Mourvèdre and Syrah. Grape varieties from the South-West may also be planted for the *vin de pays*, but they are less in evidence here than in the Hérault or the Aude *départements*, owing to the extreme heat. The rosés have an orange-pink colour, are quite high in alcohol and should be drunk when purchased and not kept. The reds are dark-coloured, full-bodied and sometimes rather rough. White wines are made from the Maccabeo grape with Ugni Blanc and Clairette. If the grapes are picked early, with a good acidity and not too much alcohol, the wines can be attractive and refreshing. Production is largely in the hands of the *caves coopératives*, and there have been great improvements in the quality of the wine in the last five years. Price mostly A.

Vins de Pays de Zone

The Pyrénées-Orientales possesses five Vins de Pays de Zone, which are listed below alphabetically.

CATALAN

Red, dry white and rosé wines from vineyards situated to the south and west of Perpignan, down to the Pyrenees in the centre and south-east of the *département*. The production is very large, around 15 million bottles (85% red, 10% rosé, 5% white). The *caves coopératives* are selling more in bottle and less in bulk, which is a sign that their wines are reaching an appreciative clientele.

COTEAUX DES FENOUILLEDES

Red, dry white and rosé wines from the north-west of the *département* on the borders of the Aude. Straightforward, everyday wines, almost all red (90%) and rosé. Production two million bottles.

COTES CATALANES

Red, dry white and rosé wines from especially well-sited vines including the cantons of Rivesaltes and Latour-de-France in the north-east of the *département*. The best wines are the reds, with a deep, warm colour and a satisfying full flavour. The large production in 1988 of 75 million bottles, 80% red, 8.5% rosé, 11.5% white, saw the first time that whites exceeded rosés.

COTE VERMEILLE

Red and rosé wine from the most recent of the *vins de pays*, created in 1987. It covers the region of Banyuls and Collioure. 17,000 bottles were produced in 1987, and only 8,000 in 1988.

VAL D'AGLY

Red, dry white and rosé wines from vines planted in the north of the *département*, in the region of some of the best Côtes du Roussillon vineyards, Caramany and Rasiguères, whose wines they resemble. Production two million bottles, 80% red, 10% rosé and 10% white.

Corsica

Vines were first planted in Corsica by the Greeks, and since Corsica is part of France, this makes the Corsican vineyards the oldest in the country. About 18,000 hectares of vineyards, mostly in the coastal regions, produce 30 million bottles of wine of which 80% is *vins de pays*. The quality has improved greatly in the last 20 years since the *vignerons* and *caves coopératives* have committed themselves to producing wines with clean fruit and distinctive style, rather than dull, heavy wines for blending purposes. During the same period the land under vines has been halved. It is the AOC wines that are now providing a solid future for the island's producers. The long sunny days make whites and rosés that are aromatic, quite low in acidity, and at their best young. The reds, always deep in colour, have a warm spiciness that is said to come from the *maquis*. They are enjoyable young, since although full-bodied they are not tannic, and really do improve with age. A small quantity of *vin doux naturel* is made, as good as the similar wines from mainland France.

AOC WINES

Vin de Corse

Red, dry and semi-sweet white, rosé wines and VDNs from vineyards planted in specific areas throughout the country. This is the global *appellation*, and wines from more closely defined regions may use the name of their region as an *appellation* alongside that of "Vin de Corse". The reds and rosés must be made from at least one-third (in practice more) of the specifically Corsican grape varieties: Niellucio and Sciacarello, to which may be added the Grenache, these three being planted to a minimum of 50%. Other grapes include Cinsaut, Mourvèdre, Syrah, Carignan and Vermentino (Malvoisie). White wines are made from the Vermentino and up to 25% Ugni Blanc. The minimum alcohol content for all wines is 11.5°, from a maximum yield of 50 hl/ha.

Most of these wines come from the east coast of Corsica, and have the typical spiciness and warm fruit of wines from a sunny climate. The whites and rosés are improving, being bottled earlier to keep their freshness and fruit and to give them an appealing pale colour. The reds in general have a lovely ruby colour and have much in common with the wines from the southern Rhône. They are more interesting and less "common" than their reputation in France suggests. The production of *vin doux naturel*, mainly from the Muscat and Grenache grapes, is quite limited. The only thing that is expensive here is the transport of wine off the island. Price B, low C.

Vin de Corse Calvi

Red, dry and *demi-sec* white and rosé wines from the region of Calvi in the north-west of the island. The Vermentino grape (which is also known as *la Malvoisie de Corse*) is dominant in the whites, producing a wine which is characterised by a light golden colour and soft, fruity taste. The reds are mainly from the Niellucio and Sciacarello grapes, and are deep-coloured, warm and full of fruit. The whites and rosés should be drunk as young as possible, since they lack acidity; the reds are at their best at 1 to 3 years. All the Vins de Corse Calvi are very good table wines, especially with the local cuisine. Price B-C.

Vin de Corse Coteaux d'Ajaccio

Red, dry white and rosé wines from a vast area of production on the lower west coast of Corsica. The Sciacarello dominates in the red wines, the Vermentino in the whites. Over 85% of the production is red, producing well-balanced, full-bodied wines with good fruit. Yield is limited to 45 hl/ha and, despite the very southern latitude, the elevation and siting of the vineyards prevent the wine from becoming too heavy. The whites are dry and fruity and should be drunk young. The best known domaine is Comte Péraldi, producing highly sophisticated wines. The Clos Capi-toro (Bianchetti Fréres) is almost as good, especially the white. Price B-C-D.

Vin de Corse Coteaux du Cap Corse

Red, dry and semi-sweet white, rosé wines and VDNs from the north-eastern tip of the island. Much less wine is produced now than a hundred years ago. The best-known wines are from the Muscat grape, picked late and sometimes laid out on straw mats to dry out the grapes and further concentrate the sugar (called *passerillage* in France), producing a wonderfully heady VDN known as "Rappu". The Malvoisie grape, or Vermentino, makes an aromatic, soft, dry white wine, of which Clos Nicrosi is outstanding. Very little red and rosé is made. Price B-C-D.

Vin de Corse Figari

Red, dry white and rosé wines from vines planted in a particularly wild and arid part of the country, directly north of Bonifacio. The Niellucio and Sciacarello are the dominant grapes for the reds and rosés, (but a local grape, the Carcagiolo is being introduced), and Vermentino for the whites. In general these wines are some of the better ones from Corsica, full-bodied with lots of character. Price B-C.

Vin de Corse Patrimonio

Red, dry and semi-sweet white, rosé wines and VDNs from vineyards to the west of Bastia. The chalky soil is particularly suitable for vines and Patrimonio was the first *appellation contrôlée* in Corsica, created in 1968. The reds and rosés must have at least 60% Niellucio in their *encépagement*, with a minimum alcohol content of 12.5° (the highest in Corsica) from a yield of 45 hl/ha. They are deep-coloured, solid, rich wines, with a fine bouquet and good keeping qualities, not unlike Châteauneuf-du-Pape. The rosés and whites are lighter and more elegant than most Corsican wines, and there is a little delicious dessert wine made as a VDN from the Muscat and Malvoisie. There are many good wines in Corsica, but Patrimonio consistently produces some of the best. Top growers are the Domaine Leccia (a superb white), Antoine Aréna and Dominique Gentile. Price C-D.

Vin de Corse de Porto-Vecchio

Red, dry white and rosé wines from mostly coastal vineyards at the south-eastern tip of Corsica. There has been great progress in winemaking here, with the result that the wines have the best of the regional characteristics from the indigenous grape varieties, and less of the faults of heaviness and oxidation. They are spicy and fruity and the whites are particularly good. Wines from the Domaine de Torraccia are superbly made, using mostly local and few "foreign" varieties, especially the *cuvée* "Oriu" from 80% Nielluccio, 20% Sciacarello. Price B-C-D.

Vin de Corse Sartène

Red, dry white and rosé wines from inland vineyards between Ajaccio and Bonifacio. Grape varieties are the same as for all Vins de Corse, with a high proportion of Nielluccio, Sciacarello and a closely related grape called Montanaccio, only planted in this region. Minimum alcohol content is 11°, from a yield of 45 hl/ha. The same granite-based soil as is found at Ajaccio, Figari and Porto-Vecchio gives the wines an elegance and firmness, while keeping the rich fruitiness of wines from a hot country. Well worth looking out for. Price B-C.

VINS DE PAYS

ILE DE BEAUTE
Red, white and rosé wines from vineyards planted throughout the island of Corsica. The principal grapes planted for the reds and rosés are the local Nielluccio and Sciacarello, with the Grenache, Cinsaut, Syrah, Mourvèdre and Carignan from the southern Rhône, Pinot Noir from Burgundy and the Cabernet Sauvignon, Cabernet Franc and Merlot from Bordeaux all admitted. The style varies, and while there has been a success with the Merlot and Cabernet Sauvignon, the majority of wine produced is still typically "Corsican", with soft deep colour and spicy bouquet in the reds, and quite full-bodied, aromatic rosés. White wines are basically from the Vermentino with some Ugni Blanc and recently some successful plantings of Sauvignon and Chardonnay. Production 14 million bottles, 65% red, 25% rosé, 10% white. The Cave Coopérative d'Alèria and the UVAL are very reliable. Price A.

Above: The Corsican vineyards are the oldest in France.
Most of them are in the coastal regions but these are planted
high in the mountains.

Fortified Wines

VINS DOUX NATURELS

Vins doux naturels are naturally sweet, fortified wines, not to be confused with *vins liquoreux*, which are wines naturally sweet from the over-maturity or botrytized condition (*pourriture noble*) of the grapes when harvested. A *vin doux naturel* (VDN) is the result of the fermentation being stopped early by the addition of alcohol before the must has fermented out all the sugar. This alcohol is a neutral grape brandy of at least 90° and is added to the must when it contains about 7° of natural alcohol and the same amount of potential alcohol. (A wine destined to become a VDN must have at least 250 grams per litre of grape sugar, giving a potential alcohol content of 14°.) This operation is called *mutage*. Depending on the stage at which the alcohol is added, and the amount (not less than 6% or more than 10%), the resulting VDN will have a total richness in alcohol plus residual sugar of between 18% and 23% by volume. The usual level is 21.5%, shown on the label as 21.5°. The finest VDNs, and indeed the vast majority, come from Languedoc-Roussillon. The principal grapes are the Grenache and the Muscat, with a little Malvoisie and Maccabeo. VDNs may be white (the Muscats), rosé and red, and the alcohol should give no sense of burning or roughness. Since the residual sugar − 100−125 grams per litre for the Muscats − will provide the balance, Muscat VDNs may be sold 2−3 months after the vintage, but Grenache based wines may not be released until September 1st the following year, and the VDNs from Maury not until the year after that. Further ageing of these wines, either in barrel or in demi-johns outside in the sun, will result in a "maderized" flavour known as Rancio. The best are at their peak at 10−15 years, and a great Banyuls may be much older. To the English palate, an aged VDN very much resembles a fine tawny port.

Banyuls

Red and tawny VDNs from the communes of Banyuls, Cerbère, Port-Vendre and Collioure in the Pyrénées-Orientales *département*. The Grenache Noir must represent at least 50%, accompanied by the Grenache Gris and Blanc, Maccabeo, Malvoisie and Muscat. The yield is a maximum of 30 hl/ha, rarely attained from these terraced hill vineyards, with a schistous soil that is very difficult to work. Banyuls must have a minimum of 21.5° alcohol plus sugar, with a maximum of 7% unfermented sugar. If the *mutage* is left until the wine is

Above: Banyuls ageing outside in the sun, in the yard of a maker above the ancient town of Collioure.

almost fermented out, the taste will be dry. These wines, becoming popular, must have less than 54 grams per litre of residual sugar, the classic Banyuls having twice this. A good Banyuls should retain the rich, grapey flavour of the Grenache with a concentrated raisiny-dried fruit taste and a sweet but not cloying finish, the natural product of a very sunny climate. Banyuls may be bottled young and carry a vintage date if it is from a single year or matured for several years in cask. A Banyuls Grand Cru must be made with a minimum of 75% Grenache to have the *appellation*, be aged in wood for at least 30 months after the vintage, and must be submitted to two official tasting panels. Banyuls Rancio has been aged in wood, with the barrels taken out into the sun during the summer to give the wine the concentrated, slightly burnt Rancio flavour. These wines lose colour in wood, and will become progressively less red, then tawny. Once in bottle, they may keep, but do not improve. In the last few years some quality growers have been making single vintage Banyuls, known as "Rimage" (Catalan for vintage), bottling them after 18 months in wood. Although the very finest Banyuls come from individual properties such as Les Mas Blanc of Dr Parcé, the Coopératives Le Cellier des Templiers and especially La Cave de l'Etoile have maintained very high standards and can still provide old vintages at reasonable prices. About six million bottles are produced, only 20% of the best quality, and for these the price is not excessive. Price C-D-E (for older vintages).

Maury

Red and rosé VDNs from 2,000 hectares north of Agly in the Pyrénées-Orientales planted soley in Grenache Noir. The schistous soil gives the wines a lightness that makes them easy to drink young, while with ageing Maury takes on the typical burnt, tangy flavour known as Rancio. The Caves des Vignerons de Maury produces most of the five million bottles a year, making several styles according to their age in cask and bottle, while the best producer is Le Mas Amiel, whose young Vintage wines and aged Tawnies can rival a fine Banyuls. The VDNs from the *appellation* Côtes d'Agly are similar if less interesting. Inexpensive. Price C-D.

Muscat de Beaumes-de-Venise

The *vin doux naturel* from Beaumes-de-Venise is made only from the Muscat à Petits Grains, known as the Muscat de Frontignan. Before fermentation the grapes must have a potential of 15° alcohol and, after the addition of pure alcohol to the must (*mutage*), a total not exceeding 21.5°. A Muscat from Beaumes-de-Venise has a lovely, sunny pale-golden colour, an extraordinarily heady perfume of fresh Muscat grapes with overtones of ripe peaches or apricots and a rich, floral finish. It should be drunk very cold, as an apéritif or with desserts as it is too aromatic to go with food. Production is almost one million bottles, mostly from the Caves des Vignerons de Beaumes-de-Venise, from whom the négociants Jaboulet Aîné, Vidal-Fleury and Les Frères Perrin buy their excellent *cuvées*. The best growers are Domaine de Durban, whose wine ages well, and Domaine de Coyeux. Like all Muscats, it is normally drunk young. Beaumes-de-Venise is the most fashionable and most expensive of the Muscat VDNs. Price D.

Muscat de Frontignan

A white VDN from the local Muscat de Frontignan grape known elsewhere as the Muscat à Petits Grains, planted on exposed, arid, stony vineyards running right down to the Mediterranean a few kilometres east of Sète in the Hérault. This is the best known of the VDN Muscats and is even richer than the equally fine Muscat de Beaumes-de-Venise. The grapes are late-harvested for the highest possible concentration of sugar and flavour, and the *mutage* only enhances the explosive Muscat fruit, to leave a wine that is golden in colour, rich, unctuous, with concentrated floral aromas and sweet, honeyed taste. Despite its richness, Muscat de Frontignan has great finesse, and is also supposed to have great restorative qualities. Most of the wine is made at the *cave coopérative* and is sold in a special bottle with carved fluting up the sides. Production is around two million bottles. Not expensive. Price high B-C.

Muscat de Lunel

White VDN from the same grape as the Muscat de Frontignan planted on stony soil with a reddish clay base. Although equally high in residual sugar (125 grams per litre), Muscat de Lunel seems less assertive than its better known neighbour. Very good wines come from the only three growers – Clos Bellevue, Château du Grès Saint-Paul and Domaine La Côte du Mazet – and quite correct ones form the *coopérative* at Verargues. Price C.

Muscat de Mireval

White VDN made from the Muscat de Frontignan grape grown between Séte and Montpellier. It is similar in style to the Frontignan, having a fine golden colour and a rich, honeyed, floral aroma and taste. The best wines come from Domaine de la Capelle and good ones from Domaine du Moulinas and Mas des Pigeonniers. Price C.

Muscat de Saint-Jean-de-Minervois

White VDN from the Muscat de Frontignan grape, planted on slopes 200 metres above sea level. The vintage here is 2–3 weeks later than for the other Midi Muscats, delivering wines that are less broadly sweet, with a finer concentration than most. Small production of high quality from Domaine de Barroubio and the Cave de Saint-Jean-de-Minervois. More expensive than Frontignan. Price high C.

Muscat de Rivesaltes

White VDN from the Muscat à Petits Grains (de Frontignan) planted in the Rivesaltes *appellation*. These wines have all the qualities of the other Muscats from the Midi, with the advantages of both new and established growers determined to make the best of their Roussillon vineyards. These include Domaines Sarda-Malet, Cazes, Boudau, Mas Canclaux, Château de Jau as well as Les Vignerons de Baixas. Such wines easily rival the Muscats de Beaumes-de-Venise and are considerably less expensive. Price C.

Rasteau

Rasteau VDN is fortified wine made from the Grenache alone. Only the ripest grapes are used, as they have the maximum degree of natural alcohol. Fermentation is stopped after 3 or 4 days by the addition of pure alcohol, distilled from wine, bringing the total to 21.5° while retaining the sweetness of the unfermented must. Rasteau VDN may either be "white" (a deep gold) or "red" (more tawny), colouration being caused by leaving the skins to ferment with the must for a few days. If it is aged in cask for several years, it takes on a flavour known as Rancio. One of the finest VDNs in France, and very rare. Perfect as an apéritif, a digestif, or poured into a melon. Price C-D.

Rivesaltes

Red and rosé VDNs from 20,000 hectares mainly in the Roussillon but a small part in Corbières. The grapes, Grenache Noir, Maccabeo and Malvoisie, are planted on well-exposed slopes to ensure complete maturation. If the VDN is made entirely from the Muscat grape, it will take the *appellation* Muscat de Rivesaltes (see above). Those made from a minimum of 50% Grenache will have a red-amber colour when young, fading to tawny. The young wines have an explosion of concentrated fruit with all the warmth of the Midi and the richness of the added alcohol. As they age in barrel, they become progressively more complex and take on the burnt, tangy flavour known as Rancio. There are many fine VDNs made, the less good in quality being able to benefit from the *appellation* Grand Roussillon VDN. Domaine Cazes Frères, Domaine Garria and Domaine Sarda-Malet are exceptional, and the Coopérative des Vignerons Catalans very reliable. Production five million bottles. Not expensive, except the older wines. Price C-D-E for older vintages.

VINS DE LIQUEUR

The difference between *vins doux naturels* and *vins de liqueur* is that the VDNs are fortified or "*muté*" with a neutral grape brandy and the VDLs are fortified with the spirit from their own region: cognac in the case of Pineau des Charentes, fine de champagne in the case of Ratafia, and armagnac in the case of Floc de Gascogne. Despite this difference, they would all be under the same *appellation*, except that cognac, fine de champagne and armagnac carry a much higher tax than distilled wine. This is why Pineau, Ratafia and Floc are more expensive than the average VDN. Price D.

Floc de Gascogne

White VDL made in the Armagnac region, from grapes allowed for armagnac production – Ugni Blanc, Colombard, Bacco – *muté* with the local spirit. Although Floc de Gascogne has been produced for many years, it only received the *appellation* in 1989.

Pineau des Charentes

Pineau des Charentes may be made from grapes grown anywhere in the Cognac region, with the proviso that the yield must be less than 50 hl/ha, much less than for cognac, with natural alcoholic degree of 10°. Pineau can be white, from the Ugni Blanc, Colombard or Sémillon grapes, or rosé, from Cabernet Franc, Cabernet Sauvignon or Merlot. The *mutage*, with cognac aged in wood, brings the total degree up to between 17° and 22°, following which the Pineau must be aged in wood for a minimum of one year. Once bottled, Pineau does not improve significantly, so it is kept in wood and bottled according to the style desired. A young Pineau des Charentes will be between 2 and 5 years old, a "vieux Pineau", the equivalent of the VDN Rancios, will be between 10 and 20. Pineau des Charentes has a more fruity – strawberries, melon – flavour than a VDN, but less concentration from the sun. It is ideal as an apéritif, served cold, or with desserts. Most cognac producers make a Pineau, and a few growers specialize in it, notably Philippe Rivière with a superb Pineau François 1er, Château de Beaulon, Domaine de Caillères, Jean-Philippe Tesseron and Domaine Cartis-Lamaure. Production 12 million bottles, 65% white.

Ratafia de Champagne

Ratafia is made in the same way as the Pineau des Charentes or a VDN, except that the fermenting must is fortified with a brandy made from champagne. Most champagne houses produce a Ratafia, but very little is exported. It is similar to the Pineau, but less sweet and appears to be stronger despite the same degree of alcohol.

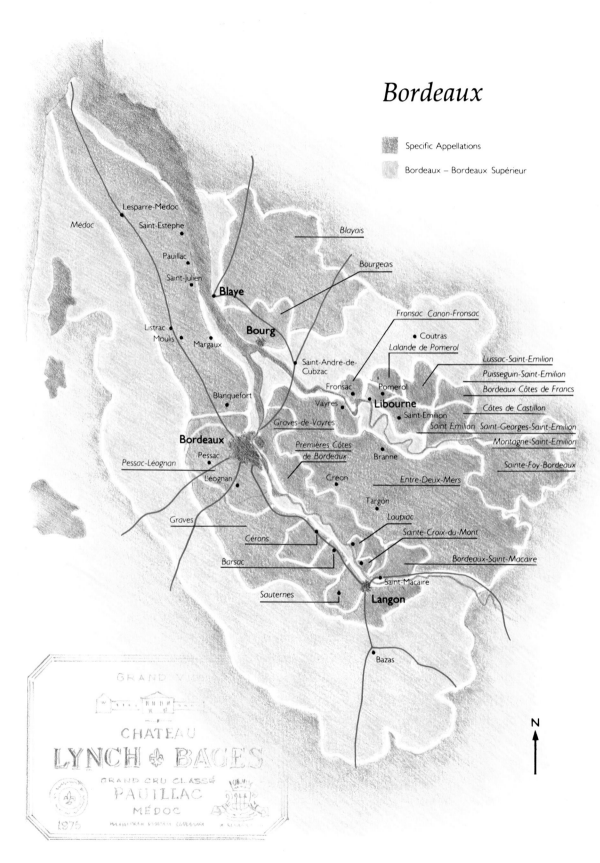

Bordeaux

Specific Appellations

Bordeaux – Bordeaux Supérieur

Médoc

Lesparre-Médoc

Saint-Estephe

Pauillac

Saint-Julien

Listrac

Moulis

Margaux

Blanquefort

Blayais

Bourgeais

Blaye

Bourg

Saint-André-de-Cubzac

Fronsac Canon-Fronsac

Coutras

Lalande de Pomerol

Fronsac

Pomerol

Vayres

Libourne

Saint-Emilion

Lussac-Saint-Emilion

Puisseguin-Saint-Emilion

Bordeaux Côtes de Francs

Côtes de Castillon

Saint Emilion Saint-Georges-Saint-Emilion

Montagne-Saint-Emilion

Sainte-Foy-Bordeaux

Graves-de-Vayres

Branne

Bordeaux

Pessac

Pessac-Léognan

Premières Côtes de Bordeaux

Creon

Entre-Deux-Mers

Léognan

Targon

Graves

Loupiac

Cérons

Sainte-Croix-du-Mont

Barsac

Bordeaux-Saint-Macaire

Saint-Macaire

Sauternes

Langon

Bazas

N

Bordeaux

The region of Bordeaux is enclosed in the *département* of the Gironde. With over 100,000 hectares under vines, producing around 600 million bottles of wine a year, all of it AOC, Bordeaux is the largest vineyard of fine wines in the world. Historically, Bordeaux has known three periods of expansion: under the Roman occupation, when vines were first planted; in the Middle Ages, when the south-west of France passed to the English crown and a thriving export business developed with the British Isles; and the period of French investment by aristocrats in the late eighteenth century and by bankers and entrepreneurs in the nineteenth century.

The Bordeaux region is vast, and its range of wines is as great among the lesser-known *appellations* as among the Crus Classés. The diversity in character and style is due to the variations in soils and climate. The wines can be divided into four categories: red wines from the left bank of the Garonne and the Gironde estuary, embracing the Médoc and the Graves; red wines from the right bank of the Gironde and the Dordogne, embracing Saint-Emilion, Pomerol, Fronsac, Côtes de Castillon, Côtes de Francs, Bourg and Blaye; red and white wines from the "Entre-Deux-Mers" region between the Garonne and Dordogne; and the great white wines from Graves and Sauternes.

Bordeaux wines can be sold as "generics" but are now usually seen with the name of the property or château more prominently displayed than that of the *appellation*. It is the *appellation* that tells you basically where the wine is from and what it should be like, while the château, domaine or négociant represents an individual interpretation of the *appellation*.

The finest wines of Bordeaux come, with few exceptions, from individual estates within the more prestigious *appellations*. These are assessed in the following pages. It will become plain that the vast majority of these are classified growths, either Grand Cru Classé, Cru Classé or Grand Cru. In Bordeaux the system of classification is not inherently geographical as it is in Burgundy where, for example, a Premier Cru in Volnay retains its classification no matter who owns it, or even if no vines are planted. In Bordeaux it is the château that is classified within the communal *appellation*, and although control is very strict, purchases or exchanges of land may take place (within the same *appellation*) between 2èmes Crus Classés, 5èmes Crus Classés and even Crus Bourgeois, with no change in the classification of the château. To balance this picture, the quality of wine produced by individual properties over even a short period of time is directly reflected in the price their wines will fetch.

This section looks first at the sub-regions that contain the classified growths, then at the regional or generic *appellations*. The wines of Bordeaux can be red, white and rosé and may be made from a single grape variety, but is more usual that two or more varieties are used. For the major châteaux the percentage of different grapes AS PLANTED is given, but it must be stressed that each vintage produces a quantity of grapes different from those percentages, and that each château may blend the resulting wine how they wish. The different grape varieties planted are given in abbreviated form as follows: red: Cabernet Sauvignon (CS), Cabernet Franc (CF), Merlot (Me), Malbec (Ma), Petit Verdot (PV); white: Sémillon (Se), Sauvignon (Sa), Muscadelle (Mu). For a brief description of these grape varieties, see pages 236–243.

The Médoc

The region known as the Médoc comprises virtually the whole of the left bank of the Gironde estuary, an area 80km long and 10km wide, running from Blanquefort, just north of Bordeaux, to Soulac at the tip of the estuary. Only red wines may carry the *appellation*, the very few whites and even fewer rosés produced are sold as Bordeaux or Bordeaux Supérieur. The grapes planted on a predominantly gravelly soil are the classic Bordeaux varieties: Cabernet Sauvignon (usually dominant, covering 52% of the *appellation*), Cabernet Franc (10%), Merlot (34%) and small amounts of Petit Verdot and, very rarely, Malbec. A Médoc should have a fine ruby colour, often a plummy, sometimes slightly briary fruit bouquet, with overtones of oak and spice and a concentrated fruit on the palate, frequently austere when young, but with good balance and a clean refreshing finish, making it the perfect wine for food. The region is divided into the *appellations*: Médoc (10° minimum alcohol from 50hl/ha), Haut-Médoc (10°, 48hl/ha), and the superior communal *appellations*: Margaux, Moulis, Listrac, Saint-Julien, Pauillac, Saint-Estèphe (10.5°, 45hl/ha). Within these *appellations*, the majority of the finer châteaux have been awarded Cru Classé or Cru Bourgeois status.

THE 1855 CLASSIFICATION

The famous 1855 classification was conceived for the 1855 Exposition Universelle in Paris and prepared by the *courtiers*, or wine-brokers, of Bordeaux, based on the quality and price of the major châteaux of the Médoc and Sauternes at that time. Since the idea of a "Château X" is basically that of a recognized *marque commerciale* or brand name, and the only official control of quality on the wine are the controls imposed by its *appellation* (unknown in 1855), this selection only classified the names of the châteaux and not, in any sense, a precise *terroir*. The many changes in ownership of these châteaux before and since 1855 and in the quality, desirability and price of these wines, have tended to bring into question the validity of the classification. The fact that a château may purchase (or sell) vines in its own *appellation* does not affect its status, and neither does the actual condition of the vineyard, *encépagement*, age of vines, or quality of winemaking, which means that the real relative quality of these brand names must constantly be under review. The INAO (Institut National des Appellations d'Origine) attempted a reclassification in 1960, which met

with strong opposition. The late Alexis Lichine also proposed a very well-researched classification, to include the Graves, Pomerol and Saint-Emilion. Meanwhile, today as in 1855, real quality tends to be reflected in the price. As the majority of Cru Classés sell through a chain of buyers – broker-négociant, importer, wholesaler – before ending up on a retail shelf or on a wine list of a restaurant, these prices "ex-Château" are further exaggerated.

The Crus Classés represent approximately 25% of the land under vines in the Médoc, 20% of the production and more than 40% of the value of wines sold. In the text the châteaux are listed in the order of the 1855 classification.

THE CRUS BOURGEOIS

The Crus Bourgeois were first officially classified in 1932, reclassified in 1966 and again in 1978, when they totalled 127. Today there are 235 châteaux entitled to put Cru Bourgeois on their labels, representing, in terms of each *appellation*: Médoc 50%, Haut-Médoc 70%, Listrac 70%, Moulis 80%, Margaux 25%, Saint-Julien 15%, Pauillac 10%, Saint-Estèphe 50%. The Syndicat des Crus Bourgeois has subdivided the châteaux into three categories: Grand Bourgeois Exceptionnel (only Haut-Médoc, château-bottling obligatory); Grand Bourgeois (barrel ageing obligatory); Bourgeois (minimum 7 hectares of vines, vinified separately, subjected to tasting). In many cases the best of the Crus Bourgeois are as good as, sometimes better than a number of Crus Classés, and sell for comparable prices. These are given prominence in the discussion under individual communes, by stating the breakdown of grapes planted for each of the Châteaux. While some of the finest *non-classé* wines do not belong to the Syndicat – Siran, d'Angludet, Lanessan, de Pez among them – its role in encouraging and promoting quality in the Médoc is undeniable.

Below the Crus Bourgeois in terms of classification come the Crus Artisans and the hardly used Crus Paysans. These are châteaux with less than 7 hectares, and in 1989, 236 of these were grouped under the Syndicat des Crus Artisans. Such wines, although a few have the quality of the Crus Bourgeois, were sold previously to the négociants under their communal *appellation* of Médoc, Saint-Julien, Pauillac, etc, depending where the vines were sited. Now they are often referred to as "Petits Châteaux".

MEDOC

Red wines only from the 3,500 hectares covering the northern part of the vineyards on the left bank of the Gironde, from north-west of Saint-Estèphe to Soulac. Permitted yield is 45hl/ha. While all the wine should share the characteristics of the *appellation* — fine ruby colour, firmness of fruit on bouquet and palate and a harmonious finish — some of the many hundred châteaux are making wine that better expresses the possibilities of soil and climate than others. In general, these have been recognized and are classified Crus Bourgeois (*qv*). Since the element of *terroir* is primordial in Bordeaux, as in all fine-wine regions, some of the more successful wines are listed below, with the names of their communes, from south to north. The high (usually over 50%) proportion of Cabernet Sauvignon in the wines of the Médoc brings tannins which, although rounder in recent years due to riper grapes from warmer vintages and a more supple vinification, need 2–3 years to soften up. A well-made Médoc may be drunk from this point, although most will continue to improve.

THE CRUS BOURGEOIS OF THE MEDOC

The most southern commune of the Médoc is Saint-Germain d'Esteuil, where **Châteaux Haute-Rive**, **du Castéra** and **Livran** produce well-made wines. To the north and inland, Ordonnac is dominated by the excellent wine from **Château Potensac** (CS 55%, Me 25%, CF 20%), which, with its other labels, Château Gallais-Bellevue, Château Goudy-la-Cardonne and Cru Lassalle, are owned by Michel Delon and made with the same care as his Léoville-Las Cases. Potensac is regularly the finest wine of the Bas-Médoc. Due north at Blaignan, **Château La Cardonne** produces a large

amount of eminently drinkable Médoc, **Château Blaignan** is almost as large but less fine, while **Château La Tour-Haut-Caussac** has more depth and *terroir* in the more complex Haut-Médoc style. Nearer the estuary at Saint-Yzans, the splendid vineyards of **Château Loudenne** run down almost to the Gironde, producing a supple, beautifully balanced red wine with a marked element of new oak and a fine, crisp, dry white (Sa 50%, Se 50%); also at Saint-Yzans, **Château Sigognac** is as delicate as Loudenne is stylish, but ages well. North-west at Couquèques is the soft, attractive **Château Haut-Canteloup** and the very impressive **Château Les-Ormes-Sorbets** (CS 65%, Me 35%), a wine with intensity of fruit, character and ageing potential. The most important commune in the *appellation* is Bégadan, with **Château La Tour De By** (CS 65%, Me 32%, CF 2%) (second label La Roque de By) making consistently fine wine, deep-coloured, aromatic, with great depth of fruit, pure Médoc, somewhat in the Pauillac style; **Château Patache d'Aux** (CS 70%, Me 20%, CF 10%) is equally well regarded. **Château Greyssac**, elegant, and plummy, has improved steadily in the 1980s, as has **Château Laujac**, while solidly fruity but fine wine comes from **Châteaux La Clare**, **du Monthil** and **Vieux-Ch.-Landon**. A little more inland, **Château Bournac** at Civrac is becoming known for its deep-coloured wines, packed with fruit and Médoc character, and at Saint-Christoly, **Châteaux Saint-Bonnet**, **La Tour Saint-Bonnet**, **Le Bosq**, **Lavallière** and **La Tour Blanche** are well made, but lack the intensity and assurance of the better wines from Bégadan. At Queyrac, **Château Carcannieux** is lightish, stylish and smooth, while at Valeyrac, **Château Bellerive** produces meaty, concentrated Saint-Estèphe and **Château Bellevue** smoother, more aromatic, quicker-maturing wine. In the very north of the *appellation*, still largely unplanted, **Château Sestignan** looks like becoming a classic Médoc.

HAUT-MEDOC

Red wine only from the 3,350 hectares of vines covering the southern part of the Médoc, between Blanquefort in the south and Saint-Seurin-de-Cadourne a little north of Saint-Estèphe. Permitted yield is 43hl/ha, two hectares lower than in the Médoc. The communal *appellations* (pages 145–158) benefit from a

soil of light gravel that historically has produced the finest wines, including all but 5 of the 61 Crus Classés. Of the 15 communes that make up the Haut-Médoc *appellation*, those with the highest incidence of gravel in the soil (logically those nearer the Gironde river) — Blanquefort, Parempuyre, Ludon, Macau, Arcins,

Lamarque, Cussac and Saint-Seurin-de-Cadourne — tend to produce wines that have an edge of finesse over the more solid wines from the inland communes — Le Taillan, Le-Pian-de-Médoc, Avenson, Saint-Laurent-du-Médoc, Saint-Saveur, Cissac and Vertheuil.

THE CRUS CLASSES OF THE HAUT-MEDOC

Châteaux La Lagune

3ème GCC (55ha; CS 60%, CF 15%, Me 20%, PV 5%)
The nearest Médoc Cru Classé to Bordeaux, the vineyards of La Lagune are planted in the light, sandy gravel of the commune of Ludon. In 1958, when it was bought and reconstituted by Georges Brunet there were only 4 hectares under vines. In the early 1960s the wine was very supple and rich, misleadingly Burgundian in style, but with the vineyard maturing, it has taken on a deeper colour and firmer structure, while keeping its particular velvety smoothness. All new oak is used for every vintage. La Lagune is particularly appealing in light years and in great vintages (1978, 1982, 1986, 1988) should be kept 12–15 years. The property is now owned by the champagne house Ayala. The second label is Ludon-Pomiès-Agassac. Production 25,000 cases. Price G + .

Châteaux La Tour Carnet

4ème GCC (32 ha; CS 53%, CF 10%, Me 33%, PV 4%)
The vineyards, in the commune of Saint-Laurent, due west of Saint-Julien, were almost entirely replanted in 1962 by the current owners, and until 1975 the wine, although charming, was not up to Cru Classé standard. The clayey-sandy soil imparts body and robustness which is now underlined by the greater age of the vines, and the wine has good colour, structure and pure Médoc style. A further 13 hectares are to be planted. La Tour Carnet is relatively quick-maturing, needing 6–8 years in good vintages. Quality is improving, but the price still places it amongst the top Crus Bourgeois rather than the Crus Classés. The second label is "Le Sire de Camin". Production 16,000 cases. Price F.

Château Cantemerle

5ème GCC (53ha; CS 45%, CF 10%, Me 40%, PV 5%)
The second most southerly Cru Classé in the Médoc, north-west of La Lagune, Cantemerle was sold in 1981

Château Margaux

to Cordier and, judging by the 1983 and subsequent vintages, the wine has regained its position as the equivalent of a 3ème Cru. The light, sandy soil and high proportion of Merlot give Cantemerle a rich charming fruit that is intensified and stiffened by the Cabernets and by two years in barrel. Cordier has doubled the land under vines, bringing it back to its original size. In good vintages, Cantemerle should be kept 10–15 years. The second label is Villeneuve de Cantemerle. Production 30,000 cases. Price G +.

Château Belgrave

5ème GCC (55ha; CS 40%, CF 20%, Me 35%, PV 5%)
The vines of Belgrave are in a single block to the west of Saint-Julien, the same commune as La Tour Carnet and Camensac. The estate changed hands in 1979, and intensive investment in the vineyards, especially in drainage, and in the *cuvier* and *chai*, had an immediate result in attractive fruity wines, robust and deep coloured in good vintages. Belgrave is made to be drunk at 6–8 years and is not yet really of Cru Classé quality. Production 20,000 cases. Price F.

Château de Camensac

5ème GCC (60ha; CS 60%, CF 20%, Me 20%)
One of the four Crus Classés in Saint-Laurent, west of Saint-Julien, Camensac was largely replanted in 1965 and has been making deep-coloured, well-structured wines since the mid-1970s. It lacks the elegance and style of the better Crus nearer the Gironde, but is very reliable. At its best at 8–10 years. Production 20,000 cases. Price E.

THE CRUS BOURGEOIS OF THE HAUT-MEDOC

Whereas in the four superior communes of Margaux, Saint-Julien, Pauillac and Saint-Estèphe, the Crus Bourgeois tend to be overwhelmed by the importance of the Crus Classés, the châteaux in the Haut-Médoc provide an extraordinary concentration of high-quality wines of great individuality. While only obsessive care in the vineyards and in the *chais* will regularly produce a fine wine, the *terroir* still gives the wine its basic character. The discussion here is of the better Crus Bourgeois, from the south of the *appellation* to the north. The nearest property to Bordeaux is **Château de Taillan**, owned by the Cruse family, producing a light, supple red wine and a dry white, called **Château La**

Left: The bars of Bordeaux, as elsewhere in France, offer a good selection of locally produced wines.

143

Dame Blanche. At Blanquefort, **Château Dillon**, grown on a sandy soil, is an elegant, attractive, medium-weight wine, while due north at Parempuyre, **Château Ségur** is in the same style but with more depth. Le Pian, inland, bears **Château Sénéjac**, back on form thanks to financial reinvestment and a brilliant young *maîtresse de chai* from New Zealand, and is making fine, intensely fruity, classic wines, as well as a little white, and **Château de Malleret**, regularly firm and elegant. Nearer to the river at Ludon, **Château Ludon-Pomiés-Agassac** is owned by and usually contains the *déclassements* of Château La Lagune, **Château d'Agassac** (CS 60%, Me 40%), a moated, fairy-tale château, produces extremely elegant wine of Margaux quality and style, while those of **Château d'Arche** are almost as fine. **Château Maucamps** and **Château Biré** at Macau (better known for Château Cantemerle) are aromatic and stylish. Just south-east of Moulis, the clayey undersoil at **Château Citran** (Avensan) adds a finesse and subtlety to a rather firm wine, while **Château Villegorge**, with vines in Moulis and Soussans (Margaux) and a high percentage of Merlot, is altogether richer and smoother. The *appellation* Margaux separates Avensan from Arcins, where the newly rebuilt **Château d'Arcins**, and also **Château Barrèyres**, produce a vast amount of correct wine, but are outclassed by the depth and breed of **Château Arnauld**, under the same ownership as Poujeaux-Theil. Further north, at Lamarque, **Château Lamarque** (CS 50%, Me 25%, CF 20%, PV 5%) is serious and satisfying, pure Haut-Médoc with good colour and fruit, and **Château Malescasse** is stylish but more reserved. The commune of Cussac is at the southern edge of Saint-Julien – and produces very similar wines: **Château Lanessan** (CS 75%, Me 20%, CF and PV 5%), owned by the Bouteillier family late owners of Pichon-Baron, has a striking bouquet and great depth and firmness of flavour that is regularly of Cru Classé standard. It is said that Lanessan was excluded from the 1855 classification only because the owner was too confident to submit a sample. **Château de Raux** is fine, meaty, but less classic. **Château Beaumont** (CS 56%, Me 36%, CF 7%, PV 1%), now under the same ownership as Château Beychevelle, is making elegant wine, deep-coloured, full of fruit, classic but quicker to mature; **Châteaux Arney**, **Fort Vauban**, and **Moulin Rouge** are interesting, but do not have the quality of Lanessan and Beaumont, while **Château La-Tour-du-Haut-Moulin** (CS and CF 70%, Me 25%, PV 5%), Beaumont's neighbour, is completely different with great colour and extract. West of Saint-Julien at Saint-Laurent, the largest estate in the Médoc, **Château Larose-Trintaudon** (CS 60%, CF 20%, Me 20%), produces 80,000 cases of smooth, well-made wines with fruit and character, while those of **Château Caronne-Sainte-Gemme** are more traditional, meaty and tannic. At Saint-Saveur, inland from Pauillac, **Château Peyrabon** (also sold as **Château Pierbone**) is known for rounded, elegant wines, aiming at the Lafite style; **Châteaux Ramage-la-Batisse** and **Touteran** have a rich, supple fruit and may be drunk young, **Château Hourtin-Ducasse** is fine and elegant, while **Château Liversan** (CS 49%, Me 38%, CF 10%, PV 3%), recently purchased by the de Polignac family, is more of a grand-style Médoc. Slightly north at Cissac, **Château Cissac** makes a deep-coloured, fruity wine of excellent quality in the Pauillac style, **Château Han-teillan** is elegant and softer, more typically Saint-Julien, and **Château du Breuil**, less fine than these, has the firmness and austerity of a Saint-Estèphe. **Châteaux Le Bourdieu, Meynieu** and **Reysson** at Vertheuil, on the south-west borders of Saint-Estèphe, are all correct and well made. The most northern commune of the Haut-Médoc, Saint-Seurin de Cadourne, has the fine gravelly soil of the best parts of the *appellation*. The wine is uniformly deep-coloured, vigorous and long-lived. **Château Sociando-Mallet** (CS 60%, Me 30%, CF 10%) stands out as the "Latour" of the commune, with dark, intense wines from a high percentage of Cabernet Sauvignon, and sells a fine second wine, **Château Lartigue de Brochon**; opposite in style is **Château Coufran**, planted in Merlot, rounder and quicker to mature; **Château Bel-Orme-Tronquoy-de-Lalande** is firm and fruity, but slightly austere, as is **Château Verdignan**; **Château Lestage-Simon** has a richer concentration of fruit and **Châteaux Bonneau, Charmail, Grand-Moulin** and the *coopérative* **La Paroisse** are firm and reliable. Price D – the better wines justifiably E.

LISTRAC

Red wine only from vineyards covering 620 hectares to the north-west of Margaux. The gravelly soil has a limestone-chalk base which, while it cannot produce wines as fine as the purer gravel soils near the Gironde estuary, encourages a deep colour and a muscular firmness that can be immeasurably improved by good vinification. Listrac lacks the suave fruit of its neighbour Moulis, but possesses a "grip" that can be compared to Saint-Estèphe or Canon-Fronsac. The wines are typically Médoc, with a rather hard fruit and lack of amiability at first, but becoming extremely satisfying if allowed to age for 7–8 years. Until the late 1970s, the finest wines in the *appellation* were without doubt the two Fourcas, **Châteaux Fourcas-Dupré** (40ha; CS 50%, Me 38%, CF 10%, PV 2%) and **Fourcas-Hosten** (46ha; CS 55%, Me 40%, CF 5%). The former, with a small proportion of its vines in Moulis, regularly achieves the colour, depth of fruit and complexity of the Crus Classés, and has had a series of excellent vintages; while the Crus Classés are progressively bringing out second labels, Fourcas-Dupré has brought out a *tête-de-cuvée* beginning with the 1975 vintage. The latter, with a high percentage of Merlot and impeccable vinification, makes a wine that is less vigorous but more polished, especially for a Listrac. The newcomer, determined to produce wine equal to the best in the Médoc, is **Château Clarke-Rothschild**

(121ha; CS 49%, Me 37%, CF 10%, PV 4%), whose first vintage was 1978. Immense investments and the advice of Professeur Peynaud resulted in a very fine deep-coloured 1982 and very good wines since, from vines now over ten years old. Rare for a Cru Bourgeois, Clarke has two second labels, Les Granges de Clarke and Château Malmaison, and also makes a rosé. Adjoining the two Fourcas vineyards is **Château Saransot-Dupré** (CS 50%, Me 50%) whose red is polished and elegant and whose very stylish white (Se 50%, Sa 25%, Mu 25%) is one of the best in the increasing number of "Médoc" whites. **Châteaux Fonréaud** and **Lestage**, under the same ownership, are very large properties on the Moulis side of the *appellation* producing fruity, well-structured wines with a certain smoothness. **Château La Bécade** and the co-owned adjoining **Château Lafon** have good colour and relatively rounded fruit, while **Châteaux Pierre Bibian, Gobinaud** and **Moulin de Laborde** are in the more old-fashioned, tough style. The Borie family owns **Château Ducluzeau**, lightish and elegant; attractive, well-made wines come from **Châteaux Peyredon-la-Gravotte** and **Cap de Léon Veyrin**. Total production in Listrac is now over 3.5 million bottles. Price D-E.

Below: Old Bordeaux vines in early spring.

MOULIS

Red wines only from 480 hectares of vines inland from the Gironde, on a highish plateau north-west of Margaux. The gravelly soil is heavier than in the vineyards nearer the river, but an underlying current of chalk gives the wines the smoothness and roundness that are characteristic of the *appellation*. In style, the best have good fruit, body and finesse and are mid-way between Margaux and Saint-Julien, the less good are rather rustic and lean. Depending on vinification and ageing (the more prestigious châteaux treat their wines in the same way as the Crus Classés), Moulis can be drunk at 3–4 years and will last 12–15. The Crus Exceptionnels and the better Crus Bourgeois are the most long-lived and attain the price of the minor 5èmes Crus. The finest wines come from the more gravelly soil around the village of Grand Poujeaux from which four are outstanding: **Château Chasse-Spleen** (62ha; CS 50%, Me 45%, CF 2%, PV 3%) is certainly of Cru Classé standard, with a very deep colour and great depth, style and complexity with a judicious use of new oak; **Château Poujeaux-Theil** (50ha; CS 35%, Me 35%, CF 15%, PV 15%) is even darker and more powerful with a suave plumminess and slight austerity that needs ageing – the second label is La Salle-de-Poujeaux; **Château Maucaillou** (55ha; CS 45%, Me 35%, CF 15%, PV 5%) is in the same vein, always impressive but less *grand*; **Château Gressier-Grand-Poujeaux** (18ha; CS 50%, Me 40%, CF 10%) is more traditional and very fine after 7–8 years. For the other châteaux, **Château Dutruch-Grand-Poujeaux** (18ha; CS 50%, Me 40%, CF 10%) is a Cru Exceptionnel of great weight and consistency, **Château Branas-Grand-Poujeaux** is more elegant, pure Médoc, **Château La Closerie-Grand-Poujeaux** is equally solid and powerful, while **Château Ruats-Petits-Poujeaux** is light and pretty and can be drunk at 2–3 years; **Château Bel-Air-La-Grave**, with a high percentage of Cabernet Sauvignon, is consistently fruity and firm. Nearer the village of Moulis-en-Médoc the wines are slightly lighter. **Château Brillette** (30ha; CS 55%, Me 40%, PV 5%) – the name comes from its pebbly soil which reflects the light – whose wines are deep coloured and aged in new oak, and **Château Biston-Brillette** have great charm yet age well; **Châteaux Moulin-à-Vent**, **Duplessis** and **Duplessis-Fabre** (under the same ownership as Fourcas-Dupré) are satisfying, medium-weight wines; **Château Mauvezin**, the largest estate in the *appellation*, with modern installations, is firm and aromatic, while **Château Moulis**, once the largest estate, is smooth and carefully made. Production of Moulis is quite limited at 2.5 million bottles. Price D, E for Crus Exceptionnels.

MARGAUX

Red wine only from an *appellation* covering the five communes of Margaux, Cantenac, Labarde, Arsac and Soussans, an area of almost 1,160 hectares. At Margaux itself, the soil is lighter and finer and the wines have a corresponding edge of elegance over the other communes. The style of Margaux has been summed up by the late Alexis Lichine in three words: finesse, elegance, subtlety. To this may be added their brilliant, deep colour and the capacity for ageing. Margaux is often thought of as the most feminine wine from Bordeaux, an idea contradicted by the sturdiness of some of the Crus Classés. Even these, however, should be most fragrant and refined. Margaux is the largest of the communes in the Haut-Médoc region and possesses not only more Cru Classés than the others but also more high-ranking ones from the original classification.

THE CRUS CLASSES OF MARGAUX

Château Margaux

1er GCC (Red: 75ha; CS 75%, Me 20%, CF and PV 5%. Bordeaux blanc: 10ha; Sa 100%)
This world-famous wine is the only Premier Cru Classé from which the *appellation*, which it represents to perfection, takes its name. The characteristics of finesse, elegance and subtlety are backed by a firmness that only heightens the whole. After a series of unspectacular vintages from the late 1960s, Margaux was sold to M. André Mentzenopoulos in 1977 and the current splendid quality of the wine is the result of much-needed investment in the vineyards and the *chais*, and of the continuing dedication of his widow and family.

The better vintages (1982, 1983, 1986, 1988, 1989, 1990) should be kept for 12–15 years. The second wine, Pavillon Rouge de Château Margaux, and the lighter vintages may be drunk at 6–8 years. The white wine, made in a separate *chai* with the most modern equipment, is dry with a flinty, floral persistence and can be drunk young or kept 3–4 years. Production 20,000 cases red, 3,500 white. Price I (white), J (red).

Château Rausan-Ségla

2ème GCC (45ha; CS 67%, CF 3%, Me 30%)
The larger part of the original Rauzan estate, whose vineyards border those of Châteaux Margaux and Palmer, Rausan-Ségla for many years did not justify its place as a 2ème Cru Classé. However, improvements begun in the late 1970s resulted in a successful 1982, and very fine wines since 1985. In 1987 the Château took the brave step of declassifying its entire crop, selling the wine under the second label, the Cru Bourgeois Château Lamouroux. Current vintages have shown great concentration and great finesse. Production 13,000 cases. Price F.

Château Rauzan-Gassies

2ème GCC (30Ha; CS 40%, CF 23%, Me 35%, PV 2%)
The smaller part of the original Rauzan estate, making correct wines, if lacking a little finesse, not really of 2ème Cru standard. In the 1980s, the guidance of Professeur Peynaud resulted in improved quality, with woodiness being replaced by a smoother fruit. Due to the low proportion of Cabernet Sauvignon and relatively short vinification and ageing, the wine can be drunk at 6–10 years. There is a second label, Enclos de Moncabon. Production 10,000 cases. Price F.

Château Durfort-Vivens

2ème GCC (25ha; CS 82%, CF 10%, Me 8%)
With the exception of a small parcel of vines almost encircled by Château Margaux, the vines of Durfort-Vivens are in Cantenac, near Brane-Cantenac, both properties being owned by Lucien Lurton. The higher proportion of Cabernet Sauvignon lends Durfort a firmness and leanness that needs up to ten years to soften. The Château showed a definite return to form in the 1980s, with very fine wines in 1983 and 1986. The second wine is Domaine de Cure-Bourse. Production 6,000 cases. Price F.

Château Lascombes

2ème GCC (93ha; CS 65%, CF 3%, Me 30%, PV 2%)
An extremely parcellated vineyard, now one of the largest in the Médoc, making deep-coloured fruity wine, almost beefy for a Margaux, but smooth and attractive. Lascombes often lacks finesse but is reliable, even in light vintages, and its roundness allows it to be drunk at 6–10 years. A more vigorous policy of vat selection produced a good 1982 and 1983 and an excellent 1985. The second wines are Château La Gombaude and Château Segonnes. Production 35,000 cases. Price G.

Château Brane-Cantenac

2ème GCC (85ha; CS 70%, CF 15%, Me 13%, PV 2%)
A large property with vines planted on light, gravelly soil with a chalk base. The relatively young vines led to a succession of quick-maturing vintages in the 1970s (with the exception of a magnificent 1975), while in the 1980s the wines had more colour and intensity, with a distinctive finesse and flavour. 1986 and 1988 were particularly good. There are two second labels: Château Notton and Domaine de Fontarney. These may be drunk at 5 years, while the *grand vin* needs 10. Production 29,000 cases. Price high G.

Château Giscours

3ème GCC (82ha; CS 75%, Me 20%, CF 3%, PV 2%)
The most southern of the Margaux Crus Classés, Giscours is an immaculately run property making extremely reliable, deep-coloured, concentrated wine, that has more robustness than delicacy, but often great style. 1975 was the last of the very tannic vinifications; current vintages now have a smooth density of fruit and softer tannins and can be drunk at 8–10 years. Having been one of the leaders in this commune in the 1970s, Giscours has now been caught up by its neighbours. Production 29,000 cases. Price H.

Château Kirwan

3ème GCC (35ha; CS 40%, CF 20%, Me 30%, PV 10%)
A well-run property in Cantenac and one of the last of the Crus Classés to adopt château-bottling, Kirwan has been considerably replanted since 1972. The wine used to be rather light and mean, but in 1979, 1982, 1986 and 1988 produced deep-coloured, firm, long-lived wines, relatively tough for a Margaux. Despite improving quality since 1978, Kirwan is still more of 5ème than 3ème Cru standard. Production 15,000 cases. Price F.

Château d'Issan

3éme GCC (32ha; CS 75%, Me 25%)
A magnificent moated Château with almost all its vines in a single block on the Cantenac-Margaux borders, d'Issan is one of the most typical Margaux, with a fragrant bouquet and soft, lissom fruit. The very high percentage of Cabernet Sauvignon gives depth and

Jean-Michel Cazes of Château Lynch-Bages. Since the 1988 vintage the wines have had a very deep colour and a rich, plummy fruit, well exemplified by the 1990. The Cru Bourgeois, Château Canuet, an adjoining estate previously used as a second label, is often more delicate and more Margaux in style than the *grand vin*. Production 16,000 cases. Price F.

Château Palmer

3ème GCC (45ha; CS 55%, CF 3%, Me 40%, PV 2%) The most prestigious property in Margaux after Château Margaux itself and, in the last two decades, often the best wine of the commune. The vineyards cover the best soil of the *appellation* and the particular *encépagement* produces a deep-coloured, intensely fruity wine, with a soft, plummy flavour, firm finish and great finesse and distinction. The absence of hard tannin allows Palmer to be enjoyed young, while good vintages can last 20 years. Recent successes, even by Palmer standards, have been 1979, 1983, 1986 and 1988. Production 13,000 cases. Price H.

Château Desmirail

3ème GCC (25ha; CS 80%, CF 9%, Me 10%, PV 1%) Desmirail was divided up and sold in 1939 to Palmer and Brane-Cantenac. The owner of the latter, Lucien Lurton, decided to re-create the property from parcels of vineyards in Cantenac and has recently exercised his right to add a further 7 hectares to the original 18. The 1982 was very successful. To maintain the quality of the *grand vin*, there is a second wine, Château Baudry, but Desmirail is still proving itself. Production 3,500 cases. Price G.

complexity, while careful vinification prevents the wine from becoming too tannic. D'Issan has been very good indeed since the mid-1970s, with splendid 1983, 1985, 1986 and 1989s. At its best at 8–12 years. Production 15,000 cases. Price G.

Château Malescot Saint-Exupéry

3ème GCC (34ha; CS 50%, CF 10%, Me 35%, PV 5%) A wine of intensity and finesse, without the charm of Margaux or Palmer, but with great breed, one of the lest well-known Crus Classés. It is hard and lean when young and needs ten years or more to show at its best. The 1985 is one of the best Margaux of that year. Second wines are Château de Loyac and Domaine du Balardin. Production 15,000 cases. Price G.

Château Cantenac-Brown

3ème GCC (40ha; CS 67%, CF 7%, Me 26%) For many years a traditionally made wine that attempted to make up in structure and body what it lacked in delicacy, Cantenac-Brown has been the object of considerable investment during the 1980s and is now owned by AXA-Millésimes, under the direction of

Château D'Issan

Château Ferrière

3ème GCC (4.85 ha; CS 47%, CF 8%, Me 33%, PV 12%)
Since 1960, the vines of Ferrière have been leased to
Château Lascombes, who make a wine that is fruity,
plummy, quite quick-maturing, but not of 3ème Cru
status. Production 1,000 cases. Price F.

Château Marquis d'Alesme-Becker

3ème GCC (10ha; CS 40%, CF 20%, Me 30%, PV 10%)
A small property, under the same ownership as
Malescot Saint-Exupéry, to the north of the Margaux
appellation in Soussans, making big, meaty, distinctive
wines. The high percentage of Petit Verdot adds colour
and fruit in good years and balances the low percentage
of Cabernet Sauvignon. The wines are very carefully

*Above: Château Margaux which produces the world-famous
Premier Cru Classé.*

made in a new *cuvier* and last 10–15 years, but do not at
present justify their rating. Production 5,000 cases.
Price F.

Château Boyd-Cantenac

3ème GCC (18ha; CS 67%, CF 7%, Me 20%, PV 6%)
This is a small property, making sturdy, rather old-
fashioned wines from old vines. The low-yielding
vines, addition of 15% *vin de presse*, and ageing for 24
months in barrels, results in a wine that contrasts with
the feminine, delicate image of a Margaux, but is pure
Médoc. Very good wines were made in 1982, 1983 and
1986. Production 8,000 cases. Price high F.

Château Pouget

4ème GCC (10ha; CS 66%, Me 30%, PV 4%)
A small property next door to Kirwan and Brane-Cantenac, Pouget was made at Boyd-Cantenac until 1983 (same ownership). The wine is similar in style, deep-coloured, full-bodied, serious, underlined by the relatively high proportion of Cabernet Sauvignon and absence of Cabernet Franc. The very successful recent vintages can be kept 10–15 years. Production 3,500 cases. Price E-F.

Château Prieuré-Lichine

4ème GCC (62ha; CS 55%, CF 12%, Me 33%, PV 5%)
An extremely parcellated property with vines in all the best parts of the *appellation*, making one of the less weighty Margaux, with purity of style and great finesse. The experience of the late Alexis Lichine combined with the advice of Professor Ribereau-Gayon, has produced a run of successful vintages, including a very fine 1983 and 1985. M. Lichine's last vintage, 1988, was exceptional, as were the 1989 and the 1990, vinified by his son, Sasha. The second label, from declassified vats, is Château de Clairefont. production 28,000 cases. Price F.

Château Marquis de Terme

4ème GCC (38ha; CS 60%, CF 3%, Me 30%, PV 7%)
In the past, this property made robust, dark-coloured wine (with up to 10% *vin de presse* added) for long-term drinking. Recent vintages are as full-bodied, but less hard than the 1970 and 1975, and can be drunk at 10 years. Quality now is satisfactory rather than exceptional. The property sells a second wine, Domaine des Gondats, under the *appellation* Bordeaux Supérieur. Production 14,000 cases. Price low F.

Château Dauzac

5ème GCC (50 ha; CS 60%, CF 5%, Me 30%, PV 5%)
Bordered by Châteaux Siran and Giscours in the commune of Labarde, Dauzac changed hands in 1978 and was once again sold in 1989. The vineyard has been expanded and replanted, and the *cuvier* rebuilt. The style of the wine is accessibly round and fruity and recent vintages are encouraging and now justify their classification. Production 15,000 cases. Price low F.

Château du Tertre

5ème GCC (50ha; CS 85%, CF 5%, Me 10%)
The vineyards of du Tertre are set apart from the other Crus Classés, in the commune of Arsac. The property is managed by the owner of Calon-Ségur and since the mid-1970s the wine, dark-coloured with a fine, Mar-gaux-style concentrated fruit, has been of high quality. 1982 and 1983 were exceptional, and the 1988 promises well. The wines of Château du Tertre can be drunk at 6–10 years. Production 15,000 cases. Price F.

THE CRUS BOURGEOIS OF MARGAUX

Since Margaux possesses the largest number of Grands Crus Classés, it is not surprising that the Crus Bourgeois are to be found on the perimeter of the *appellation*, where the wines are a little sturdier and less delicately balanced. There are, however, four properties that stand out from the rest, whose wines are regularly of Cru Classé standard: **Château Siran** (35ha; CS 50%, CF 10%, Me 25%, PV 15%), in Labarde, whose vines touch those of Giscours and Dauzac, makes extremely fine deep-coloured, suave wine, pure Margaux and quite exceptional in great years (1961, 1970, 1975, 1982); **Château d'Angludet** (30ha; CS 45%, CF 15%, Me 35%, PV 5%), in Cantenac, set apart from but almost surrounded by Crus Classés, with all the *sève*, elegance and length one expects from a Margaux, has been very successful in recent vintages; **Château Bel-Air-Marquis d'Aligre** (17ha; CS 30%, CF 20%, Me 35%, PV 15%), in Margaux and Soussans, on a chalky soil, produces wines of arresting elegance, style and depth; **Château La Tour de Mons** (30ha; CS 45%, CF 10%, Me 40%, PV 5%), at Soussans, is full-bodied, with high extract and acidity, a slow-maturing wine with a great deal of fruit. Since the mid-1980s, two other châteaux have come very much to the fore: **Château Monbrison** (14ha; CS 30%, CF 30%, Me 35%, PV 5%), with rich, ripe, densely concentrated wines that regularly outclass the lesser Cru Classés, and which permits itself, quite rare for a Cru Bourgeois, a second label, Clos Cordet; and **Château La Gurgue** (12ha; CS 70%, Me 25%, PV 5%), with vines very near Château Margaux, now under the direction of Mme Bernadette Villars of Château Chasse-Spleen. Nearly on the level of these wines is **Château Labégorce-Zédé**, at Soussans, which has more breed and elegance than the good but rather rich **Château Labégorce**. Also at Soussans, **Château Tayac** is rather lean but quite distinguished, and **Château Paveil de Luze** is smoother and more straightforward. At Margaux itself, **Château Charmant** is as delicious as its name suggests. At Cantenac, the iron content in the soil produces wines that are more muscular and tannic, such as **Château Montbrun** and the well-situated **Château Pontac-Lynch**, while **Château Martinens** is suppler and of good quality. At Arsac, to the south of the *appellation*, **Château d'Arsac**, classified Haut-Médoc, is a large, well-run property. Price E – low F.

SAINT-JULIEN

Red wine only from the smallest of the finer *appellations* of the Médoc, with 820 hectares under vines, of which four-fifths were classified in 1855. The soil is the same *graves* as at Margaux, but deeper and with more clay, and the wines are correspondingly richer. The vineyards nearer to the estuary, Beychevelle, Ducru-Beaucaillou, the Léovilles, produce wines of great breed and finesse, while those further inland, Talbot, Gruaud-Larose, and Lagrange, are meatier. Saint-Julien is "quintessential claret", combining deep colour, a rich cedary bouquet and fine balanced flavours.

THE CRUS CLASSES OF SAINT-JULIEN

Château Léoville-Las Cases

2ème GCC (95ha; CS 65%, CF 12%, Me 20%, PV 3%) The largest and most prestigious of the three Léovilles. The soil is slightly lighter than at Latour, whose vines it touches, but none the less, Léoville-Las Cases is the firmest of the Saint-Juliens, blending the austerity of Pauillac with the charm of Saint-Julien. It is a top-class wine of great breed and distinction, whose better vintages need at least 15 years. Las Cases has shown more than two decades of high quality, rivalling that of the 1ers Crus. 1982 is quite exceptional. The excellent second wines are Clos de Marquis and Domaine de Bigarnon. Production 32,000 cases. Price H.

Château Léoville-Poyferré

2ème GCC (75ha; CS 65%, CF 2%, Me 25%, PV 8%) The middle part of the Léoville estate, Léoville-Poyferré, has improved since 1975, with the wine again showing some of the depth and class of a 2ème Cru. The wines are less fragrant than Léoville-Barton but are very well made with 1982 and 1983 representing a real break from the past; 1985 is impressive, and 1989 and 1990 are exceptional. The second label is Château Moulin-Riche. Production 33,000 cases. Price G.

Château Léoville-Barton

2ème GCC (45ha; CS 70%, CF 8%, Me 25%, PV 2%) The smallest, most traditional and most Saint-Julien of the Léovilles, Léoville-Barton is a ripe, elegant wine, never obvious, even when young, and blossoming out to show a fragrant, rose-like bouquet with great purity and length of flavour. Recent vintages have been very successful, particularly 1982 and 1985 with an exceptional 1986, 1988 and 1990. In some years the lighter wines were declassified into a generic Saint-Julien, which now carries the label Lady Langoa. The death in 1986 of the much-loved Ronald Barton, after 50 years of making this wine and that of Château Langoa-Barton, was a great loss to the Médoc. Production 16,000 cases. Price low G.

Château Gruaud-Larose

2ème GCC (82ha; CS 64%, CF 9%, Me 24%, PV 3%) A large property set well back from the Gironde, producing dark, rich, full-bodied but classic Saint-Julien from a high proportion of old vines. The wine (and that of Talbot) showed a certain lack of elegance from the mid-1960s, reversed recently, coinciding with the return to the traditional Bordeaux bottle from the Cordier bottle in 1979. 1982 and 1988 are exceptional. Gruaud-Larose is fruity enough to be drunk at 6–8 years, but really needs 12–15. The excellent second wine, since 1979, is Le Sarget de Gruaud-Larose. Production 38,000 cases. Price high G.

Château Ducru-Beaucaillou

2ème GCC (49ha; CS 65%, CF 5%, Me 25%, PV 5%) A very fine property, with most of the vines situated between Beychevelle and the Gironde, making a wine that only Léoville-Las Cases and, recently, Léoville-Barton can rival. Ducru is a little more open and softer than Las Cases, with a great depth of fruit, impeccably made by Jean-Eugène Borie. The second wine, for much earlier drinking, is Château La Croix. Production 20,000 cases. Price H.

Château Lagrange

3ème GCC (81ha; CS 66%, Me 27%, PV 7%) Set well back between Gruaud-Larose and the Haut-Médoc vineyards of Belgrave, Lagrange has made a considerable effort to improve its vinification. The relatively high proportion of Merlot used to give the wine a softness that allowed it to be drunk at 6–8 years, but new planting has increased the proportion of Cabernet Sauvignon and the wine is becoming more serious. The property was sold in 1983 to a Japanese group who have installed the most modern vinification system. 1985, 1986 and 1988 are very successful and Lagrange is once again worthy of its classification. The second wine, since 1983, is Les Fiefs de Lagrange. Production 20,000 cases. Price high C.

Château Langoa-Barton

3ème GCC (15ha; CS 70%, CF 8%, Me 20%, PV 2%)
The Château at which Léoville-Barton is made and whose vines are in the heart of the *appellation*. A traditional vinification produces a ruby-coloured, finely bouqueted wine, slightly more round than the Léoville and with equal balance. At 8–10 years Langoa is delicious, but good vintages may last longer. Some lighter *cuvées* are sold as generic Saint-Julien under the name Lady Langoa. Production 7,000 cases. Price F.

Château Saint-Pierre

4ème GCC (17ha; CS 70%, CF 10%, Me 20%)
A small property well situated between Talbot, Gruaud-Larose and Langoa-Barton making deep-coloured, meaty wines from old vines. In 1983 Saint-Pierre changed hands, with Jean-Eugène Borie of Château Ducru-Beaucaillou purchasing the *cuvier* and *chai* in which to make his Cru Bourgeois Château Lalande-Borie, and the late Henry Martin of Gloria purchasing all the vines except two small parcels enclaved by Gruaud-Larose, which went to Cordier. The very reliable second wine, Château Saint-Louis-le-Bosq, has been discontinued. A most dependable property. Production 7,000 cases. Price F.

Château Branaire-Ducru

4ème GCC (48ha; CS 73%, CF 5%, Me 20%, PV 2%)
Very well run property with some vineyards opposite Beychevelle, the rest parcellated across the centre of the commune, making extremely elegant wine with good colour, relatively light in body but not in flavour, one of the most harmonious wines of the Médoc. Branaire-Ducru seems to typify Saint-Julien and is much underrated as a 4ème Cru. Most vintages bear this out, especially 1982 and 1985. May be drunk at 8–10 years. The second wine is Château Duluc. Production 20,000 cases. Price G.

Château Talbot

4ème GCC (98ha; CS 70%, CF 5%, Me 20%, PV 5%)
One of the largest estates in the Médoc, the largest in a single block, with vines running from Léoville-Poyferré to Gruaud-Larose, Talbot produces a full-bodied, richly textured Saint-Julien. While it often lacks the elegance of the Léovilles, it is very satisfying, particularly in recent (1979, 1982, 1985) vintages. It is slightly quicker-maturing than its Cordier-owned stable-mate Gruaud-Larose. Five hectares are planted with white grapes (Sa 80%, Se 20%) to make the attractive, dry "Caillou Blanc", and the whole vineyard has recently been expanded by a further 25 hectares. The second wine, since 1979, is Le Connétable de Talbot. Production 40,000 cases. Price G.

Château Beychevelle

4ème GCC (70ha; CS 70%, Me 30%)
A splendid estate, with vines separated from the Gironde by those of Ducru-Beaucaillou, making fine, elegant wines, as typically Saint-Julien as those from Branaire opposite, and rather fatter. After over 100 years in the Achille-Fould family, the Château was sold in 1983 to an insurance company. Beychevelle has for many years been considered "supérieur à son classement" and the 1985 once again proves this is so. The second wine, for early drinking, is Réserve de l'Amiral. Production 30,000 cases. Price G.

THE CRUS BOURGEOIS OF SAINT-JULIEN

With most of the commune occupied by the Crus Classés, there are few Crus Bourgeois in Saint-Julien. The largest is **Château Gloria** (45ha; CS 65%, CF 5%, Me 25%, PV 5%), regularly on a par with the Crus Classés and often beating them in blind tastings, with two second labels, Château Haut-Beychevelle-Gloria and Château Peymartin. Only a little smaller, sometimes unreliable and less distinguished is **Château du Glana**. **Château Terrey-Gros-Caillou** produces a delicate, supple wine, **Château Hortevie**, under the same ownership (35ha; CS + CF 70%, Me 25%, PV 5%) is fuller-bodied and very good, and **Château Moulin-de-la-Rose**, almost entirely surrounded by Crus Classés, is concentrated and tannic. **Château Lalande-Borie** (18ha; CS 65%, CF 10%, Me 25%,), formerly part of Château Lagrange and often erroneously described as the second wine of Ducru-Beaucaillou, is naturally of high quality, **Château Teynac** used to be part of Saint-Pierre-Sevaistre and still makes good wine, and **Château La Bridane** is also reliable. On the borders of Pauillac, Michel Delon of Léoville-Las Cases produces the very elegant wines of **Château du Grand-Parc**. Price E–F.

PAUILLAC

Red wines only from the third-largest fine wine producing commune in the Médoc, with 1,050 hectares under vines and more Crus Classés than any other commune except Margaux. The soil is a deep gravel with some clay and chalk in the base, becoming heavier towards the west of the *appellation*. The wines of Pauillac should share a dark, garnet colour and intense fruit, with an almost metallic hardness when young that never really softens out and is known as *le goût de capsule* or "lead-pencil taste". Pauillacs, Lafite-Roths-

Above: Château Pichon-Longueville Baron surrounded by its predominantly gravel vineyards.

child excepted, are seldom feminine or delicate, but possess a structure and "presence" that is most classic in fine claret. The fragrance of Lafite, the severity of Latour and the sumptuousness of Mouton are all characteristic of these classic Médocs.

THE CRU CLASSES OF PAUILLAC

Château Lafite-Rothschild

1er GCC (100ha; CS 70%, CF 10%, Me 20%)
One of the finest and most prestigious wines of Bordeaux, justifiably back at the top since the mid-1970s, with a run of brilliant successes since 1976. The vineyards of Lafite are at the northern edge of the commune and border those of Château Mouton-Rothschild. A small parcel of vines is actually in Saint-Estèphe. The wine is made as carefully as possible: long vinification in wooded vats, with 2.5 years in new oak. Rigorous selection at bottling (two-thirds of the 1980 vintage was declassified), the age of the vines and the intentional low yield, add to the quality that comes from the gravelly, slightly chalky soil. Lafite has the most fragrant bouquet of the Pauillacs, where the aroma of violets is unmistakable, and despite great delicacy, it can be firm and long-lived. Lighter vintages are charming and can be drunk at 7–8 years after the vintage, the better wines needing 12–15 years to show their complexity. The second wine is Le Moulin des Carruades. Production 25,000 cases. Price J+.

Château Latour

1er GCC (60ha; CS 80%, CF 4%, Me 15%, PV 1%)
The most consistently great wine of Bordeaux, Latour has its vineyards in the southern part of the commune, on the borders of Saint-Julien, with the vines running down towards the Gironde. Everything that can be done to improve and maintain the quality of the wine is done, in the vineyards as in the *chai*, and only the very best goes into the *grand vin*. In style, Latour is majestic, with an immense colour and terrific structure, perhaps the only wine in the Médoc that is not approachable in great vintages until 15 years, yet its power does not result in heaviness, but in breed and depth. The second wine, Les Forts de Latour, comes from vines outside the walled vineyard of Latour and from younger vines within it, it is very much in the Latour style, the quality being that of a 2ème Cru Classé. Production 16,000 cases Grand Vin de Château Latour, 3,000 cases Les Forts de Latour. Price J+.

Château Mouton-Rothschild

1er GCC (1973) (80ha; CS 85%, CF 7%, Me 8%)
Producing one of the most spectacular wines of Bordeaux, the vineyards of Mouton-Rothschild adjoin those of Lafite in the north of the commune. The wine is the result of the most single-minded dedication to quality at all costs, in the history of the Médoc. Due to the very high percentage of Cabernet Sauvignon leading to an intense concentration of flavour, the wine

resembles Latour more than Lafite, but is flamboyant where Latour is severe. Except in very tannic years (1961, 1970, 1975), this rich concentrated firework display of flavour from low-yielding old vines will begin to open up at 10 years; the greater vintages need 20. The 1982 is quite extraordinary. There is no second wine from Mouton-Rothschild. Production 25,000 cases. Price J+.

Château Pichon-Longueville Baron

2ème GCC (55ha; CS 75%, Me 25%)
The smaller of the two Pichons, with vines opposite Latour on the west of the Médoc road, making deep-coloured, sturdy wines that repay keeping. The high percentage of Cabernet Sauvignon and absence of Cabernet Franc emphasizes the structure of this wine that has been rather less fashionable than Pichon-Comtesse. 1978, 1979 and 1982 were excellent, among the best wines of the commune, but outstanding wines have been produced since the 1988 vintage as a result of the investment made by AXA-Millésimes. This is now one of the very best Pauillacs. Production 20,000 cases. Price low H.

Château Pichon-Longueville Comtesse de Lalande

2ème GCC (75ha; CS 45%, CF12%, Me 35%, PV 8%k)
An exceptionally stylish wine from the larger of the Pichons, from vineyards next to those of Latour, Pichon-Baron and the commune of Saint-Julien. Although the Château is actually on the Latour vineyards, the style of wine is more Saint-Julien, with the suppleness of the Merlot and the charm of the Cabernet Franc pointing up a contrast to the more dense and unyielding Pauillacs. Vintages since the 1970s have been very successful, and by the mid-1980s, the wine was selling on a par with Château Ducru-Beaucaillou and Cos d'Estournel as one of the "super seconds". Despite their smooth fruit, good vintages should be kept at least 10 years. The second wine is La Réserve de la Comtesse, on a par with a 5ème Cru. Production 30,000 cases. Price high H.

Château Duhart-Milon-Rothschild

4ème GCC (60ha; CS 70%, CF 5%, Me 20%, PV 5%)
A vineyard purchased by the Lafite-Rothschilds in 1964, replanted, and, since 1976, producing top-class wines with both body and elegance. The situation of the vineyards, the same *encépagement* as Lafite, the same intentional low yield from vines now of a respectable age, and very careful vinification, combine to produce a wine of exceptional promise, as shown by the 1983, 1986 and 1988. The second label is Moulin de Duhart. Production 25,000 cases. Price G.

Château Pontet-Canet

5ème GCC (70ha; CS 70%, CF 4%, Me 26%)

A large estate due south of Château d'Armailhac, with one of the highest productions in the Médoc. From 1964 to 1974 the wines were unimpressive, but since 1975 matters have improved under the administration of Guy Tesseron and the recent vintages, especially 1990, have been very good, albeit in a rather firm style. A second wine is made called Les Hauts de Pontet. Production 30,000 cases. Price F.

Château Batailley

5ème GCC (50ha, CS 70%, CF 5%, Me 22%, PV 3%)

The larger of the two Batailleys, separated in 1942. The vineyards are set well back from the Gironde in the south-west of the commune and the wine is deep-coloured and firm, sometimes lacking in charm, but quite satisfying and always good value for money. Recent vintages have had an excellent fruit, more new oak flavours and less rustic tannin so may be drunk at 8–10 years. Production 22,000 cases. Price E-F.

Château Haut-Batailley

5ème GCC (21ha; CS 65%, CF 10%, Me 25%)

The smaller of the two Batailleys, owned by the same family as Ducru-Beaucaillou and Grand-Puy-Lacoste, making a very elegant, supple wine, slightly in the Saint-Julien style. The comparison is similar between Batailley-Haut-Batailley and Pichon-Baron-Pichon Comtesse: sturdy versus stylish Pauillacs. Professeur Peynaud was the consultant to the latter two estates. The second label is Château La Tour d'Aspic for drinking at 6–8 years. Production 7,000 cases. Price F.

Château Grand-Puy-Lacoste

5ème GCC (48ha; CS 70%, CF 5%, Me 25%)

This excellent property, separated from the Gironde by the Bages plateau, was purchased in 1978 by the Borie family from the remarkable Raymond Dupin. The wine, very dark in colour, with the Pauillac goût de capsule or "lead-pencil" impression on the palate, has remained one of the most striking and typical wines of the appellation, often equal in quality to a 3ème Cru. The better vintages need at least 10 years before drinking. A second wine was introduced in 1982, Château Lacoste-Borie. Production 14,000 cases. Price G.

Château Grand-Puy-Ducasse

5ème GCC (35ha; CS 62%, Me 38%)

A parcellated estate with vines near Pontet-Canet, Lynch-Bages and Batailley, now under the same ownership as Chasse-Spleen and Rayne-Vigneau. The young vines were high yielding, which made for a pleasant wine that could be drunk at 5–8 years. Although the wines are much firmer now, they are not in the same league for quality (or price) as Grand-Puy-Lacoste. The second wine is Château Artigues-Arnaud. Production 12,000 cases. Price E-F.

Château Lynch-Bages

5ème GCC (85ha; CS 75%, CF 10%, Me 15%)

These vineyards consist of five parcels across the Bages plateau, where the soil makes for dark, full-bodied wines. The high proportion of Cabernets, the age of the vines and the lowish yield at Lynch-Bages underline this character to make a wine packed with intense fruit that dominates the natural austerity of Pauillac. Very reliable wines, both for quality and ageing, for 30 years consistently better than its classification. The second wine, a Grand Cru Bourgeois, with 4 hectares of its own, is the very successful Château Haut-Bages-Avérous. A very little Sémillon-based dry white is also made. Production 35,000 cases. Price high G.

Château Lynch-Moussas

5ème GCC (25ha; CS 70%, CF 5%, Me 25%)

The furthest inland of the Crus Classés, surrounded by woods on the borders of the appellation, Lynch-Moussas is experiencing a renaissance under the same ownership as neighbouring Batailley. The wine is still light for a Cru Classé, but is improving with each vintage. Production 12,500 cases. Price high E.

Château d'Armailhac

5ème GCC (45ha; CS 70%, CF 10%, Me 20%)

The old Mouton d'Armailhac estate, renamed Mouton-Baron-Philippe in 1956 and Mouton-Baronne-Philippe in 1974, then in 1991 renamed once again as Château d'Armailhac, runs between Mouton-Rothschild and Pontet-Canet. The light, sandy soil would lead the style of wine towards the latter, but the low-yielding vines and exemplary vinification give it a depth and polish that is associated with the former. Can be drunk at 6–8 years. Production 18,000 cases. Price F.

Château Haut-Bages-Libéral

5ème GCC (26ha; CS 74%, Me 23%, PV 3%)

A small property with the majority of its vines just north of Latour, but on a lighter soil. The high percentage of Cabernet Sauvignon and the absence of Cabernet Franc result in a deep-coloured, chewy, slow-maturing wine that has shown very well in recent vintages due to a change in management from Cruse to Madame Villars of Château Chasse-Spleen. The 1985, 1986, 1988 and 1989 are ripe and elegant wines.

Château Latour

Château Pédesclaux

5ème GCC (20ha; CS 70%, CF 7%, Me 20%, PV 3%)
The vineyards of Pédesclaux are split into two main parcels, one to the west of the town of Pauillac near Lynch-Bages, the other to the north by Pontet-Canet and Mouton. The wines are firm and complete, perhaps lacking finesse, but successful and long-lasting in the classic vintages. Wine not sold as Pédesclaux goes into the two Crus Bourgeois, Châteaux Bellerose and Grand-Duroc-Milon. Production 8,000 cases. Price E.

Château Clerc-Milon

5ème GCC (30ha; CS 75%, CF 5%, Me 20%)
An estate in the north of the commune adjoining Lafite and Mouton, purchased by Baron Philippe de Rothschild in 1970, Clerc-Milon produces firm, complete wine, less supple but more structured that Mouton-Baron-Philippe. Classic vintages like 1978, 1982, 1985 and 1988 will repay 15 years ageing. Production 15,000 cases. Price G.

Château Croizet-Bages

5ème GCC (24 ha; CS 37%, CF 30%, Me 30%, PV + Ma 3%)
With vines between Lynch-Bages and Grand-Puy-Lacoste, the encépagement and vinification of Croizet-Bages does not correspond to its neighbours. The wine is more muted, with less intensity of fruit and, until 1979, rather woody. A very marked improvement was seen in the 1981, as with the sister-Château, Rauzan-Gassies. Can be drunk at 6–8 years, but will improve for longer. Production 8,500 cases. Price E-F.

THE CRUS BOURGEOIS OF PAUILLAC

With 12 5ème Crus in the commune, not to speak of the three 1er Crus, the Crus Bourgeois of Pauillac tend to be overshadowed by their grander brothers. Apart from the many Cru Classé châteaux which use their Cru Bourgeois properties for the second wine, there are some fine individual properties: **Château La Couronne** (4ha; CS 70%, Me 30%), owned by the Borie family and adjoining Haut-Batailley, produces a perfectly balanced, stylish wine; **Château Fonbadet** (15ha; CS 60%, CF 15%, Me 19%, Ma 4%, PV 2%), is firm, fruity and distinguished, a true Pauillac, and worthy of a higher rating. **Château Haut-Bages-Montpelou**, part of Duhart-Milon until 1948 and now owned by the Castéjas of Batailley, is softer, but very correct; **Château La Fleur-Milon**, well situated next to Clerc-Milon, makes some firm, meaty wine that deserves to be better known; **Château Pibran** and **Château La Tour Pibran**, touching Pontet-Canet and Grand-Puy-Ducasse, produce deep-coloured wine with good acidity; **Château Colombier-Montpelou** is less lively, but a serious wine made by the owner of Pédesclaux; **Château La Bécasse** is not a Cru Bourgeois, but due to its high percentage of Cabernet Sauvignon and lavish use of new oak, has been described as a "mini-Mouton-Rothschild". The Cave-Coopérative "La Rose Pauillac" also produces some good wine, but not of Cru Bourgeois status. Price high E.

SAINT-ESTEPHE

Red wines only from the second largest of the fine-wine *appellations* in the Médoc, with 1,140 hectares under vines. The vineyards are more hilly than in the communes to the south, and the soil, while still predominantly gravel, has more clay. In style, Saint-Estèphe is always sturdy (a delicate Saint-Estèphe is a contradiction in terms), with a firm fruit and great staying power. It is far from Margaux, both geographically and in terms of character, near to Pauillac, and what it lacks in charm it makes up in "wineyness". When young, or from non-sunny years, the wines tend to be tough, even astringent, but with recent progress in vinification, fruit now tends to dominate wood and tannin.

THE CRU CLASSES OF SAINT-ESTEPHE

Château Cos d'Estournel

2ème GCC (70ha; CS 60%, CF 2%, Me 38%)
The vines of Cos d'Estournel occupy a stretch of rising ground overlooking those of Lafite. The property belongs to the Domaines Prats, owners until 1989 of

Above: Château Cos d'Estournel – there is no house but the Chinese pagoda-style architecture makes it a landmark in Saint-Estèphe.

Petit-Village in Pomerol. The grapes are picked as late as possible to ensure high sugars and to avoid harsh tannin and acidity, while the long fermentation captures the maximum amount of colour and bouquet. This, helped by the high percentage of Merlot, makes Cos a deep-coloured, rich, plummy wine, with great breed and elegance, that relies on intensity of fruit rather than tannin for its long life. Lesser *cuvées* are destined for Bruno Prats' nearby Cru Bourgeois, Château de Marbuzet. Production 20,000 cases. Price low H.

Château Montrose

2ème GCC (68ha; CS 65%, CF 10%, Me 25%)
A fine estate to the north of Saint-Estèphe with its vines planted in a single block on an easy slope towards the Gironde. The more temperate climate (due to the proximity to the estuary) limits the risk of spring frost and aids the grapes to ripen early, but the secret of Montrose is in the classic *encépagement* and the

157

determination to make a *grand vin*. The wine has great colour, structure and integrity, while the packed fruit can take over 15 years to emerge. This is Saint-Estèphe at its most vigorous, although the wines of the 80s are more supple than those of the 70s and earlier. The lesser *cuvées* are reserved for the personnel (1,800 cases a year) and for the second labels La Dame de Montrose and Château Demereaulement. Production 24,000 cases. Price low H.

Château Calon-Ségur

3ème GCC (50ha; CS 65%, CF 15%, Me 20%)
The most northern Cru Classé and the one at the lowest altitude (2–12m above sea-level), with vines planted on a gravelly, chalky soil that adds a lightness to the Saint-Estèphe style. If not as consistently good as Cos d'Estournel and Montrose, Calon-Ségur is full of flavour and charm and can be strikingly elegant, as seen in 1982 and 1985. Recent vintages have been very successful. The second label is Le Marquis de Ségur. Production 20,000 cases. Price G.

Château Lafon-Rochet

4ème GCC (40ha; CS 60%, CF 6%, Me 34%)
The vineyard of Lafon-Rochet, which is just north of Lafite and Duhart-Milon, and south-west of Cos d'Estournel, was entirely replanted in the early 1960s by Guy Tesseron, who bought the estate (and rebuilt the château) in 1961. The high percentage of Cabernet Sauvignon (for a Saint-Estèphe) and a long vinification, result in a deep-coloured, intense, austere wine with a rich fruit that repays 10 years keeping. Recent vintages, as the vines age and the Saint Estèphe-Pauillac style is confirmed, have been very good. Recently a second label has appeared: Numèro 2. Production 15,000 cases. Price low F.

Château Cos Labory

5ème GCC (15ha; CS 40%, CF 20%, Me 35%, PV 5%)
A small vineyard, with parcels adjoining Cos d'Estournel and Lafon Rochet, but far from these in style, Cos Labory is fruity and supple rather than firm and intense. The roundness of the wine approaches Moulis or Saint-Julien, and it may be drunk at 5–6 years. Production 7,000 cases. Price E-F.

THE CRUS BOURGEOIS OF SAINT-ESTEPHE

With over 1,100 hectares under vines and only five Crus Classés, the idea of a Crus Bourgeois Château comes into its own in Saint-Estèphe. If one estate has to be singled out as producing consistently fine wines in the Médoc outside the 1855 classification, it might be **Château de Pez** (23ha; CS 70%, CF 15%, Me 15%). These are perfectly made wines, with every quality one could desire in a Saint-Estèphe: colour, bouquet, firmness and depth of fruit, elegance and ageing potential. From the same village comes **Château Les Ormes-de-Pez** (30ha; CS 50%, CF 10%, Me 35%, PV 5%), owned by the Cazes family of Lynch-Bages: rich, rounded and very good. Nearer to the river are **Château Phélan-Ségur**, with finesse, elegance and style, right back on form with an exceptional 1989, **Château Capbern-Gasqueton**, an excellent, well-structured wine under the same ownership as Calon-Ségur, **Château Meyney** (50ha; CS 70%, CF 4%, Me 24%, PV 2%), a strikingly rich, concentrated wine owned by Cordier, with a second label Prieur de Meyney, and **Château Haut-Marbuzet** (38ha; CS 40%, CF 10%, Me 50%), whose use of new barrels gives the wine a polish and enhances the fruit. In the southern part of the *appellation* are **Château de Marbuzet** (see Cos d'Estournel), **Château Macarthy**, with good depth, **Château Le Crock**, more supple and elegant, and **Château Andron-Blanquet**, which is made at Cos Labory. In the centre, **Châteaux Pomys** and **La Haye** are quite full-bodied and complex, **Château Houissant** tends to be lean at first but softens out, **Château Lafitte-Carcasset-Padirac** is a large estate with a good reputation, and **Château Tronquoy-Lalande** produces dark, plummy wines almost in the style of Meyney. The excellent *cave coopérative*, **Le Marquis de Saint-Estèphe**, has its *chai* in this part of the *appellation*. To the north, around the village of Saint-Corbian, are **Château Beausite** and **Château Beausite-Haut-Vignoble** – the former full and round, the latter firm and reserved – **Château Morin**, **Château Domayne** and the excellent **Château Le Boscq**, the last vineyard before the *appellation* ends and the Médoc begins. Price E.

Graves

The Graves *appellation* extends from where the Médoc ends, at La Jalle de Blanquefort, north of Bordeaux, to south of Langon, where it surrounds the *appellations* of Cérons, Barsac and Sauternes. The actual area is 60km long and about 15km wide, but most of the vineyards close to Bordeaux (with the exception of Château Haut-Brion, La Mission-Haut-Brion, Les Carmes-Haut-Brion and Pape-Clément) have been sold for building land. The region takes its name from the nature of the soil, gravel on a sandy base with a little clay, generally flat but with excellent drainage. As in the Médoc, with a similar soil and a climate influenced by the Atlantic, the Cabernet Sauvignon flourishes, and is the major grape variety of all but one of the Crus Classés. The Graves region is unique in Bordeaux in that it covers both red and white wine of equal *appellation* status, with the white being dry or possibly *demi-sec*. Production of red wine has recently overtaken white, and this trend seems confirmed. The white, with almost no *demi-sec*

made these days, is at its finest in the north, where certain Crus Classés make an extremely fine wine, increasingly vinified and aged in new oak barrels, and which repays ageing in bottle. The white wines south of Léognan can be elegant and fruity, but are less interesting and may be drunk young. Red Graves has the same clean, dense fruit as a Médoc, a similar austerity when young and a soft charm with sometimes a hint of roses in the bouquet. They are perhaps less striking that the grand Médocs, come round a little earlier, but are their equal in finesse. The red must be at least 10° and the white 11°, from a maximum yield that was increased in 1983 from 40hl/ha to 50hl/ha.

Until 1987, the whole region was classified under the *appellation* of Graves. The presence of all the Crus Classés around the communes Pessac and Léognan in the north, led to the creation of a new *appellation* for this area: Pessac-Léognan, while the wines of Portets and the south retain *appellation* Graves.

PESSAC-LEOGNAN

Red and white wines from an *appellation* created in 1987 to recognize the historic superiority of the wines from around Pessac and Léognan, including those from the communes of Villenave d'Oron, Cadaujac and Martillac. The red wines have much in common with the finer Médocs, possessing a more floral aroma to add charm to their natural intensity of fruit. The whites represent the finest dry whites from Bordeaux and in the last decade their quality (and price) has begun to rival the better white burgundies from the Côte d'Or. The total area under vines is currently 910 hectares: 710 for red wines and 200 for white, producing a total of 6 million bottles.

THE GRANDS CRUS CLASSES OF THE GRAVES

The Grands Crus Classés are all situated in the north of the region, to the west and south of Bordeaux itself, and all are therefore under the new *appellation* Pessac-Léognan. The two most prestigious wines, from the communes of Pessac and Talence, actually have their vineyards surrounded by the western suburbs of

Bordeaux and, as a result, enjoy a warmer climate than those in Léognan, Villenave d'Oron, Cadaujac and Martillac. Of these, Léognan is the most extensive, with 6 of the 14 Crus Classés and a *cave-exposition-vente* in the town itself. Only Château Haut-Brion was classified (Premier Grand Cru Classé) in the 1855 classification, the remaining châteaux being temporarily classified in 1953, with a final, official, classification taking place in 1959. There is no official order of quality, so the châteaux are listed alphabetically, after Haut-Brion and La Mission-Haut-Brion.

Château Haut-Brion

1er GCC (40ha; CS 50%, CF 15%, Me 35%; Pessac)
The doyen of the Bordeaux châteaux, well known since the seventeenth century, Haut-Brion produces wines of great elegance and breed, with a fine sweetness of fruit and harmonious finish. Even in great vintages, the wine may be drunk after only 7–8 years due to the softness of the tannin, but reaches its peak at 15 years. Haut-Brion was the first property in Bordeaux to install stainless-steel vats to control the vinification (1960). The second wine, Château Bahans-Haut-Brion, used to be a non-vintage blend using only young vines and

hence much lighter than the *grand vin*. Since 1976, however, a proportion of Bahans-Haut-Brion has carried a vintage date, and this wine is much closer in style to Haut-Brion itself. Under 1,000 cases of very fine white wine are made at Haut-Brion (3ha; Se 55%, Sa 45%), with the panache and *sève* of a Montrachet and just as expensive. Production of red wines is 12,000 cases. Price J.

Château La Mission-Haut-Brion

GCC (20ha; CS 50%, CF 10%, Me 40%; Talence)
For many years the great rival of Haut-Brion, La Mission-Haut-Brion was purchased by Haut-Brion in 1983. The style of wine is quite different: much darker in colour, as dark as the most intense Médoc, more tannic with a rich spiciness that is very particular. The 1975, 1982 and 1990 are quite exceptional, and the wine has a reputation for successes in light vintages – as in 1974 and 1990. Slow maturing, the best vintages need to wait 20 years. Production 7,000 cases. Price J.

Above: Château La Mission-Haut-Brion, now surrounded by the suburbs of Bordeaux.

Château La Tour-Haut-Brion

GCC (4ha; CS 65%, CF 10%, Me 25%; Talence)
Similar to La Mission-Haut-Brion in colour and tannin (more *vin de presse* is used) and very firm, but showing less of the rich spiciness. With the exception of years like 1975, it matures earlier than La Mission. Now under the same ownership as Haut-Brion, the intention is to treat La Tour-Haut-Brion as a separate vineyard and not as the second wine of La Mission-Haut-Brion. Accordingly, half the vines have been re-allied to La Mission with a resulting change in *encépagement*. Production 1,500 cases. Price H.

Château Laville-Haut-Brion

GCC (4ha; Se 60%, Sa 40%; Talence)
The white wine of La Mission-Haut-Brion. High proportions of Sémillon give the wine richness and *sève* to surpass other white Graves, and permitting it to age beautifully. Fermentation and ageing in new wood leave a marked impression on the wine. Of its type, the best dry white wine in Bordeaux. Should be drunk at 1–2 years or after 10. Production 1,200 cases. Price I.

Château Bouscaut

GCC (45ha; Me 50%, CS 35%, CF 15%; Cadaujac)
The high proportion of Merlot (unique in the Graves) produces a wine that is firmer and more tannic than in Saint-Emilion or Pomerol, with good structure but perhaps lacking in finesse. Since 1978 the wines are richer and better balanced and Bouscaut's recent (1980) acquisition by Lucien Lurton and the increasing interest of Jean-Bernard Delmas, *directeur-oenologue* at Haut-Brion, should see this trend continue. The Cru Classé white comes from 7ha, 60% Se, 40% Sa, and is barrel-fermented and wood-aged to produce a wine of good quality that can age well. Production 15,000 cases of red, 6,000 of white. Price E-F.

Château Carbonnieux

GCC (Red: 45ha; CS 60%, CF 7%, Me 30%, Ma + PV 3%. White: 45ha; Sa 60%, Se 35%, Mu 5%; Léognan)
The largest property of the Graves Cru Classés, Carbonnieux is divided equally between the production of red and white wine, the latter being better known. The red has a good colour, is never overly fruity and is sometimes a little tart when young, but softens after 7–8 years. The white ferments in stainless steel and spends three months in wood before being bottled in May or June the year after the vintage. It is very fresh but a little closed when young and needs 2–3 years to show complexity. Both wines have shown a marked increase in quality in the late 1980s. Production 40,000 cases, both red and white. Price E-F.

Domaine de Chevalier

GCC (20ha; CS 65%, CF 10%, Me 25%; Léognan)
A vineyard unique in the Graves, with all the vines planted in a single square block, surrounded by woods. The soil is light and gravelly, the vines intentionally low-yielding, and a long fermentation gives a deep colour and firm structure to the wine, which has great purity of style and incomparable finesse. It is often more successful than other châteaux in poor vintages, and can be drunk at 7–8 years, but good years are better at 10–15. The Domaine de Chevalier 1981 is the finest wine of the vintage. Two hectares are devoted to white wine (Sa 70%, Se 30%), which is barrel-fermented and then barrel-aged for 18 months before bottling. It is firm and delicate at the same time and is, for many, the finest dry white wine produced in Bordeaux. In 1983 the Ricard family sold the Domaine to the Bernard family of Bordeaux. Production 7,000 cases of red, 800 of white. Price I.

Château Couhins

GCC (White: 6ha; Sa 50%, Se 50%; Villenave-d'Ornon)
The property is owned by the Institut National de la Recherche Agronomique (INRA), who took back the running of the vineyards from André Lurton in the late 1970s. The vines are relatively young and the wine is straightforward modern-style Graves. 1983 was the first vintage that the wine was vinified at the Château. Production 1,000 cases of *non-classé* red, 1,500 of white. Price E.

Château Couhins-Lurton

GCC (6ha; Sa 100%; Villenave-d'Ornon)
This beautifully made, aromatic yet dry white wine is made by André Lurton at Château La Louvière. It is almost Californian in its strikingly modern, clean, fruity/oaky style. Drink young, at 1–3 years. Production of 2,000 cases includes 4 hectares recently planted. Price E.

Château de Fieuzal

GCC (40ha; CS 65%, Me 30%, CF 5%, PV 5%; Léognan)
With its high proportion of Cabernet Sauvignon, controlled fermentation at high temperatures to extract deep colour and with no hard tannins, Fieuzal is almost more Médoc than Graves. The 1979, 1982 and 1983 were particularly successful and the 1984 was almost the best Graves of that year. Since then Fieuzal has gone from strength to strength. The rich fruit allows it to be drunk at 5–6 years, but the wine is not at its peak in good vintages until after 10 years. Under 3,000 cases of *non-classé* white comes from 50% Sa and 50% Se, the grapes being cold-fermented and aged in new barrels for drinking young or keeping. A second wine, Château le Bonnat is made in both red and white. Production 15,000 cases. Price F.

Château Haut-Bailly

GCC (28ha; CS 65%, CF 10%, Me 25%; Léognan)
Very stylish wines (red only), with a purity of fruit, a deceptive suppleness on the palate and the classic "faded-roses" Graves finish. After a few light vintages in the 1970s, Haut-Bailly returned to form with a fine 1977 (100% Cabernet), an excellent 1978 and an exceptional 1979. This performance has been sustained during the 1980s. The wine is attractive quite young, at 6–7 years, but good years should be kept twice as long. The second wine, La Parde de Haut-Bailly, is a lighter, quite delicious reflection of the *grand vin*. No white wine is made. Production 10,000 cases. Price H.

Château Malartic-Lagravière

GCC (17ha; CS 50%, CF 25%, Me 25%; Léognan)
A small *vignoble* covering a single block of land around the Château with the highest yields per hectare of all the Crus Classés. The wine has a strikingly pretty, deep carmine colour, a high proportion of new wood in recent vintages, and is one of the most successful "modern" wines made under the influence of Professeur Peynaud. It is very good at 5–8 years, to appreciate the fruit. The white, from 100% Sauvignon planted on under 2 hectares, is bottled in the spring following the vintage after a few months in new oak, and seems to defy the generalization that Sauvignon on its own does not age well. In 1990 this property was purchased from the Marly-Ridoret family by champagne house Laurent-Perrier. Production 7,500 cases of red, 800 of white. Price F.

Château Olivier

GCC (Red: 18ha; CS 65%, CF 10%, Me 25%. White: 16ha; Se 65%, Sa 30%, Mu 5%; Léognan)
Until 1981, the proprietor, M. de Bethmann, had left the running of this estate to Louis Eschenauer & Co., who undertook a programme of replanting, especially for the less well-known red. With the estate now under the family's control, personal effort is showing results. The wines are well made, with a fine colour, clean fruit and pleasantly tannic Graves finish. The 1978 and 1981 are very successful, and both can be drunk at 7–8 years. As the vines mature, the wine will perhaps need more time. The white is much better than in the past and, despite a high percentage of Sémillon, should be drunk quite young. Production 19,000 cases of red, 9,000 of white. Price E-F.

Château Pape-Clément

GCC (29ha; CS 60%, Me 60%; Pessac)
The oldest vineyard in the Graves, created in 1300 by Bertrand de Goth, who later became Pope Clément V. The wine is not one of the deepest coloured Graves, yet it possesses a rich, supple fruit and a harmonious softness. In certain vintages (1955, 1962, 1970, 1978) it is spectacular, at its best after 12 years, while lighter vintages may be drunk at 5–6 years. There is a tiny amount (1,500 bottles) of *non-classé* white that is not commercially available. Production 10,000 cases. Price low H.

Château Smith-Haut-Lafitte

GCC (55ha; CS 65%, CF 11%, Me 25%; Martillac)
Much recent replanting as part of an expansion programme by the owners (Louis Eschenauer & Co., négocians and also owners of Château Rausan-Ségla) has resulted in a wine of clean fruit and charm that is good to drink at 5–8 years. The 1978 was richer than many wines of that year, the 1982 very complete, the 1985 and 1986 both of high quality. The second red wine is Les Hauts de Smith. The white, *non-classé*, is 100% Sauvignon, crisp and dry for early drinking. Production 20,000 cases of red, 2,500 of white. Price F.

Château La Tour-Martillac

GCC (Red: 19ha; CS 60%, CF 5%, Me 30%, Ma + PV 5%. White: 5ha; Se 55%, Sa 40%, Mu 5%; Martillac)
The high proportion of old wines (average age 30 years, with some from the late 1920s) and old-fashioned vinification produces a full-bodied wine that is rather rough at first, but quite quick to mature and at its best at 10 years. Much improvement has been seen since 1979, particularly with 1982 and 1983. There is now a second label, La Grave-Martillac. The high proportion of Sémillon gives the white the traditional Graves style that improves with age. The Château has been in the hands of the Kressmann family since 1930. Production 9,000 cases of red, 2,500 of white. Price F.

NON-CLASSIFIED PESSAC-LEOGNAN

If one region had to be singled out for overall improvement in quality during the 1980s, it would be the Graves. The high proportion of Cabernet Sauvignon and Cabernet Franc has kept the yields relatively low, and across the two *appellations* red wines have retained the sense of "*terroir*", while whites have improved out of all recognition. The following châteaux are all of Cru Bourgeois standard, some above, and are listed alphabetically. **Château Baret**, red and white, good, not exciting; **Château Brown**, from Léognan, full-bodied and supple; **Château Les Carmes Haut-Brion** (CS 10%, CF 40%, Me 50%), a 3.5-hectare property next door to Haut-Brion, producing a richly textured wine of high quality; **Château de Cruzeau** (40ha), entirely replanted by André Lurton in 1973, good, but less fine and less expensive than the same owner's Château La Louvière; **Château Ferran**, red and white, not to be confused with Château Ferrande further south; **Château de France**, with very well-placed vineyards adjoining de Fieuzal, now making wines of almost Cru Classé quality; **Château Haut-Bergey**, equally well placed, red wines only; **Château Haut-Gardère**, red and white wines of exceptional elegance from Léognan; **Château La Garde**, red and white, a large property distributed by the négociant Eschenauer; **Château Larrivet Haut-Brion** (mostly red, 15ha, CS 60%, Me 35%, Ma + PV 5%), good concentration and fruit; **Château La Louvière** (38ha red, CS 70%, CF 10%, Me 20%; 10ha white, Sa 85%, Se 15%), whose superbly firm reds and crisp stylish whites are the best *non-classé* wines of the region; **Château La Tour Léognan**, the second label of Château Carbonnieux; **Château Rochmorin**, another very large (61ha red, 23ha white) property owned by André Lurton, with wines mid-way between his La Louvière and his Cruzeau; **Château Le Sartre**, red and very good white from the Perrin family of Carbonnieux.

GRAVES

Red and white wines from the centre and southern part of the region, south of Léognan. While most of the finest wine undoubtedly comes from the conscientious Grands Crus Classés winemakers, and while the wines from the north generally have more bouquet, style and concentration than those from the south, there are some excellent *non-classé* wines made in the Graves communes of Portets, Podensac, Illats, Langon and Saint-Pierre-de-Mons. Many may be considered the equivalent of the Crus Bourgeois of the Médoc. The proportion of white wine is much higher here – 600 hectares, nearly 4 million bottles, compared to 900 hectares and 5.5 million bottles of red – than in the Pessac-Léognan *appellation*, and with no reputation to sell on, it was here that the greatest progress was made in the 1970s to produce fresh, fruity, dry white wines. Many are now vinified and matured in new oak barrels to add depth and complexity. The red wines have a soft plumminess that the wines further north lack, and they are ready to drink at 3–5 years. In general they are not expensive and represent some of the best-value-for-money fine wines in Bordeaux. The better ones are listed alphabetically. **Château d'Archambeau**, very stylish red and white wines made by Jean-Philippe Dubourdieu; **Château d'Ardennes**, a property of similar size (25 hectares) from the same commune of Illats, making more sturdy, but equally good wine; **Château d'Arricaud**, a big property at Landiras, south of Barsac; **Château Cabannieux**, at Portets; **Château de Cardaillan**, a fine red wine from the estate of Château de Malle in Sauternes; **Château Cazebonne**, fine red and white wine from the southern commune of Saint-Pierre-de-Mons; **Château de Chantegrive** (50 hectares, half red, half white), the principal property at Podensac, making quite excellent wines; **Château Chicane**, a rich, meaty wine made by Pierre Coste, the Langon propriétaire-négociant; **Château Doms**, Portets; **Château Duc d'Arnauton**, well-made red and white wines from the owners of Château Gravas in Barsac; **Château Ferrande**, a prestigious 40–hectare property in Portets; **Clos Floridène**, a tiny property owned by Denis Dubourdieu, the precursor of fine white wine from the region, rich in floral aromas, but with a clean dry finish; **Domaine de Gaillat**, another splendid red wine from Pierre Coste; **Château Lamouroux**, white wine only from the Lataste family, better known for their Grand Enclos du Château de Cérons; **Château Landiras**, recently purchased by Peter Vinding-Diers (winemaker for some years at Château Rahoul), whose first vintages have been outstanding; **Château Magence**, one of the early producers of fine red and white wine from the south of the *appellation*, and still very good indeed; **Château Mayne-Leveque**, owned by the Leveque family of Château de Chantegrive; **Château Millet** (65ha, red: Me 60%, CS + CF 40%, white: Sa 50%, Se 50%), the largest and most prestigious property in Portets, with long-lasting wine and a quicker maturing second label Château du Clos Renon; **Château Pique-Caillou**, stylish wines from near to Bordeaux; **Château Rahoul**, the second major property in Portets, making excellent

red and white wine; **Château de Respide**, a fine property near Langon, but outclassed in terms of quality by the exceptional wines of **Château Respide-Médeville**, made by the owners of Château Gilette in Preignac; **Château Roquetaillade La Grange** (30ha red, 15ha white), top-quality wines from near to Langon; **Château de Saint-Pierre**, also very fine from a little further south at Saint-Pierre-de-Mons, as good as its neighbour, **Château Toumilon**; **Château Tourteau-Chollet**, an important property east of Portets making red and white wines, distributed by the négociants Mestrézat-Preller.

Graves Supérieurs

Dry, *demi-sec* and sweet white wines from the Graves region, with a minimum alcohol content of 12°. Most producers of dry white wine do not bother with this *appellation*, preferring the simple *appellation* Graves and the name of their château. Most of the Graves Supérieurs produced come from the southern part of the *appellation*, between Portets and Langon, and have all the Graves characteristics, together with a certain softness and richness. The current fashion for dry white wine has meant that much of their market has been lost. Price C-D.

Cérons

Dry and sweet white wines produced in the commune of Cérons, an enclave of the Graves between Podensac and Barsac on the left bank of the Garonne. In recent years, the volume of Cérons has diminished in favour of a dry wine, which may take the *appellation* Graves, or Cérons *sec*, although in the latter case the wine must correspond to the 12.5° of alcohol and 40hl/ha limit imposed at Cérons, instead of the 11° and 50hl/ha for Graves. The classic Cérons is a fully sweet wine, but less luscious than a Sauternes, and even less rich than a Barsac, Loupiac or Sainte-Croix-du-Mont, with a clean honeyed fruit and a pleasant touch of acidity in the finish. The two finest of these sweet (*moelleux* rather than *liquoreux*) wines are the Grand Enclos du Château de Cérons, a wine of great raciness and finesse, and the Château de Cérons, while the wines produced by Châteaux Haura, Mayne-Binet and Archambeau are very good. Since Cérons is not a well-known *appellation* the wines are generally interesting and good value for money. Price C.

Sauternes and other Sweet Wines

The sweet white wines of Bordeaux, or *vins liquoreux* as they are called, come from vineyards on the left bank of the Garonne, from Podensac in the Graves to Langon, and from the slopes opposite on the right bank. The sole grape varieties planted are the Sémillon (always dominant), Sauvignon and Muscadelle (a very small proportion, and often omitted). The particular microclimate of the region, with coolish, misty mornings during the harvest, with the sun burning off the moisture during the day, will precipitate and encourage the development of a fungus called the *Botrytis cinerea* (*pourriture noble* or noble rot), which attacks the grapes and reduces the volume of water in each berry with the consequent increase in sugar and potential flavour. If the weather during the vintage is too cold (as in 1974, 1977), the Botrytis will not appear; if it is too sunny and dry (1976, 1978) there is not enough moisture in the air, and the bunches will become roasted (*rôti*) and not *pourri*; finally, if the noble rot sets in well and the weather breaks (1964, 1982, 1984 and 1989) anything not harvested before it rains is lost.

The actual picking is often spread over several weeks, during which the pickers make successive *tries*, passing many times over the same vineyard to pick the bunches most affected by rot. Fermentation is longer and more difficult than for a dry white or a red wine, where residual sugar is neither required nor allowed, and short cuts, by over-chaptalization or over-sulphuring, are only too evident in the bottle. A fine sweet wine should have a yellow-golden colour, a pronounced floral, fruity, honeyed aroma, a rich, luxurious flavour, clean and not cloying, and a refreshing finish. Of the best-known wines, Barsac is less intensely sweet than Sauternes, although it may sell under the same *appellation*. The minimum alcohol content is 12.5°, and most Sauternes will aim for a minimum of 14° plus 3–4° of unfermented sugar. The low yield of 25hl/ha is almost never reached owing to the natural concentration due to the *pourriture noble*, and the risks inherent in its appearance.

Below: At Château d'Yquem pickers make successive "tries" in the vineyards to pick the bunches – sometimes individual berries – that are most affected by Botrytis.

SAUTERNES

Sauternes must be made with grapes already attacked by *pourriture noble*. They are harvested at the point when the sugar is concentrated to maximum, the pickers going through the vines several times, even picking grape by grape. The major grape variety is Sémillon with also Sauvignon, and a little Muscadelle. The *appellation* Sauternes covers five communes: Barsac (which may, and usually does, use its right to use Barsac as an *appellation* on its own, see page 168), Bommes, Fargues, Preignac and Sauternes. These incredibly luscious, intense, elegant wines are known mostly through their Grands Crus Classés. Sauternes may be drunk young for the explosive, honeyed fruit, but better vintages from better châteaux should really be kept up to 10 or 20 years.

THE CRUS CLASSES OF SAUTERNES

Château d'Yquem

1er GCC (102ha; Se 80%, Sa 20%; Fargues)
Château d'Yquem is the greatest of all the sweet white wines of France, a vineyard of almost mythical reputation, the most extreme in the Bordeaux region in its search for quality and perhaps the most notable example of what is meant by "fine wine". In modern terms, everything is exaggerated at Yquem: the length of the harvest, sometimes lasting into December, with up to eleven *tries*; the refusal to enrich the wine by chaptalization; the minute yield, averaging one glass of wine per vine at 8hl/ha, the use of only new barrels for fermentation and the three and a half years ageing, even the simplicity of the label. The result is a wine of great richness and perfect balance, an extraordinary mixture of fruit, alcohol and residual sugar that develops into a true work of art as it matures. Great vintages are still stunningly young after 40 years. In certain vintages, Yquem will produce a dry wine sold under the name of Y (Ygrec), made from 50% Sémillon, 50% Sauvignon, with some affinity to Laville-Haut-Brion due to the heady Sémillon nose and roundness of flavour. The *appellation* Sauternes is naturally disallowed, and Ygrec is sold as a Bordeaux Supérieur. The Lur-Saluces family, also own Château de Fargues, a Cru Bourgeois with the same *encépagement*, which is less opulent than Yquem, but is none the less a wine of exceptional quality (average production 1,000 cases). At Yquem total production averages 6,500 cases (2,000 of Ygrec, price I). Price J +.

Above: Cellar workers beside a stack of bottles of Sauternes at the tiny property of Clos Haut-Peyraguey.

Château Guiraud

1er GCC (85ha; Se 54%, Sa 45%, Mu 1%; Sauternes)
The sale of Guiraud to Canadian owners in 1981 arrested a decade of decline for this property, famous for its rich, racy, honeyed Sauternes. Heavy investment in vinification equipment, rigorous selection at the harvest and after fermentation, and a high proportion of new oak barrels, swiftly restored Guiraud's reputation. The *grand vin* should be drunk at 5–15 years, the second wine, Le Dauphin de Lalague, at 3–6. There is some excellent, deep-coloured, soft red wine made at Guiraud and some crisp Sauvignon-style dry white. Production 6,500 cases. Price H.

Clos Haut-Peyraguey

1er GCC (15ha; Se 83%, Sa 15%, Mu 2%; Bommes)

This tiny property occupies some of the best *terroir* in Sauternes, and the wine is made with great care. The Sauvignon is harvested when ripe but not botrytized and the Sémillon when fully botrytized (if the year permits), to produce a wine allying bouquet, richness and elegance. It can be drunk young, but ages well, up to 15 years for exceptional vintages like 1975 and 1986. The Pauly family also own Château Haut-Bommes, well situated next door to Yquem, which makes excellent wine. Production 3,000 cases. Price G.

Château Lafaurie-Peyraguey

1er GCC (30ha; Se 93%, Sa 5%, Mu 2%; Bommes)
A medium-sized but parcellated property, Lafaurie-Peyraguey produces elegant Sauternes that is rather pale in colour, not overly sweet during the 1970s but firm and long-lasting. No wine was bottled in 1974, but otherwise quality has been high, particularly since 1979, with outstanding wine in 1981, 1983, 1986 and 1988. It is best drunk at 8–12 years. Lafaurie-Peyraguey is regularly one of the most prized Sauternes. Production: 5,000 cases. Price H.

Château La Tour Blanche

1er GCC (27ha; Se 77%, Sa 20%, Mu 3%; Bommes)
Donated to the State in 1912, La Tour Blanche doubles as a producer of Sauternes and a School of Viticulture and Oenology. The vineyards are on the borders of Barsac, and the wine is correspondingly lighter than many other 1er Cru Sauternes. It used to be sometimes lacking in personality – to be drunk at 5–6 years – but great improvement in vinification since 1985 has produced a finer and more concentrated wine.

Château Rabaud-Promis

1er GCC (33ha; Se 80%, Sa 18%, Mu 2%, Bommes)
The vineyards of Rabaud-Promis represent the larger part of the Château Rabaud estate classified in 1855, due to a separation in 1903. The wines are rich but sometimes rather weighty and lacking complexity, spending 3–4 years in vat before final selection and bottling. No Rabaud-Promis was bottled in 1972, 1973, 1974 or 1977. The 1975 was excellent and the 1979 very good and, like most châteaux, the wines have been very good in the 1980s. They are at their best at 5–10 years. Production 5,000 cases. Price F.

Château Rayne-Vigneau

1er GCC (72ha; Se 85%, Sa 20%; Bommes)
One of the largest properties in Sauternes, Rayne-Vigneau was much modernized in the early 1970s and now produces a pleasant *vin liquoreux* and a crisp dry wine (Se 50%, Sa 50%) from the highest-yielding vines

in the *appellation*. It is rare among 1ers Crus in that it is regularly found in supermarkets in France. May be drunk at 4–5 years, although the 1986 and 1988 will last longer. Production 16,500 cases. Price low F.

Château Rieussec

1er GCC (66ha; Se 80%, Sa 18%, Mu 2%; Fargues)
The vines of Rieussec cover the highest point in the same commune as Yquem, to make a very stylish wine that is a little less rich than their neighbour's. The 1976 was untypical, being rather caramelized, but 1975 and 1979 were classic. A *cuvée speciale*, corresponding to the old *appellation "crème de tête"*, was introduced in 1975, while the less concentrated *cuvées* sell under the second label, Clos Labère. A dry white wine is also made at Rieussec, called "R" de Rieussec, from the first *trie* of non-botrytized grapes. It is more Sémillon in style than the other dry white Sauternes, with the exception of "Y". In 1984 the vineyard was purchased by Domaines Rothschild of Château Lafite. Their influence is clear in the excellent 1988. Production 9,000 cases. Price H.

Château Sigalas Rabaud

1er GCC (14ha; Se 90%, Sa 10%, Bommes)
The smaller part of the Rabaud property, making wines of greater finesse than Rabaud-Promis, Sigalas Rabaud is one of the lighter, but most elegant and aromatic Sauternes. The floral, peach-like bouquet is preserved by ageing in vats rather than barrels and the wine can be drunk with pleasure after 4–5 years. Production 2,500 cases. Price F.

Château Suduiraut

1er GCC (70ha; Se 80%, Sa 20%, Preignac)
Suduiraut is generally recognized as being potentially the second-greatest wine in Sauternes after Yquem. It is one of the most rich wines, both in colour and flavour, of the *appellation* which in great years (1967, 1976) comes near to perfection. Three years were totally declassified (1973, 1974, 1977), and the final selection produced only 4,160 cases in 1975 and 2,900 in 1976. 1982 was exceptionally rich for the year, but 1983 disappointing. By 1986 it was back on form. Suduiraut ages well and is at its best at 10–20 years. Production 10,000 cases. Price H.

Château d'Arche

2ème GCC (30ha; Se 90%, Sa 10%; Sauternes)
Well-made, rich and honeyed wine from a property situated between La Tour Blanche and Guiraud. The 1980 is remarkable for the vintage. A tiny amount of *crème de tête* is selected in successful vintages, the most recent being 1967, 1971 and 1975. Until 1980, the

second wine was sold under the label Château d'Arche-Lafaurie, an adjacent property. Lesser *cuvées* are now sold to the Bordeaux trade in order to maintain the quality of the *grand vin*. Recent vintages have been of 1er Cru standard. Production 4,000 cases. Price high F.

Château Filhot

2ème GCC (60ha; Se 50%, Sa 40%, Mu 5%; Sauternes) The most southern of the Crus Classés, Filhot has family connections with the Lur-Saluces at Yquem, but the wine is quite different in style, being much less opulent. The light sweetness and marked finesse of flavour allow the wines of Château Filhot to be drunk relatively young, at 3–4 years, while the best vintages (1979, 1986) are very fine at 10 years old. A dry white wine, Le Vin Sec de Château Filhot, has been made for many years. Production 10,000 cases. Price F.

Château Lamothe

2ème GCC (8ha; Se 70%, Sa 15%, Mu 15%; Sauternes) The 8-hectare portion of Lamothe owned by M. Despujols produces a straightforward Sauternes with no ambitions to rival the 1ers Crus. Production 1,700 cases. Price E.

Château Lamothe-Guignard

2ème GCC (15ha; Se 90%, Sa 5%, Mu 5%) The 11 hectares purchased by the Guignard family after the death of the owner (M. Bastit Saint-Martin of Château d'Arche) in 1980, produced their first wine from the 1981 vintage under the Lamothe-Guignard label, a wine of great promise. Since then, a further 4 hectares have been planted, increasing the proportion of Sémillon, while the racy quality is confirmed each year. Production 2,000 cases. Price E.

Château de Malle

2ème GCC (24ha; Se 75%, Sa 23%, Mu 2%; Preignac) Château de Malle appears to be one of the sweetest Sauternes, rich, golden and unctuous, with not quite the complexity of a 1er Cru. The same property makes some very fruity red Graves, Château de Cardaillan, and a dry white, Chevalier de Malle. The second wine of de Malle is Domaine de Saint-Hélène. Production 5,000 cases. Price E.

Château Romer du Hayot

2ème GCC (16ha; Se 70%, Sa 25%, Mu 5%; Fargues) The wine from this property, which adjoins Château de Malle, is well balanced and fruity but, in common with all but the finest *vins liquoreux*, it takes a fine vintage (1975, 1979, 1983, 1986) for it to achieve great richness and complexity and for it to last for more than 5–6 years. Production 4,000 cases. Price E.

CRUS BOURGEOIS

As the image of Sauternes improves and the 1ers Crus Classés begin to sell at a realistically high price, more notice is being taken of a few fine wines in the *appellation* that were less well known through lack of classification and their sales being concentrated in the home market. The ex-*régisseur* from Château d'Yquem, Pierre Méslier, owns **Château Raymond-Lafon** (20ha; Se 80%, Sa 20%), making luscious, stylish wines from vines situated between Yquem and Sigalas-Rabaud. **Château Bastor-Lamontagne** is a large property, well situated at Preignac, of which **Château de Pick** used to be a part, both now making fine Sauternes; **Château Haut-Bergeron**, also at Preignac, has a part of its vines next to Yquem, and practises a rigorous selection — there is an excellent second label, Château Farluret; **Château Saint-Amand** makes wine worthy of a 2ème Cru; **Domaine d'Arche-Pugneau** is entirely surrounded by 1ers Crus; finally, at **Château Gilette** (3.5ha; Se 85%, Sa 15%, Mu 2%), the Médeville family have been making outstanding Sauternes since the 1930s. The 1937 *crème de tête* rivalled the Yquem and Climens of that year, and the 1953 is no less extraordinary. At Gilette different *cuvées* are produced of varying degrees of richness, which will be stated on the label. It is quite justifiably almost a "cult" wine in France. The Médevilles also own **Château les Justices**, producing fine Sauternes as well as an excellent Bordeaux rouge. Price D-F.

BARSAC

Sweet white wine from vineyards on sandy-gravelly soil to the south of Cérons and to the north of Sauternes on the left bank of the Garonne. Only the classic Bordeaux grapes (Sémillon, Sauvignon and Muscadelle) may be used, and if the wine is vinified dry, it loses the Barsac *appellation*, and becomes Bordeaux or Bordeaux Supérieur. Grapes are picked late, affected by *pourriture noble*, and must have the same degree of alcohol and yield as Sauternes. Barsac has all the qualities of Sauternes, and may in fact be sold under that *appellation*, but is more usually sold under that of Barsac-Sauternes. It differentiates itself from the rich, luscious Sauternes by being slightly lighter in style, more lemony. The best Barsacs, 1ers and 2èmes Grands Crus Classés, produce some of the finest sweet white wines in the world. Price D.

THE CRUS CLASSES OF BARSAC

Château Climens

1er GCC (35ha; Se 98%, Sa 2%)
Climens shares with Coutet the privilege of being one of the two 1ers Crus in Barsac. It is the richest, most complete of the Barsacs, and in some years (1937, 1947, 1971, 1983, 1988) has been compared with the wines of Château d'Yquem. Under the ownership of Lucien Lurton, Climens remains dedicated to quality: four *tries* during the vintage, fermentation and two years' ageing in barrel, and careful final selection. The wines are rich and complete and develop their full potential over 10–20 years. Production 6,000 cases. Price H.

Château Coutet

1er GCC (37ha; Se 75%, Sa 23%, Mu 2%)
Climens' rival in Barsac, producing smooth, stylish wines, with less power but equal finesse. The slight hint of a lemony acidity after the honeyed taste is pure Barsac. Coutet is fermented and aged in wood, bottled after two years and is at its best at 8–10 years. A tiny amount of *crème de tête* is produced in great years, named Cuvée Madame, after the late owner, Mme Rolland-Guy. The current owner, M. Baly, will continue this practice. Production 6,000 cases. Price F.

Château Broustet

2ème GCC (16ha; Se 63%, Sa 25%, Mu 12%)
Broustet is owned by M. Eric Fournier (also proprietor of Château Calon in Saint-Emilion) who makes a rich, smooth Barsac. No wine was bottled in 1974, 1976 and 1977, but 1979 and 1985 showed well. The lesser wines (all 1976, for example) are sold under the label Château de Ségur. Since 1986 quality has been very high. Production 2,000 cases. Price E.

Château Caillou

2ème GCC (15ha; Se 90%, Sa 10%)
The vineyards of Caillou touch those of Climens and the now replanted Château Myrat, and produce a wine with good fruit and rich flavour that spends 2–3 years in wood before bottling. It is a concentrated, long-lived wine, with a loyal French clientèle. Production 4,000 cases. Price F.

Château Doisy-Daëne

2ème GCC (15ha; Se ;70%, Sa 20%, Mu 10%)
Once the best known of the three "Doisy" vineyards, Doisy-Daëne is now rivalled by Doisy-Védrines. Pierre Dubourdieu vinifies in stainless steel and ages the wine for one year in new oak, to produce a lively *vin liquoreux* of great style and finesse. A very clean and aromatic dry white wine is made under the *appellation* Graves. Production 4,500 cases. Price high E.

Château Doisy-Dubroca

2ème GCC (3.3ha; Se 80%, Sa 20%)
This tiny property, purchased by Lucien Lurton in 1971 at the same time as his purchase of Climens, is sandwiched between Doisy-Daëne and Doisy-Védrines. The influence of Professeur Peynaud on the vinification here, as at Climens, has resulted in a harmonious balance of roundness and long-lived richness. Production 400 cases. Price F.

Château Doisy-Védrines

2ème GCC (21ha; Se 80%, Sa 20%)
A very traditional property, like Climens and Coutet, fermenting and ageing in barrel and making rich, long-lived wine from a small yield. 1975 was exceptional, 1976 and 1980 were very fine, and 1986 was one of the best wines of the vintage. Doisy-Védrines can be drunk at 5–6 years but repays keeping. A clean, crisp dry white wine, Le Chevalier de Védrines, is made in some quantity, as well as a red wine, Latour-Védrines, reducing the average production of Doisy-Védrines to 3,000 cases. Price E.

Château de Myrat

2ème GCC (22ha, Se 85%, Sa 10%, Mu 5%)
Due to the uneconomic status of most of the 2èmes
Crus Sauternes over several decades, the owner of
Château de Myrat decided to uproot his vines in 1976.
His son has now replanted, and the first official vintage
was the 1990.

Château Nairac

2ème GCC (16ha; Se 90%, Sa 6%, Mu 4%)
Perhaps the first example of the new confidence in the
future of the wines of Barsac was the purchase in 1971
of Nairac by Nicole Tari of Château Giscours and her
then husband Tom Heeter. Since 1971 the best possible
wine has been made when the vintage permits (there
was no Nairac in 1977, 1978 or 1984), and the
dedication to quality is on a par with the finest of the
1ers Crus. Production 2,000 cases. Price high E.

Château Suau

2ème GCC (6.5ha; Se 80%; Sa 10%, Mu 10%)
A straightforward, rather sweet Barsac under the same
ownership as Château Navarro in the Graves. No
pretensions to rival the 1ers Crus. Production 1,650
cases. Price D.

*Above: The damp mists over the vineyards of Barsac
encourage the noble rot that is the secret of Sauternes.*

CRUS BOURGEOIS

As there are only two 1ers Crus Classés in Barsac, the
Crus Bourgeois have not been overshadowed as they
have been in Sauternes. Next door to Climens and
Doisy-Védrines, **Château Roumieu** produces 3,000
cases of excellent wine, and Simone Dubourdieu makes
a Barsac with great *sève* at **Château Roumieu-Lacoste**;
the wines from **Château Piada** are successful, as are the
fine, aromatic wines of **Château Liot**; **Château
Cantegril** is lightly sweet, with a lemony edge;
Château Guiteronde-du-Hayot is less sweet but
more fruity, with a high proportion of Sauvignon;
Château Gravas, originally named Doisy-Gravas, is
fine and unctuous, of Cru Classé quality, especially the
very concentrated *cuvée speciale*; **Château du Mayne**,
owned by Jean Sanders of Haut-Bailly, is in the classic
mould, while **Château Padouën**, directed by Peter
Vinding-Diers, uses cold fermentation and new barrels
to produce a small quantity of exciting wine; **Château
de Rolland** has a large production of pleasant wine, the
smaller **Château Saint-Marc** and **Château Simon** are
reliable, and an old Lur Saluces property, **Château
Pernaud**, has recently been replanted by the manager
of Château Suduiraut. Price D.

THE OTHER SWEET WINES OF BORDEAUX

The *appellations* that follow adhere to the same principles as those of Sauternes: the Sémillon grape is dominant, with a complement of Sauvignon and sometimes a little Muscadelle; sweetness is usually attained as a result of overripe and hopefully botrytized grapes; chaptalization is discouraged, for it affects the overall balance of the wine. While the overall trend is towards dry white wines, the growing interest in *vins liquoreux* and the recent run of fine vintages in the 1980s, has seen a welcome renaissance in the sweet wines of Bordeaux.

Bordeaux-Haut-Benauge

Sweet white wine from the middle of the Entre-Deux-Mers region, made from Sémillon, Sauvignon and Muscadelle. Minimum alcohol content 11.5°, basic yield 45hl/ha. Not often seen, owing to the fall from favour of inexpensive sweet white wine. Most of the *appellation* is vinified dry and sold as Entre-Deux-Mers, but there has been a renaissance of this style recently, especially in Châteaux de Bertin and Haut Mallet.

Cadillac

Semi-sweet and sweet white wines from the commune of Cadillac on the right bank of the River Garonne in the southern part of the Premières Côtes de Bordeaux region, opposite Cérons and Barsac. Only the classic white grapes of Bordeaux – Sémillon, Sauvignon and Muscadelle – are permitted, and the wine used to be sold under the rather cumbersome Premières Cotes de Bordeaux-Cadillac label. Production is small from an area that has been reduced to 80 hectares. Drink quite young and serve very cold. Price C.

Cérons

See page 163.

Côtes de Bordeaux Saint-Macaire

Semi-sweet or sweet white wine from vines planted on the right bank of the Garonne, across the river from Langon, at the south end of the Entre-Deux-Mers *appellation*. The grape varieties permitted are the classic *cépages nobles* of Bordeaux white winemaking: Sémillon, Sauvignon and Muscadelle. Minimum alcohol content is 11.5° from a yield of 40hl/ha, producing fruity, honeyed wines, a little less rich and intense than Saint-Croix-du-Mont and Loupiac. At the best young, served very cold. Price B-C.

Loupiac

Sweet white wine only, from a small *appellation* between Cadillac and Sainte-Croix-du-Mont on the right bank of the Garonne, opposite Barsac. The Sémillon, Sauvignon and Muscadelle grape varieties are late-picked to make a smooth, honeyed wine in the style of a minor Sauternes. Many châteaux make only a small proportion of their wine in this manner, preferring the more commercial quality of a dry wine, but there has been a revival of interest since the early 1980s. For many years the finest wines, rivalling the best Sauternes, were the *crèmes de têtes* of Château de Ricaud, which should now re-emerge under the new ownership, and fine wines are also made at Château Loupiac-Gaudier, Château du Cros, Clos Jean and Château Mazarin. Price C.

Sainte-Croix-du-Mont

Sweet white wine from hillside vineyards on the right bank of the Garonne opposite Sauternes. The Sémillon, Sauvignon and Muscadelle grapes ripen well into the autumn to produce a small quantity of *vin liquoreux* often comparable to a good Sauternes. In common with Loupiac, the minimum alcohol content must be 12.5° from a yield (much higher than in Sauternes, but very seldom reached) of 40hl/ha, leading many growers to pick early and make a Bordeaux *blanc sec*. True Sainte-Croix-du-Mont is pale gold in colour when young, deepening to amber with age, it is honeyed, rich and unctuous, with great finesse. The better wines are fine and long lasting. They may be drunk young, to appreciate the explosive richness of fruit, or kept for up to 25 years. Such wines may come from Château Loubens, the acknowledged "1er Cru" of the *appellation*, Château La Rame, Château Laurette, Château de Tastes and the excellent Château Lousteau-Vieil. Price C-D.

Saint-Emilion

Saint-Emilion is by far the largest fine wine *appellation* in Bordeaux, with over 5,000 hectares under vines, not counting the 3,000 hectares in the "Satellite" Saint-Emilions to the north-east of the main *appellation*. The vineyards are to be found on the right bank of the Dordogne in the region known as the Libournais, named after Libourne, the town that is the capital of the right-bank wine industry. Grapes planted are principally the Merlot, with the balance being made up of Cabernet Franc, and a little Cabernet Sauvignon and Malbec (Pressac). Consequently, the wine has a richness and suppleness from the Merlot, that is a contrast to the rather hard intensity of the Cabernet Sauvignon-based Médocs. The wines of Saint-Emilion are divided into two styles by nature of the soil: the "Graves", sandy, gravelly soil adjacent to Pomerol, giving wines with a pronounced bouquet and rich, almost sweet fruit; and the "Côtes", undulating vineyards with a clayey soil on a limestone base, where wines are rather firmer, close-knit and less easy when young. Both are quite robust, with a minimum alcohol content of 11° from a yield of 45hl/ha, 11.15° for the Grands Crus from a lower yield of 40hl/ha. There are many different styles of wine in the *appellation*, due to soil, *encépagement* and vinification, but if there is a Saint-Emilion type, it is a rich, full-coloured wine, with a warm concentrated fruit and an apparent ripenesss due to a relatively low degree of tannin. They may be drunk younger than a Médoc or a Graves, the minor wines at 2–3 years, the better ones at 5–6, while, like all fine claret, the best wines need 10 years. Production varies greatly, but averages 35 million bottles.

THE CLASSIFICATION OF THE WINES OF SAINT-EMILION

The *appellation* Saint-Emilion classified its wines in 1954, selecting two châteaux (Ausone and Cheval-Blanc) as 1ers Grands Crus Classés "A" and a further ten as 1ers Grands Crus Classés "B", these last being on a par with the 2èmes or 3èmes Crus Classés of the Médoc. Further down the scale come the Grands Crus Classés, the equivalent of the 5èmes Cru or Crus Bourgeois, of which there were originally 72 châteaux. These are followed by the Grands Crus, where the châteaux re-apply each year and their wine can be refused by a tasting panel. Everything else is plain Saint-Emilion. This system underwent slight changes in 1969, and in 1985, 31 years after the first official classification, the system was once again revised, reducing the different levels of officially classified wines from four to two. From the 1985 vintage, there are 74 Grand Cru Classé Saint-Emilions, and then Saint-Emilions *tout court*. Within the Grand Cru Classé category, there are 11 Premiers Grands Crus Classés, down from 12, following the controversial demotion of Château Beauséjour-Bécot, and 63 Grands Crus Classés.

THE PREMIER GRANDS CRUS CLASSES

Château Ausone

(7ha; Me 50%, CF 50%)
The vines are planted on the edge of the town of Saint-Emilion, facing east-south-east on a clayey soil with a limestone base. The protection from the north and the west, the slope of the vineyards and the age of the vines, combine to offer the finest raw material, which since 1975 has been complemented by the brilliant vinification of Pascal Delbeck. Ausone has a deep garnet-ruby colour, an intense, smooth flavour, with no hint of heaviness, and a long harmonious finish. It is the most sophisticated of the Saint-Emilions. New barrels are used every year and the wine matures perfectly in the cellars (originally limestone quarries) and is bottled after 15–20 months with no filtration. It has no harsh tannins and may be drunk at 7–8 years, while the finer vintages last 15–20. Production 2,000 cases. Price J + .

Château Cheval Blanc

(35ha; CF 66%, Me 33%, Ma 1%)
The other 1er Grand Cru Classé "A" of Saint Emilion, from the Pomerol side of the *appellation* known as the "Graves". The soil, basically gravel, with sand and clay in parts, and the virtual absence of slope is particularly suited to the Cabernet Franc, lending to this varietal a richness that is not found elsewhere in Bordeaux. Cheval Blanc is always a big wine, or potentially so, with a roundness, richness and certain plummy sweetness that is a pure contrast to Ausone. It is more often compared either to Pétrus, across the road in Pomerol, or to Figeac, of whose vineyard it used to be a part. Really great vintages (1961, 1975, 1982, 1985, 1988) where the low yield concentrates the flavour, will last 20–30 years, while the good ones may be drunk at 10–12. Production 12,500 cases. Price J + .

Left: Wine maturing in oak casks in the chai of a Bordeaux château.

Château Beauséjour-Duffau-Lagarrosse

(7ha; Me 60%, Cf 25%, CS 15%)

The smaller part of the Beauséjour property, bordered to the north by Beauséjour-Bécot and to the south and west by Canon. The wines are classic Saint-Emilion, deep-coloured, high in alcohol and extract, with the rich fruit of the Merlot balanced by the firmness of the Cabernets. Good vintages (1979, 1982, 1988 and the spectacular 1990) need at least 10 years and the best wines will last 20 years or more. Production 3,300 cases. Price G.

Château Belair

(13ha; Me 60%, CF 40%)

Under the same ownership and management as Ausone, of whose vineyards it is a north-western continuation, Belair is similar in style and has been extremely successful in recent vintages. The slightly higher percentage of Merlot, the ageing in barrels of which only one-third are renewed each year, and the "younger" vines (35 years average, as opposed to 45 years at Ausone) tend to make a faintly less striking wine. The 1979 and 1989 however, are among the best of the *appellation*. At 10 years Belair is perfect. Production 4,000 cases. Price H.

Château Canon

(18ha; Me 55%; CF 40%, CS 3%, Ma 2%)

Canon is entirely surrounded by other 1er Grands Crus Classés, Beauséjour, Clos Fourtet, Belair and Magdelaine, and corresponds the archetypal Saint-Emilion "Côtes": deep-coloured, aromatic, firm yet welcoming, with an admirable seriousness and length. The cellars, old limestone quarries, are the finest in Saint-Emilion, vinification is very traditional and the wine stays for 22 months in wood (two-thirds renewed each year) before bottling. It is ideal at 8–10 years, but the best vintages need longer. Production 7,000 cases. Price high G.

Château Figeac

(38ha; Me 30%, CF 35%, CS 35%)

One of the largest of the 1ers Grands Crus Classés, situated in the "Graves" Saint-Emilion, adjoining Cheval Blanc which, until the 1830s, was part of the Figeac estate. The gravelly hillocks that make up most of the vineyard at Figeac are particularly suited to the Cabernet, and the one-third of Cabernet Sauvignon gives the wine a length and *sève* that complement perfectly the natural sweetness of the Merlot. Figeac is less massive than Cheval Blanc, equally firm, but more

Above: Ploughing between the rows of vines in a Saint-Emilion vineyard.

seductive. Vinification is impeccable, and the whole of the crop is aged in new barrels. The harmony and sweetness of Château Figeac allow the wine to be enjoyed young, yet the same qualities do not fade with age. The second wine is La Grangeneuve de Figeac. Production 20,000 cases. Price I.

Clos Fourtet

(18ha; Me 70%, CF 20%, 10%)

The vines of Clos Fourtet are planted on the eastern edge of the town of Saint-Emilion on a clayey soil with a solid limestone base, from which the famous cellars have been hewn. The wine used to be hard and old-fashioned, often dried out before the tannin had time to soften, but since the 1978 vintage the influence of the new owner, André Lurton has resulted in a more modern vinification to extract more fruit and less tannin. It fairly resembles Canon, with less intensity and is quicker maturing. A forthright, well-made wine. Production 4,500 cases. Price high G.

Château La Gaffelière

(22ha; Me 65%, CF 25%, CS 10%)
The oldest vineyard in the *appellation*, created in the fourth century, and possibly (owing to the discovery in 1969 of the ruins of a Roman palace, complete with mosaics showing bunches of grapes) the site of Ausonius' house. The vines are planted away from the town, surrounded by Belair and Magdelaine to the north-west and Pavie to the east. The dominance of Merlot, mostly vines over 40 years old, and a long vinification give the wine a blend of richness and solidity which is typically Saint-Emilion. The recent successful vintages of La Gaffelière (1979, 1983, 1985, 1988, 1989) will be at their best at 10–12 years. Production 8,000 cases. Price G.

Château Magdelaine

(11ha; Me 90%, CF 10%)
A small property with vines planted on south-facing slopes away from the town, flanked by Canon and Belair to the north and east. Magdelaine is owned by Ets J.-P. Moueix of Libourne and the wine made by the Moueix oenologist Jean-Claude Berrouët. The high proportion of Merlot, the highest among the Grands Crus Classés, picked at optimum ripeness by a large team of *vendangeurs*, gives the wine a sweetness and suppleness that is almost Burgundian. It is the most feminine of the finest Saint-Emilions and, apart from naturally tannic vintages such as 1970 and 1975, may be drunk at 6–8 years. Production 5,000 cases. Price H.

Château Pavie

(37ha; Me 55%, CF 25%, CS 20%)
In production terms, one of the largest of the 1er Grands Crus Classés (but equal in size to Figeac), Pavie occupies a superbly situated south-facing slope outside the town of St-Emilion. It also possesses some 100–year-old vines, the most ancient of the *appellation*. A more modern vinification since the mid-1970s has combined with a run of good vintages (a good 1978 and exceptional 1979, 1982, 1985, 1986 and 1988) enabling Saint-Emilion to put Pavie firmly in the top rank. It is less austere than Canon or even than Clos Fourtet, another Peynaud-advised estate. The current stylish fruitiness of the wines of Pavie makes it difficult to wait the 10–12 years that they deserve. Production 15,000 cases. Price G-H.

Château Trottevieille

(10ha; Me 50%, CF 25%, CS 25%)
The vineyard of Trottevieille is situated to the east of Saint-Emilion, set apart from the other 1ers Grands Crus Classés "Côtes", which are to the west and south.

The wine always has a good colour and vigorous fruit but has sometimes lacked finesse and intensity of flavour. It is reliable, very much improved since 1985 and shows best at 5–8 years. Production 4,200 cases. Price F.

THE GRANDS CRUS CLASSES

The last but one classification of the châteaux of Saint-Emilion was in 1969, which confirmed Grand Cru Classé status for 72 châteaux. In the 1985 classification this number was reduced to 63. Some of these are almost of 1er Grand Cru standard, others are definitely not. Most of the wines are very good at 5 years, at their best at 7–8, and fading after 12. In cases where production is pushed to the limit, the wines will be lighter and quicker to mature. Price is usually indicative of quality, and while some of the larger properties have acquired a reputation that ensures them a good price, the smaller estates often do as well by selling to a regular clientèle of private buyers. Since 1985 high yields have been avoided, and quality once again matches the price. The list that follows is in alphabetical order.

The Saint-Emilion "Côtes"

Château L'Angélus, a large property below Beauséjour, producing round, full wines, quite expensive, but recently of exceptional quality; **Château L'Arrosée**, well-made, concentrated wine with 40% Cabernet Sauvignon; **Château Balestard-la-Tonnelle**, rich, full-bodied wine with length, finesse and class; **Château Beauséjour-Bécot** (16ha; Me 70%, CF 24%, CS 6%), formerly a 1er Grand Cru Classé, demoted for having extended its vineyard through the purchase in 1979 of two adjoining properties, Château La Carte and Château Trois Moulins, thus almost doubling its size; continues to make nice, meaty wine of high standard, with a second wine, La Tournelle des Moines; **Château Bellevue**, sound, quick maturing; **Château Bergat**, not far from Trottevieille, is managed and sold by Borie-Manoux; **Château Berliquet**, a very fine property deservedly promoted to Grand Cru status in 1985; **Château Cadet-Piola**, smooth, elegant wines with good colour and one of the prettiest labels in Bordeaux; **Château Canon-la Gaffelière**, stylish, elegant wine, good but rather expensive; **Château Capdemourlin**, **Château Cap de Mourlin**, the wines are made separately but in the same cellar and are of the same depth and quality as Balestard-la-Tonnelle; **Château La Carte**, integrated with Beauséjour-Bécot; **Château Chapelle-Madeleine**, a tiny 0.2-hectare property owned by Mme Dubois-Challon and since 1970 absorbed into Ausone; **Château Le Châtelet**, small property, not far from Beauséjour, with well-made wine; **Château La Clotte**, well-situated vineyard near to Pavie, lovely, elegant, Merlot-style wines; **Château La Clusière**, adjoined to and owned by Pavie, but not so fine; **Château Couvent des Jacobins**, excellent, meaty, high-quality wines, as good as the **Clos des Jacobins**, a Cordier-owned vineyard where the wines are improving; **Château Curé-Bon-La-Madeleine**, excellent little property near to Belair and Canon, making well-structured wines; **Château Faurie-de-Souchard**, well-made, good soft fruit, quick maturing; **Château Fonplégade**, large property making very reliable sturdy wine; **Château Fonroque**, owned by J.-P. Moueix, dark, full-bodied, very different from Moueix's Magdelaine; **Château Franc-Mayne**, well-positioned property acquired in 1984 by AXA-Millésimes and now making concentrated elegant wine; **Château Grand-Mayne**, elegant wines from 50% Cabernets; **Château Grand-Pontet**, firm fleshy wines, lacking in charm; **Château Guadet-Saint-Julien**, a small, well-run property near Montagne-Saint-Emilion; **Château Haut-Sarpe**, owned by the Janoueix family, making serious, complex wine; **Château Laniote**, a Merlot-dominated property next door to Fonroque; **Château Larcis-Ducasse**, an excellent property just east of Pavie, full-bodied, concentrated wines from old vines; **Château Larmande**, producing some deep-coloured, stylish wines of top quality; **Château Laroze**, big property with sandy soil, next to the "Graves" in situation and style, well-made wines; **Clos La Madeleine**, tiny property beside Belair and Magdelaine, 50% Cabernets, should be very fine; **Château Matras**, next door to L'Angélus, with a low proportion of Merlot, fine, carefully made wines; **Château Mauvezin**, small property near to Soutard and Balestard-la-Tonnelle, making very solid wine from old vines, but now replanting; **Château Moulin du Cadet**, well situated, just north of Saint-Emilion among the other Cadets, making firm, stylish wine; **Clos de L'Oratoire**, largish property making fairly rich, straightforward wines; **Château Pavie Decesse**, well-placed property above Pavie and under the same ownership since 1970, making firm, elegant, long-lived wines; **Château Pavie Macquin**, traditionally made, Merlot-dominated wines with potential for expansion; **Château Pavillon-Cadet**, small property making fine wines with 50% Cabernet Franc; **Château Petit-Faurie-de-Soutard**, solid, high-class wines from a property managed by M. Capdemourlin; **Château Le Prieuré**, deep-coloured, firm wines made by the same owner as Vraye-Croix-de-Gay (Pomerol) and Siaurac (Lalande-de-Pomerol); **Château Saint-Georges-Côte-Pavie**, well-made, elegant wines from a vineyard next to La Gaffelière and Pavie; **Château Sansonnet**, small property near Trottevieille; **Château La Serre**, meaty wines from a Merlot-dominated property not far from Ausone, under the same ownership as La

Pointe; **Château Soutard**, classic, distinguished, long-lived wines from a large estate well situated just north-west of Saint-Emilion; **Château Tertre-Daugay**, well-placed vineyards adjoining Magdelaine and Belair, recently bought by the owner of La Gaffelière and being replanted; **Château Trimoulet**, serious, carefully made wine owned by the négociant Pierre Jean; **Château Troplong-Mondot**, one of the largest and the best of the Grands Crus Classés, owned by the Valette family of Pavie, producing consistently fine wine; **Château Villemaurine**, at the north-eastern edge of the town, producing sturdy, rather lean wines.

The Saint-Emilion "Graves"

Château Chauvin, on the Saint-Emilion-Pomerol border, producing fleshy wines with a certain sweetness; **Château Corbin**, deep-coloured, meaty wine but lacking finesse; **Château Corbin-Michotte**, wines of exceptional quality and breed, painstakingly made by Jean-Noël Boidron; **Château Croque-Michotte**, situated between Cheval Blanc and Pomerol, making a full-bodied, plummy wine of good quality; **Château Dassault**, big property, where the wines are as elegant as the label; **Château La Dominique**, next door to Cheval Blanc, with rich, generous, stylish wine; **Château Grand-Barrail-Lamarzelle-Figeac**, big property opposite Figeac whose wine it resembles, but in a lighter, sweeter style; **Château Grand-Corbin**, big, chewy wine from old vines, in the same style as Corbin; **Château Grand-Corbin-Despagne**, producing serious, deep-coloured wines of high quality; **Château Haut-Corbin**, small property making smooth, modern Saint-Emilion; **Château Ripeau**, next door to the declassified Jean-Faure, which it used to own, making smoother, softer wines; **Château La Tour-Figeac**, separated from Figeac in 1879, this is the best of the three La Tour-Figeacs; **Château la Tour-du-Pin-Figeac (Giraud)**, well-made wines but not up to the Figeac name; **Château La Tour-du-Pin-Figeac (A. Moueix)**, a more elegant, leaner wine, high in Cabernet Franc; **Château Yon-Figeac**, opposite Figeac, adjoining Grand-Barrail, producing firm, consistent wine.

SAINT-EMILION

In rare cases these wines may be the equal of the Grands Crus Classés, but generally their quality is of good generic standard. With 72 Grands Crus Classés already in existence before 1985, some 200 wines were awarded Grand Cru status, but could lose this on a decision from a tasting panel. These wines are henceforth classified simply as Saint-Emilion. Listed

alphabetically are some of the finer estates deserving serious consideration: Châteaux Bellefont-Belcier, Cardinal Villemaurine, Carteau Matras, Cormeil-Figeac, Ferrand, La Fleur, La Fleur Pourret, Fombrauge, Franc Pourret, La Grâce Dieu, Grand-Corbin-Manuel, Haut Simard, Jean Faure, Laroque, Magnan-La-Gaffelière, Monbousquet, Montalabert, Peyreau, Simard, Vieux Sarpe. The *cave coopérative*, l'Union des Producteurs de Saint-Emilion, is extremely large and capable of showing some well-made, quite quick to mature wines under a variety of château names.

THE "SATELLITE" SAINT-EMILIONS

The communes surrounding Saint-Emilion have the right to the *appellation* if it is preceded by the name of their commune. They share the same 45hl/ha maximum yield (very often exceeded) as Saint-Emilion and the 11° minimum alcohol, and tend to be less concentrated but similar in style. With the merging of Sables-Saint-Emilion into the St-Emilion *appellation* and Parsac-Saint-Emilion to Montagne-Saint-Emilion, there are now four "satellites".

Above: Early morning in the vineyards of Saint-Emilion, the largest high-quality wine appellation in France.

Lussac-Saint-Emilion

Red wines from the slopes north of Saint-Emilion to the west of Pomerol. Lussac-Saint-Emilion is ready to drink young, at 3–4 years, and fades after about 8 years. The best are as good as, and the same price as, the Saint Emilion Grands Crus. Recommended Châteaux are: Bel-Air, Haut-Milon, de Lussac, Lyonnat, Mayne-Blanc and Tour de Cirenet. Price D.

Montagne-Saint-Emilion

Red wines from vineyards to the north of Saint-Emilion and to the west of Pomerol. Vines planted on the higher slopes on a chalky-clayey soil give a more robust wine than those planted on the gravelly soil towards Pomerol. Recommended Châteaux include: Calon (also in Saint-Georges-Saint-Emilion), Corbin, Faizeau, Montaiguillon, Plaisance, Roudier, Vieux Château Saint André. Price D.

Puisseguin-Saint-Emilion

Red wines from the north-east of Saint-Emilion. The same grape varieties are planted on a stony clayey-chalky soil, and produce wines that are full-coloured and robust, very much in the Saint-Emilion style, and keep well. None the less, Puisseguin is generally less fine than either Saint-Georges or Montagne Saint-Emilion. The best Châteaux are: Branda, Bel-Air, Guibeau, Roc de Boissac. Price C-D.

Saint-Georges-Saint-Emilion

Red wines from vineyards which are planted to the north-east of Saint-Emilion, bordering those of Montagne-Saint-Emilion. All the vines are planted on the "Côtes", and produce a more robust wine, with a deep colour, powerful yet elegant, that ages beautifully. These wines are the finest of the "satellite" Saint-Emilions, along with Montagne-Saint-Emilion, under which *appellation* they may be sold. Very good value. Recommended Châteaux include: Calon (also in Montagne-Saint-Emilion), La Croix-de-Saint-Georges, Saint-Georges, Tour du Pas Saint-Georges (owned by Château Ausone). Price D, best F.

Right: A Saint-Emilion winemaker at work.
Below: Harvesting in Saint Emilion.

Pomerol

With only 749 hectares in production (out of a possible 785), Pomerol is the smallest of the regions of Bordeaux producing fine wine. It is also the most parcellated, with 185 growers, one-third of whom own less than one hectare. The *appellation* is bordered by Lalande-de-Pomerol and Néac to the north, Saint-Emilion to the east and the town of Libourne to the south. The soil is perfect for vines, a flinty, clayey gravel mixed with sand on a hard clay and iron base, the iron giving Pomerol its particular richness. The wine is a mixture of velvety softness, richness and firmness, much nearer in style to a Saint-Emilion than a Médoc and with some affinity with good Burgundy. The dominant grape is the Merlot, aided by the Cabernet Franc rather than the Cabernet Sauvignon and a very little Malbec or Pressac. The soft fruit of the Merlot and the liveliness of the Cabernet Franc (known locally as the Bouchet) combine to give Pomerol an immediacy that is not found in Cabernet Sauvignon-based wines. However, while a fine Pomerol is very attractive and open 5 years after the vintage, it will, unless the vines have over-produced wildly, last 10–15 years more. All Pomerol is red, with a minimum alcohol content of 10.5° from a maximum yield of 42hl/ha. Production varies, since the Merlot can be very prolific (1973, 1979, 1982, 1985) or suffer from cold or rot (1977, 1984, 1986, 1987), but the average is four million bottles a year.

There has been no official classification of Pomerol. Pétrus is universally recognized as an honorary 1er Grand Cru Classé, followed by a handful of châteaux on a par with the 1ers Grand Crus Classés B of Saint-Emilion or the 2èmes or 3èmes Crus Classés of the Médoc. Two dozen or so properties that are not quite in this league also make very fine wine.

Château Pétrus

(11.5ha; Me 95%, CF 5%)
An extraordinary wine from the most perfectly kept property, managed and part-owned by the J.-P. Moueix family. The soil contains more clay than elsewhere in the *appellation*, with a thin sandy topsoil. The grapes are harvested at their optimum ripeness by an army of pickers who can finish the *vendange* in three afternoons, thus avoiding possible dilution of the wine by the morning dew. Vinification, in cement tanks, extracts a deep colour and the wine spends 20 months in new oak casks before bottling. Pétrus is generally a huge wine, very dark in colour, with plummy, blackcurranty flavours and great richness, structure and "presence". The 1982 is probably the most remarkable

wine of the vintage. It can be drunk at 7–8 years, but the better vintages demand and deserve much more time. Despite the high proportion of old vines, production is a respectable 4,000 cases, a tribute to the health of the vineyard. Price J+.

Château Le Bon Pasteur

(7ha; Me 90%, CF 10%)
A rich, sensuous wine made by Michel Rolland, the best-known consultant winemaker in the *appellation*. This luscious, high-extract style is approachable young, but has the balance to last. Production 3,500 cases. Price G.

Château Certan de May

(5ha; Me 70%, CF 25%, CS 5%)
Superbly situated next to Vieux Château Certan and Pétrus, the concentration and depth of this wine, also known as Château de May de Certan, puts it among the best of the *appellation*. Production 2,000 cases. Price H.

Château Clinet

(7ha; Me 75%, CS 15%, CF 10%)
Having produced firm, long-lasting wines for some years, Clinet reduced yields and improved its quality dramatically in the 1980s. The owner, Georges Audy, died in 1989 but his son-in-law, Jean-Michel Arcaute, had already taken over vinification. The 1988, 1989 and 1990 are marvels of concentration. Production 3,000 cases. Price H.

Château La Conseillante

(13ha; Me 45%, CF 45%, Ma 10%)
This vineyard lies on the Saint-Emilion side of the *appellation*, between Pétrus and Cheval Blanc. The Malbec adds firmness to the fragrance of the Cabernet Franc and the soft fruit of the Merlot. It is a wine of deep, silky elegance, a Chambolle-Musigny of Pomerol, and is harmonious enough to last 10–15 years. This is a vineyard on top form. Production 5,000 cases. Price H-I.

Château L'Evangile

(13ha; Me 67%, CF 33%)
Situated, like La Conseillante, right on the edge of Saint-Emilion, L'Evangile makes a sturdier, meatier wine, with less finesse but more structure. It has much

the same weight and tannin as Trotanoy, but is less intensely rich. Good vintages (1971, 1975, 1979, 1982) need over 10 years to develop their potential. In 1990 Domaines Rothschild (Lafite) took a majority interest. Production 4,500 cases. Price H-I.

Château La Fleur-Pétrus

(9ha; Me 80%, CF 20%)
A Moueix-owned property, near Pétrus and Gazin. Old vines and the gravelly-clay, iron-based soil produce a fine, firm Pomerol with good colour ·and structure, but less plummy and intense than either Pétrus or Trotanoy, perhaps more Médoc in style. Very good at 8–12 years. Production 2,500 cases. Price high H.

Château Le Gay

(9ha; Me 80%, CF 20%)
Under the same ownership as the exceptional Château Lafleur, Le Gay is slightly to the north of Lafleur, and the wine, although deep coloured and rich from old vines, just lacks the class of Lafleur. Production 2,400 cases. Price high H.

Château Gazin

(18ha; Me 80%, CF 15%, CS 5%)
One of the largest properties, in the north-east of the *appellation*, Gazin produces well-made wines although they lack balance and sweetness in light years. Recent vintages (1979, 1982 and especially 1989), with more colour, body and fruit, will last well. Production 8,500 cases. Price high F.

Château Lafleur

(4.8ha; Me 50%, CF 50%)
A tiny property on the Pétrus plateau making exquisite, deep-coloured wines with a strikingly floral bouquet and great purity of flavour. Lafleur is a beautifully made, long-lasting wine from a high proportion of old vines. The 1990 is a triumph. Production 1,500 cases. Price high I.

Château Latour à Pomerol

(7.5ha; Me 80%, CF 20%)
Owned by the Lacoste-Loubat family, who still retain a share of Pétrus, and vinified by Jean-Claude Berrouet of J.-P. Moueix, this is a full, meaty, richly textured Pomerol. Production 2,400 cases. Price I.

Château Nenin

(25ha; Me 50%, CF 30%, CS 20%)
The vineyards lie on the southern slope of Pomerol, towards Libourne, where the soil has more gravel and less sand. The style of Nenin is straightforward, full-bodied and satisfying, but without the depth and panache of the finest *crus*. The wines mature well. One of the rare château in Pomerol to make enough wine to have a second label, Château Saint-Roch. Production 10,000 cases. Price high F.

Château Petit-Village

(11ha; Me 80%, CF 10%, Ma 10%)
This property was extremely well run, since 1970, by Bruno Prats of Cos d'Estournel, who made a wine almost more Médoc than Pomerol, complex and rather firm, not a wine to drink young. In 1989 the Prats family sold to AXA-Millésimes, the insurance company that owns, among others, Château Pichon-Longueville-Baron and Château Cantenac-Brown. Petit-Village is now under the control of the equally dedicated Jean-Michel Cazes. Production 4,500 cases. Price G.

Château Trotanoy

(7.5ha; Me 85%, CF 15%)
The second star in the Moueix stable, after Pétrus, Trotanoy produces a deep-coloured, intensely flavoured wine with perfect structure from some of the oldest vines in Pomerol. While it is not the firework display that is Pétrus, it is often a more serious wine, needing more time to be totally satisfying. In light years (1974, 1980) it is stylish and elegant and can be drunk at 4–5 years; in great vintages (1964, 1970, 1982, 1985, 1989, 1990) it can last 20 years. A splendid wine. Production 2,500 cases. Price J.

Vieux Château Certan

(13.5ha; Me 50%, CF 25%, CS 20%, Ma 5%)
One of the most famous properties in Pomerol, whose wines are relatively Médocain in style due to the presence of Cabernet Sauvignon and ageing in new barrels. The wood and the briary fruit of the Cabernets can dominate the young wine, giving an impression of astringency, but (in years of restrained production) Vieux Château Certan will acquire a smoothness and depth of fruit that make it one of the most elegant wines in Bordeaux. Production 6,500 cases. Price I.

THE "CRUS BOURGEOIS" OF POMEROL

The following Châteaux may be considered equal in quality terms to some of the 5èmes Crus Classés or the Grands Crus Bourgeois of the Médoc. **Château Beauregard** (13ha; Me 50%, CF 50%), a full-flavoured wine of great charm, due to the high proportion of Cabernet Franc, elegant, supple and quite quick to mature; **Château Certan-Giraud** (7ha; Me 65%, CF 35%) has vines situated on the highest part of the Plateau de Certan, and one could wish for more finesse from this deep-coloured, generally satisfying, sturdy wine; **Château Certan-Marzelle** is under the same ownership, the wine is made at Certan-Giraud and is of the same style; **Château Croix-du-Casse**, owned by Château Clinet, but softer, slightly sweeter and quicker to mature; **Clos du Clocher**, owned by J.-B. Audy, négociants at Libourne, is deep coloured, smooth and full-bodied, reliable rather than exciting; **Clos de L'Eglise** (6ha; Me 55%, CS 25%, CF 20%) has very old vines which give a rich wine with a lot of flavour: impressive and typically Pomerol; under the same ownership, **Château Plince** is lighter and less interesting; **Château L'Eglise-Clinet** (4.5ha; Me 60%, CF 30%, Ma 10%), a small property, well situated in a clayey-gravelly soil near the church, producing well-made wines, as generous and as stylish as Clinet; **Château L'Enclos**, situated just north of Clos René, produces a serious wine with deep fruit and warmth of flavour which ages well. **Château La Croix**, a large property for Pomerol, touching Nenin, Petit-Village and Beauregard, owned by J. Janoueix and Co. of Libourne, who also own **Château La Croix Saint Georges**, these straightforward, meaty wines are made together; **Château La Croix de Gay** (11ha; Me 80%, CF 10%, CS 10%), from the northern part of Pomerol towards Néac, produces carefully made, deep-coloured, solid wines; **Château La Vraye Croix de Gay** (3.5ha; Me 80%, CF 15%, CS 5%), a small property near the best *crus* of Pomerol (Le Gay, Lafleur), makes delicious racy wine with a bouquet of violets and truffles; **Château Feytit-Clinet** (6.5ha; Me 85%, CF 15%), with its vines planted on the best gravelly-clay, iron-based soil and the vinification of Jean-Claude Berrouet, the winemaker for all the J.-P. Moueix properties, is a lightish but elegant and stylish Pomerol; **Château La Fleur-Gazin** (7 ha; Me 90%, CF 10%), another property managed by Moueix, next door to Gazin, Lafleur and La Fleur Pétrus, producing fairly intense wines of great elegance; **Château La Grave-Trigant-de-Boisset** (8ha; Me 90%, CF 10%), owned by Christian Moueix, is one of the most stylish, vibrant and seductive Pomerols, impeccably made — a lovely wine; **Château Lagrange** (8ha; Me 90%, CF 10%),

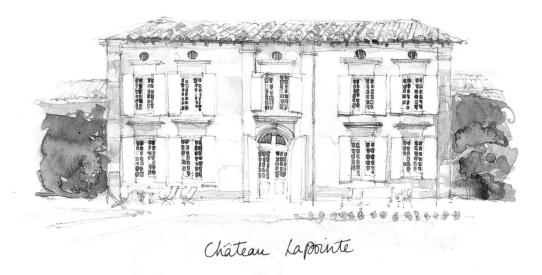

Château Lapointe

another J.-P. Moueix property on some of the best soil in Pomerol, producing firm, racy wines; **Château Mazèyres**, a well-kept property on the far west border of the *appellation*, makes fine if rather lean wines; **Château Moulinet**, one of the larger and older châteaux, produces a velvety, soft, very accessible Pomerol; **Château La Pointe** (20ha; Me 80%, CF 15%, Ma 5%), a big property on the outskirts of Libourne, where the sandy soil gives a less intense colour and fruit than the more clayey, iron soil of the Pétrus plateau; well-made wines, of good structure; **Clos René** (11ha; Me 60%, CF 30%, Ma 10%) produces solid, consistently well-made wine with a deep colour and plummy, long-lived fruit; **Château Moulinet-Lasserre** is part of the same property; **Château Rouget** (18ha; Me 90%, CF 10%), from the north of the *appellation* near Néac, was classified as the fifth finest Pomerol in 1868 – dark-coloured, powerful wines with long life; **Château de Sales** (48ha; Me 66%, CF 17%, CF 17%), the largest property in the *appellation*, producing very sound, fruity, slightly earthy wines; **Château La Violette**, with most of the vines next to Nenin, produces a pretty wine with a soft fruit.

The Wines of the Libournais

The Libournais, named after the merchant town of Libourne on the right bank of the Dordogne river, the second port in the Gironde after Bordeaux itself, embraces the major *appellations* of the right bank. The wines produced are almost 100% red – there is a tiny amount of white produced in the Côtes de Francs – and the principal grape here is the Merlot (whereas the Cabernet Sauvignon dominates on the left bank). In style the wines are sturdy rather than flashy with a good depth of fruit and not overly reliant on new oak. The *appellations* of Saint-Emilion and Pomerol have already been discussed – see page 171ff.

BORDEAUX-COTES DE FRANCS

Red, dry and sweet white wines from an *appellation* touching the "Satellite-Saint-Emilions" (see page 176), and covering 300 hectares, to the north of the Côtes de Castillon. Red wines, of 11° minimum alcohol, are made from the Cabernet Sauvignon, Cabernet Franc, Merlot and Malbec grapes, with the Merlot dominant. White wines, of 11.5° minimum alcohol, are made from Sémillon and Sauvignon with a little Muscadelle. The production is 90% red, with around 1,200 bottles a year, compared to the 16.5 million bottles of Côtes de Castillon, which they resemble in style, although these wines are a little more supple and quicker to mature due to the limestone soil and high elevation. The best come from Château Puygueraud and Château Laclaverie, (which are both owned by the Thienpont de Berlaere family of Vieux Château Certan in Pomerol), from Château de Francs and the *cave coopérative*. The dry whites are pleasant, but less interesting than Entre-Deux-Mers, and the sweet whites are virtually non-existent. Attractive wines, good value for money. Price C-D.

COTES DE CASTILLON

Red wines made from the Cabernet Sauvignon, Cabernet Franc, Merlot and Malbec, with a predominance of Merlot. The vines are grown on the right bank of the Dordogne, just west of Saint-Emilion, and cover 2,640 hectares, producing 16.5 million bottles. Minimum alcohol content is 11°, from a maximum yield of 40hl/ha. These wines are as good as, sometimes better than, the lesser Saint-Emilion wines, usually underrated, and represent excellent value. They have a fine colour, generous fruit and some finesse, and may be drunk at 2–6 years. Château de Pitray and Château Moulin-Rouge are good examples. Such has been the regularity of quality in this region, that from 1989 the appellation has been upgraded from Bordeaux-Côtes de Castillon to Côtes de Castillon. Very good wines come from the following Châteaux, many of whose owners possess more prestigious properties in Saint-Emilion: Bréhat, de Clotte, Labesse, Lacoste, Moulin Rouge, du Palanquey, de Pitray and de Saint-Philippe.

CANON-FRONSAC

Red wine only from the smaller but finer of the Fronsadais *appellations*, covering 300 hectares of hillside vineyards 2.5km north-west of Libourne. Of the Bordeaux grape varieties the Merlot and the Cabernet Franc dominate, with Cabernet Sauvignon and Malbec used for balance and colour. The wines of Canon-Fronsac are the best of the "minor" *appellations*, often outshining many Médocs, Saint-Emilions, Pomerols or Graves. They have a fine, deep colour, a clean, quite concentrated aroma of fruit with a little spice and the firm vigorous flavour of well-made wine. They are very satisfying wines that have not succumbed to over-production, as have many Saint-Emilion wines. They can be drunk at 4–5 years, but the better wines need 10 years to underline their complexity and high quality. Canon-Fronsacs are relatively sturdy, with a minimum of 11° alcohol from a yield of 47hl/ha.

Some of the finest, most elegant wine in the *appellation* comes from the tiny Château Canon, owned by Christian Moueix, Château Canon de Brem (recently purchased by the Moueix company which intends great things for the *appellation*), and its second label, Château Pichelèbre, produce classic, intensely flavoured wines that improve over 15–20 years; Châteaux Coustolle, Vincent and Vrai-Canon-Bouché are almost of this standard, while Château Vrai-Canon-Boyer is lighter and quicker to mature; other fine wines come from Châteaux Dalem, Grand Renouil, Haut-Ballet, du Gaby, du Gazin, Junayme, Mazeris, Haut-Mazeris, Moulin-Pey-Labrie, du Pavillon and Touma-

lin. Production is 1.6 million bottles. Price D–E.

FRONSAC

Historically, the wines of Fronsac, known as le Fronsadais, were better known than those of Pomerol. The entire *appellation* covers 1,100 hectares, of which nearly 800, on the lower slopes, are classified as Fronsac, producing 4.5 million bottles a year. The grape varieties planted and the style of wine are similar to Canon-Fronsac, except that Fronsac may be lighter (10.5° minimum) and less intense, and can therefore be ready to drink earlier. Many proprietors have châteaux in both *appellations*. Fine châteaux here include: de Carles, La Dauphine (another de Brem property, now part of the J.-P. Moueix stable), La Grave, Jeandeman, Mayne-Vieil, Moulin-Haut-Laroque, La Rivière, Rouët, La Valade, La Vieille Cure and the excellent Villars. The wines of Canon-Fronsac have an edge of concentration but Fronsacs are better value for money. Price D.

LALANDE-DE-POMEROL

Red wine only from an *appellation* north of Pomerol and bounded on the east by Montagne-Saint-Emilion. Although the finest wines come from the *appellation* Néac, the more prestigious-sounding Lalande-de-Pomerol *appellation* is used, following a merger of the two areas in 1954. The vineyards are flat, with a gravelly soil which is mixed with clay or sand. The grapes planted are the Cabernet Sauvignon, Cabernet Franc, Merlot and Malbec, with Merlot dominant as in Pomerol. The wines have some similarities; a deep colour and rounded flavour, but Lalande-de-Pomerol tends to be tougher and leaner, with less of the soft Merlot charm, and requires some time in bottle to become attractive. The marked financial success of neighbours Pomerol and Saint-Emilion have encouraged better vineyard management since the early 1980s, while improvements in vinification and a run of good vintages have tended to increase quality even further. Good properties include Château La Croix-Saint-André, Château Siaurac and Château de Viaud. One of the best values for money from the Libournais. Price D-E.

Néac

Red wine only from the better part of the Lalande-de-Pomerol-Néac *appellation*, now sold under the name of Lalande-de-Pomerol. Most of the châteaux with vines in this commune, like Château Tournefeuille, will state their Néac origins on the label as their address.

The Regional Wines of Bordeaux

The heading of this section is in no way derogatory. Over half of the wines made in the Gironde department do *not* come from the grander *appellations* and, as can be the case elsewhere in France, the better wines from these lesser known *appellations* are markedly superior to the less good efforts from more important regions. Where possible, these *appellations* have been grouped geographically.

GENERIC BORDEAUX

Bordeaux

Red, dry and sweet white, and rosé wines grown in any part of the Bordeaux region, exclusively in the Gironde *département*. Red and rosé wines must be made with the following grape varieties: Cabernet Sauvignon, Cabernet Franc, Merlot, Malbec, Petit Verdot and Carmenère. The minimum alcohol content is 10°, from a maximum basic yield of 50hl/ha. White wines must be from the Sémillon, Sauvignon and Muscadelle grapes for the most part, with the minor varieties of Merlot Blanc, Colombard, Mauzac, Ondenc and Saint-Emilion (also known as Ugni Blanc) being allowed to a maximum of 30% in principle, but a much lower percentage is used in practice. Minimum alcohol content is 10.5°, and if the wine has less that 4 grams per litre of residual sugar, it must state *sec* (dry) on the label. Yield is the same as for the reds. This basic, or generic, *appellation* covers not only the everyday wine of Bordeaux, but also those wines which are declassified from higher-quality regional or communal *appellations* and, in addition, wines made in certain *appellations* that are not accepted as part of that particular classification. In the latter case, a white wine made in the Médoc, an *appellation* exclusively for red wine, will have to take the *appellation* Bordeaux (or Bordeaux Supérieur if it is of a higher degree of alcohol), as will a *dry* white wine made in Barsac or Sauternes, where the appellation is purely for sweet wines. Generic red Bordeaux is usually of good quality and should be drunk 1–4 years after the vintage. Great progress has been made in the vinification of white Bordeaux, of which the dry, crisply fruity whites are deservedly popular, very good value and should be drunk young. The smaller amount of sweet white is pleasant and should be served very cold, as should the very small production of Bordeaux rosé.

Bordeaux Clairet

Dry rosé wines from red grapes with more colour than a Bordeaux rosé. The English word "Claret" is said to have found its origin in this style of wine, which was once the way all wines of Bordeaux were made. Today, it is often more like a very light red wine. A few owners of red Crus Classés make a Clairet for home consumption, and it is a speciality of the village of Quinsac in the Premières-Côtes-de-Bordeaux. Drink young, served cold but not iced. Worth looking out for. Price B-C.

Bordeaux Mousseux

White sparkling wine from the accepted Bordeaux grape varieties, made sparkling by the *méthode champenoise*. They may be dry or *demi-sec*, determined by the amount of *liqueur d'expedition* that is added after *dégorgement*, and are quite pleasant to drink as an inexpensive alternative to champagne, or in a Kir Royal. Recent increases in champagne prices and progress in vinification ensure a growing market.

Bordeaux Rosé

Dry rosé wines made from the red grape varieties permitted for generic Bordeaux, with a minimum of 11° alcohol from a yield of 50hl/ha. The *appellation* Bordeaux Supérieur Rosé may be used if the yield is not more than 40hl/ha. Very pleasant, particularly if the must is cool-fermented to preserve the freshness of the fruit. Drink very young. Good value and goes with all types of food. Price B.

Bordeaux Supérieur

Red, dry and sweet white, and rosé wines of much the same type as the generic "Bordeaux *simple*", except that the minimum alcohol content must be higher: 10.5° for reds and rosés, 11° for the whites; the basic maximum yield comes down from 50hl/ha to 40hl/ha; and only the *cépages nobles* may be used. They are therefore fuller wines with more character and intensity of flavour. Drink as for Bordeaux. There are many very good wines in this *appellation* representing excellent value for money. Such has been the increase in quality, encouraged and aided by the Syndicat des Vins de Bordeaux, that these wines have become the real ambassadors of their region. Bordeaux and Bordeaux Supérieur represent 50% of the surface under vines in the Gironde and 52% of the production. Value for money in this *appellation* has never been better. Price B-C.

THE BLAYAIS AND THE BOURGEAIS

Blaye-Blayais

Red, dry and sweet white wines from the right bank of the Gironde estuary. The region's vineyards cover 4,100 hectares across three *appellations* of which these are the most simple. To the basic red grape varieties may be added the Cot, and to the whites the Folle Blanche and the Frontignan. Red and white wines have the same minimum alcohol content, 10°, from a yield of 45hl/ha for the whites, 50hl/ha for the reds. The quantity of red wine which is produced is tiny, most of it being upgraded to Premières Côtes de Blaye. The white wines, which are predominantly dry, are pleasant and should be drunk very young. Price B-C.

Côtes de Blaye

Dry or sweet white wines, from the same region as the Blayais wine, but with a higher minimum alcohol content of 10.5°. In general the sweet wines have given way to the fruity, dry wines from the Sauvignon and the Sémillon grapes. Good value, but without the floral finesse of the best Entre-Deux-Mers. About two-thirds of the production of 2 million bottles comes from *caves coopératives*. Price B-C.

Premières Côtes de Blaye

Red, dry, *demi-sec* and sweet white wines grown on the right bank of the Gironde, opposite the Médoc. Same yield as for the Blayais wine, but with 0.5° more alcohol. Only Cabernet Sauvignon, Cabernet Franc, Malbec and Merlot are permitted for the reds, which have a good colour and a straightforward, soft, fruity taste. The limestone-clay soil is particularly favourable for the Merlot, making the wines softer but with more finesse on the nose than their neighbour the Côtes de Bourg. Fine examples include Châteaux Bourdieu, Charron, Crusquet-le-Lagarche, L'Escadre, Peyrèyre and Segonzac. A great deal of good-value red wine is produced and a very small amount of white, which is usually sweet. Price B-C.

Bourg-Bourgeais

Red, dry, *demi-sec* and sweet white wines from the canton of Bourg-sur-Gironde, south of the Blayais on the right bank of the Gironde opposite the Haut-Médoc. Both red and white wines are made only from the *cépages nobles* of Bordeaux. Over 95% of the production from 2,900 hectares is red, making a deep-coloured, robust, high-quality Bordeaux with good ageing potential. They are excellent at 2–6 years, can last even longer, and are much underrated in compari-son with the Médocs from across the river. They are better known than the Côtes de Blaye, thanks to excellent Châteaux such as de Barbe, Brulesecaille, Le Clos du Notaire, Falfas (under new ownership since the 1988 vintage and making exceptional wine), de la Grave, Guerry, Guionne, Laroche, Lidonne, Mendoca, Rousset and Tayac. Very good with chicken, red meats and cheese. Production (including Côtes de Bourg) is 20 million bottles of red, with 300,000 bottles of white. Price C.

Côtes de Bourg

Red and dry white wines from the Bourgeais. This *appellation* is now generally used as an alternative to that of Bourgeais and covers the vast majority of red wines, but the white wines must be dry. Price C-D.

THE ENTRE-DEUX-MERS

This region, which is also the name of an *appellation* producing dry white wine, is found in the vast triangle formed by the Garonne and the Dordogne rivers. Vines cover 23,000 hectares, just under one quarter of the total in Gironde. Many excellent sweet wines are made in this region – Côtes de Bordeaux Saint-Macaire, Loupiac, Sainte-Croix-du-Mont – and these are des-cribed on page 170.

Entre-Deux-Mers

Dry white wines, grown in the triangle formed by the Garonne and the Dordogne rivers, but excluding all red wines, sweet whites and other wines with specific *appellations*. While the minor white Bordeaux grapes, such as Colombard, Merlot, Ondenc and Ugni Blanc, are allowed, in reality only Sauvignon (now becoming dominant) Sémillon and Muscadelle are planted, in an effort to keep up the quality. The soil is clay-limestone, clay-silicon and gravel, and the wines produced must have a minimum of 10° and a maximum of 13° alcohol, with less than 4 grams per litre of residual sugar. Wines are only accepted as Entre-Deux-Mers after a vigorous tasting, and that rejected is declassified into Bordeaux *sec*. Entre-Deux-Mers is light, fresh and fruity, with a particular *goût de terroir* that makes it the perfect match for shellfish, especially the local oysters from Arcachon. It is also excellent with hors d'oeuvres and fish. It should be drunk young. Excellent examples are to be found from André Lurton's Château Bonnet and from Châteaux Canet, Thieuley, Tour de Mirambeau and Turcaud. A good part of the Entre-Deux-Mers region

Right: Early Summer in the vineyards of Saint-Emilion.

has been replanted with red grapes, which make an attractive, soft, fruity Bordeaux or Bordeaux Supérieur. Sold under these *appellations* are Château Bonnet and Grand Monteil. Both the white Entre-Deux-Mers, with an average production of 18 million bottles, and the red bordeaux are extremely good value. Price B-C.

Entre-Deux-Mers-Haut-Benauge

Dry, semi-sweet and sweet wines from a sub-*appellation* of Entre-Deux-Mers. The wines are aromatic and attractive, the best-known being from Château Toutigeac. Price B-C.

Graves de Vayres

Red, dry white and *demi-sec* white wines from an enclave in the north of the Entre-Deux-Mers region, on the left bank of the Dordogne. This *appellation* is not to be confused with the Graves *appellation* between Bordeaux and Langon. Here, classic Bordeaux grape varieties produce soft, fruity, Merlot-based reds, and pleasant dry whites, both to be drunk young. The original *appellation* dates from 1931 and was limited to dry and sweet whites. Currently there are 350 hectares producing white wine, 650 producing red. A high proportion of the latter sells under the generic Bordeaux or Bordeaux Supérieur *appellations*. The best-known property, for red and white wine, is Château Pichon-Bellevue.

PREMIERES COTES DE BORDEAUX

Red and dry whites from the right bank of the Garonne, along a 60-km stretch from the outskirts of Bordeaux to Cadillac, made from the classic Bordeaux grape varieties. The northern part, nearer Bordeaux, produces red and Clairet wines, the southern part of the vineyard being better known for its semi-sweet and sweet wines, although much replanting of red grapes has been done. The *appellation* covers 3,600 hectares for red wines, 2,700 for whites — which includes the *appellation* Cadillac (*qv*) and Côtes de Bordeaux Saint-Macaire (page 170) — whose production of semi-sweet and sweet white wines has fallen to only 60 hectares. Production is limited to 40hl/ha, minimum alcohol content is 10.5°

for the reds (11.5° if the name of the commune is added, e.g. Premières Côtes de Bordeaux-Quinsac), 12° for the whites. The red wines are soft and generous, with a fine ruby colour, a little harsh *en primeur*, but acquiring suppleness and depth with age, up to 6–7 years. The sweet whites which used to go under this *appellation* have been allowed, since 1981, to use the *appellation* Cadillac (see page 170). They are late-picked in the Sauternes manner and are now well vinified, rich and perfumed. The red wines have made great progress in qualitative as well as quantitative terms in the last decade, and the best are the equal of a middle-range Cru Bourgeois. These include Châteaux Brethous, Cayla (a superb barrel-aged white), de la Closière (both red and white), Lagarosse, de le Meulière, Lezongars, Nenine, du Peyrat, Plaisance (red and white), Reynon, Suau (extremely polished wines), and the excellent Château Fayau from the Médeville family of Château Gilette.

SAINTE-FOY-BORDEAUX

Red, dry white and sweet white wine from the north-eastern extremity of the Gironde *département*, on the left bank of the Dordogne. Geographically, it is part of the Entre-Deux-Mers region, although the wines are quite different. They are made from the classic Bordeaux varieties and must have 10.5° minimum alcohol for the reds, 11° for the whites, from a maximum yield of 45hl/ha. In the past, the wines were *demi-sec* or sweet, and were known as the "poor-man's Sauternes", but now that Sauvignon is increasingly planted the wines are mostly dry and pleasantly fruity. The reds, usually sold under the *appellation* Bordeaux or Bordeaux Supérieur, have a good deep colour and are full bodied with an attractive soft fruit that allows them to be drunk young. The Cave Coopérative Univitis is the principal producer. Price B-C.

VINS DE PAYS

There are no VDQS wines in the Gironde *département*, for all Bordeaux wines have full AOC status. There is, however, one *vin de pays*, Vin de Pays de la Gironde — see page 191.

The South-West

The South-West covers a large range of wines from the *départements* of the Aveyron, Cantal, Dordogne, Gers, Haute-Garonne, Hautes-Pyrénées, Pyrénées-Atlantiques, Tarn and Tarn-et-Garonne. With more than 40,000 hectares under vines covering an area that runs from Bergerac to the Basque country, from the Atlantic Ocean to the Massif Central, the South-West is not really homogeneous. There is as little resemblance between Bergerac and Madiran as there is between Sancerre and Vouvray, yet they have more in common with each other than with wines outside the region. Perhaps where the white wines of the Loire Valley share a spirited liveliness, the wines of the South-West share an earthy robustness. Typical of this style, smoothed in recent years by more polished winemaking, are the wines of Cahors, whose *goût de terroir* cries out for a *confit de canard* as does Madiran for a *cassoulet*. Such wines are not to everybody's taste, and lighter, more quaffable wines are produced from the Gamay grape, a recent immigrant to the area. Red wine dominates. Historically the Rosé de Béarn was one of the (many) favoured wines of Henry IV; today lighter rosés from the Gamay are in vogue, but the South-West is not rosé country. The wines are diverse: Jurançon and Monbazillac put the region on a par with Bordeaux or the Loire for fine sweet white wine; dry whites vary between crisp, modern Sauvignons and the more interesting Gaillacs from the local Mauzac. Much sparkling wine is made, those from *la méthode rurale* being among the best in France. Across the colours and appellations, the wines of the South-West are enjoying a deserved popularity. Perhaps this is because they go so well with food, and are so accessible in terms of price and style, placed as they are between the more bourgeois bottles of Bordeaux and the sun-filled products of the Midi.

In the text that follows, they have been divided into three sub-regions: Bergerac and the Dordogne; the Centre; Béarn and the Pyrenees.

Bergerac and the Dordogne

This region covers the vineyards to the north and east of the Bordeaux *appellations*, from both banks of the River Dordogne. The dominant grape varieties here are the Cabernet Sauvignon, Cabernet Franc, Merlot and Malbec for reds and rosé wines, and the Sauvignon, Sémillon and Muscadelle grapes for the whites.

AOC WINES

Bergerac

Red and rosé wines from the Bergerac region covering a vast 10,000 hectares in the *département* of the Dordogne. The white wines can only be sold under the

The South-West

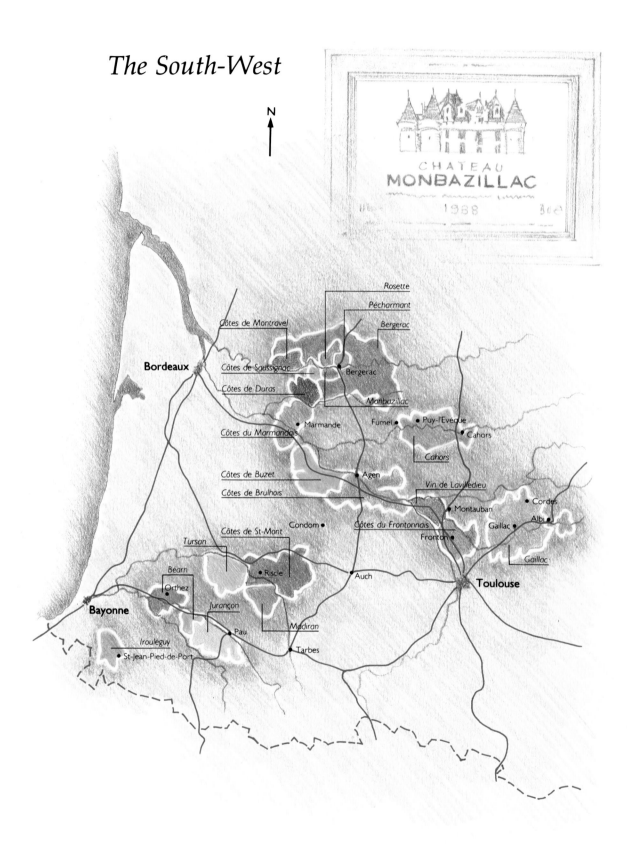

N

CHATEAU
MONBAZILLAC
1988

Côtes de Montravel

Rosette

Pécharmant

Bergerac

Bordeaux

Côtes de Saussignac

Bergerac

Côtes de Duras

Monbazillac

Marmande

Fumel

Puy-l'Eveque

Côtes du Marmandais

Cahors

Cahors

Côtes de Buzet

Agen

Côtes de Brulhois

Vin de Lavilledieu

Cordes

Montauban

Albi

Côtes de St-Mont

Condom

Côtes du Frontonnais

Gaillac

Tursan

Fronton

Gaillac

Béarn

Riscle

Auch

Toulouse

Orthez

Jurançon

Madiran

Bayonne

Pau

Irouléguy

St-Jean-Pied-de-Port

Tarbes

appellation Bergerac *sec*. Already well known in the late Middle Ages, they are now just recovering their reputation. Grapes permitted are the Bordeaux varietals: Cabernet Sauvignon, Cabernet Franc, Merlot and Malbec, as well as the Fer. The wines must reach a minimum alcohol content of 10°, from a yield of 50hl/ha. The Dordogne divides the wines into two styles: those from the right bank are softer and have more finesse, those from the left bank are deeper in colour, fuller-bodied and more tannic. Bergerac resembles the red Bordeaux from the region of Entre-Deux-Mers with a lighter, more pronounced fruit, and they may be drunk relatively young, at one to three years. The rosés have a pretty pink colour, are refreshing and vivacious, but are less interesting than the reds. With around 30 million bottles of red and rosé produced each year, the quality and price of this appellation varies from the least interesting and cheapest cooperative wines found in French supermarkets to those from serious producers producing wines of character. These include Domaine de Gouyat, Château La Jaubertie, Château La Raye and Domaine de Richard. A good alternative to Bordeaux rouge. Price B-C.

Bergerac sec

Dry white wine from the Bergerac region. Grape varieties are the Sémillon, Sauvignon and Muscadelle, with a little Ondenc and Chenin Blanc, producing a wine with a minimum alcohol content of 11°, from a yield of 50hl/ha. In the past, white Bergerac used to be sweet, but this is being reversed with the increased planting of Sauvignon. The wines are aromatic, crisp and dry with a pleasant fruit, the finest from Château du Chayne, Domaine de Gouyat, Château Le Ray and Château Tour des Gendres. Production 25 million bottles. Drink very young, with *charcuterie*, fish and poultry. Price A-B.

Côtes de Bergerac

Red wines from the Bergerac region, made with the same grapes as Bergerac, but with a minimum alcohol content of 11°. The difference between Bergerac and Côtes de Bergerac is similar to that between Bordeaux and Bordeaux Supérieur: the wines have more depth and personality, and are well worth the little extra money. Due to the still questionable reputation of simple Bergerac, most quality wines – certainly those with ageing potential – are found under Côtes de Bergerac, including: Château Belingard, Château Combrillac, Château de Géraud, Château La Mayne, and Château Tour des Gendres. Production about three million bottles. Price B-C.

Côtes de Bergerac Moelleux

Sweet white wine from the Bergerac region, made from the Sémillon, Sauvignon and Muscadelle grapes. The wines should have between 12° and 15° alcohol and residual sugar combined. These delightful, soft, fruity wines are still popular in France and northern Europe, and are relatively inexpensive. They are much less sweet than the neighbouring Monbazillacs. Price B.

Côtes de Duras

Red, dry white and sweet white wines from 1,200 hectares, from the north of the Lot-et-Garonne *département*, between the vineyards of Entre-Deux-Mers and Bergerac. The red wines are from the Cabernet Sauvignon, Cabernet Franc, Merlot and Malbec, with a minimum alcohol content of 10° from a yield of 50hl/ha. They are pleasant and fruity, with a good colour, quite easy to drink young. The white wines, whose production at around 5.5 million bottles is more than that of the red, are from Sémillon, Sauvignon and Muscadelle, with the local grapes Mauzac and Ondenc, and up to 25% Ugni Blanc. The sweet white used to dominate, but now the crisp dry Sauvignon-based whites are more popular. Both, with a minimum degree of 10.5°, have a distinctive flowery bouquet and a clean, fruity finish. They are not yet well known and in addition to the excellent *cave coopérative* (especially their prestige brand, Duc du Berticot) there are some very good growers (such as Domaine de Laulan and Domaine de Savigriattes). Price B.

Côtes de Montravel – Haut Montravel

Sweet white wine from the region of Montravel. These two *appellations* are for wines from the hillside vineyards planted in certain specific communes. The more simple Montravel comes from vineyards on the plain, and represents 85% of the global Montravel *appellation*. Here, however, only the Sémillon, Sauvignon and Muscadelle grapes are permitted, and the wines must have a minimum of 12° alcohol, a maximum of 15° plus residual sugar. They resemble the better Premieres Côtes de Bordeaux. Very small production. Price C.

Monbazillac

Sweet and very sweet white wine, from 2,500 hectares of vineyards along the left bank of the Dordogne, to the south of Bergerac. Grape varieties are the same as for Sauternes and the other great sweet wines from the Bordeaux region: Sémillon for flavour and richness, Sauvignon for finesse and body and a little Muscadelle for the heady, slightly muscat aroma. Monbazillac has to have a minimum of 13° alcohol plus residual sugar, from a yield of 40hl/ha, which is almost never attained, due to the obligatory late harvesting of grapes affected by Botrytis, where quantity is sacrificed to quality. In good years, Monbazillac is even more rich than a Sauternes, with 14–15° natural alcohol and 80–100 grams of residual sugar per litre. The wine is enjoying something of a comeback after years of decline, and the winemakers are paying more attention to see that their wines are clean, do not have too much sulphur and live up to the fame of the *appellation*. Monbazillac may be drunk young, straw-gold in colour, honeyed and luscious, but it is best kept five to ten years to acquire the complexity that all fine *vins liquoreux* attain with age. Drink very cold, as an apéritif, with *pâté de foie gras* or with fruit-based desserts. Production is large, 6–8 million bottles a year, much of it from the *coopérative* whose wines include Château la Brie, Château de Monbazillac and Château Septy. A good Monbazillac, like these and Château Le Fagé or Château Truil-de-Nailhac, is extraordinarily good value. Price C.

Montravel

Dry, *demi-sec* and sweet white wine from vineyards only ten kilometres east of Saint-Emilion. Montravel is actually an enclave of the Bordeaux region and it is only because it is in the *département* of the Dordogne that it is not classified among the wines of Bordeaux. Grapes permitted are the Sémillon, Sauvignon and Muscadelle, plus a little Ondenc, Chenin Blanc and Ugni Blanc. The minimum alcohol content is 11°, more if the wine is sweet, from a yield of 50hl/ha. In reality, the wines of Montravel are usually dry, the *appellations* Côtes-du-Montravel and Haut-Montravel (above) being used for semi-sweet and fully sweet wines. These are well-made wines, with a light golden colour, soft fruit and a certain charm. Red wine made in Montravel is sold under the *appellation* Bergerac. Good value is to be found from Domaine de Gouyat and Domaine de Roque Peyre, and there is an exceptional, wood-aged Sémillon-dominated wine from Domaine de Krével. Production is just over two million bottles. Price B.

Pécharmant

Red wine from the slopes on the right bank of the Dordogne in the Bergerac region. Grape varieties are limited to Cabernet Sauvignon, Cabernet Franc, Merlot and Malbec. Pécharmant must have a minimum alcohol content of 11°, as opposed to 10° for simple Bergerac, from a maximum yield of 40hl/ha. The wines are rich in colour, almost purple when young, meaty and generous with a good deal of class. They are at their best at 3–6 years, to be drunk with *charcuterie*, white, but preferably red, meats, game and cheese. Pécharmant is the best red wine from the Bergerac region, the rival of Saint-Emilion or Médoc, exemplified by the Château de

Tiregand, Domaine du Haut Pécharmant, Domaine La Métairie and Domaine de Bertranoux. Price C-D.

Rosette

Semi-sweet white wine from well-exposed slopes to the north of Bergerac. The Sémillon, Sauvignon and Muscadelle grapes find the limestone-clay soil particularly suitable to producing a wine that is fragrant, delicately sweet but full-bodied and distinctive. Minimum alcohol plus residual sugar is 12°, never more than 15°, from a yield of 40hl/ha. Not being over-sweet, Rosette is good with fish, poultry and white meats, especially if served with a rich sauce. Production is very small, around 20,000 bottles, and most of it is drunk locally. One of the few producers left is the Château Puypézat. Price C.

Saussignac

White wine, usually dry, from five communes around Saussignac in the Bergerac region. The wines must reach 12.5° alcohol to have the right to the *appellation* Saussignac, which makes them a bigger, more mouth-filling wine than Bergerac *sec*. Good with *charcuterie*, fish and white meats. Less than 300,000 bottles are produced. One of the rare producers is Pierre Sadoux at Château Court-les-Muts. Price B.

VDQS WINES

Côtes du Marmandais

Red and dry white wines from vines planted on either side of the Garonne, about 40 kilometres upstream from Langon in the Lot-et-Garonne *département*. The red wine is made from at least 50% "local" grape varieties: the Fer, Abouriou, Malbec, Gamay and Syrah, the balance being made up by the Bordeaux grapes, Cabernet Sauvignon, Cabernet Franc and Merlot. Minimum alcohol content is 10°, from a yield of 50hl/ha. Côtes du Marmandais red is pleasant, well balanced with a soft earthy fruit. The very small (under 5%) proportion of white wine is made from the Sauvignon, Ugni Blanc and Sémillon and is dry, pleasantly fruity but sometimes lacking in acidity. Both are unpretentious and inexpensive. The two *cave coopératives* of Beaupuy and Cocumont control virtually all the production. Production is around seven million bottles. Price A-B.

VINS DE PAYS

Production of *vins de pays* is very small in this part of the South-West. Those of the Charentais have been included, for though they are further north, they have more in common with this region than with the Loire Valley. Price A-low B.

VIN DE PAYS DE LA DORDOGNE

Red, dry white and rosé, the red (from Merlot and the Cabernet family) attractive and fruity, like a Bergerac, the white (mostly Sémillon with a little Sauvignon and Ugni Blanc) clean and flowery for everyday drinking. Production nearly one million bottles, usually over 50% white.

VIN DE PAYS CHARENTAIS

Red, dry white and rosé from the Charente and Charente-Maritime; the red wines have a lively colour, slight acidity and go well with food; the whites (70% of the production, but the reds and rosés are increasing) are aromatic and refreshing, with a little aftertaste. Production has gone from 600,000 to over four million bottles since 1982. Made principally from Ugni Blanc.

VIN DE PAYS DE LA GIRONDE

White wine from a few vineyards in the north of the Gironde *département*, not classified as Bordeaux. Principally dry white wines from Ugni Blanc and Colombard, not unlike the light table wines from Charentes. Production 70–80,000 bottles.

The Centre

Vineyards from the Lot, Lot-et-Garonne, Tarn, Tarn-et-Garonne and the Gers, including the outlying departments of the Avéyron, Cantal and the Haute-Garonne. The Bordeaux varieties are still widely planted, and indeed are dominant in the Buzet *appellation*, but with few exceptions the style owes more to tradition and *terroir* than to a specific mix of grapes.

AOC WINES

Buzet

Red, dry white and rosé wines from 1,250 hectares in the region between Agen and Casteljaloux on the left bank of the Garonne, in the Lot-et-Garonne *département*. The red wines are made from the Cabernet Sauvignon, Cabernet Franc and Merlot, with a very little Malbec, essentially the *encépagement Bordelaise*. The majority of the wine is vinified by the *cave coopérative* at Buzet-sur-Baïse, and has an excellent colour, with all the elegance of the Cabernets and the soft fruit of the Merlot. They are excellent dinner wines, to be drunk between three and eight years. The Château de Gueyze is the prestige wine, aged in new oak casks and has the quality of a good Médoc. The other major property is Château de Padère, acquired in 1989 by the *cave coopérative*. White wines, only 4–5% of the *appellation*, are made from Sémillon, Sauvignon and Muscadelle and resemble the everyday dry, white Bordeaux with a little more body. The production of rosé is insignificant. All wines have a minimum of 10°

alcohol from a yield of 40hl/ha. The vineyards of Côtes de Buzet are in full expansion, as the wine is justifiably popular. Good value, even the more expensive *cuvées*. Price B-C.

Cahors

Red wine from 3,500 hectares of vineyards planted on both banks of the Lot river, in the Quercy *département*. The vineyards of Cahors are some of the oldest in France, being already well known under the Roman occupation. The *encépagement* is most original: a minimum of 70% Malbec (known locally as the Auxerrois, and in the Loire Valley as the Cot), a maximum of 20% Merlot and Tannat, with 10% Jurançon Noir. The wine produced is very deep in colour, a dark crimson, and is solid, meaty, pleasantly rough at first, smoothing out after three years into a wine of great harmony and distinction. The relative lightness in alcohol, 10.5° minimum with a maximum of 13°, from a yield of 50hl/ha, belies the body and flavour. The expression "Vieux Cahors" is for wines aged for three years in wood. Cahors is perfect with the local Quercyois cuisine, fabulous with *confit de canard* and is a rival to Madiran to accompany a *cassoulet*. There has been much replanting in the region, and while most of the *appellation* produces good-quality wines, a few are distressingly light. Those that are typical, albeit of different styles, include Château du Cayrou, Château du Cèdre, Domaine Eugénie, the famous Clos de Gamot, Domaine de Grauzils, Château de Haute-Serre, Clos la Coutale, Clos de Lagarde, Château Lagrezettre, the Domaine de la Pineraie of M. Burc and Clos Triguedina. The *cave coopérative* accounts

for almost half of the production of nearly 25 million bottles.

After a very successful period in the early 1970s, Cahors lost ground in the 1980s to the more quality-minded growers of Madiran. Work is under way to redress the balance, including the formation of "Les Seigneurs de Cahors", a club of Châteaux-Domaines who feel that they represent the best the *appellation* can produce. Prices are still reasonable. Price C-D.

Côtes du Frontonnais

Red and rosé wines from a recently recreated vineyard area north of Toulouse in the *départements* of the Haute-Garonne and Tarn-et-Garonne. The grapes are up to 70% the local Negrette, with a distinctive sweetish raspberry-like aroma, the balance being made up with Cabernet Sauvignon, Cabernet Franc, Malbec, Cinsaut, Syrah, and Gamay. Minimum alcohol content is 10.5°, maximum 13°, from a yield of 50hl/ha. The wines have a very good colour, and are fruity and well structured. They may be drunk young, but can last 3 to 4 years. Some of the best wines come from the commune of Villaudric, whose name may be added to Côtes du Frontonnais on the label. Château Bellevue le Fôret was responsible for the rejuvenation of the *appellation* and has been followed by Domaine de Baudare, Château Cahuzac, Domaine de la Colombière, Château Flotis and Château Montauriol. There are now over 1,000 hectares of vines planted, producing around ten million bottles. Price B.

Gaillac

Red rosé, dry and *demi-sec* whites and sparkling wines from the Tarn *département*, around the towns of Albi and Castres. The Gaillac vineyards, now covering 1,600 hectares, are some of the oldest in France, dating from the pre-Christian era. Its wines are quite diverse: fruity, aromatic reds and rosés, clean dry whites, sweet whites, and wines fully sparkling, slightly sparkling or simply *perlé*. The Tarn river divides the region into two styles of wine: those from the chalky slopes on the right bank tend to be richer and more aromatic; those from the granitic soil on the left bank are crisper and more lively. The white wines, representing around 40% of the total production of 12 million bottles, are made from the Mauzac Blanc a minimum of 15% of the curiously named L'En de l'El (from the local dialect *loin de l'oeil*, roughly "out of sight"), the rest made up with Ondenc, Muscadelle, Sémillon and Sauvignon. They are deliciously aromatic, the dry wines having a good

Left: Château Monbazillac, which is owned by the Monbazillac cooperative, also has an excellent restaurant.

acidity, and should be drunk young. The reds and rosés come from a wide range of grapes: a minimum of 60% must be made up with the Fer, Negrette, Duras, Gamay and Syrah, the rest from the Cabernet Sauvignon, Cabernet Franc, Merlot, Portugais Bleu, Jurançon Rouge and Mauzac. They have a good colour and fruit, some personality, are light and easy to drink and go with anything – the perfect country wine. Many reds are being made by carbonic maceration, and may be drunk young, even *en primeur*, served cool. The best of these particular wines come from Cunac and Labastide-de-Levis. Both red and white wines have a minimum alcohol content of 10.5°, from a yield of 45hl/ha (which is often exceeded). Most of the production is from *caves coopératives* and is particularly good from the Cave de Técou and the Coopérative de Labastide-de-Levis. There are also some fine growers, including Domaine Jean Cros, Domaine de Labarthe, Château des Lastours, Mas d'Aurel, Domaine de Mazou, Château des Salettes and the superb wines of Robert Plageoles. Price A-B-C.

Gaillac Doux

Sweet white wine subject to the same rules as Gaillac blanc, but with a minimum of 70 grams per litre of residual sugar. These wines are getting more and more rare as the taste for dry wines increases. Price C.

Gaillac Mousseux

Sparkling wine from grapes grown in the Gaillac region, made sparkling by the traditional method called *gaillaçoise*. No sugar is added, no *liqueur de tirage* as in the *méthode champenoise*, but fermentation is stopped by successive filtrations, leaving some residual sugar which will produce the sparkle at the secondary fermentation in bottle in the spring following the vintage. The result is a wine with a fine natural sparkle, a delicate bouquet and an attractive softness on the palate. The *méthode champenoise* is in fact used in the region, as it is less risky, but it leaves the wine with less fruit and lacking in charm. Gaillac Mousseux is much appreciated in the local restaurants. The most respected producer in the *appellation* is Jean Cros. Price D.

Gaillac Perlé

Slightly sparkling white wine from the Gaillac region. The wine is fermented at a cool temperature to enchance the bouquet, and is kept for several months on its lees after malolactic fermentation to retain a slight sparkle that enhances the fruity, refreshing taste. It is delicious as an apéritif or throughout the summer meal. There are excellent wines from the Cave de Técou. Price C.

Gaillac Premières Côtes

White wine, dry or semi-sweet, from the Gaillac region with a minimum of 12° alcohol from a yield of 40hl/ha. Very seldom seen, as the wines from Gaillac sell well enough under the less strict *appellation simple*. Price B.

Marcillac

Red and rosé wines upgraded in 1990 from VDQS to AOC, from around the town of Rodez in the Aveyron *département*. The principal grape planted is the Fer (minimum 80%), the rest being made up by Cabernet, Merlot, Jurançon Noir and Gamay. Marcillac, made almost entirely at the *cave coopérative*, is a deep-coloured, robust, rather rough wine with lots of fruit. It is good with all *charcuterie*, red meats, stews and cheese. A fine, straightforward country wine. Price B.

VDQS WINES

Côtes de Bruhlois

Red and rosé wines from 180 hectares of vines planted *en coteaux* on either side of the Garonne, in the south-east of the Lot-et-Garonne and the west of the Tarn-et-Garonne. They are made from the Bordeaux grapes, Merlot, Cabernet Franc and Cabernet Sauvignon, with the addition of Tannat and Cot. The quality of the wines, which is similar to the Côtes de Marmandais (see page 190), caused Côtes de Bruhlois to pass from *vin de pays* to VDQS in 1984. Production is around one million bottles, mostly in the hands of two *coopératives* at Donzac and Layrac. Price A-B.

Vins d'Entraygues et du Fel

Red, dry white and rosé wines from the north of the Aveyron *département* and the southern part of the Cantal *département*. The reds and rosés are principally from the Cabernet Sauvignon, Cabernet Franc, Fer, Jurançon Noir, Gamay, Merlot, Negrette and even the Pinot Noir. They are light, with a minimum of 9° alcohol, and fruity, with a pleasing local character. White wines are from the Chenin Blanc and Mauzac, light, with a minimum of 10° alcohol, and attractively crisp. Production is tiny, totalling 6,000 bottles of white, twice that of red and rosé combined, and it is all consumed locally. Price B.

Left: Grapes being tipped into an old-fashioned hand-operated "fouloir" or crusher at Gaillac.

Vins d'Estaing

Red, dry white and rosé wines from the commune of d'Estaing in the Aveyron *département*. Production of the white wine is insignificant – less than 1,000 bottles a year – from the Chenin Blanc and Mauzac grapes. The reds, from a similar range of grapes to the Vins d'Entraygues et du Fel, are much the same in style: light, fruity and unpretentious. Best drunk on the spot. With only seven hectares currently planted, this is the smallest VDQS in France. Price B.

Vins de Lavilledieu

Red wines (with a minute production of white and rosé), from the *départements* of the Tarn-et-Garonne and Haute-Garonne centred on Montauban. The wine is made principally from the Negrette (minimum 35%) plus a wide mixture of varieties, including the Fer, Gamay, Jurançon Noir, Picpoul and Mauzac Noir. The wines resemble those of Gaillac and the Côtes du Frontonnais, pleasant, fruity and slightly rustic. Production is around 10,000 bottles. Price B.

VINS DE PAYS

With such a range of old established *appellations*, whose wines come largely from grape varieties that have been planted in the South-West over the centuries, it is not surprising that the tendency is for *vins de pays* – a relatively new creation – to come from grapes grown outside the region, such as the Gamay, the Cabernets, Merlot or Syrah. In many cases, these grapes are blended with the indiginous varieties, the robust Fer Servadou, Cot (Auxerrois) or Tannat, to give softness and fruit, while retaining a South-West character. A growing percentage of white wines are based on Ugni Blanc, Colombard and Sauvignon. Price A, low B.

Vins de Pays Régionaux

VIN DE PAYS DE COMTE TOLOSAN

Red, dry white and rosé wines from all the *départements* in the South-West: the Ariège, Avereyron, Haute-Garonne, Gers, Landes, Lot, Lot-et-Garonne, Pyrénées-Atlantiques, Hautes-Pyrénées, Tarn, and Tarn-et-Garonne. As such, it is a similar *appellation* to the Vins de Pays du Jardin de la France in the Loire and Vins de Pays d'Oc in the Midi. The full range of grape varieties from Bordeaux and the South-West is admitted as well as Gamay and Syrah, and wines may be blended from across these *départements*. This is particularly interesting for big buyers, who want a large volume with a regular and defined style. Production in 1988 was two million bottles, 90% red, 9% rosé, 1% white.

Vins de Pays Départementaux

VIN DE PAYS DE LA HAUTE-GARONNE

Red and rosé wines mostly from the north of the *département*, in the Frontonnais region. Grape varieties are the Negrette, completed by the Merlot, Cabernet Franc and Sauvignon, Syrah and Jurançon Noir. Deep-coloured reds (90%), fruity rosés. Production 800,000 bottles. The best producer is Domaine de Ribonnet.

VIN DE PAYS DU TARN-ET-GARONNE

Red and rosé wines from the region of Lavilledieu as well as from the Frontonnais to the west of Montauban, from the Gamay, Tannat, Cabernet Franc and Sauvignon, Syrah and Jurançon Noir. Deep-coloured wines, with a lively fruit due to the Gamay. Production 1.2 million bottles, mostly red, 95% made by two *caves coopératives* at Lavilledieu and Campsas.

Vins de Pays de Zone

AGENAIS

Red, dry white and (very little) rosé from the Lot-et-Garonne. The red with a deep ruby colour can be quite tannic, much resembling Côtes de Duras. The white is pale and fruity with refreshing acidity. Reds travel, whites do not. Production 1.5 million bottles.

COTEAUX DE GLANES

Red and rosé from the northern Lot on the left bank of the Dordogne. Light, soft and fruity wines mostly red from the Gamay and Merlot grapes. Production 100,000 bottles, usually all red.

COTEAUX DE QUERCY

Red and rosé from the Lot below Cahors, and the Tarn-et-Garonne. The Gamay grape makes light, fruity, commercial wines, but the better wines are made from the local Cot, Tannat and Cabernet grapes. Excellent table wines, with good colour and definition. The best are those grown around Cahors. Production two million bottles, 95% red.

COTEAUX ET TERRASSES DE MONTAUBAN

Red and rosé from around Montauban in the Tarn-et-Garonne. They have good colour and fruit and a liveliness due to the silica-based soil. In style they quite resemble wines of Gaillac and Lavilledieu. Production, almost all red, 300,000 bottles.

COTEAUX DE MONTESTRUC

Red, dry white and rosé from around Auch in the middle of the Gers *département*. Very like the Côtes de Gascogne and may be sold under its name, as may the Côtes de Condomois, hence the low production, mostly red, of 120,000 bottles.

COTES DU TARN

Red, dry white and rosé from the western half of the Tarn. These are some of the best *petits vins* from the South-West: the reds (with Gamay-based wines for early drinking and those based on the Duras, Syrah and Cabernets for keeping) are a brilliant ruby colour with good fruit, the rosés very good, the whites everyday wines with some character. These wines are rarely disappointing. Very large production of 15 million bottles, 60% red, 30% white, 10% rosé, two-thirds made by *coopératives*.

GORGES ET COTES DE MILLAU

Red, dry white and rosé from both banks of the Tarn. Reds on the left bank, from the Gamay, are quite light in colour, fruity with pleasant acidity, the rosés perhaps better, the whites pale, crisp, with distinctive fruit and good acidity. Reds, from the right bank from the Syrah, Cabernet, Cot and Fer, are much firmer and age better. Their quality puts them into the VDQS category.

Production 200,000 bottles, 80% red and 90% made by the *coopérative* at Aguessac.

SAINT-SARDOS

Almost entirely red wine from west of Montauban in the Tarn-et-Garonne, and the north-west corner of the Haute-Garonne. Reds and rosés are fruity (Cabernet Franc, Tannat, Syrah), easy to drink; whites resemble the minor dry whites of Bordeaux. Production 700,000 bottles, mostly from the *coopérative* of Saint-Sardos.

COTES DU CONDOMOIS

Red, dry white and rosé from the Gers and four communes in the Lot-et-Garonne. The white is light with good acidity (drink young), the red (90%) quite full, best drunk locally (very little rosé is made). Production is approaching one million bottles. With a yield limited to 70hl/ha (as opposed to 80hl for other *vins de pays*), these wines have good structure. An upgrade to VDQS has been applied for.

Béarn and the Pyrenees

This region covers the departments of the Landes, Pyrénées-Atlantiques, Hautes-Pyrénées and part of the Gers. The wines are most distinctive, remaining totally original in their *encépagement* – the Baroque, Petit and Gros Manseng, and Courbu for the whites, Tannat and Fer Servadou for the reds – while accepting the sophistication of the Bordelais for winemaking. The quality of wine currently produced in the historic *appellations* of Jurançon and Madiran is as satisfying as is the success of the Vin de Pays de Côtes de Gascogne.

AOC WINES

Béarn

Red, rosé and dry white wines, principally from the *département* of the Pyrénées-Atlantiques. The province of Béarn also covers the wines of Irouléguy, Jurançon, Pacherenc du Vic Bihl and Madiran. Reds and rosés must be from the local grape, the Tannat, to a maximum of 60%, and other indigenous varietals such as Manseng Noir, Fer, Pinenc, Courbu Noir, along with Cabernet Sauvignon and Cabernet Franc from Bordeaux. They are fruity, agreeable and quite light, perfect with the Basque cuisine. Most are produced by *caves coopératives* such as Les Vignerons de Bellocq and much is drunk by locals and tourists at one to two years

old, although the red may be kept longer. The white wine, under 10% of the *appellation*, is from a mixture of local grapes: Petit-Manseng, Gros-Manseng, Courbu, Lauzat, Baroque, with the addition of Sémillon and Sauvignon. They are light and dry, but lack a little character and acidity and do not travel well. All Béarn wines must have 10.5° minimum alcohol from a basic maximum yield of 50hl/ha. Average production is 750,000 bottles, mostly rosé. Price B.

Irouléguy

Red, white and rosé wines from a small vineyard area of nearly 116 hectares to the west of Saint-Jean-Pied-de-Port, not far from the Spanish frontier. The whites, in the same style as the Béarn blanc, are virtually non-existent. The reds must be made from the Tannat to a minimum of 50%, the other grapes being the Fer, also indigenous to the South-West, the Cabernet Sauvignon and Cabernet Franc. The minimum alcohol content is 10°, from a yield of 50hl/ha, and Irouléguy is one of the rare wines in France to have a maximum alcohol level at 14°. The production of rosés dominates that of red, the wine having a pretty orangey-rosé colour (the opposite of the violetty-pink rosés from Bourgueil in the Loire, for example), quite a full flavour and should be drunk young. The reds have more character, an irresistible ruby colour, full of fruit and a spicy *goût de terroir*, without the weight of a Madiran. Both are

Above: Cabernet Sauvignon grapes awaiting collection by the Buzet cooperative.
Left: Vintage time in the very rural Landes département.

perfect with the local cuisine, and go very well with egg dishes. Average production is 200,000 bottles a year. Virtually all from the *cave coopérative*. Well worth looking out for. Price B.

Jurançon

Sweet white wine from the Pyrénées-Atlantiques, to the south-west of Pau. If, as is common today, the wine is vinified dry, it must be sold under the *appellation* Jurançon *sec*. The sweet Jurançon, the finest wine from the South-West, famous from the time of Henry IV, is becoming easier to find as *vignerons* have once again taken the risk of producing a *vin liquoreux*. The vineyards are very parcellated and the local vines – Petit Manseng, Gros Manseng and Courbu – are planted "high", growing to between 1.5 and 2 metres off the ground, supported by trellises. The very low yield of 25hl/ha is seldom attained as the minimum of 12.5° alcohol is the result of extremely late picking, by which time the grapes have become dried out or raisiny, with the desired concentration of sugar. Low producing but very fine, the Petit Manseng is usually the only grape found in the best *cuvées*. The wine, with the same weight as a Vouvray Moelleux or a Sauternes, is quite different from these and most individual: the colour is golden, the bouquet rich, honeyed, with hints of nutmeg and cinnamon, even cloves and ginger, the taste luscious with a refreshing lemony acidity in the finish. Jurançon may be drunk young either as an apéritif, with certain hors d'oeuvres such as *pâté de foie gras*, or with fruit desserts. It is one of the finest, and until recently most underrated, wines of France. This opinion is especially borne out by wines from Clos Cancaillau, Domaine Cauhapé, Cru Lamouroux and Clos Uroulat. Not expensive for the quality. Price D.

Jurançon sec

Dry white wine from the same region and the same grapes as Jurançon. The permitted yield is double at 50hl/ha and the minimum alcohol content 11° with a maximum of 12.5°. Jurançon *sec*, easier to make and to sell than the sweet wine, accounts for about nine-tenths of the average production of three million bottles. This is a tenfold increase from the 1970s, due to a renaissance in the *appellation*, which now covers 500 of a possible 560 hectares. The wine is pale in colour, with just a hint of honey and spices on the nose, good clean fruit and a slightly tart finish. It is good as an apéritif or with hors d'oeuvres, fish or chicken. The wines from the *coopérative* are reliable and inexpensive, but those of Domaine Cauhapé and the Clos Uroulat are better. Price C.

Madiran

Red wine from 1,000 hectares planted in the *départements* of the Pyrénées-Atlantiques, Hautes-Pyrénées and the Gers, to the north-east of Tarbes. Grapes planted are the Tannat (minimum 40%, maximum 60%), the Fer, Cabernet Sauvignon and Cabernet Franc. Minimum alcohol content is 11°, basic maximum yield 45hl/ha. Madiran rivals, and in fact surpasses, Cahors to be the deepest-coloured, longest-lived wine of the South-West. The Tannat makes a wine that is very rough when young, and even if it is tempered with the Cabernet Franc it still legally has to spend 20 months in wood before it is bottled. A good Madiran has a splendid purple-ruby colour, a rich, fruity bouquet and a full taste. It is perfect with the local cured ham, excellent with meat and game, unsurpassed with *cassoulet*. It may be drunk at two or three years but is best between five and ten. The wines from the *coopérative* are inexpensive, but the growers' wines are better. These are divided between the fine old-fashioned style, high in Tannat from Domaine Picard, Domaine du Crampilh, Cru du Paradis, Domaine Barréjat, and the more modern Cabernet-influenced wines of Château de Peyros and Jean-Marc Laffite. Between these styles are wines from the two largest

Domaines in the *appellation*: Château Montus and Domaine Boucassé of Alain Brumont and Château d'Aydie of Laplace Frères. These two forward-looking growers have kept to the traditional grape varieties, while investing in the most modern winemaking equipment as well as new oak barrels, to produce a series of wines that have redefined the *appellation* from a wine of rustic power to one combining elegance with intensity of flavour and *goût de terroir*. Their influence has also encouraged the renaissance of Pacherenc du Vic Bilh. Price C-D.

Pacherenc du Vic Bilh

Dry, semi or fully sweet white wine from the same region as Madiran. It is made from the local grapes, the Ruffiac, Gros Manseng, Petit Manseng and Courbu, with a little Sémillon and Sauvignon. Minimum alcohol content is 12°, from a yield of 40hl/ha. The vines are trained high, as at Jurançon, two metres above the ground in *pachets-en-rang* (the local dialect for *piquets-en-rang*, "posts-in-a-line"), hence the name. The wine produced is rich and lively at the same time, not unlike Jurançon, but usually less concentrated and lacking Jurançon's lemony acidity, and finishes fruity and slightly honeyed, if it is dry, the label must carry the word *sec*. Good as an apéritif, with hors d'oeuvres and especially the local river-fish. Smallish production of 500,000 bottles, made almost exclusively by the better domaines from the Madiran *appellation*. Still reasonable, but prices are rising as quality increases. Price B-C.

VDQS WINES

Côtes de Saint-Mont

Red, white and rosé wines from the *département* of the Gers and the eastern Landes. Reds are made from a high proportion (70%) of Tannat, plus Cabernet Sauvignon, Cabernet Franc and Merlot. They have a deep colour and a clean, slightly rough fruit, resembling a more simple version of Madiran. The whites, from the local grapes Meslier, Jurançon, Sauvignon and Picpoul, are pale straw in colour, quite distinctive, dry but not acidic, well worth trying in the local restaurants. There is an excellent *coopérative*, Les Producteurs de Plaimont, whose prestige *cuvée* Château de Sabazon is excellent. Price B.

Tursan

Red, dry white and rosé wines from the Landes *département*, around the towns of Géaune and Aire-sur-Adour. The reds and rosés must be made principally from the Tannat grape, with Cabernet Sauvignon,

Cabernet Franc and Fer. The wine is solid and well structured, having a minimum of 10.5° alcohol from a yield of 45hl/ha, quite full in tannin like a minor Madiran. The rosés are simple and fruity, but not so interesting as the reds. The white Tursan, which used to represent most of the production, comes from its own particular grape, the Baroque, to a minimum of 90%. The wine is quite straightforward, having more flavour than bouquet, and goes very well with the local hors d'oeuvres and fish. It should be drunk very young. Most of the wine is made by the Coopérative des Vignerons de Tursan. Michel Gérard, the famous 3–star chef from nearby Eugénie-les-Bains, has recently planted his own vineyard, Château de Bachen, to make a very floral, stylish white wine. Coincidentally, an application has been made to upgrade Tursan to a full *appellation*. Production is currently 1.5 million bottles, 50% white. Price B.

VINS DE PAYS

Apart from the high quality of the red wines from the local varieties, one of the marked successes in the *vin de pays* category has been the fresh, fruity dry whites from the Côtes de Gascogne. Price A, low B.

Vins de Pays Regionaux

VIN DE PAYS DE COMTE TOLOSAN
See page 196.

Vins de Pays Départementaux

VIN DE PAYS DES LANDES
Red, dry white and rosé from the south-east of the *département*. The reds made from Tannat and the Cabernets, are full in colour, more or less robust depending on the proportion of Tannat. Rosés are from the same grapes – Baroque, Arrufiac, Colombard and Gros Manseng. Production 500,000 bottles, 75% white, 15% red, 10% rosé.

Vins de Pays de Zone

BIGORRE
Red, dry white and rosé wines from the north of Tarbes in the Hautes-Pyrénées near to Madiran. The reds and rosés (90%) are mostly from the Tannat and Cabernet Franc, the whites from the local Arrufiac grape, with Ugni Blanc and Colombard. Both are light and fruity for drinking young. The creation of this *vin de pays* was very recent and no wine was declared in 1987 and 1988.

COTES DE GASCOGNE
Red, dry white and rosé from the west of Auch in the Gers. Very good wines, 65% white from Ugni Blanc and Colombard, which have started to gain more than a local reputation. Production 18 million bottles, 80% white, a complete revolution in the region. Excellent wines from Château de Tarriquet, Domaine des Bordes and the *coopérative* at Plaimont.

TERROIRS LANDAIS
Red, dry white and rosé from the Landes. Reds and rosés are based on the Tannat and Cabernet grapes, whites on the Baroque, Ugni Blanc and Colombard. Production in 1988 almost one million bottles, 50% white, 40% red, 10% rosé.

THEZAC-PERRICARD
A new *vin de pays*, from the Lot-en-Garonne whose first year of production was 1988, declaring 100,000 bottles, all red. They resemble those of the Agenais.

The Loire Valley

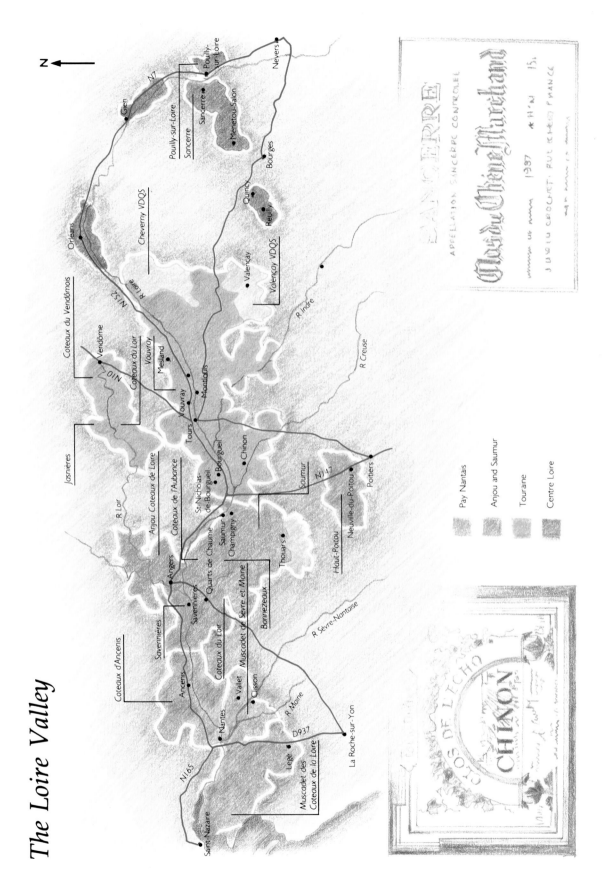

N

Saint-Nazaire

N165

Muscadet des
Coteaux de la Loire

Coteaux d'Ancenis

Ancenis

Nantes

Legé

La Roche-sur-Yon

D937

R Maine

Clisson

Vallet

Coteaux du Loir

Muscadet de Sèvre et Maine

Savennières

Savennières

Angers

Quarts de Chaume

Bonnezeaux

R Sèvre-Nantaise

Anjou-Coteaux de Loire

Coteaux de l'Aubance

St-Nicholas-
de-Bourgueil

Saumur-
Champigny

Thouars

Haut-Poitou

Neuville-du-Poitou

Poitiers

N147

Saumur

Josnières

R Loir

Bourgueil

Chinon

Tours

Vouvray

Montlouis

Vouvray

Coteaux du Loir

Mesland

N10

Vendôme

Coteaux du Vendômois

N152

R Loire

Orléans

Cheverny VDQS

Valençay

Valençay VDQS

R Indre

R Creuse

Reuilly

Quincy

Bourges

Menetou-Salon

Sancerre

Sancerre

Pouilly-sur-Loire

Pouilly-sur-Loire

Nevers

Gien

N7

Pay Nantais

Anjou and Saumur

Touraine

Centre Loire

The Loire Valley

The Loire is the longest river in France and, since it meanders across the middle of the country, south of Champagne, north of Bordeaux, it is to be expected that vineyards are found on both banks. Over nearly 1,000 kilometres more than 80,000 hectares produces, with great variation, between 330 and 460 million bottles of wine each year. If Loire wines have one characteristic in common, it is a certain *nervosité*, or liveliness, a product of the temperate climate.

Virtually every style of wine is to be found in the Loire Valley, from the driest whites to rich, honeyed dessert wines, from light, fruity reds to be drunk young, to more serious reds to be treated like claret, the complete range of rosés, and the second most famous sparkling wine in France. Many, are perfect "local" wines, delicious to drink on the spot, yet requested the world over.

The river Loire rises in the Auvergne, on the same latitude as Beaujolais, so it is not surprising to find the Gamay grape widely planted, making characteristically fruity wines with a discernible *goût de terroir*. As the river winds northwards, the white burgundy grapes, Chardonnay and Aligoté, are seen alongside the Sauvignon, and the Pinot Noir makes one of its rare appearances outside the Côte d'Or to make wines at Saint-Pourçain that are not yet typically Loire in style. The wines become more what we expect as the river enters the Nivernais: Pouilly-Fumé and Sancerre and the similar-tasting Quincy and Reuilly. Further north still, very little wine is now made around Gien, where a century ago there were 800 *vignerons*. Even the vineyards around Orléans are being engulfed by the city suburbs.

When the river turns west towards the sea, entering the château country, vines begin in earnest and are planted with hardly a break right up to the mouth of the Loire at Nantes. The white wines of Touraine witness the change from Sauvignon to Chenin Blanc, while the Pinot Noir, still in evidence at Sancerre, disappears in favour of the Cabernet family. Attractive, mostly white wines come from Cheverny and Chambord; Amboise produces good wines under the *appellation* Touraine, while the finest wines are from the region of Tours. From the east come Montlouis and Vouvray, similar white wines both made from the Chenin Blanc, able to become bone-dry, *demi-sec*, lusciously rich or sparkling. From the west, on the outskirts of the Saumurois, come the best red wines in the Loire valley, Chinon and Bourgueil, made from the Cabernet Franc.

As the river enters the province of Anjou, the style changes again. With the exception of the excellent Anjou-Villages and Saumur Champigny, red wines become less interesting, though still typically Loire in style, fruity and slightly rustic. The rosés, dry or *demi-sec*, are well known, but the white wines of Bonnezeaux, Coteaux du Layon and Quarts de Chaume are the jewels of the Loire, honey-sweet, long underrated and now firmly back in fashion. The dry whites, also from the Chenin Blanc, are good, especially at Savennières.

The Pays Nantais bring another change in style. Here the wines are dry and almost exclusively white. Some pleasant reds and rosés are made at Ancenis, but the best-known wine is the Muscadet, the pale, almost crackingly crisp white wine synonymous with shellfish throughout the world. Even drier than Muscadet, often too tart for most tastes, is the Gros Plant du Pays Nantais.

The four regions are looked at from west to east. *Vins de pays* appear at the end of the chapter.

The Wines of the Atlantic Coast and the West

"La région Nantaise", as it is known in France, comprises 12,900 hectares of vines planted across the Loire-Atlantique *département* south of Nantes, and produces almost 100 million bottles of wine annually, nearly all white. It is dominated by the wines from the Muscadet region. These light, crisp, slightly acidic wines have a tanginess that has perhaps more in common with the sea than with the river. All wines – red, white and rosé – from this part of the Loire Valley are light, low in alcohol, and should be drunk young.

AOC WINES

Muscadet is the name of the grape variety as well as the name of the wine. The grape originated in Burgundy, where it was called "Melon de Bourgogne", because of the rounded form of its leaves, but it is no longer planted there. The name "Muscadet" probably comes from the slightly "musky" flavour of the wine. Muscadet is the archetypal dry white wine: harvested early to keep the freshness and fruit, very pale in colour, dry but not generally acid, with a certain finesse and lively charm and a well-defined character. It goes perfectly with shellfish, and well with hors d'oeuvres, fish, white meats and even goat's cheese. As a popular wine, its only rival is Beaujolais. The annual production of Muscadet is around 80 million bottles from nearly 11,000 hectares, which is divided between three *appellations*.

Muscadet

Dry white wine only from the Muscadet grape; minimum alcohol content 9.5°, maximum 12° from a yield based on 50hl/ha but always much more due to the PLC or *plafond limite de classement* (see page 11), whereby the legal yield can be increased on a yearly basis. It is to be drunk as young as possible. The label may add *sur lie* (bottled on its lees) to the *appellation*, if the wine has not been racked off its lees after fermentation, and if it is bottled before 30 June following the vintage. In fact, most straight Muscadets are bottled before the summer. The production of Muscadet *tout court* represents not more than 10% of the *appellation*. A proportion of this style of wine is sold "en primeur" from the middle of November, which is when it is at its best. Price B.

Muscadet des Coteaux de la Loire

From vines planted on the right bank of the Loire, up-river from Nantes towards Ancenis. Minimum alcohol content is 10°, otherwise the same conditions as for Muscadet apply. The wine is clean and fruity, possibly a little fuller in style than Muscadet *tout court*, but rather more tart and less flavourful than Muscadet de Sèvre-et-Maine. It represents not more than 5% of the total production. The best grower here is Domaine Guindon, whose wines have a bouquet of spring flowers to balance the natural dryness, and which can be aged. Price B.

Muscadet de Sèvre-et-Maine

From south-east of Nantes, in the Sèvre-et-Maine *département*, this *appellation* represents 85% of the total production. The best Muscadet wines come from this region with its rolling hills and stony-clayey soil, and must show 10° of alcohol from a yield of 50hl/ha, a yield generally exceeded. The finest wine comes from the cantons of Vallet, Clisson and Loroux-Bottereau, delicate, with much finesse and great length of flavour. The success of these wines on the home and export markets has encouraged growers and négociants alike to upgrade their best wines into *cuvées spéciales*, some of them aged in new oak, which is a departure from the classic style. While these wines underline, and some exaggerate, the potential of the *appellation*, a Muscadet de Sèvre-et-Maine in the hands of a good grower is one of the most "French" of French wines. There are very many fine producers and it seems hardly fair to single out the following: Donatien Bahuaud, Château de Chasseloir, Château du Cléray and the wines from Sauvion Frères, Domaine des Dorices, Jean Douillard, Marquis de Goulaine, Domaine la Haute Févrie, Serge Luneau, Marcel Martin, Louis Metaireau, Château de l'Oiselinière, Clos des Rosiers and Francis Viaud. Most producers bottle their wine *sur lie*. They should be drunk young 1–2 years after the vintage. None improve after 2 years, but the best survive up to 5. Still reasonably priced according to the quality. Price B-C.

VDQS WINES

Coteaux d'Ancenis

Little-known red, dry white and rosé wines from 300 hectares on the right bank of the Loire around Ancenis. The label must state the name of the grape from which the wine is made: Pineau de la Loire (the local name for Chenin Blanc), Pinot Beurot and Malvoisie (white); Gamay and Cabernet Franc (red and rosé). With the exception of the slightly sweet wine from the Malvoisie, the Coteaux d'Ancenis are light, dry, fruity and refreshing, best drunk young. The Gamay now represents 80% of production. Minimum alcohol must be 10° for a low yield (much less than in the Muscadet) of 40hl/ha and most of the 1.3 million bottles produced are light, fruity with a lively acidity. The exceptions are the wines from Domaine Guindon, where the extraction of character and flavour is astounding: their Malvoisie is unique in the *appellation*. Generally very inexpensive; Guindon's wines cost more, but are worth it. Price B.

Fiefs Vendéens

Red, dry white and rosé wines from the 380 hectares in the Vendée *département*. Reds and rosés are from the Gamay, Cabernet Franc, Cabernet Sauvignon, Pinot Noir and Pineau d'Aunis; whites from the Gros Plant, Chenin Blanc, Sauvignon and Chardonnay, light and refreshing, and should be drunk young. These wines were upgraded from *vin de pays* to VDQS from the 1985 vintage. The better communes are Mareuil, Pissotte (Domaine Xavier Coirier) and Brem-sur-Mer (Pierre Richard). Most of the production is of light red and rosés, but the quantity of white is increasing. All are best drunk locally. Inexpensive. Price A-B.

Gros Plant du Pays Nantais

Dry white wine grown from the grape of the same name, also known as the Folle-Blanche, which originated in the Cognac region, directly to the south. Gros Plant is "greener" than Muscadet, appears much drier, and should be drunk very young as an apéritif or with shellfish. As with Muscadet, the better wines are bottled *sur lie* to retain flavour. Many producers in Muscadet make an excellent Gros Plant, exceptional examples being the Clos des Rosiers at Vallet and Domaines des Herbauges at Bouaye. Production: 25 million bottles from 3,000 hectares. Minimum alcohol content 9°, yield 50hl/ha, always exceeded. Price B.

VINS DE PAYS

This region produces wines under the regional Vins de Pays du Jardin de la France, under the Departmental Vins de Pays de la Loire-Atlantique and de la Vendée and under two Vins de Pays de Zone, Marches de Bretagne and Retz. See page 222.

The Wines of Anjou and Saumurois

The ancient royal province of Anjou corresponds roughly to today's *département* of Maine-et-Loire. Vines are planted along the banks of the Loire and its tributaries and benefit from the clear light and temperate climate. The wines of Anjou have a reputation stretching back to the twelfth century and while historically the white wines are the most sought after, offering a complete range of styles from bone-dry to honey-sweet and even sparkling, there are some excellent red wines being produced, as well as the ever-popular rosés.

The wines of Saumur have a reputation as old as those of Anjou and they are officially classified with Anjou, yet perhaps they have more in common with the wines of Touraine. The white wines are generally dry or *demi-sec*, with sweet wines being made only in the best years. The soil, a hard chalky-clay known as *le tuffeau*, produces long-lasting wines of great character. Vines grown on a more sandy soil are fine, but lighter. The region around the town of Saumur itself is particularly well known for sparkling wines made by the *méthode champenoise*, while the red wine made at Champigny can claim to be among the finest in the Loire. The total area under vines slightly exceeds 20,000 hectares.

AOC WINES

Above: Mechanical harvesters have not yet reached this vineyard near Nantes.

Anjou

Red, white and rosé wines mainly from the *département* of the Maine-et-Loire, but also from parts of the *département* of Deux-Sèvres and the Vienne. Within these geographical limits, wines may be made from the following grapes: Reds: Cabernet Franc, Cabernet Sauvignon, Pineau d'Aunis. Rosés: Cabernet Franc, Cabernet Sauvignon, Pineau d'Aunis, Gamay, Cot, Groslot. Whites: Chenin Blanc (Pineau de la Loire) to a minimum of 80%, with a maximum of 20% made up by Chardonnay or Sauvignon. There are about 5,200 hectares in production, with a basic yield of 50hl/ha.

Anjou is the global *appellation* that covers several

regional or communal *appellations* (see below) as the *appellation* Bourgogne covers Pommard, Nuits-Saint-Georges and so on. The white wines are generally dry, with a soft, honeysuckle fruit in good years, the rosés are light in colour, charming, often with a touch of sweetness and the reds have a good colour, lots of fruit and a delightful, raspberry-scented *goût de terroir*. Since the mid-1980s, white and red Anjou have emerged from obscurity, due to a combination of good vintages and improved winemaking. The red wines especially have proved to be an alternative to Saumur-Champigny, Chinon or Bourgueil, at a lower price. The superb quality made in 1989 and 1990 have confirmed Anjou as a major producer of fine, country-style red wines, which are still inexpensive.

Anjou Coteaux de la Loire

White wines only, dry and semi-sweet from both sides of the Loire around Angers. The vineyard area is small but well exposed; only the Pineau de la Loire may be planted, producing a wine with a bouquet of summer flowers and a discreet fruit flavour, to be drunk on its own, or with light entrées and white meat. The *demi-sec* is softer and slightly honeyed, but not as intense as the sweet wines from the Coteaux de l'Aubance or Coteaux du Layon. Domaine du Fresche and Gilles Musset are the principal growers. The minimum alcohol content is quite high at 12°, with a low yield of 30hl/ha with no marked acidity, these are wines to drink young. Production is 200,000 bottles and is falling due to replanting with red grapes. Domaine du Fresche and Gilles Musset are the principal producers. Price B.

Anjou Gamay

Mostly red wines made from the Gamay grape only, and this must be stated on the label. Light, easy to drink, less interesting than red Anjou from the Cabernet, but attractive when drunk young and cool. Much of the 1.3 million bottles produced are sold in bulk to négociants. The best grower is Domaine de Sainte-Anne. Price low B.

Anjou Mousseux

Very small production of white and rosé wines made sparkling by the *méthode champenoise*. The principal grape is Pineau de la Loire, but up to 60% of Cabernet, Gamay, Cot, Groslot and Pineau d'Aunis may be added to the press to make the white wine. The sparkling wines from Saumur are more popular. The total production is sold locally. Price C.

Anjou-Villages

Red wines only from several villages on the banks of the Loire and its tributaries the Aubance and the Layon. This *appellation* was created in 1987, retroactive to the 1986 vintage, in recognition of the progress made in Anjou reds. Only Cabernet grapes may be planted, with a preference for Cabernet Franc. Although the permitted yield is, as for Anjou, 50hl/ha, these wines may not leave the producers until the September after the vintage, encouraging growers to use low-yielding or older vines to obtain the necessary concentration of fruit. Reserved for the Anjou-Villages wines is the typical tall Anjou bottle with the coat of arms of the province embossed on the neck. They have a deep violet-red colour and are packed with a direct, slightly earthy fruit with a satisfyingly rounded finish. While a simple Anjou rouge can be drunk within the year, the

Villages need 3–4 years to show at their best. Most of the growers who have been producing fine Coteaux du Layon have made some equally exciting and impressive Anjou-Villages, including: Domaine du Closel, Château de Passavant, Château des Rochettes, Jacques Lecointre, Domaine Ogereau, Domaine de Pierre-Bise, Domaine de la Motte and the Coopérative Les Caves de la Loire. Justifiably more expensive than Anjou rouge, and good value. Price high B.

Bonnezeaux

Produced from the south-facing right bank of the river Layon in the commune of Thouarcé, Bonnezeaux is a Grand Cru of the *appellation* Coteaux du Layon, and, alongside the other Grand Cru *appellation* Quarts de Chaume, produces the finest sweet white wines in Anjou. Only the Pineau de la Loire (Chenin Blanc) is planted, and the bunches of grapes are left on the vines to increase the sugar content and await the *pourriture noble*. In good years Bonnezeaux is rich and perfumed, with an unctuous fruit and a refreshing lemony acidity that prevents it from becoming cloying. It can be drunk young, in the year after the vintage while it is still exploding with fruit, and it ages beautifully. It is naturally sweet and high in alcohol (minimum 13.5° total after fermentation) and is perfect as an apéritif, with fish in a cream sauce, with fruit desserts or in the middle of a summer's afternoon. Such wines are justifiably coming back into fashion. The best wine is the Château de Fèsles of Jacques Boivin. Domaine de la Petite Croix and Domaine du Petit Val are almost as good. Production is small at around 120,000 bottles (rarely attaining the permitted 25hl/ha from 50 hectares), but is increasing since recent vintages have shown such quality. A total of 130 hectares. Becoming expensive. Price E, and F for older vintages.

Cabernet d'Anjou

Semi-sweet rosés from the Anjou region, made from the Cabernet Franc and/or Cabernet Sauvignon grapes exclusively. Minimum alcohol required is 10°, plus 10 grams per litre residual sugar; yield 40hl/ha, average production per year 1.5 million bottles. This prettily coloured, semi-sweet rosé enjoyed a great success from the 1890s to the 1950s when (not helped by rather poor winemaking overall) this style of wine began to lose favour. If well made and drunk young, it has a soft salmon-pink colour, violets or raspberry bouquet and a *tendre* or soft finish. Best drunk on its own, quite cold, or with *petits fours*. Better vintages and improved winemaking, have given these delicious, discreetly fruity and appealing wines a new lease of life. Wines from Château de Tigné, Domaine Bertrand, Domaines des Maurières and Domaine Poupard are among those of note. Same price or less than Anjou rouge. Price B.

Cabernet de Saumur

Semi-sweet rosés from the Saumur region, with the same *appellation* conditions as the Cabernet d'Anjou. The colour is perhaps paler, often as light as a *vin gris*, and the taste a little lighter and firmer, less rich. Small production, around 120,000 bottles. Price B.

Coteaux de l'Aubance

Semi-sweet and sweet white wines from 80 hectares of vines grown along the banks of the river Aubance, a tributary of the Loire. These soft, charming, fruity wines are grown on the same schistous soil as the Coteaux du Layon and from the same grape (Chenin Blanc), they are similar in character but usually less intense in flavour. The yield is low, 30hl/ha, and the production has been declining in favour of dry whites made from the Chenin Blanc or reds and rosés made from the Cabernet or Gamay, which are more popular but have only the right to the *appellation* Anjou. However, the recent upsurge in demand for the sweet white wines of Anjou, following the spectacular 1989 vintage, has encouraged the growers to continue. Excellent, long-lasting wines from Domaine Richou, and very good from Domaines de Montgilet, du Fresche, du Pélican and Dittière. Only 130,000 bottles are produced, always less expensive than a Coteaux du Layon. Price C (Coteaux de l'Aubance); B (Anjou).

Coteaux de Saumur

Tiny production (12,000 bottles) of *demi-sec* white wine from Chenin Blanc grapes grown on the *tuffeau* soil of the Saumur region. Not unlike Vouvray, with a bouquet of honey and flowers, followed by crisp, well-defined fruit flavours. It is almost all drunk locally. Price B.

Coteaux du Layon

Semi-sweet and sweet white wines produced from the Chenin Blanc from a possible 3,000 hectares, of which only 1,300 are under vines, on the banks of the Layon, a tributary of the Loire. The fall in demand and the economic risk of making sweet white wine has seen some of the region planted in Cabernet Franc and a little Cabernet Sauvignon to make a red or a rosé under the *appellation* Anjou, while much of the white wine is vinified dry and is sold as Anjou blanc. Coteaux du Layon is limited to 30hl/ha as opposed to 50hl/ha for Anjou, and must have at least 12° alcohol before any addition by chaptalisation of which 11° may be fermented alcohol and 1° residual sugar. This high degree is obtained by harvesting the grapes as ripe as possible, hopefully with the effects of *pourriture noble*. The result is a pale golden, sometimes green-tinted wine, with a summery, honeyed, slightly spicy bouquet and sweet but not cloying finish. The high sugar allows the wine to age beautifully and the natural acidity of the Chenin Blanc provides a refreshing liveliness in even the richest years. The finest communes in the *appellation* – Beaulieu, Faye, Rablay, Rochefort, Saint-Aubin and Saint Lambert – are now grouped as Coteaux du Layon-Villages, and may add their name to the label if the wine is richer and more intense in sugar and fruit. Each of these communes produces a slightly different style of wine – Faye and Rablay are more racy, Beaulieu and Saint-Aubin more unctuous, Saint-Lambert and Rochefort more concentrated, even earthy – which clearly stands out in great vintages like 1989 and 1990. The commune of Chaume is considered superior to the others (Château de Plaisance, Château de la Roulerie, Domaine de la Soucherie), but may only add its name if the yield does not exceed 25hl/ha, the same as for Sauternes. Winemaking is improving and these delicious wines are coming strongly back into fashion. Very fine wines come from the following properties: at Beaulieu: Château de Breuil, Domaine de Pierre-Bise; at Faye: Châteaux de Montbénault, Nouteau-Cerisier; at Rochefort: Domaine de la Motte, Domaine Grosset, Château de la Guimonière; at Saint-Aubin: Château de Bellevue, Domaine Cady, Domaine de la Pierre Saint-Maurille; at Saint-Lambert: Domaine Ogereau, Jean-Paul Jolivet; at Rablay: Domaine La Pierre Blanche (Lecointre); and also Domaine de Millé, Château des Rochettes and Domaine Cochard. There are very few *négociants* of note in Anjou, and the *caves coopératives* wines do not approach those of the growers. No longer cheap, but still half the price of a comparable Sauternes. Production in good years is around 5.5 million bottles. Price C-D. E for older vintages.

Coteaux du Layon-Chaume

The same style and character as above, with the grapes coming exclusively from the commune of Chaume. Minimum total alcohol content is 13° from a maximum yield of 25hl/ha. Only a handful of *vignerons* use this *appellation*. Price D-E.

Crémant de Loire

Sparkling wines from the accepted grape varieties grown in the Anjou, Saumur and Touraine regions, made by the *méthode champenoise*. A crémant is less "bubbly" than a fully sparkling wine, with an atmospheric pressure of 3.5kg as opposed to 5kg. This *appellation* covers any bottle-fermented sparkling wines from Anjou, Saumur and Touraine. Crémant de Loire Rosé now comprises about 10% of the 3 million bottles of sparkling wine production of the Loire, increasing yearly as an alternative to champagne, but also a pleasant wine in its own right. Inexpensive for a *méthode champenoise*. Price C.

Quarts de Chaume

Sweet, perfumed, luscious wines from the Chenin Blanc grown on 40 hectares in a micro-climate of the Coteaux du Layon *appellation*. The permitted yield is the lowest in France, 22hl/ha, with a minimum of 13° alcohol plus residual sugar. Quarts de Chaume, with Bonnezeaux, is the richest and most elegant of the sweet wines of Anjou. Harvesting is the result of successive *tries* to select only the most ripe bunches or those satisfactorily affected by noble rot, to produce a stunningly aromatic wine (peaches, apricots) with a fully sweet flavour and a fine, reserved finish. It can be drunk very young, or aged, but is best at 8–12 years. The Château de Belle Rive of the Lalanne family is once again making superb wines, and there are some lovely wines from Jean Baumard, Domaine des Maurières and the Château de Suronde. The name Quarts de Chaume comes from the habit of the ancient Dukes of Anjou of keeping the wines of the finest part of the Chaume vineyards for themselves. At its best, it is the rival of any sweet wine in France. Production is less than 100,000 bottles and it is expensive. Price F.

Rosé d'Anjou

Slightly sweet rosés made from any or all of the red wine varieties planted in Anjou: Cabernet Franc, Cabernet Sauvignon, Pineau d'Aunis, Gamay, Cot and Groslot, but particularly the last, also known as Grolleau. They are light in alcohol (9° minimum), with a minimum of 9 grams per litre residual sugar, very pretty to look at and refreshing to drink. Best drunk on their own, at the start of a meal, or throughout a summer's lunch. The same yield as Anjou: 50hl/ha. With 20–30 million bottles produced a year, this is the largest *appellation* by volume in Anjou. Quality, previously doubtful, is now much improved due to cleaner winemaking. Inexpensive. Price B.

Rosé d'Anjou Pétillant

The still rosé from Anjou, made *pétillant* by the *méthode champenoise*. This is a lengthy and expensive process, and since the demand for semi-sweet, semi-sparkling rosés is small, this is a wine which is hardly made any more. Price C.

Rosé de Loire

A dry rosé made in Anjou, Saumur and Touraine from the same grapes as the Rosé d'Anjou, Cabernets must represent a minimum of 30%, and no more than 3 grams per litre residual sugar are allowed. It is lighter and brisker than Anjou, attractively fruity and should be drunk young. Most of the production of 2.5 million bottles is made in Touraine. Inexpensive. Price B.

Saumur

White, both dry and sweet, and red wines made from the same grapes as are the red and white wines of Anjou (page 206). The dry white wines, with a minimum of 10° alcohol and a yield of 45hl/ha, are very fine, clean, fruity, harmonious and last well. The difference between Saumur and Anjou is the chalky-clayey *tuffeau* soil, which produces wines more in the style of Vouvray. They are delicious with hors d'oeuvres, fish, and light meat dishes, particularly pork, and can be particularly attractive, avoiding the acidity of Vouvray and the aggressiveness of Sancerre. Excellent wines come from Château de Villeneuve, Château de Parnay and the Cave de Saint-Cyr-en-Bourg. The sweeter wines from Saumur come under the *appellation* Coteaux de Saumur. The red wines, quite low in alcohol (10° minimum) with a low yield of 40hl/ha, may be light in colour, but are straightforward, fruity and pleasantly regional in character. The finest of these wines comes from Saumur-Champigny, which has its own *appellation*. Two-thirds of wines produced in Saumur are white, from a total of 4 million bottles. Price B.

Saumur-Champigny

Red wine from the Cabernet Franc planted on the most favourable limestone-chalk-based slopes on the left bank of the Loire to the east of Saumur. Champigny is the finest red wine in the Anjou-Saumur region, with a deep violet-ruby colour, an immediate aroma of crushed fruit (raspberries), a generous clean flavour and, when young, a slightly rough finish. It is delicious when drunk young and cool, while the better vintages can last 5–10 years. Until the early 1980s, Saumur-Champigny was the least known of the Saumur-Touraine red wines, but unexpected popularity in Paris restaurants brought recognition followed by replanting and increased prices. The lesser wines – Anjou rouge and particularly Anjou-Villages – are now set to take advantage of the price difference, but quality in this *appellation* has never been higher. Fine wines come from Denis Duveau, Domaine Filliatreau (especially the Cuvée Lena Filliatreau from old vines), Château de Chaintre, Clos des Cordeliers, Château de Villeneuve, Château du Hureau, Alain Sanzay and René-Noël Legrand and the Cave des Vignerons de Saint-Cyr-en-Bourg. Production 4.8 million bottles. Price C.

Saumur Mousseux

White and rosé sparkling wines. The whites, since they are made by the *méthode champenoise*, may include the permitted red grapes in the *cuvée* to a maximum of 60%. If either Chardonnay or Sauvignon is used it must be to a maximum of 20%, the rest being Chenin Blanc. The *méthode champenoise* involves the addition of alcohol (*liqueur de tirage*) to encourage the secondary fermentation, so wines to be made into Saumur Mousseux may be as low as 8.5° from a high yield of 60hl/ha. In any event, wines high in alcohol do not make good sparkling wines. They are mostly sold under brand names (Ackermann, Bouvet-Ladubay, Gratien et Meyer, Langlois Château, Veuve Amiot, etc.) as are the majority of champagnes. Either *crémant* or fully sparkling, they are fine quality sparkling wines and are justifiably successful. The production of rosé is about 5% of the total. The success of Crémant de Loire, in the manner of Crémant de Bourgogne and Crémant d'Alsace, has persuaded many producers to opt for this *appellation*. Price C.

Saumur Pétillant

These wines have virtually ceased to exist, since, although made in the same way as Saumur Mousseux, they could not legally use the champagne *habillage* or presentation (champagne cork held in place by wire, silver foil around the neck, etc.) and had to look like a still wine. Those wines that are produced are very much appreciated locally. Price probably C.

Savennières

Dry and sometimes semi-sweet white wine from parcellated vineyards covering only 60 hectares on the right bank of the Loire to the south-west of Angers. The wine is made from the Chenin Blanc and has the highest minimum alcohol content (12°) and the lowest yield (30hl/ha) for a dry white wine in Anjou. The soil contains a high proportion of slate, which gives the wine a flinty, rather austere acidity, and which needs a sunny vintage to provide the Chenin's floweriness and fruit. A good Savennières is less honeyed and direct than a Vouvray, but perhaps more refined, and benefits from a little bottle-age. Low sales led many proprietors to plant Cabernet Franc, producing an attractive Anjou rouge, but recently demand has increased, particularly for the modern, softer and lightly aromatic style of wine. Fine wines come from Jean Baumard, Château d'Epiré, Château de Chamboureau and the Domaine du Closel. The recent, continuing success of the sweeter white wines from the region has persuaded some growers to make a *demi-sec* if the vintage lends itself. Some replanting is under way, and there is a possibility of 120 hectares in all. Due to the low yields and the preference of most growers to sell their wine with a little bottle-age, these wines are relatively expensive. The two finest wines have their own *appellation*. Savennières-Roche-aux-Moines produces a rounder, more concentrated and complex wine (Domaine de la Bizolière, Château de la Roche-aux-Moines), mid-way between the classic Savennières and the famous Savennières-Coulée-de-Serrant. This wine, owned as a *monopole* by Madame Joly, covers less than 7 hectares and produces no more than 20,000 bottles of slow to mature but impressive wine. It was deemed by Curnonsky, the French gastronome, to be one of the four greatest white wines of France. The balance between a floral bouquet and firm, minerally flavour is unique. La Coulée-de-Serrant is tough and acidic at first, and needs five years to open up, whereas the lighter Savennières can be drunk sooner. Price C-D (La Roche-aux-Moines), F (La Coulée-de-Serrant).

Haut Poitou

Red, dry white (still and sparkling) and rosé wines, mostly from the Vienne *département* around Poitiers. Whites are from the Sauvignon, Chardonnay, Pinot Blanc and Chenin Blanc (to a maximum of 20%, the opposite of what pertains in Anjou). Reds and rosés are made principally from the Gamay, Pinot Noir, Cabernet Sauvignon, Cot and Groslot (also known as Grolleau) grapes. The wines are generally, except in very hot years, light in both colour and body, fresh and fruity and should be drunk young and chilled. The Sauvignon and the Gamay are typical of their grape varietal and are very popular, and the Chardonnay is crisp and distinctive. The Cave Coopérative de Neuville controls 90% of the 8 million bottle production, having relaunched the vineyards of the region in the early 1960s. This is one of the success stories of French viticulture, the wines have steadily improved, awarded VDQS status in 1970 and deservedly being promoted to a full *appellation* in 1989. Prices are still reasonable for such well-made wines. Price B.

VDQS WINES

Vins du Thouarsais

Red, dry white and rosé wines from around Bressuire in the Deux-Sèvres *département*. The white is made from Chenin Blanc, the reds and rosés from Cabernet Sauvignon and Cabernet Franc. Light (9.5° minimum alcohol for the whites, 9° for the reds), pleasant, fruity wines in the Anjou style. Drink young and cool, even the reds. Production: 80,000 bottles. Price B.

VINS DE PAYS

The Anjou and Saumurois produce *vins de pays* under the regional Vin de Pays du Jardin de la France, the Departmental Vin de Pays de Deux-Sèvres and Vin de Pays de la Vienne. See page 222.

Above: Le Clos de la Coulée de Serrant in the Loire Valley.

The Wines of Touraine

The province of Touraine is known as "the garden of France", and its wines were esteemed even before those of Anjou. The styles are similar to those in Anjou and the Saumurois, the climate ideal and the soil, be it the chalky-clayey *tuffeau* or the sandy-gravelly alluvial plains, is perfect for the vine. The Pineau de la Loire is at its best and most diverse in Touraine, while the Cabernet Franc (le Breton) and the Gamay produce the most attractive reds and rosés. Touraine is at the centre of the Loire Valley and represents, more concisely than the other provinces, the wines of the Loire valley at their most typical and distinctive. Across the *départements* of the Indre, Indre-et-Loire, Loir-et-Cher and the Sarthe are planted 10,000 hectares, producing up to 80 million bottles of wine.

AOC WINES

Dry, semi-sweet and sweet white, red and rosé wines made in the *départements* of Indre-et-Loire, Loir-et-Cher and a very little in the Indre. The permitted grape varieties are: White: Pineau de la Loire (Chenin Blanc), Menu-Pineau (or Arbois), Sauvignon and Chardonnay, which is limited to 20% of the area planted. Red: Cabernet Franc (Breton), Cabernet Sauvignon, Cot, Pinot Meunier, Pinot Gris, Pineau d'Aunis, Gamay. Rosés: as for reds, plus the Groslot.

The minimum alcohol content is 9° for the reds and 9.5° for the whites and rosés, from a basic yield of 45hl/ha. The Sauvignon is planted to the east of the *appellation*, as is the Gamay. These fresh young wines, packed with fruit, are often seen under the names "Sauvignon de Touraine" and "Gamay de Touraine", in order to benefit from both the popularity of the grape varieties and the regional *appellation*. They are an excellent, and less expensive, alternative to the Sauvignons from the centre of France (Sancerre, Pouilly-Fumé) and the Gamays from Beaujolais. The name of an individual commune may be added to Touraine on the label, if the wines are particularly distinctive. Around 40 million bottles of wine are produced annually as Touraine, the style following more the grape variety than the actual *appellation*. The Chenin Blanc produces wines which have much in common with the Saumur whites, and finds the best expression of its honeysuckle-lemony fruit in the wines of the Vouvray. The rosés are drier than in Anjou, perhaps more elegant as well. A sub-denomination, not an *appellation*, has been revived: Les Vins de Noble Joué, the wines are of the palest pink with a particular aroma of peaches. The reds made from the Breton (Cabernet Franc) are important wines of great fragrance and fruit, while those made from the minor varieties are more simple, "country wines" personified.

The nearer the vineyards are to Tours, the more the Cabernets and Chenin dominate. Once east of Amboise, Gamay and Sauvignon take over, with excellent wines from Henry Marionnet (Domaine de la Charmoise), Domaine de la Garenne, Domaine de la Presle, Jacky Preys, the négociant Paul Buisse and the excellent Cave des Vignerons d'Oisly et Thesée. Some white and rosé sparkling wines are made, favouring the *appellation* Crémant de Loire. Prices B-C.

Touraine-Amboise

White, red and rosé wines from the same grape varieties as Touraine, but grown around Amboise. These wines must have one more degree of natural alcohol than the Touraine *tout court*, hence more concentration of flavour. The whites are generally dry, with a pale greeny-gold colour, soft fruit and good acidity. They can age well and are at their best with hors d'oeuvres, especially pâtés, fish, white meats and goat's cheese. The rosés are attractive and fruity and the reds slightly rough and acidic, but go well with food. The *appellation* covers 150 hectares, producing 1.5 million bottles, 65% red, 25% white and 10% rosé. White and rosé wines are often semi-sweet, but with an attractive balancing acidity. Mostly sold in the region. Inexpensive. Price B, worth looking out for.

Touraine-Azay-le-Rideau

A small production of white and rosé wines from 50 hectares of vines planted on both banks of the Indre. The wines are made from the Pineau de la Loire, and the

rosés must have a minimum of 60% Groslot (or Grolleau) in their make-up, with 40% coming from other varieties. Both wines may be very slightly sweet, and are excellent for picnics, light lunches and everyday drinking. They do not taste as good away from the local cuisine. Price B.

Touraine-Mesland

White, red and rosé wines as found in the *appellation* Touraine, but grown in the region of Mesland. The extra natural degree of alcohol gives these wines an extra degree of character and style, as it does to the Touraine-Amboise. Mesland produces wines that are slightly higher in acidity than Amboise, but with as much if not more personality. The wines are generally made from single grape varieties: Chenin, Sauvignon, Cabernet Franc, Gamay, even Cot, and will mention this on the label. Each varietal is distinctive, the Chenin and the Cabernet producing the more typical Touraine style. A particularly good producer here is the Domaine Girault-Artois. Wines from the 250 hectares are 75% red, and are generally inexpensive. Price B.

Touraine Mousseux

All white and rosé wines that are in the Touraine *appellation* may be made sparkling by the *méthode champenoise*. The reds have to come from the *appellations* Bourgueil, Saint-Nicolas-de-Bourgueil and Chinon, of which none is nowadays sold as *mousseux*. In fact, this *appellation* has been largely replaced by the Crémant de Touraine, which sells under the *appellation* Touraine. It is very agreeable, but less good than a Vouvray. Price C.

Touraine Pétillant

The same rules apply as above, except that, as for Saumur Pétillant, the bottles may not be confused with those made and presented like champagne, which makes them impossible to sell on the export market. The wine is still made and drunk locally. Price C.

Bourgueil

Red and rosé wines principally from the Cabernet Franc (with the Cabernet Sauvignon tolerated to a maximum of 20%) covering 1,200 hectares on the right bank of the Loire between Tours and Saumur. The most important communes are Bourgueil, Restigné, Ingrandes and Benais, where the marked difference in the soil produces quite different styles of wine. The gravelly-alluvial soil on the plain (Restigné, Ingrandes) produces quick-maturing wines with much bouquet and finesse; the *coteaux* (Benais, Bourgueil), where the top-soil is gravel with a clay-limestone base (*le tuffeau*), produces deeper-coloured, meatier wines that need more time. A good Bourgueil (often a blend of the two styles) will have a lovely garnet-ruby colour, a bouquet reminiscent of raspberries, with a lively, sometimes rustic fruit and clean, dry finish. In poor years they tend to be rather thin, while in very sunny vintages (1976, 1985, 1989, 1990) they can have a huge colour and intensity of fruit that puts them in the category of fine wines, easily the equal of a Médoc. Red Bourgueil can be drunk (served cool) a year or two after the vintage, while the best wines last 10 years or more. The rosé has a delightfully pale, violet-pink colour and is the perfect summer wine.

The wines of Bourgueil have a reputation for honesty — 'the scandal in Bourgueil is that there IS no scandal', wrote Pierre-Marie Doutrélant in his book *Les bons vins et les autres* — and straightforwardness. While these wines are not widely seen outside France, the current interest in the Cabernet wines of the Touraine and Anjou, fuelled by a series of fine vintages in the late 1980s, and high prices elsewhere (but due in fact to inherent quality), has concentrated attention on the following growers: Domaine de la Coudray, Pierre-Jacques Druet, Caslot-Galbrun, Jean-François Démont, Gustave Goré, Marc Mureau, Domaine des Raguenières, Gérard Rouzier and Lamé-Delille-Boucard, who have kept back some old vintages. Production, from a maximum base yield of 40hl/ha before the PLC, is nearing six million bottles. Prices are still reasonable: C (D for older vintages).

Chinon

Red, rosé and white wines from an *appellation* covering 1,500 hectares on the left bank of the Loire and both banks of its tributary the Vienne, between Tours and Saumur. The tiny production of white wine is from the Chenin Blanc (Pineau de la Loire), with the typical floral bouquet and lively character of the grape. The reds (and rosés) are made from the Cabernet Franc, known locally as "le Breton", grown on three different types of soil: the sandy-gravelly soil along the banks of the Vienne produces light, fruity wines for early drinking; the more gravelly soil with some clay on the plateau produces a wine with more body and depth; while the heavier *tuffeau* lends a further element of intensity and flavour, particularly if the vines are planted *en coteaux*. These are the finest wines of the *appellation*, exemplified by the Clos de l'Echo of Couly-Dutheil and the Clos de la Dioterie of Charles Joguet. The best vineyards are at Chinon itself, Cravant-lès-Coteaux, Savigny-en-Véron and Sazilly. A good Chinon should have an entrancing ruby colour, a pronounced aroma of crushed flowers (violets) and an impression of soft fruit with a refreshing finish, where the *terroir* is matched by the elegant smoothness of the Cabernet Franc. The wines have great charm and can usually be drunk the year

after the vintage, while the better *cuvées* and better vintages can improve for 5–15 years. As at Bourgueil, with which it is often compared, the quality is as much if not more dependent on how the wine is made than where it is grown: it is the opinion of Charles Joguet, the most innovative winemaker in Chinon, that if the *appellation* had an image of "rusticity", it was more the result of poor winemaking than an inherent *goût de terroir*. Overall quality has seen a great improvement in the 1980s due in part to Professeur Jacques Puisais of Tours, whose influence has encouraged cleaner cellars, lower yields and longer vinification. Chinon has more polish and finesse than either Bourgueil, Saint-Nicolas-de-Bourgueil or Saumur-Champigny, and is beginning to achieve an international reputation. Excellent wines from: Gérard Chauveau, Domaine Dozon, Château de Ligré (with a superb white), Charles Joguet, Domaine de la Perrière, Jean-Maurice, Olga and Raymond Raffault, and the important grower-négociant Couly-Dutheil. Production is a little over 7 million bottles, less than 1% of which is white. Prices are reasonable, about the same as a good Beaujolais. Price C-D.

Coteaux du Loir

Red, dry white and rosé wines grown on the slopes of both banks of the river Loir, about 40 kilometres north of Tours in the Sarthe *département*. Although historically these vineyards were as well known as any in Touraine, they are virtually extinct today, with only 20 hectares under vines. The whites are made from the Pineau de la Loire (Chenin Blanc), and resemble the wines from Vouvray, but with a bit more acidity; the reds may be made from the Pineau d'Aunis, Gamay, Cabernet Franc and Cot, they have a good colour and are well made and fruity, if slightly rustic in character; rosés may be made with the same grapes plus up to 25% of Groslot. The whites age well, owing to the acidity, while the reds and rosés should be drunk young. All three styles of wine go very well with the local *rillettes*. Price B.

Crémant de Loire

See under Anjou, page 206.

Jasnières

White wine from the global *appellation* Coteaux du Loir, but which must come from the communes of L'Homme and Ruillé-sur-Loir. Made from the Pineau de la Loire, the minimum alcohol content is 10° and the yield is very small at 25hl/ha. The wine produced has great delicacy, finesse and character, and at its best Jasnières is the equal of the finest wines in Touraine. Although in poor years it is rather green and acidic, in very sunny years it acquires vanilla-honeyed aromas

Above: The newly opened leaves of a vineyard in late Spring. This one is in the appellation *of Chinon.*

Left: The Château de Chinon set above the river Vienne.

and a natural sweetness. Difficult climatic conditions combined with the low yield, impose a severe financial burden on the small number of *vignerons* who still make the very rare Jasnières, although three good and plentiful years – 1988, 1989 and 1990 – have improved matters. The best of these remarkable wines come from Joël Gigou and Domaine de Cézin (François Fresneau), both of whom also produce Coteaux du Loir. Price C-D.

Montlouis

White wines, either dry or sweet, from the left bank of the Loire, opposite the vineyards of Vouvray in the Indre-et-Loire *département*. The wine is made from the Chenin Blanc (Pineau de la Loire), and the soil, methods of cultivation and vinification are so similar to the wines made on the other bank that, until 1938, Montlouis was sold as Vouvray. Wines from this *appellation* may be dry, *demi-sec*, fully sweet or *liquoreux*, semi-sparkling and sparkling. The still wines are the most interesting, with the fresh, honeysuckle aromas of the Chenin Blanc, the great finesse of the *terroir* and the lemon-fruit finish. They may be drunk soon after the vintage, or kept for several years. Montlouis used to be

215

much underrated, not even popular enough to attract purchases by négociants except to be made into sparkling wine, but since the early 1980s it has seen an encouraging revitalization. 300 hectares are now planted from a maximum of 400 to produce an average of 1.5 million bottles. Recent vintages have seen some excellent Montlouis *moelleux* which will last for 20 years. Fine wines from Yves and François Chidaine, Domaine Delétang, Claude Levasseur, Jean Guestault and the Comtesse de Montenay. Not expensive for the quality: Price C-D (for sweet wines).

Montlouis Mousseux

Montlouis still wine (9.5° minimum alcohol, yield 45hl/ha), made sparkling by the *méthode champenoise*. Production is about five times that of the still wines, since *vins mousseux* are very popular in France, and sparkling Montlouis justifiably so. It is usually *brut*, but may be *sec*, *demi-sec* or *moelleux*. Price C.

Montlouis Pétillant

White semi-sparkling wines from Montlouis. As the *appellation* suggests, they are only slightly effervescent, and reflect more of the original quality of the still wine. Very little is made, yet it makes a superb apéritif. The wine of Guy Delétaing is a perfect example. Price C.

Rosé de Loire

See under Anjou, page 206.

Saint-Nicolas-de-Bourgeuil

Red and rosé wines from a separate *appellation* within the Bourgueil region, covering not quite 500 hectares planted with the Cabernet Franc. The two specific types of soil – sandy-gravel and limestone-clay – exist in Saint-Nicolas, but there is more sand and the wine is correspondingly lighter than at Bourgueil and is usually drunk younger. Well-made wines come from Audebert Père & Fils, Max Cognard-Taluau, Pierre Jamet, Jean-Paul Mabileau and Daniel Moreau. Permitted yield is inexplicably lower than at Bourgueil, at 35hl/ha, producing a total of 2 million bottles, including a little rosé. On the other hand, these wines may be sold under the *appellation* Bourgueil, while the reverse is not allowed. They sell for the same price. Price C.

Vouvray

Vouvray produces a complete range of white wine from the Chenin Blanc, planted on 1,750 hectares of vineyards on the right bank of the Loire to the east of Tours. Depending on the weather throughout the vintage and the decision of the vigneron, Vouvray may be dry (*sec*), off-dry (*demi-sec*), sweet (*moelleux*) and very sweet (*liquoreux*), as well as semi-sparkling and sparkling. The soil is of heavy limestone-clay, and the *tuffeau* of Touraine, with some chalk and a gravelly topsoil that is perfect for the Chenin Blanc. The minimum degree of alcohol is 11°, which gives a firm backbone to the flowery honeysuckle-scented wine, whose fruit is always balanced by a marked acidity. The maximum yield of 45hl/ha is generally exceeded for the less good *cuvées* that are normally destined for the sparkling wine, but the yield is very much lower, nearer 25hl/ha, for the sweet, late-harvest wines. In poor years (1972, 1977, 1984) the still wines have an unacceptable amount of acidity when young, and even when mature they never have the charm associated with wines from the Loire. In good or great years (1959, 1964, 1976, 1981, 1985, 1989) the dry wines will be perfectly balanced, with more style and length than even the best Sauvignons, and the late-picked bunches will produce wines with an intensely floral, fresh fruit aroma and honeyed richness of taste that can rival the finest Sauternes. While a dry Vouvray may be drunk young, but can improve over several years, the sweeter wines may last several decades, and domaines are now prepared to go to the trouble to produce these wines. Vouvray Pétillant, less sparkling than the Vouvray Mousseux and less easy to make successfully, is quite delightful. First-class wines, many with the names of the individual *clos* from which they are made, come from: Daniel Allias, Philippe Brisebarre, Didier Champalou, Philippe Foreau (Clos Naudin), Château Gaudrelle, Domaine Huët (Le Haut Lieu, Le Bourg, Le Mont, probably the greatest wines of the *appellation*), François Mabille, Prince Poniatowski (Clos Baudouin) and Domaine Villain. Wines from the *cave coopérative* are not, as yet, impressive. Prices vary from inexpensive to very expensive – for the great *vins moelleux* – but in the latter category these are among the finest wines of France. Production is currently 12 million bottles. Price C-D (G for older vintages).

Vouvray Mousseux

White wine from the Vouvray region with a minimum of 9.5° alcohol before the addition of the *liqueur de tirage*, made sparkling by the *méthode champenoise*. Depending on the dosage, sparkling Vouvray may be *brut*, *sec*, *demi-sec* and very rarely *moelleux*. If red grapes are planted in Vouvray, they carry the *appellation* Touraine, and some proprietors make a delightful sparkling Touraine rosé. Sparkling Vouvray is one of the best alternatives to champagne, but is mostly drunk on its own merits. Price C-D.

Vouvray Pétillant

White wine from vineyards in the Vouvray region, less sparkling than the Vouvray Mousseux. Since the flavour of the wine is of more importance than its bubbliness, Vouvray Pétillant is particularly agreeable, as none of the quality of the wine (or lack of it) is covered up by the sparkle, but merely enhanced by the slight effervescence. Very little Pétillant is made and most of it is drunk in the local restaurants. Price C.

VDQS WINES

Cheverny

Red, white and rosé wines produced on 200 hectares in the region of Cheverny, to the south of Blois, in the *département* of Loir-et-Cher. This is one of the relatively new (1973) VDQS *appellations*, whose wines are of generally high quality and very typically "Loire" in style. The whites are made from the Chenin Blanc, Sauvignon, Menu-Pineau (or Arbois), Chardonnay and Romorantin (very rare, rather unyieldingly acid in poor years, beautifully floral in good ones). They are very attractive, fresh, fruity wines to be drunk young. The grape is unsually specified on the label, the Chenin Blanc resembling a light Touraine and the very popular Sauvignon a minor Sancerre. The reds may be made from the Gamay, Cabernet Franc or Cabernet Sauvignon, Pinot Noir or Cot, and these grapes may be vinified as rosés, as may the Pineau d'Aunis and the Pinot Gris. Both reds and rosés are light in colour and body (minimum alcohol content 9°, as opposed to 9.5° for the whites, both from a yield of 50hl/ha) and are to be drunk young, especially the Cheverny-Gamay. A little sparkling wine is made by the *méthode champenoise*, mostly for local consumption. The *vignerons* in this *appellation* are serious, very proud of the VDQS status, and continue to produce wines to rival some regional *appellations*. The best growers are: Bernard and François Cazin, Domaine Gendrier (a superb Romorantin), Domaine de la Plante d'Or and Philippe Tessier. Production is nearly 2 million bottles. Still not expensive. Price B.

Coteaux du Vendômois

Red, white and rosé wines from vineyards planted over 60 hectares in the commune of Vendôme in the *département* of Loir-et-Cher. The white grape is the Chenin Blanc, with Chardonnay admitted up to 20%, Pineau d'Aunis and Gamay for the rosés, to which may be added Pinot Noir and Cabernet for the reds. White wine resembling Coteaux du Loir, represents only 10% of the total production. The reds have a pretty ruby colour and a soft fruit, and should be drunk young. They are attractive, minor wines, the most interesting of which are the very pale rosés from the Pineau d'Aunis (Domaine Claude Norguet). About 500,000 bottles are produced, mostly drunk locally. Inexpensive. Price low B.

Valençay

Dry white, red and rosé wines from the region of Valençay in the *département* of the Indre. The *encépagement* is not classically Touraine, with 60% minimum Menu-Pineau (Arbois), the rest from Sauvignon, Chardonnay, Pineau de la Loire (Chenin Blanc) and Romorantin. The style is clean and firm with good fruit, but perhaps less flowery than the other Touraine whites from the Pineau de la Loire. The reds are more than three-quarters made from Cabernet Sauvignon, Cabernet Franc, Cot, Gamay and Pineau d'Aunis. They are light in alcohol, 9° minimum, but have good fruit and local character. Eighty percent of the total production is red or rosé. These wines from only 20 or so hectares are delightful drunk on the spot, but taste a little thin away from home. Inexpensive. Price low B.

VINS DE PAYS

Vins de pays from Touraine include the Regional Vins de Pays du Jardin de la France and the Departmental Vins de Pays de l'Indre, de l'Indre-et-Loire, de Loir-et-Cher, and de la Sarthe. See page 222.

Above: Vineyards of Saint-Nicholas-de-Bourgeuil.

Wines of The Centre and The East

While the wines from these regions are as delightful and diverse as those from the more western parts of the Loire Valley, there are notable differences in style. For white wines, the Chenin Blanc (Pineau de la Loire) gives way to the Sauvignon, while for reds and rosés, the Cabernet disappears in favour of the Pinot Noir and the Gamay. To the north are the wines of Orléans, now much better known for its vinegar, and the light wines around Gien. Up river, but to the south, are the famous wines of Sancerre and Pouilly-Fumé, as well known as Vouvray and Muscadet, and the similar but lesser-known Quincy, Reuilly and Ménétou-Salon. Following the river and its tributaries, the Cher and the Allier, to their source, the style changes to the more simple wines of the Auvergne, which seem to have more in common with Burgundy or with Beaujolais than the Loire Valley.

Below: The soil of Vouvray is perfect for the Chenin Blanc.

AOC WINES

Pouilly-Fumé

Dry white wine made from the Sauvignon grape, covering 650 hectares of magnificently situated south-south-east-facing vineyards around the town of Pouilly-sur-Loire in the Nièvre *département*. Throughout the *appellation* the Chasselas may be planted, to produce a minor, fruity *vin de carafe* that must be sold as Pouilly-sur-Loire, but this represents less than 10% of the land under vines. A Blanc Fumé de Pouilly (the Sauvignon is known locally as *le Blanc Fumé*) must have over 11° of alcohol from a maximum yield of 45hl/ha, and while the degree is usually exceeded in good years, production is often curtailed by spring frosts. The soil has a chalky-clay base, with a limestone element in the two best-known *climats*, Les Loges and Les Berthiers. The wine should be pale yellow, sometimes with green

tints, with a fragrant red or whitecurranty aroma, slightly spicy, pleasantly lively, more subtle than a Sancerre, with a firm fruit flavour and elegant finish. An initial acidity or "leanness" softens after one year and, contrary to the other Sauvignon-based wines from the Loire Valley, good examples may improve for two or three years more. The most important person in the wine community is Patrick de Ladoucette, who commercializes over 60% of the production with two brands, Château de Nozet and Le Baron de L. The excellent Château de Tracy is the equal of these wines in quality if not in volume. Other good growers, making flowery but firm wines, are Bailly Père & Fils, Jean-Claude Chatelain, Didier Dagueneau, Jean-Claude Dagueneau, Paul Figeat, Jean-Claude Guyot, Landrat & Guyollot, Roger Pabiot, Michel Redde and Guy Saget. Production is over 4 million bottles. The price is reasonable for the quality, always a little more than a Sancerre. Price C-D.

Ménétou-Salon

White, red and rosé wines from 500 hectares of vines grown around the villages of Ménétou-Salon and Moroques in the Cher *département* north of Bourges. The whites, from the Sauvignon grape grown on the same chalky soils as at Sancerre, are in the same style, but with less pronounced character. However, they have the same highly aromatic redcurranty nose and crisp fruit finish. The reds and rosés, made from the Pinot Noir grape, are also very similar to their Sancerre counterparts. Production has been growing as the reputation of these wines has spread from Parisian restaurants to the export market. The local *coopérative*, Les Vignerons de Jacques Coeur, sells 120,000 bottles a year of acceptable wine, about 10% of the total production. Individual domaines are much more interesting, proud to rival Sancerre or Pouilly-Fumé: Domaine de Chatenoy, Georges Chavet, Domaine Henry Pellé (the leader of the *appellation*), and Jean Tellier. Reasonably priced, about 20% less than Sancerre. Price C.

Pouilly-Sur-Loire

Dry white wine made from the Chasselas grape in the same region as Pouilly-Fumé. The Chasselas, which is also grown in Alsace and the Savoie, makes a light wine, 9° minimum, from the same yield as the Blanc Fumé. It is a dry, fruity, light wine which is easy to drink, the perfect *vin de comptoir*. Production is only 300,000 bottles, and falling in favour of Pouilly-Fumé. There used to be a thriving sparkling wine industry in this region based on the Chasselas grape. None of the wine is exported, as it would lead to confusion with Pouilly-Fumé. Drink very young. Price low C.

Quincy

Dry white wines made exclusively from the Sauvignon in the communes of Quincy and Brinay in the Cher *département*. The wines of Quincy are very aromatic and of great finesse, and used to be sold under the *appellation* "Quincy Vin Noble". While its fruit is a little gooseberry-like and green in poor years, Quincy is usually softer, less assertive than Sancerre or Pouilly-Fumé, often more distinctive than the neighbouring Ménétou-Salon and Reuilly. Well-known producers are Domaine Mardon, Gérard Meunier-Lapha, Raymond Pipet and Jacques Rouzé. Can be kept, but should be drunk young for its charm. Minimum alcohol content 10.5°, yield 45hl/ha, production 450,000 bottles from not quite 100 hectares. Price C.

Reuilly

Dry white, red and rosé wines from the Sauvignon (whites), the Pinot Noir and Pinot Gris (reds and rosés) on 30 hectares of vineyards planted on the banks of the Arnon, a tributary of the river Cher. The whites are typically "Sauvignon du Centre de la Loire", fruity, aromatic and dry. They are comparable to Quincy in style, but more austere. The reds and rosés are lighter than the Sancerres, but have an interesting Pinot spiciness. Henri Beurdin, Robert Cordier, Charles Lafond and Didier Martin are the *vignerons* to look out for. Production is very small, averaging 150,000 bottles of white and 35,000 red and rosé, and the wines are drunk mostly in local restaurants, where they show at their best. Price C.

Sancerre

Red, white and rosé wines from 14 communes around the town of Sancerre in the Cher *département*, with 1,900 hectares under vines and a further 100 in course of plantation. The grapes permitted are Sauvignon for the whites and Pinot Noir for the reds and rosés, the latter two representing 20% of the production. The rosés have a lovely, pale, salmon-pink colour, a refreshing acidity (a little too marked in poor years) and, like most rosés, must be drunk young. The reds, particularly if the vines are south-facing, can have a good colour and pure Pinot Noir bouquet, a certain intensity of fruit with sometimes a slightly hard finish. In good years (1982, 1985, 1988, 1989) from good growers (Jean Vacheron, André Dezat), they can be very interesting. The most popular and the best wine in Sancerre is the white, a lively wine with a pale colour, a striking aroma of redcurrants and gooseberries, a certain grassiness or tart fruitiness that does not age elegantly, and a cheerful, fruity finish. Well made, they are exciting, satisfying and harmonious; poor examples, from over-production, over-chaptalization, over-sulphuring, are either thin and acidic or heavy and dull.

The most important influence in Sancerre is the *terroir*, which is of three different types and produces three distinctive styles of wine. At Bué, the largest wine commune, the soil is stony on a heavy clay *tuffeau* base, producing round, strikingly fruity wines, very stylish and quite fat. The best vineyards here are Le Clos de Chêne Marchand, Le Grand Chemarin and Le Clos du Roy. Around Chavignol and Verdigny, the steeper slopes have a thin, pebbly top-soil on a base of chalky-clay, producing elegant, firm wines, with more reserve and often more finesse that those at Bué. The steepest slopes above the village, Le Clos de Beaujeu, Les Monts Damnés and Les Comtesses, produce the finest wines. Around Ménétréol and Saint-Satur and on the easy slopes leading up to the hill-village of Sancerre, the soil is a mixture of clay and flint, producing slight austere, less obviously charming wines, with a fine steely finish. The first two types of soil represent 80% of the vineyard, and a Sancerre that is a blend of wines from two or three *terroirs* is the exception rather than the rule. Most wines are at their best in the two years following the vintage. As in neighbouring Burgundy, Sancerre is a region of small growers who have remained on their land throughout many generations, and the skill and dedication of the winemaker is as important as the *appellation*. The many fine producers include B. Bailly-Reverdy, Balland-Chapuis, Philippe de Benoist, Domaine Cherrier, Paul Cotat, Lucien Crochet, Domaine Jean Delaporte, Vincent Delaporte, Gitton Père & Fils, Henri Natter, Roger Neveu, Pierre Prieur & Fils, Lucien Picard, Jean Reverdy, Jean-Max Roger and Jean Vacheron. Production: 13 million bottles of white, 3 million of red and rosé. Becoming expensive. Price C-D.

VDQS WINES

Châteaumeillant

Red and rosé wines from the south of the Cher *département*. The wines are made from the Gamay, Pinot Noir and Pinot Gris, with the Gamay dominant. Vines were already planted in this area in the twelfth century, and were very popular until phylloxera destroyed the vineyards. Less than 100 hectares are planted now. The red is very agreeable, light and fruity, with a pretty deep-cherry colour. It should be drunk quite young. The rosés are fruity and dry; especially good is the *vin gris* style of rosé, with very little colour but great delicacy of taste. Total production 600,000 bottles, mostly from the very good Cave des Vins de Châteaumeillant. Price B.

Coteaux du Giennois

Red, dry white and rosé wines made from 100 hectares of grapes planted throughout the *départements* of Loiret and Nièvre, principally around Gien and Cosne-sur-Loire. These light, fruity, dry wines are made from the Sauvignon and Chenin Blanc for the whites and from the Gamay and Pinot Noir for the reds and rosés. They are light (9° minimum alcohol for reds and rosés, 10° for whites) and refreshing, and are perfect everyday table wines. Production is small, about 600,000 bottles, and mostly consumed locally. Domaine Balland-Chapuis and SCEA Hubert Veneau produce wines similar to Sancerre deserving recognition. Price B.

Côtes d'Auvergne

Red, dry white and rosé wines form the region of Clermont-Ferrand and Riom, in the *département* of Puy-de-Dôme. These are considered to be Loire wines, but they have little in common with the wines of Anjou and Touraine. The grape varieties for the red and rosé wines are the Gamay and a little Pinot Noir, which produce a wine of 9.5° minimum alcohol content from a basic yield of 45hl/ha. The style is similar to Beaujolais, sometimes with a little more depth, and an interesting *goût de terroir* of wild cherries. They should be drunk young and served cool. Although 2.5 million bottles are produced annually from around 500 hectares, much of this is drunk locally, as the wine goes so well with the world-renowned *charcuterie d'Auvergne*. The better communes in the *appellation* may add their name to that of Côtes d'Auvergne on the label, thus: Côtes d'Auvergne-Boudes, Côtes d'Auvergne-Chanturgue (historically the most famous), Côtes d'Auvergne-Corent, Côtes d'Auvergne-Madargues. White wine, from Chardonnay, is made in very small quantities. The reds and rosés are perfect country wines. Quality has been improving for some years and as a result, a demand has been made for full AOC status. Price B.

Côtes Roannaises

Red and rosé wines from 100 hectares in the *département* of the Loire in the region of Renaison and Roanne. Wines are made from the Gamay, with a minimum alcohol content of 9° from a basic yield of 40hl/ha. The style varies from a light, Beaujolais-type of wine from Maurice Lutz to a deeper-coloured, more sturdy and more rustic wine from "old-fashioned" growers such as Paul Lapandéry. A mid-way style, the equal of a Beaujolais-Villages, comes from Felix Vial. Production is around 600,000 bottles and very little is exported, since the wines are much sought after by the French themselves. Price B.

Côtes du Forez

Red and rosé wines grown on 180 hectares on the right bank of the upper stretches of the Loire, almost opposite Lyon. The only grape allowed is the Gamay, which makes light (9° minimum alcohol from a basic yield of 40hl/ha), fruity wines, sometimes a little acidic in poor years, but generally very pleasing, Beaujolais in style, to be drunk young. They are perfect with the local cuisine, where the wine's fruity acidity tempers the richness of the food, and are having a great success in Paris bistros. The Cave Coopérative des Vignerons Foréziens represents most of the 1 million bottles produced, and is very good. Price B.

Saint-Pourçain-Sur-Sioule

Red, dry white and rosé wines from 450 hectares of vines in the Allier *département*, south-west of Moulins. These wines are considered as Loire wines, although by their *encépagement* they have more in common with Burgundy. The white wines must be from the local grape Tressalier (known as the Sacy in the region of Chablis), Chardonnay, Sauvignon, Aligoté and not more than 10% Saint-Pierre-Doré. They are light (9.5° minimum alcohol), with a transparent yellow-green colour, a fragrant, floral aroma and a deliciously refreshing, slightly appley taste. The red and rosé wines are made from the Pinot Noir and Gamay, and their style depends on the proportion of Pinot Noir. The lighter, Gamay-based wines closely resemble Beaujolais, those with more Pinot Noir are closer to Burgundy, while both have an attractive *goût de terroir*. The *vignerons* in Saint-Pourçain are determined to regain for their wines their historic reputation, and the wines represent excellent early drinking. Domaine du Bellevue and Ray Père & Fils are very good. Les Vignerons du Saint-Pourçain are reliable. Price B.

Vins de l'Orléanais

Red, white and rosé (especially *gris*) wines produced from just over 100 hectares on both banks of the Loire in the region of Orléans. The white wines, under 10% of the production of 700,000 bottles, are made from the Pinot Blanc and the Auvergnat Blanc (Chardonnay). The reds and rosés are made from the Auvergnat Noir (Pinot Noir), Pinot Meunier and Cabernet Franc, known locally as the Moir Dur. The red has a soft fruit (that belies its northern situation), owing to a short vinification, and should be drunk the year after the vintage. The best-known wine is the rosé from the Pinot Meunier, usually sold under the label Gris Meunier d'Orléans, which is very aromatic with a natural fruitiness. Many of the vineyards are owned by farmers more concerned with other crops, and little leaves France, but growers are encouraged by the burgeoning interest in these wines, due partly to the quality of the Cave Coopérative de Mareau-aux-Prés, Jacky Legroux and Clos Saint-Fiacre. Price B.

VINS DE PAYS FROM THE LOIRE VALLEY

The Loire Valley, which would seem to be the obvious place to find a large number of local *vins de pays*, actually represents only 6% of the total production. Each *département* has its own *vin de pays*, but there are very few regional Vins de Pays de Zone. Perhaps one of the reasons is that the Loire Valley is one of the oldest vineyards in France, and its many local wines have become established earlier with their own *appellations*. As in the Rhône Valley, the *vins de pays* found in the Loire generally represent local grapes planted outside the accepted *appellation* or "foreign" grapes planted within an already defined region. Production of *vin de pays* varies from year to year between 50 and 60 million bottles, divided into 60% red, 30% white and 10% rosé. Of this, 85% is sold under the regional denomination, du Jardin de la France, 10% under the name of the *département* and only 5% under a more restricted zone. Most of them (about 65%) are from a single grape variety, the name of which is usually on the label. Price A.

Vins de Pays Régionaux

VIN DE PAYS DU JARDIN DE LA FRANCE
The Vin de Pays du Jardin de la France is the largest of the three regional *vins de pays*, with a combined production of over 50 million bottles. Red, dry white and rosé wines are produced from the following *départements*: Cher, Indre, Indre-et-Loire, Loir-et-Cher, Loire-Atlantique, Loiret, Maine-et-Loire, Deux-Sèvres, Vendée, Vienne and the Haute-Vienne. This includes all the Val de Loire, and excludes the Nièvre and the Sarthe, and the varietals permitted are all those recommended in the Loire, as well as the Pinot Noir, Aligoté and Chardonnay from Burgundy. The wines, in general, are as delightful as their name: light, crisp whites, fruity, light-coloured reds and pretty, refreshing rosés. The style is typically Loire, and the wines are often as good as some of the lesser-known VDQS wines. They should all be drunk young and even the red wines are better drunk cool, especially the Gamay.

Vins de Pays Départementaux

Thirteen *départements* across the Loire Valley have the right to their own *vin de pays*, the production in 1988 ranging from 4 million bottles in the Maine-et-Loire to under 9,000 in the Sarthe. However, the name du Jardin de la France has proved much more popular than the single *département* name, leading to a fall in production declared from several *départements*.

CHER
Red, dry white, *gris* and rosé wines made mostly from the Gamay and the Sauvignon, with a little Pinot Noir, Pinot Gris and Chardonnay. The Sauvignon whites resemble a "petit" Sancerre, and the Gamay reds the wines of Châteaumeillant or a very light Beaujolais. All these wines have a refreshing acidity. Production 300,000 bottles, 65% red, 25% white, 10% rosé.

DEUX-SEVRES
Red, dry white and rosé wines from the north of the *département*, most of the land being too rich to bear vines. They resemble the wine of Thouarsais, are mostly Gamay reds and Sauvignon or Grolleau (Groslot) whites, and are light, low in alcohol and easy to drink. Production 150,000 bottles, 60% red.

INDRE
Red, dry white, *gris* and rosé wines made from a large variety of Loire Valley grapes, including the Cabernet Sauvignon centred around Valençay. The rosés and light reds are the best, the whites tending to be a little tart. If the wine comes from a single grape varietal, it will say so on the label. The Gamay grape is most often used on its own. Production is under 150,000 bottles, most of the wines being declared as Jardin de la France.

INDRE-ET-LOIRE
Red, dry white and rosé wines from the heart of the Touraine vineyards, especially to the east of Tours around Amboise. The excellent Sauvignon and Gamay wines from this *département* were all *vin de pays* until the better vineyards got the Touraine *appellation*. Sauvignon still plays a big part in the 500,000 bottles sold, but Chenin Blanc and Chardonnay are also used. These are some of the best in the Loire Valley, the rosés are delightful, and the reds have colour and flavour.

LOIR-ET-CHER
Red, dry white, *gris* and rosé wines from the château country around Blois, Chambord and Cheverny. Big production of fruity but rather tart white wines from the Chenin Blanc and Sauvignon, light reds and rosés from the Gamay, Cot and Cabernet Franc. They resemble the wines of Cheverny and Coteaux du Vendômois, the two VDQS *appellations* in the *département*. Production 1.4 million bottles.

LOIRE-ATLANTIQUE
Red, dry white, *gris* and rosé wines, mostly from the Sèvre-et-Maine region, that have much in common with Marches de Bretagne et du Retz (below) and Coteaux d'Ancenis. Production 400,000 bottles.

LOIRET

Red, dry white and *gris* wines from the southern part of the *département* around Orléans and Gien. Gamay, Pinot Noir, Cabernet and Pinot Meunier are the grapes most used, with a little white made from the Sauvignon or the Chardonnay. The total production is limited, no more than 100,000 bottles, and the wines are very light and do not travel.

MAINE-ET-LOIRE

Red, dry white and rosé wines from the Anjou and Saumur country from the same grapes as the wines of Anjou (page 206) plus Gamay for the reds. The whites have a crisp, lemony flavour, and the reds and rosés are dry and fruity. Production is currently 4 million bottles, but this is falling in favour of the more popular alternative name, Vins du Pays du Jardin de la France, as is the case for most of these Départementaux. 85% red.

NIEVRE

Red and dry white wines. Production is small, 250,000 bottles, and mostly white, concentrated on La Charité-sur-Loire, fruity but with quite high acidity. Reds are made from the Gamay and Pinot Noir.

PUY DE DOME

Red, dry white and rosé wines from vines in the Côtes d'Auvergne region. Very small (100,000 bottles) production of mostly red and rosé wines from the Gamay and the Pinot Noir.

SARTHE

Tiny production (9,000 bottles) of very little white wine from the Chenin Blanc, and a few reds and rosés from the Gamay, Cot and Cabernet Franc. The Sarthe is one of the few *départements* in France where the vine seems to be dying out.

VENDEE

Small production (about 150,000 bottles) of wines similar to the local VDQS Fiefs Vendéens.

VIENNE

Red and dry white wines made from the same grape varieties as the Vins du Haut Poitou (page 210). Light and fruity wines. Very small production of around 30,000 bottles.

Vins de Pays de Zone

COTEAUX DU CHER ET DE L'ARNON

Red, dry white, *gris* and rosé wines from the *départements* of the Indre and the Cher. The better-known AOCs are Reuilly and Quincy. Reds and rosés are from the Gamay, with Pinot Noir and Pinot Gris; whites from the Sauvignon and Chardonnay, with Pinot Blanc up to 30%. These are delightful summer wines. Production 60–70,000 bottles.

MARCHES DE BRETAGNE

Red, dry white and rosé wines from the south of the Loire-Atlantique *département*, the west of the Maine-et-Loire and the southern tip of the Vendée. Whites, from the Muscadet, Folle Blanche, Sauvignon and Chenin, with a little Chardonnay; reds and rosés mostly from the Gamay and Cot. These are summer wines. Big production, around 1.5 million bottles, 70% red, hardly any white.

RETZ

Red, dry white and rosé wines from the south-west of the Loire-Atlantique *département* and part of the Vendée, a region named after the infamous Gilles de Retz ("Bluebeard"). A few whites, from the Folle Blanche, Chenin Blanc and Sauvignon, but mostly light, aromatic rosés made from the Gamay, Groslot and Cot, and some clean, pleasantly fruity reds. Production 1.5 million bottles.

URFE

Red, dry white and rosé wines from the north of the Loire *département* alongside the Côtes de Forez and Côtes Roannaises *appellations*. Reds and rosés from the Gamay and Pinot Noir; very few whites from the Chardonnay, Aligoté, Pinot Gris and Viognier. The reds are not unlike Beaujolais in style. Production 150,000 bottles and on the increase.

Champagne

The ancient province of Champagne produces wines of the same name from the most northerly vineyards in France. The vines are spread across 5 *départements* – the Marne, the Aube, the Seine-et-Marne, the Aisne and the Haute-Marne – with a possible 34,000 hectares accepted as suitable for vineyards by the INAO, of which almost 25,000 hectares are actually planted. Of the land under vines, 80% is in the Marne, 15% in the Aube and the rest extends over the other three *départements*. The Champagne vineyards can be divided into three regions of production: the centre of production, around the towns of Reims and Epernay, comprising the Montagne de Reims, the Vallée de la Marne and the Côte des Blancs; the vineyards of the Aube, 75 kilometres to the south-west; and the "marginal" vineyards on the edge of the Champagne region that are in the process of being replanted. While the last rwo regions possess no Grands Crus or Premier Crus, and do not, on their own, produce the finest bottles of champagne, their wines are found in some of the finest blends.

Only three grape varieties may be planted in Champagne: Pinot Noir, Pinot Meunier and Chardonnay. The Pinot Noir represents 28% of the vineyard area and is concentrated on the Montagne de Reims, where it ripens well on the easy south-south-east-facing slopes and gives wines of depth and finesse from the chalky-sandy soil. The Pinot Meunier, covering 12,000 hectares, 48% of the area under vines, is a more sturdy varietal that ripens later than the Pinot Noir and is particularly suited to the more fertile soils of the Vallée de la Marne and the Aube. Pinot Meunier is not admitted in the Grands and Premiers Crus vineyards, but its reliability and high yield make it the most planted grape in Champagne. The Chardonnay is at its best on the very chalky soil of the Côte des Blancs, where it is the only grape permitted. It flowers later than Pinot Noir and is therefore less exposed to the risk of spring frosts and has a higher yield. Its qualities of lightness and finesse are essential for balancing the richness and weight of the Pinot Noir, and are very desirable on their own as a Champagne Blanc de Blancs.

The Champagne vineyards are made up of flatlands and easy slopes at a height of 100–150 metres above sea-level. The soil is chalk base with a thin layer of top-soil. The chalkiness and poverty of this soil are responsible for the special quality and elegance found in the wines produced in Champagne by the Pinot Noir and Chardonnay grapes, which give a more intense wine in their native Burgundy. The climate is cool and, at an average of 10°C over the year, it is at the limit for the survival of the vine. Apart from providing at the same time excellent drainage and useful water retention, the chalk soil absorbs and reflects the sun's rays to give much needed extra light and warmth to the vine. The cool spring nights carry a high risk of frost, especially in the Vallée de la Marne, where for this reason the more resistant Pinot Meunier is planted. The most desirable exposition is full south (Bouzy), but there are some north-facing slopes on which the vines manage to ripen, and the slopes on the Côte des Blancs mostly face east.

Champagne

Premiers Crus

Grands Crus

R. Aisne

Montagne de Reims

Reims

Vallée de la Marne

Verzency

Verzy

R Vesle

A4

R Marne

Ay

Bouzy

Château Thierry

Epernay

Cramant

Châlons-sur-Marne

N3

Oger

Côtes des Blancs

Vertus

Sézanne

Vitry-le-François

N4

Côtes de Sézanne

N77

Brienne-le-Château

Troyes

R Seine

Vignoble de l'Aube

Bar-sur-Aube

N71

Bar-sur-Seine

Les Riceys

CHAMPAGNE
BOLLINGER
GRAND ANNÉE
1985

AOC WINES

Champagne

To have the right to the *appellation* Champagne, the wines must be made from the Pinot Noir, Pinot Meunier or Chardonnay grapes grown in the *départements* of the Marne, Aube, Aisne, Seine-et-Marne and Haute-Marne. The still wines must be made sparkling by the process of secondary fermentation in bottle, known as *méthode champenoise* (see page 228), and no stage of this process may be undertaken outside the Champagne region. Maximum yield is in terms of kilograms of grapes per hectare, and is limited to 13,000 kilograms and may in no case exceed one hectolitre per 150 kilograms of grapes, a maximum yield of 85hl/ha. Non-vintage wines must spend at least one year in bottle before *dégorgement*, and vintage wines (which must have a minimum of 11° natural alcohol and of which 100% of the *cuvée* must be from the stated vintage) has to remain in bottle three years. Finally, all corks must be marked with the word "Champagne" and the date of the vintage if there is one. With such strict controls, Champagne is the only *appellation* in France that may, and does, omit *appellation contrôlée* from its label. Production is very variable, with an average of 250 million bottles a year, of which 7% are Champagne Rosé. Price F-G-H-I.

Below: Immaculately kept vineyards on slopes above Vertus, showing the light, chalky Champagne soil.

Coteaux Champenois

Red, white or rosé wines from the same grapes as for champagne from the same vineyard area. This still wine used to be called "Vin Nature de la Champagne", which was a simple *vin de table*, and the current *appellation* only dates from 1974. Wines from the Grand Cru and Premier Cru villages are often used unblended, and in this case the name of the village will appear on the label; the best known include Bouzy, Ambonnay and Avize. The whites are flowery, clean and fresh, with an appley acidity that is sometimes too pronounced. The finest, as well as the only regularly successful wines, are from the Grands or Premiers Crus vineyards on the Côte des Blancs (Chardonnay de Laurent Perrier, Moët & Chandon's Château de Saran). The rosés are very rare, the best coming from the red grape villages on the Montagne de Reims and not usually seen outside France. The reds are the most famous, led by the soft, elegantly fruity Bouzy Rouge (Georges Vesselle, Jean Vesselle, Paul Bara), and wines from Ambonnay, Aÿ (Bollinger Le Côte aux Enfants), Mareuil (Philipponat) and Vertus. The whites should be drunk young, while the reds can age if kept in a cool cellar. Production varies with that of champagne, being insignificant in years of low volume and never more than 1% of the total crop. Price E-F-G.

Rosé Des Riceys

Non-sparkling rosé made from the Pinot Noir planted in the commune of Les Riceys in the Aube departement. The wine must have a minimum alcohol content of 10°, from a yield not exceeding that of champagne. Only the grapes from the slopes facing due south ripen sufficiently to make a good rosé, the rest being destined for champagne. Rosé des Riceys is a natural rosé that gains its colour from two to four days maceration, and the moment that the wine is drawn off the skins is the key to the special *goût des Riceys*: if the wine is too pale, too dark or has not the required character, it is declassified. The wine should be an onion-skin rosé, with a delicate bouquet but a firm, slightly nutty flavour. Average production totals only 7,500 bottles (Alexandre Bonnet, Horiot Père & Fils). Price E.

THE CRUS IN CHAMPAGNE

The *cru* system in Champagne differs from that in Burgundy or Bordeaux since, while it is geographical, it is also an index to the price of grapes from a particular vineyard. In 1919 a scale of quality was imposed on the different communes, beginning at 100% for the finest (Grands Crus) and descending to 50%. Today, Premiers Crus are indexed at 90–99%, Deuxièmes Crus at 80–89% with the least good grapes selling at 77%. The index refers to the price for one kilogram of grapes that is determined between the négociants and the growers before the vintage. Thus grapes from Grand Cru vineyards will sell for 100% of the declared price, those from a Premier Cru for 90–99% of this price, and so on. A Grand Cru vineyard may often mention "Grand Cru 100%" if the champagne or Côteaux Champenois is the produce of that single commune. Until 1985 there were only 12 Grands Crus: **Ambonnay, Avize** (white), **Aÿ, Bouzy, Cramant** (white), **Louvois, Mailly, Puisieulx, Sillery, Tours-sur-Marne, Verzenay** and **Vesle**; five well-known Premiers Crus – **Chouilly, Le Mesnil-sur-Oger, Oger, Oivy** and **Verzy** were awarded Grand Cru status in that year, leaving **Chigny-lès-Rosés, Cuis, Dizy, Ludes** and **Rilly-la-Montagne** as Premier Crus. The quality of a négociant's or grower's champagne will be closely related to the quality of grapes he uses. Virtually no Grandes Marques Champagnes have an average classification of under 90%, and many still average at over 95%.

THE METHODE CHAMPENOISE

The *méthode champenoise* is the process whereby still wine is made sparkling by undergoing a secondary fermentation in bottle. While this method is used in many other parts of France and throughout the world, the actual making of champagne is more elaborate and disciplined than elsewhere. The system begins in the vineyards, where the grapes are sorted, poor-quality grapes discarded and particular attention paid to keeping the grapes unbroken before pressing, to avoid pigment from the skins of the black grapes colouring the must. For the same reason, the grapes are pressed as quickly as possible in large, low, vertical presses unique to the region (although horizontal presses have now been introduced) in units of 4,000 kilograms. From this unit (known as a *marc*) a maximum of 2,666 litres of juice may be extracted, obtained by three separate pressings: the first, *la cuvée*, produces 2,050 litres, the second, *la taille*, 410 litres and the third, *la deuxième taille*, 206 litres. The more the grapes are pressed, the darker in colour and the more tannic is the must, and many of the champagne houses use only the *cuvée*, selling off the two tailles to houses whose standards are not so high. The impurities in the must are then allowed to settle (*débourbage*) before the alcoholic fermentation (now mostly carried out in stainless steel vats instead of in oak casks), and this is followed, in most houses, by the malolactic fermentation to lower the total acidity. At this point, the wine resembles most other still white wines, but this is changed by the making of the final blend (*assemblage*) and the *champagnisation* of this blend or *cuvée*.

The *assemblage*, along with the *terroir* of Champagne, is what sets champagne apart from other sparkling wines. The aim of the blender, whose skill is a major influence on the future of his particular house, is to create each year a champagne from the wines available to him from the current vintage, plus the reserve wines, that corresponds to the "house" style. Vintage champagnes must follow the house style (unless there is a decision to alter this), while reflecting the particular characteristics of the vintage. Once the blend is created, from as little as three or four and as many as 60 or 70 different wines, the wine is bottled (*le tirage*) with the addition of cane sugar dissolved in old wine and impregnated with selected yeasts (*liqueur de tirage*) and is taken to the cellars to undergo its second major fermentation *in the bottle*. This fermentation (*la prisse de mousse*) should take place as slowly as possible over many months to result in a constant presence of many extremely small bubbles once the wine is in the glass. A poor prisse de mousse will result in a reduced number of bigger bubbles that will quickly dissipate. The pressure of the gas or sparkle thus produced is normally between five and six atmospheres for a fully sparkling champagne, and only 3.6 for a Champagne Crémant.

The secondary fermentation takes place with the bottles lying horizontally and, apart from creating the sparkle, leaves a deposit consisting mostly of dead yeasts along the side of the bottles. The process of eliminating this deposit begins with placing the bottles in specially designed racks (*pupitres*) at an almost horizontal level, where they are turned daily (*le remuage*) over a period of weeks to arrive at an almost vertical position with the deposit shaken down to rest on the cap or cork. (Much progress has been made in automatic *remuage* in large *gyropalettes*, replacing the individual *remueur* and doing the job more quickly and cheaply.) At this stage the bottles are removed from the *pulpitres* or *gyropalettes* and placed nose-to-tail vertically (*mise sur pointe*) to mature slowly and await the operation known as *dégorgement*. For this, the bottles are taken from the cellar, still in their upside-down position, and placed in a conveyor machine that passes the neck of the bottle through a freezing (-18°C) liquid that captures the sediment or deposit in a tiny block of frozen wine. The *dégorgeur* then up-ends the bottle, removes the cap or cork, and allows the pressure of the gas to expel the pellet of ice, leaving the wine clear. The final operation (*le dosage*) follows immediately, where by the loss of champagne is compensated by an addition of still champagne with a little sugar-cane solution, known as *le liqueur de dosage*.

Depending on the percentage of liqueur the wine will be more or less sweet. Some champagnes, of only the finest provenance (otherwise they would taste too rough or acidic), receive no liqueur, just more of the same wine; they are bone dry and may be called Brut Zéro, Brut Intégral, Brut *non-dosé*, Brut 100%, although

the official designation is Extra Brut. In general, a champagne is considered brut if it has up to 1% liqueur added, extra-sec at 1–3%, sec at 3–5%, demi-sec at 5–8% and doux at 8–15%. The finer *cuvées* are always reserved for the Brut. Following *dégorgement* and *dosage* the bottle is corked with the classic champagne cork, wired down to prevent explosion, and may be either returned to the cellar for further maturing, for the *dosage* to "take", or labelled, capsuled (*habillage*) and cartoned up ready for sale. Throughout the whole process, it is vital that sufficient time is allowed for the various stages. The minimum period is one year, from bottling to sale: most responsible champagne houses extend this to three years, and five years or more for their vintage wines.

STYLES OF CHAMPAGNE

NON-VINTAGE
A blend across several vintages, although dominant in wines from the latest year, the reserve being added at the *"assemblage"*. Three-quarters of champagne production is non-vintage.

VINTAGE
Wine from only the best years (1979, 1982, 1983, 1985, 1986 in recent years) using up to 80% of the harvest, leaving the 20% for non-vintage wines. They are aged three years in bottle and are not normally released until 1–2 years later.

BLANCS DE BLANCS
Wine from only white grapes, Chardonnay in the case of champagne, to make a bottle of great elegance and finesse, but with potential for long ageing. The finest come from the Grands Crus of the Côte des Blancs: Cramant, Chouilly, Le Mesnil-sur-Oger.

BLANCS DE NOIRS
Wine from black grapes only. Pinot Noir and Pinot Meunier, producing a champagne fuller in colour and more "meaty" than a blend or a Blanc de Blancs. Very little is made, and only in the Grand Cru villages of the Montagne de Reims.

CHAMPAGNE ROSE
Champagne Rosé is the only wine in France in the making of which red and white wine (not grapes) may be blended. This will happen at the time of the *assemblage* (above), when a tiny quantity of still red wine (obligatorily from Champagne) will be added to the still white wine to achieve the colour, character and "weight" of rosé desired by the particular champagne house. Champagne Rosé may also be made from red grapes left overnight in the press, so that the must is

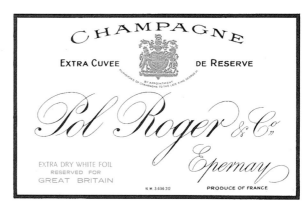

Left: Champagne bottles in racks, where they stand cork downwards at an angle of 45 degrees to enable the yeast to sink down towards the cork for later removal. Every day for up to three months each bottle is slightly shaken, slightly twisted and tipped slightly nearer the vertical by skilled "remuers".

lightly coloured, or by the *saignée* process, whereby the red grapes begin to ferment in vat and the wine is drawn off when the desired colour has been attained. These last two are true *rosés de noirs*. A shorter maceration period will result in the very rare *oeil de perdrix* champagnes, where the colour is mid-way between a blanc and a rosé. Champagne Rosé, very popular in the 1890s, regained its status as the celebration wine in the 1980s. The style varies according to the négociant or grower, being restrained and delicate from Krug and rounded and fleshy from Veuve Clicquot.

CREMANT

Champagne (or other sparkling wines) that contains only 3.6 atmospheres of pressure after the "prise de mousse". The impression is of an effervescence more "foamy" or "creamy" than a classic champagne. Elegance is key in a good Crémant, and the proportion of Chardonnay grapes is always high.

CUVEES DE PRESTIGE

The luxury blends from the major champagne houses. The best known is Moët et Chandon's Dom Pérignon. Other prestige *cuvées* are Cristal Roederer, Taittinger Comtes de Champagne, Pol Roger *Cuvée* Winston Churchill and anything from Krug.

THE CHAMPAGNE LABEL

The label will carry the name of the producer, or owner of the brand, the address where the champagne was produced and a registration number preceded by two letters which represent the status of the producer. The letters are: RM (Récoltant-Manipulant), a grower who can only vinify and sell the produce from his own grapes, although in some cases the vinification is carried out by his *coopérative*; NM (Négociant-Manipulant), a producer who makes the champagne, but has to buy in some or all of the grapes; CM (Coopératives de Manipulation), *caves coopératives* who vinify the grapes of their members and sell under many different labels; RC (Récoltant Coopérateur), a grower who sells grapes to a *coopérative* and receives champagne to sell under his own label; SR (Société de Récoltants), a group of growers who make their champagne together but sell it separately; and MA (Marque Auxiliaire or Marque Autorisée), the brand name belonging to a buyer who may purchase his champagne from RMs, NMs or CMs. Since almost all champagne is a blend of wine from different vineyards, it is very rare for the name of a single vineyard (Clos des Goisses from Philipponat, for example) to appear on a champagne label.

THE GRANDES MARQUES

The "Grandes Marques" houses, the oldest-established companies in Champagne, are the ambassadors for the region's wine throughout the entire world. They are generally the biggest and certainly the best known of the *Négociants-Manipulants* who, as a whole, own only 13% of the vines in Champagne, but commercialized (in 1981) 66% of the production. Eighty per cent of the wines are sold as non-vintage Brut, the balance being made up of vintage champagne, Champagne Rosé, *cuvées* Spéciales or de Luxe and a declining amount of Sec and Demi-sec. The non-vintage will follow as closely as possible the house style and it is the wine on which the reputation of the Grandes Marques is based. Vintage wines will certainly have more class and probably more body and may be kept for 10 to 12 years from the vintage date. The luxury *cuvées* are the best the house can do, both in terms of the wine's presentation and its quality, which in some cases is quite extraordinary, and well worth the high price. Listed below are the major Grandes Marques, with a comment on their house style and specialities.

Ayala (1 million bottles, Aÿ) possesses no vineyards of its own, but has contacts with many growers and sells a mature non-vintage from 2/5 black and 1/3 white grapes and a very fine Blanc de Blancs. **Bessert de Bellefon** (2.3 million bottles, Reims), best known for its light Crémant Blanc and the only Crémant Rosé made in Champagne. **Billecart-Salmon** (0.5 million bottles, Mareuil-sur-Aÿ) sells a delicately fruity non-vintage, a superb Blanc de Blancs, and an especially fine, pale rosé. **Bollinger** (1.5 million bottles, Aÿ), an immensely prestigious house, with its own vineyards covering 70% of its needs. Even in the non-vintage, the average classification of the *crus* is 98%, with the Pinot Noir dominant. The whole range is classic, slightly old-fashioned champagne that can age well. The luxury *cuvée*, the recently disgorged "Tradition", that has spent 6–10 years *sur pointes*, is even more robust and complex than the vintage. Bollinger also owns 0.41 hectares of un-grafted French vines, which produce a 100% Pinot Noir of a biscuity colour and unforgettable flavour. **Canard-Duchêne** (3.2 million bottles, Ludes) makes a pleasant, if soft, non-vintage and a well-presented luxury *cuvée*, Charles VII. **De Castellane** (3.3 million bottles, Epernay) has a fine 75% black grape non-vintage, an excellent vintage Blanc de Blancs and a luxury *cuvée* Commodore from only Grand Cru vineyards. **A. Charbaut & Fils** (1.2 million bottles, Epernay), with vineyards on the Montagne de Reims, produces a rare vintage Blanc de Blancs from Grand Cru vines. **Veuve Clicquot** (10.5 million bottles, Reims) possesses one of the three largest holdings of vines in the region, well balanced between the "noirs"

Bouzy, Ambonnay, Verzenay and the "blancs" Cramant and Avize: big, rich, recognizable champagnes, with a prestigious non-vintage, vintage Rosé and luxury *cuvée* La Grande Dame. **Deutz** (1 million bottles, Aÿ) produces well-aged Brut non-vintage wines with a high proportion of Pinot, an extraordinary vintage Blanc de Blancs from Avize and Le Mesnil and a very fine *cuvée* William Deutz with 60% Pinot Noir. **Gosset** (0.35 million bottles, Aÿ) is the oldest *maison de vin* (which celebrated its 400th anniversary in 1984) and has a good non-vintage, but makes a speciality of Rosé (in a clear bottle) and a very fine Grand Millesime luxury *cuvée*, where the elegance of the presentation is matched by the wine inside the bottle. **George Goulet** (0.35 million bottles, Reims) makes a fine, mature non-vintage and an excellent Crémant. **Heidsieck Monopole** (2 million bottles, Reims), produces a meaty, Pinot Noir-based non-vintage and vintage, mostly from its own vineyards, and a very fine Chardonnay-Pinot luxury *cuvée*, Diamant Bleu. **Charles Heidsieck** (4.2 million bottles, Reims) owns no vineyards, yet its full-bodied non-vintage is usually very good. **Henriot** (1.5 million bottles, Reims) has made a name for its very dry Blanc de Blancs and the Pinot Noir-based Réserve du Baron Philippe de Rothschild. It is now part of the Veuve Clicquot group. **Jacquesson et Fils** (0.4 million bottles, Dizy) high quality champagnes and an exceptional Blanc de Blancs. **Krug** (0.5 million bottles, Reims) represents champagne at its most luxurious and uncompromising: the non-vintage Grande *Cuvée* is 35% Chardonnay, 50% Pinot Noir and 15% Pinot Meunier, with an average classification of 97%, and is commercialized at six years as opposed to the normal three. The vintage is less opulent than it used to be, but very fine, and the very small quantity of Rosé, launched in September 1983, is a work of art. **Lanson** (5 million bottles, Reims), with 210 hectares of vines, bases its reputation on the fruity, lively non-vintage Black Label, the Blanc de Blancs-style vintage and the recently introduced luxury Nobel *Cuvée* de Lanson, a non-vintage 80% Chardonnay, 20% Pinot Noir (Lanson was sold in December 1990 to the Moët-Hennessey group and later sold to Ste-Marne et Champagne). **Laurent-Perrier** (7.5 million bottles, Tours-sur-Marne) relies on long-term contracts with 200 growers working 700 hectares of vines to provide the grapes for a well-made non-vintage, a *non-dosé* Ultra-Brut, the non-vintage but extraordinarily fine *cuvée* Grand Siècle and one of the best Côteaux Champenois Blanc de Blancs. **Abel Lepitre** (0.6 million bottles, Reims) specializes in Crémant Blanc de Blancs. **Ste-Marne et Champagne** (10 million bottles, Epernay), one of the newest houses, is now the second-largest producer of champagne. Most of the wine is sold under *sous-marques* such as A. Rothschild and Georges Martel, in early 1991 this company purchased Lanson from the Moët-Hennessy group. **Mercier** (5.5 million bottles, Epernay) sells a

non-vintage Brut Blanc de Noirs of average quality mostly on the French market. **Moët & Chandon** (25 million bottles, Epernay) is the largest champagne house and has remained one of the most prestigious. The Brut Impérial, 90% Blanc de Noirs, is sometimes sold a little young, but improves in bottle as do all good champagnes, while the finest Chardonnay and Pinot Noir grapes are reserved for the impeccable *cuvée* Dom Pérignon, always vintaged and sold 6–7 years after *tirage*. The *vin nature* Château de Saran from the company's vineyards at Cramant is one of the best Côteaux Champenois Blancs. **Mumm** (12 million bottles, Reims), one of the largest houses, is best known for the non-vintage Cordon Rouge with an average classification of 95% but rather heavily *dosé* at 1.5%, and the very fine half Chardonnay-half Pinot Noir *cuvée* René Lalou. The small production of Crémant de Cramant (non-vintage) is quite exceptional. **Joseph Perrier** (0.65 million bottles, Châlons-sur-Marne) produces an elegant, fairly light non-vintage (despite it being 66% Pinot Noir and Pinot Meunier), a very reliable vintage and a very good Côteaux Champenois rouge from their own vineyards at Cumières. **Perrier-Jouët** (3.1 million bottles, Epernay) makes very good, meaty non-vintage from grapes with an average classification of 95%, a fine vintage and two excellent luxury *cuvées*, Blason de France, with Pinot Noir dominant, and Belle Epoque (also Belle Epoque rosé) where Chardonnay from Avize and Cramant is blended with Pinot Noir from the Montagne de Reims. **Philipponat** (0.5 million bottles, Mareuil-sur-Aÿ), one of the smaller houses, now linked with Gosset, makes some correct non-vintage, an interesting Mareuil rouge Côteaux Champenois and a quite exceptional vintage Le Clos des Goisses, from their own 98% vineyard at Mareuil-sur-Aÿ. **Piper-Heidsieck** (5 million bottles, Reims) commercializes a lively non-vintage that is sold relatively young and rather over-*dosé*, and the excellent luxury *cuvée* Florens-Louis (60% Chardonnay) in which the 12 *crus* that make up the *assemblage* are nearly identical to those in a *cuvée* elaborated for Marie-Antoinette. **Pol Roger** (1.5 million bottles, Epernay) is one of the finest houses in Champagne, making classic, elegant non-vintage, perfect vintage wines and a Rosé (Pinot Noir 100%), a Chardonnay (100%) and Réserve Spéciale PR (half Chardonnay 100%, half Pinot Noir 100%) of exceptional quality. **Pommery & Greno** – since 1990 part of the Moët-Hennessey group – (4 million bottles, Reims) possesses one of the largest vineyard holdings of the region concentrated on the Montagne de Reims, producing wines of great class, 66% Noir, 33% Blanc, elegant and dry from a light *dosage*. The vintage is from vineyards classified 100%, and the non-vintage *Cuvée* de Prestige de Pommery was released in 1985. **Louis Roederer** (2.7 million bottles, Reims) produces big, creamy champagnes of great class, an excellent vintage

Left: Pinot Noir grapes for Champagne.
Above: The Bollinger headquarters in Aÿ.

Blanc de Blancs and is especially known for the original *cuvée prestige* Cristal Roederer, a rich, long-lived wine, and the very pale Cristal Rosé. **Ruinart** (1.5 million bottles, Reims), the first house to sell champagne as opposed to still wine, produces a good non-vintage and a superlative pure Chardonnay *cuvée de luxe* Dom Ruinart, which is also available as a Rosé by the addition of some Pinot Noir. **Salon** (60,000 bottles, Le Mesnil-sur-Oger) only makes a vintage Blanc de Blancs from the 99% *cru* Le Mesnil-sur-Oger, a wine of great breed. **Taittinger** (4.5 million bottles, Reims), a very prestigious house, makes a lively, dry non-vintage, a well-balanced vintage and an exceptionally fine Blanc de Blancs Comte de Champagne. **De Venoge** (1.5 million bottles, Epernay) commercializes some good Blanc de Blancs.

THE GROWERS

The Récoltant-Manipulant and the *caves coopératives* possess 87% of the vines in Champagne and commercialize 36% of the production. While the 1970s saw a rise in the number of growers making and selling champagne under their own label, this seems to have stabilized in the 1980s, partly due to the high price for the grapes offered by the négociants. The best growers' wines come from the Grand Cru and Premier Cru vineyards, and although it is in the nature of champagne to be a wine blended from different *crus*, the Récoltant-Manipulant champagnes have the interest to be almost without exception *mono-crus*, the product of one single *cru*. Some notable wines are made at **Bouzy** by Paul Bara, Alain Vesselle, George Vesselle, Jean Vesselle, Brice-Barancourt; at **Avize** by Michel Gonnet, Jacques Selosse; at **Chigny-les-Rosés** by Albert Lassalle, Cattier; at **Chouilly** by Legras, Vazart-Cocquart; at **Cramant** by Bonnaire, Guiborat, Pertuis, at **Cuis** by Pierre Gimonnet; at **Cumières** by Leclerc-Briant; at **Louvois** by Yves Beautrait.

CHAMPAGNE BOTTLES

Champagne comes in many sizes, but only the half-bottle, bottle and magnum are always sold in the bottle in which they were *champagnise*. Jeroboams sometimes are, but it is more normal that this size, the even larger sizes and the quarter-bottles will be decanted under pressure from ordinary bottles. The different sizes with volume are listed here:

Quarter	18.7 cl
Half	37.5 cl
Bottle	75 cl
Magnum	2 btts
Jeroboam	4 btts
Rehoboam	6 btts
Methuselah	8 btts
Salmanazar	12 btts
Balthazar	16 btts
Nebuchadnezzar	20 btts

Grape Varieties

The grape variety and the *terroir* (soil, sub-soil, microclimate) are the two vital elements that make up the profile, style or character of a wine. The human factor, which covers viticulture, vinification, *élevage* and bottling, is to a large extent controlled by these two basic elements. The weather will determine the overall quality of each year, the grapes producing more or less concentrated juice, depending on ripeness and yields, whose character will be enhanced or diminished according to the vintage, but not substantially altered by it. In France, the interaction between grape variety and soil has been ratified in the Appellation Contrôlée system to set down ground rules for the production of some of the finest wines in the world. For example, only Pinot Noir and Chardonnay may make burgundy, these two grapes plus Pinot Meunier are the only grapes allowed in Champagne, Sancerre must come from the Sauvignon, Hermitage from the Syrah, and so on. In Bordeaux, the South-West of France and the southern Rhône Valley, more than one varietal may be used, in proportions consistent with the style of the *appellation* or responsible for a wine's difference within its *appellation*. At the same time, varietals with distinctive character and quality (known as *cépages nobles*) have been replanted in "foreign" soils in France and throughout the world, to produce wines of intrinsic quality and recognizable style. It has been said that the character of a wine comes from the grape, its soul from the *terroir*.

Even where *appellations* use just a single varietal, the name of the grape rarely appears on the label, for the grape is "given" in the name of the wine. As the *appellation* diminishes in importance from the communal to the generic, grape varieties are used, as in Bourgogne-Pinot Noir or Touraine-Sauvignon, this is to emphasize its importance relative to the much broader place name. Increasingly, *vins de pays*, which often have even less regional definition, will stress the grape variety on their wine labels.

MAJOR RED GRAPES

Cabernet Franc

The more fragrant of the two Cabernets, making wine with a fine, deep carmine colour, a delightful aroma of raspberries or violets and a firm, sometimes earthy, but not hard fruit finish. It is at its best in Touraine, Anjou, the Pomerol and Saint-Emilion regions of Bordeaux where it is called the "Bouchet", and northern Italy. The Cabernet Franc is a minor, but important, element in the Médoc and the Graves. It also makes a fine rosé.

Cabernet Sauvignon

The principal grape of the Médoc, a late-ripening varietal with small, very dark berries producing a wine of intense colour, striking blackcurrant, bell-pepper aroma, hard, even austere, tannin-backed flavour with great depth and ageing potential. The Cabernet Sauvignon is planted throughout the Bordeaux region and the South-West, and has spread up to the Loire Valley and across to the Midi. In France it needs a relatively warm climate, is often blended with Cabernet Franc and Merlot to offset its firmness, and benefits greatly from being allowed to age in wood and then in bottle. It is synonymous with high-quality red wine in Italy, Spain, Bulgaria, South Africa, Australia and North and South America.

Gamay

The single grape of the Beaujolais, where it is perfectly suited to the granite-based .soil, the Gamay gives a deep violet-red colour, flavour bursting with fruit and is generally low in tannin.

It prefers a cool to a warm climate, and flourishes throughout the Loire Valley, in the Savoie and in parts of the South-West. Although generally drunk young, wines from the best *crus* in the Beaujolais will improve for several years.

Grenache

Less fine than the Syrah, with a tendency to overripeness leading to high alcohol and low acidity, the Grenache flourishes in the warm climates of the southern Rhône, Provence and the Midi, Spain and California. It produces a full-bodied, fruity, "warm" wine, and also makes a fine fleshy rosé and the best red *vins doux naturels*.

Merlot

A dark-coloured grape, ripening relatively early, but which is very prone to rot in humid vintages, the Merlot is planted in Bordeaux (where it is the perfect foil for the Cabernet Sauvignon in the Médoc, and dominant in Saint-Emilion and Pomerol) and the South-West of France, northern Italy and with great success in California. The wine is rich in colour, with a plummy smoothness, needing less ageing than the Cabernets, but on the right soil can produce equally impressive wine.

Mourvèdre

A late-ripening varietal making dark-coloured, firmly structured wines with a welcome acidity. It is the principal grape of Bandol and a necessity in Châteauneuf-du-Pape to add stature and ageing potential to the "fat" wines of the Grenache. It is irregular in ripening and needs careful vinifying, but is a much underrated grape, now achieving world-wide recognition.

Pinot Noir

The traditional grape of Burgundy and Champagne, also planted in Alsace and the Jura, Pinot Noir is a fragile grape that prefers a cool climate. The wine has a medium-deep colour, a rich strawberry-cherry-blackcurrant aroma with sweet, fleshy fruit and a firm but not overly tannic finish. Except in Champagne, where it is pressed and the juice blended with that of Chardonnay and Pinot Meunier, it loses its character if blended with other grapes. The richly delicate flavour of the Pinot Noir shows well in the cooler regions of northern California.

Syrah

A very dark-coloured grape suited to warm climates and making rich, powerful wine with a blackcurrant, spicy aroma and concentrated fruit flavour. It is at its best in the northern Rhône, adds backbone and style in the southern Rhône and is very successful in South Africa and Australia. If the yield is kept low (Hermitage, Côte-Rôtie), the wine is very intense and long-lived.

Tannat

The principal grape in Madiran, and now playing an increasing role throughout the South-West, the Tannat produces dark-coloured wines with a dense fruit and sturdy backbone. Ageing in wood and in bottle is necessary for them to soften out.

SECONDARY RED GRAPES

ALICANTE BOUSCHET
A "teinturier" grape still planted in the Midi and Corsica, but being progressively replaced.

ARAMON
Also known as the Ugni Noir, used as a blender grape in the Midi, but its importance is falling fast.

CARIGNAN
This is the most planted grape in the Midi, producing dark-coloured, intense wines which have a certain bitterness and lack of finesse if not vinified properly.

CESAR
An historic varietal that is still planted in the Yonne, principally in Irancy, to make firm, interestingly old-fashioned red burgundy.

CINSAUT (CINSAULT)
A widely planted variety in the southern Rhône, Provence and the Midi. Lightish in colour, with good fruit and acidity, wines from the Cinsaut are an important foil to the Grenache for red wines, and essential for rosés, notably Tavel.

Above: Merlot

COUNOISE
A Mediterranean varietal, very useful in Châteauneuf-du-Pape and wines from the Midi, adding firmness and fruit.

COT OR MALBEC
Also known as the Auxerrois in Cahors, where it is dominant, and Pressac in Saint-Emilion. Generally used with other grapes for its colour and body, except in the Loire. It produces wines with a firm, vibrant fruit, with more character than charm.

FER OR FER-SERVADOU
Important indigenous grape in the South-West, making deep-coloured, slightly rustic wines with a firm backbone. Blends well with the Cabernet Franc and the Tannat.

GAMAY TEINTURIERS
The Gamay "Beaujolais" has a colourless pulp, as do all red grapes for making fine wine. The juice of the Gamay Teinturiers is red, hence the name, and is used for adding colour to *vins ordinaires* and a few *vins de pays*.

GROSLOT OR GROLLEAU
Red grape mostly planted in the Loire, where it is used principally for Anjou and Touraine rosés.

MONDEUSE
Traditional grape of Savoie and the Bugey, giving ruby-coloured wines, with good body and flavour, and superior to those from other local red grapes.

NIELLUCIO
Grape variety indigenous to Corsica, responsible for the fine wines of Patrimonio.

PETIT VERDOT
One of the blender grapes used in Bordeaux, hardly seen now except in the Médoc. Ripens fully only in good years, giving the wine colour and tannin.

PINEAU D'AUNIS
Grape planted in Touraine and Anjou, used as a blender grape for red wine, but more often and more successfully on its own for Loire rosés.

PINOT MEUNIER OR GRIS MEUNIER
Grape of the Pinot family making light red wines in the Orléanais (Vin Gris d'Orléans) and one of

Above: Delas Freres' Syrah vines on the hill of Hermitage.

the three grapes permitted in the making of champagne, where it shows an immediately appealing style.

POULSARD
Varietal specific to the Jura, where it gives a light-coloured wine, more rosé than red.

SCIACARELLO
Corsican varietal making fine, deep-coloured wines with body and fruit. Particularly successful in the southern part of the island.

TROUSSEAU
Varietal from the Jura, making a deep-coloured, long-lasting wine, a complement to the Poulsard and Pinot Noir.

MAJOR WHITE GRAPES

Chardonnay

The grape of white burgundy and champagne, Chardonnay prefers a lightish soil and coolish climate, but adapts remarkably well to different *terroirs*. The colour ranges from almost colourless yellow to a full gold, often with green tints, the aroma is elusive, with appley, buttery or nutty overtones, and the flavour is high in fruit, sometimes lean and sometimes rich, with good acidity. Complexity is added by the *terroir*, barrel fermenting and ageing and a year or two in bottle. Planted with great success in the Loire Valley, the Jura, the Midi and in all fine-wine producing countries, it epitomizes fine, dry white wine.

Chenin Blanc

This underrated varietal produces the finest wines, ranging from a lemony dryness to a luscious richness in the Loire Valley, where it is known as Pineau de la Loire. Here it ripens evenly in good vintages, often becoming botrytised, yet never losing its balancing acidity which guarantees the wines a long life. It is not planted elsewhere in France, but produces excellent wines, both dry and sweet, in South Africa, New Zealand and California. The high natural level of acidity permits the wines to age beautifully.

Gewurztraminer

One of the most important varieties in Alsace, producing richly flavoured, spicily aromatic wines, which can be vinified bone dry or, in good years, attain exceptionally high levels of sugar. It is hardly seen in France outside Alsace, then usually on an experimental basis. See page 29.

Muscat à Petits Grains

This versatile, highly aromatic variety is found principally in Alsace (see page 29), where, apart from some exceptional *vendanges tardives* and SGN wines, it is vinified dry, and in the southern Rhône and the Midi, where it is responsible for the finest white *vins doux naturels*.

Pinot Gris

Best known in Alsace (see page 32), where for decades it was known only under the name of Tokay, the Pinot Gris produces broad flavoured wines with firm fruit and a suave complexity. Under the name of Pinot Beurot it is seen in the Côte d'Or, and under Malvoisie in the Midi, where it is mostly used for fortified wines.

Riesling

One of the finest and most complex of the white wine grapes, with the range of the Chenin Blanc and the complexity of Chardonnay, Riesling has a distinctive fruit, purity of style and lemony acidity (even at its sweetest) that transcends differences in region and climate. This and the other *cépages nobles* from Alsace are described on pages 29–32. Riesling is perhaps more closely allied to Germany than France, and is very successful in all the wine-growing countries of the New World.

Sauvignon

An extremely versatile grape that ripens early but can attain *pourriture noble* in the right conditions. Sauvignon is at its most marked in the Loire Valley, where its aggressively fruity blackcurrant/gooseberry aroma and crisp acidic finish are typified by Sancerre and Pouilly-Fumé. In Bordeaux it is a minor grape in the *encépagement* for sweet wines, and was temporarily the dominant grape in the dry wines of Graves in the South-West. It is also planted in northern Burgundy, the Midi and with great success in the New World, where it is made in dry, sweet and late-harvest styles.

Sémillon

The principal grape of the great sweet wines of Bordeaux due to its ability to attain *pourriture noble*, and important in many white Graves and wines of the South-West. Its mellow softness made it, for a time, less fashionable than the crisper Sauvignon, but winemakers have now returned to it for its smooth depth of flavour.

SECONDARY WHITE GRAPES

ALIGOTE
Traditional Burgundy grape planted from Chablis to the Mâconnais, making light, dry wine, quite high in acidity. At its best at Bouzeron in the Saône-et-Loire, where it produces a lively rival to the Chardonnay.

ALTESSE
Grape variety planted in Savoie and the Bugey, making firm, dry and very aromatic white wines of high quality.

ARBOIS OR MENU PINEAU
A member of the Pineau family, cousin of the Pinots (Chardonnay) grown in the upper Loire, producing refreshing but rather tart wines.

AUXERROIS
A member of the Pinot family, known in Alsace as Klevner, producing firm, aromatic wines with more grip but less aroma than the Pinot Blanc.

BOURBOULENC
Southern grape variety seen in the Côtes du Rhône Méridionales, throughout the Midi and in the Minervois, where it is called Malvoisie, producing fine aromatic wines that capture the fruit and should be drunk young.

CHASSELAS
Better known as a table grape, the Chasselas produces pleasant, fruity wines for early drinking in Alsace, the Savoie and at Pouilly-sur-Loire.

CLAIRETTE
Traditional grape variety from the Midi and the Côtes du Rhône, producing a heady, aromatic wine that should be drunk young. Very good as a base for aromatic sparkling wines.

COLOMBARD
Planted in the South-West, the Colombard makes a straightforward, fruity white wine, as well as being one of the principal grapes used to produce armagnac. Must be drunk young.

FOLLE BLANCHE
Grape used principally for distillation into cognac and armagnac, but capable of producing a pleasant white wine on its own, especially in the Loire-Atlantique, where it is known as the Gros Plant du Pays Nantais.

GRENACHE BLANC
Planted almost exclusively in the southern Rhône, Provence and the Midi, to make an attractive fruity white wine, best blended with crisper varietals.

JACQUERE
One of the basic varietals for the *vins de Savoie*, light, slightly smokey bouquet, with a crisp fruit and pleasant acidity.

MACCABEO OR MACCABEU
Widely planted in the Languedoc-Roussillon, where it makes a full-bodied, aromatic, quite attractive white wine.

MARSANNE
Now the major white grape variety in the northern Côtes du Rhône, also planted in the south. Producing fine, scented, full-bodied wines; at its best in Hermitage.

MAUZAC
Traditional grape variety of the South-West, around Gaillac and Limoux. Light and fresh, with an aromatic appley flavour, it is very good *champenisé* and makes a charmingly fruity *vin moelleux*.

MELON DE BOURGOGNE
The single grape for Muscadet, and now synonymous with this *appellation*.

MUSCADELLE
One of the three grapes used to make the great sweet wines of Bordeaux and the South-West (with Sémillon and Sauvignon), normally used in small proportions owing to the very heady musky bouquet and rich sweet flavour.

PINOT BLANC
A grape of the Pinot family, still planted in Burgundy although it is inferior to the alternative, Chardonnay (with which it has no connection). At its best in Alsace, where it produces aromatic, firm-flavoured wines that may be drunk young or kept.

Above: The Chenin Blanc grape which produces a range of fine wines.

Left: Sémillon

ROLLE
A fine, aromatic grape from Provence, where it is still planted, despite its fragility, for its elegance. Also known as the Vermentino.

ROMORANTIN
Hardly seen outside the centre of the Loire Valley, this grape is often unforgivingly acidic, but shows fine individual flavours in warm years.

ROUSSANNE
Traditional grape from the northern Côtes du Rhône with more aroma and finesse than the Marsanne, with which it is being replaced.

SAVAGNIN
Grape variety planted exclusively in the Jura, where it makes very particular, full-bodied wines, with a distinctive sherry-like bouquet.

SYLVANER
Planted principally in Alsace (see page 32) where it makes dry, attractively fruity wine with more character than it is given credit for.

UGNI BLANC
Widely planted in the south, producing large quantities of straightforward wine, with an attractive flavour and acidity if the grapes are picked early. Also known as the Saint-Emilion in Charente, where it is distilled into cognac.

VERMENTINO
Grape originally from Provence, but now mostly seen in Corsica under the name of Malvoisie de Corse, producing full-bodied, aromatic wines.

VIOGNIER
A rare and very fragile varietal originally only planted in the northern Rhône Valley, making the intensely aromatic, richly flavoured wines of Condrieu and Château Grillet. Some experimental plantings have been made in the southern Rhône, Provence and the Midi, with great success.

Regional Food and Wine

The chart below gives the major gastronomic regions of France, which happily correspond to the wine regions (omitting, necessarily, the Ile de France, Brittany and Normandy, where no wine is produced) and attempts to match a few local dishes with the major wines of the region, adding suggestions from other parts of France. It does not cite any *vins de pays*, since these go perfectly with the local cuisine.

	Dish	Local Wines	Other Wines
Alsace	Aperitif: Muscat d'Alsace		
	Foie gras d'oie en brioche (*Goose foie gras in brioche*)	Tokay	Sauternes; Jurançon
	Grenouilles au Riesling (*Sautéed frogs' legs*)	Riesling	Graves blanc
	Tarte aux oignons (*Onion tart*)	Sylvaner, Pinot Blanc	Mâcon blanc
	Truite au bleu (*Trout poached in court-bouillon*)	Pinot Blanc; Riesling	Puligny-Montrachet
	Carpe farcie à l'alsacienne (*Stuffed carp*)	Gewürztraminer; Tokay	Chassagne-Montrachet blanc
	Sandre aux pommes (*Perch with apples*)	Pinot blanc; Riesling	Pouilly-Fuissé
	Choucroute garnie (*Sauerkraut with smoked pork and sausages*)	Pinot blanc; Riesling	Crémant d'Alsace
	Rôti de cochon de lait (*Roast sucking pig*)	Riesling; Tokay	Hermitage blanc; Saint-Julien
	Cuissot de chevreuil aux poires (*Roast roe-deer with pears*)	Riesling; Pinot Noir	Crozes-Hermitage rouge
	Munster	Gewürztraminer	Juliénas
	Kugelhopf	Tokay; Gewürztraminer Vendange Tardive	Champagne demi-sec
	Digestif: Marc de Gewürztraminer; Eau-de-vie Blanche		
Jura and Savoie	Aperitif: L'Etoile Mousseux; Crépy		
	Salade d'écrevisses (*Crayfish salad*)	Côtes du Jura blanc; Seyssel	Pouilly-Fumé
	Croustade jurassienne (*Cheese puff pastry turnovers*)	Arbois blanc; Apremont	Chablis; Rully blanc
	Pâté chaud au ris de veau (*Hot pâté with veal sweetbreads*)	Arbois blanc or rosé; L'Etoile	Meursault
	Mousselines d'écrevisses (*Crayfish mousselines*)	Arbois blanc; Chignin	Champagne Crémant
	Omble chevalier braisé (*Braised char*)	Marestal; Roussette de Savoie	Bâtard Montrachet
	Coq au vin jaune (*Cockerel cooked with yellow wine*)	Arbois blanc; Côtes du Jura blanc	
	Perdreau aux fidés (*Partridge with noodles, bacon and cheese*)	Côtes du Jura rouge or rosé; Mondeuse	Madiran
	Escalope de veau belle comtoise (*Veal escalope with ham and cheese*)	Arbois rouge or rosé; Mondeuse	Saint-Emilion
	Comté	Côtes du Jura blanc or rouge	Médoc
	Vacherin	Arbois blanc; Vin de Savoie blanc	Pinot Noir d'Alsace
	Morbier	Arbois blanc; Chautagne Gamay	Côte-de-Brouilly
	Gâteau grenoblois (*Walnut cake*)	Vin de paille	Tokay Vendange Tardive
	Digestif: Vin de paille; Marc de Château d'Arlay		
Rhône Valley	Aperitif: Saint-Péray Mousseux		
	Tomates provençales (*Grilled tomatoes with olive oil and garlic*)	Lirac blanc	Graves blanc
	Saucisson lyonnaise aux pistaches et aux truffes (*Pork sausage with pistachio nuts and truffles*)	Crozes-Hermitage blanc or rouge	Fleurie
	Melon rafraîchi (*Chilled Cavaillon melon*)	Condrieu; Rasteau Rancio	Banyuls
	Chausson aux truffes (*Drôme truffle enclosed in puff pastry*)	Château Grillet; Hermitage blanc	Bâtard-Montrachet
	Pavé de poisson (*Cold terrine of fish and shellfish*)	Saint-Joseph blanc; Hermitage blanc	Graves blanc, Chablis
	Encornets farcis (*Squid stuffed with tomato and rice*)	Tavel rosé; Lirac rosé	Provence rosé
	Perdreau aux choux verts (*Partridge casserole with cabbage*)	Côte-Rôtie; Cornas	Aloxe-Corton
	Sauté de lapin aux herbes (*Rabbit sauté with herbs*)	Côte-Rôtie; Côtes du Rhône-Villages	Bourgueil; Santenay
	Gigot d'agneau en croûte (*Leg of lamb in pastry*)	Châteauneuf-du-Pape rouge; Gigondas	Médoc
	Picodon	Cornas; Vacqueyras	Sancerre rouge
	Saint Marcellin	Lirac; Côtes du Rhône-Villages	Moulin-à-Vent
	Gâteau aux marrons glacés (*Chestnut cake*)	Muscat de Beaumes-de-Venise	Muscat de Frontignan
	Digestif: Frigolet; Marc de Château Rayas		
Provence and the Midi	Aperitif: Muscat de Beaumes-de-Venise		
	Pissaladière (*Onion, olive and anchovy tart*)	Provence blanc or rosé	Sylvaner
	Ratatouille (*Provençal vegetable stew*)	Châteauneuf-du-Pape blanc; Tavel rosé	Crozes-Hermitage blanc
	Soupe au pistou (*Vegetable soup with basil*)	Provence blanc	Pinot Blanc d'Alsace
	Loup de mer au fenouil (*Sea bass with fennel*)	Bellet blanc; Provence blanc	Hermitage blanc
	Rouget à la niçoise (*Baked mullet with tomatoes and anchovies*)	Bellet rosé	Rosé des Riceys
	Bouillabaisse (*Mediterranean rockfish soup*)	Cassis blanc; Provence blanc	Graves blanc
	Canard aux olives (*Duck with olives*)	Bandol; Provence rouge	Saint-Joseph rouge
	Poulet au riz au safran (*Chicken with saffron rice*)	Provence rosé; Tavel rosé	Rosé de Marsannay
	Filet de boeuf froid à la niçoise (*Cold roast beef in tarragon aspic*)	Vin de Corse; Provence rouge	Lirac rouge
	Banon	Coteaux d'Aix-en-Provence; Corbières	Côtes du Rhône-Villages
	Sorbet au citron (*Lemon sorbet*)	Muscat de Frontignan	Champagne demi-sec
	Digestif: Banyuls Rancio		

Dish	Local Wines	Other Wines

Champagne

Aperitif: Champagne Crémant; Champagne Blanc de Blancs

Terrine de lapin en croûte *(Rabbit terrine in pastry)* ⎫	Coteaux Champenois blanc	Montagny; Rully blanc
Boudin blanc *(Chicken, veal and pork sausage)* ⎬	Champagne Blanc de Blancs	Vouvray
Feuilleté d'escargots à la champenoise *(Snails in puff pastry with champagne sauce)* ⎭	Champagne non-vintage	Chablis

Matelote champenoise *(Eel, pike and carp stew)*	Champagne non-vintage	Meursault
Truite aux amandes *(Trout with almonds)*	Champagne Blanc de Blancs; Champagne non-vintage	Riesling
Paupiettes de saumon au champagne *(Stuffed fillets of salmon with champagne sauce)*	Blanc de Blancs Crémant; Blanc de Blancs vintage	Chassagne-Montrachet blanc

Potée champenoise *(Champagne pot au feu)*	Champagne 'monocrus'; Champagne non-vintage	Chinon; Chénas
Rognons de veau sautés à la crème *(Calves' kidneys with cream)*	Champagne vintage; Champagne rosé	Beaune
Poulet au Bouzy *(Chicken in red wine)*	Bouzy rouge; Coteaux Champenois rouge	Savigny-lès-Beaune
Cuissot de sanglier au genevièvre *(Roast leg of wild boar with juniper berries)*	Champagne vintage, type Blanc de Noirs	Pomerol; Hermitage

Chaource ⎫	Coteaux Champenois rouge	Volnay
Carré de l'est ⎬	Champagne Blanc de Noirs	Mercurey
Pierre Robert ⎭		Brouilly

Poires à la champenoise *(Pear tart with frangipane)*	Champagne demi-sec	Vouvray demi-sec

Digestif; fine or marc de champagne

Burgundy

Aperitif: Kir; Kir Royale

Jambon persillé *(Parsleyed ham)*	Bourgogne Aligoté; Chablis	Anjou blanc
Escargots à la bourguignonne *(Snails in garlic butter)*	Chablis; Bourgogne blanc	Ménétou-Salon
Gâteau de foies de volaille *(Chicken liver pâté)*	Côte de Beaune blanc or rouge	Pouilly-Fumé

Pochouse *(Fresh-water fish stew with white wine)*	Meursault	Pinot Blanc d'Alsace
Quenelles de brochet *(Pike dumplings)*	Saint-Romain; Corton Charlemagne	Sancerre
Andouillette à la lyonnaise *(Fried chitterling sausage with onion and vinegar)*	Pouilly-Fuissé; Saint Véran	Vouvray sec

Coq au Chambertin *(Cockerel in Chambertin sauce)*	Chambertin; Gevrey-Chambertin; Morey-Saint-Denis	Châteauneuf-du-Pape
Côtes de veau dijonnaise *(Veal chops with mustard)*	Fixin; Mercurey; Morgon	Fronsac
Boeuf bourguignonne *(Burgundy beef stew)*	Pommard; Moulin-à-Vent	Cornas
Râble de lièvre *(Saddle of hare)*	Corton; Nuits-Saint-Georges	Hermitage rouge

Saint-Florentin	Chablis Grand Cru	Arbois blanc
Epoisses	Chablis Grand Cru; Irancy rouge	Pinot Noir d'Alsace
Montrachet	Fleurie; Pommard	Bouzy rouge

Sorbet de cassis *(Cassis sorbet)*	Crémant de Bourgogne rouge	Champagne demi-sec

Digestif: Marc or Fine de Bourgogne

Loire Valley

Aperitif: Vouvray Pétillant

Andouille/Rillettes/Rillons *(Mixed local meats)*	Anjou blanc; Quincy	Bourgogne Aligoté
Mousse chaude de foies de volaille *(Warm mousse of chicken livers)*	Sancerre; Pouilly-Fumé	Chablis Premier Cru
Feuilleté d'asperges *(Asparagus in puff pastry with butter sauce)*	Pouilly-Fumé; Vouvray sec	Riesling; Saint-Joseph blanc

Saumon à l'oseille *(Salmon with sorrel)*	Pouilly-Fumé; Savennières	Corton-Charlemagne
Brochet au beurre blanc *(Pike with white butter sauce)*	Anjou blanc; Vouvray sec	Bourgogne blanc
Petite friture *(Fried whitebait)*	Sancerre; Pouilly-Fumé	Mâcon blanc; Entre-Deux-Mers

Rôti de porc aux pruneaux *(Roast pork with prunes)*	Chinon; Sancerre rouge	Côte de Beaune-Villages
Fricassé de volaille/lapin *(Fricassé of chicken/rabbit)*	Saint-Nicolas-de-Bourgueil; Champigny	Médoc
Canard sauvage grillé *(Grilled wild duck)*	Chinon; Anjou rouge	Pomerol

Crottin de chavignol	Sancerre blanc	Beaujolais-Villages
Port Salut	Chinon	Saint-Amour
Sainte-Maure	Sancerre; Bourgueil	Saint-Emilion

Tarte tatin *(Caramelized upside-down apple tart)*	Quarts de Chaume; Coteaux du Layon	Jurançon doux

Digestif: Marc de Vouvray; Cognac

Bordeaux and the South-West

Aperitif: Champagne; Lillet blanc

Jambon de Bayonne *(Cured Bayonne ham)*	Cahors; Madiran	Bourgueil
Terrine de gibier *(Game terrine)*	Fronsac; Pomerol	Crozes-Hermitage
Foie gras de canard chaud aux raisins *(Duck liver with grapes)*	Barsac; Sauternes	Tokay
Huîtres et saucisses chaudes *(Hot oysters and sausages)*	Entre-Deux-Mers; Bordeaux blanc or rouge	Muscadet

Alose poché froid sauce verte *(Cold poached shad with green herb mayonnaise)*	Graves blanc	Savennières
Lamproies au vin rouge *(Eel stew with red wine)*	Saint-Emilion; Graves rouge	Bouzy rouge
Cabillaud à la bordelaise *(Baked cod steaks)*	Graves blanc or rouge	Cassis blanc

Entrecôte à la bordelaise *(Beef steak with marrow)*	Médoc; Graves rouge	Chinon
Ris de veau aux truffes *(Sweetbreads with truffles)*	Margaux; Saint-Emilion	Volnay
Salmis de pigeon *(Salmis of pigeon)*	Pomerol; Saint-Estèphe	Gigondas
Gigot d'agneau pré salé *(Leg of lamb from the salt marshes)*	Pauillac; Saint-Julien	Chambolle-Musigny

Gouda	Médoc	Vosne-Romanée
Roquefort	Sauternes; Jurançon doux	Saint-Joseph rouge

Pignola *(Pine nut cake)*	Barsac; Loupiac	Vouvray demi-sec

Digestif: armagnac; cognac

245

Comités Interprofessionnels des Vins et Spiritueux

These semi-public bodies, which are made up both of delegates of the producers and the négociants, and of representatives of the various administrative services, play an important role at all levels of wine production and marketing. One of their functions is to inform the consumer: most of them have a secretariat and a variety of informational material, such as maps and brochures. Anyone who requires information about a specific wine-producing area should apply to the organization responsible for that particular region.

ALSACE
CIVA, Comité interprofessionnel des vins d'Alsace, 8 place de-Lattre-de-Tassigny, 68003 Colmar Cedex.
ANJOU/SAUMUR
CIVAS, Conseil interprofessionnel des vins d'Anjou et de Saumur, 21 boulevard Foch, 49000 Angers.
BEAUJOLAIS
UIVB, Union interprofessionnelle des vins du Beaujolais, 210 boulevard Vermorel, 69400 Villefranche-sur-Saône.
BERGERAC
CIVRB, Comité interprofessionnel des vins de la région de Bergerac, 2 place du Docteur-Cayla, 24100 Bergerac.
BORDEAUX
CIVB, Conseil interprofessionnel du vin de Bordeaux, 1 cours du 30 juillet, 33000 Bordeaux.
BURGUNDY/MÂCON
CIVBM, Comité interprofessionnel des vins de Bourgogne et Mâcon, Maison du tourisme, avenue du Maréchal-de-Lattre-de-Tassigny, 71000 Mâcon.
CHAMPAGNE
CIVC, Comité interprofessionnel du vin de Champagne, BP 135, 51204 Epernay Cedex.
CORSICA
GIVIC, Groupement interprofessionnel des vins de l'Isle de Corse, 6 rue Gabriel Péri, 20000 Bastia.
COTEAUX D'AIX EN PROVENCE
Syndicat des Coteaux d'Aix-en-Provence, Maison des Agriculteurs, avenue Henri Poutier, 13626 Aix-en-Provence Cedex 01.
COTE D'OR/YONNE
CIVB, Comité interprofessionnel de la Côte-d'Or et de l'Yonne pour les vins AOC de Bourgogne, rue Henri-Dunant, 21200 Beaune.
COTES DE PROVENCE
CIVCP, Comité interprofessionnel des vins des Côtes de Provence, 3 avenue Jean-Jaurès, 83460 Les-Arcs-sur-Argens.
COTES DU RHONE
CIVDR, Comité interprofessionnel des vins des Côtes du Rhône, Maison du tourisme et du vin, 41 cours Jean-Jaurès, 84000 Avignon.
FITOU/CORBIERES/MINERVOIS
CIVFCM, Conseil interprofessionnel des vins de Fitou, Corbières et Minervois, RN 113, 11200 Lézignan-Corbières.
Syndicat du Cru Corbières, RN113, 11200 Lézignan-Corbières.
Syndicat des Côteaux du Languedoc, Le Mas de Saporta, BP 9, 34972 Lattes Cedex.
Syndicat du Cru Minervois, 10 boulevard Louis Blazin, 34210 Olonzac.
GIP Côtes du Roussillon, 19 avenue de Grande-Bretagne, 66000 Perpignan.
JURA
Société de Viticulture du Jura, avenue du 4ème RI, BP 396, 39016 Lons le Saunier Cedex.
PAYS NANTAIS
CIVOPN, Comité interprofessionnel des vins d'origine du Pays Nantais, 17 rue des Etats, 44000 Nantes.
SOUTH WEST
CIVG, Comité interprofessionnel des vins de Gaillac, 8 rue du Père Gibrat, 81600 Gaillac.
Union interprofessionnel du Vin de Cahors, BP 61, 46002 Cahors Cedex.
Syndicat de Défense des Vins de Jurançon, 2 rue des Ecoles, 64110 Jurançon.
Syndicat de Défense et de Contrôle des Vins de Madiran, 65700 Maubourguet.
TOURAINE
CIVT, Comité interprofessionnel des vins de Touraine, 19 square Prosper-Mérimée, 37000 Tours.
VINS DOUX NATURELS
CIVDN, Comité interprofessionnel des vins doux naturels, 19 avenue de Grande-Bretagne, 66000 Perpignan.

Bibliography

Benson, Jeffrey and Mackenzie, Alastair, *The Wines of Saint-Emilion and Pomerol*, Sotheby Publications, 1983.

Blanchet, Suzanne, *Les Vins du Val de Loire*, ed Jema SA, Saumur, 1982.

Brejoux, Pierre, *Les Vins de la Loire*, ed Revue du Vin de France.

Broadbent, Michael, *The Great Vintage Wine Book*, Mitchell Beazley, 1980.

Brunel, Gaston, *Guide des Vignobles et Caves des Côtes du Rhône*, ed L-C Lattes, Paris, 1980.

Coates, Clive, *Claret*, Century, 1982.

Coates, Clive, *The Wines of France*, Random Century, 1990.

Debuigne, G, *Dictionnaire des Vins*, ed Larousse.

Dovaz, Michel, *Encyclopédie des Crus Classés du Bordelais*, Julliard, 1981.

Dovaz, Michel, *L'Encyclopédie des Vins de Champagne*, Julliard, 1983.

Duijker, Hubrecht, *Grands Bordeaux Rouges*, Fernand Nathan, 1977.

Duijker, Hubrecht, *Les Bons Vins de Bordeaux*, Fernand Nathan, 1982.

Duijker, Hubrecht, *Les Grands Vins de Bourgogne*, Fernand Nathan, 1980.

Duijker, Hubrecht, *The Loire, Alsace and Champagne*, Mitchell Beazley, 1982.

Dumay, Raymond, *Guide du Vin*, ed Stock.

Feret et Fils, *Bordeaux et ses Vins*, Bordeaux, 1982.

Forbes, Patrick, *Champagne*, Gollancz, 1967.

George, Rosemary, *French Country Wines*, Faber, 1990.

Hanson, Anthony, *Burgundy*, Faber, London, 1982; Boston 1983.

Hugel, Jean, *Gastronomy and Wines of Alsace*, private printing.

Johnson, Hugh, *The Wine Companion*, Mitchell Beazley, 1983.

Johnson, Hugh, *The World Atlas of Wine*, Mitchell Beazley, London, 1985; Simon and Schuster, New York, 1985.

Le Guide Hachette des Vins, Hachette, Paris, 1991.

Le Guide Gault-Millau des Vins, Paris, 1991.

Lichine, Alexis, *Encyclopedia of Wines and Spirits*, Alfred A Knopf, New York, 1974; Cassell, London, 1978.

Livingstone-Learmonth, John and Master, Melvyn, *The Wines of the Rhône*, Faber, London, 1983; Boston 1983.

Parker, Robert, *Bordeaux*, Dorling Kindersley, 1986.

Parker, Robert, *Burgundy*, Dorling Kindersley, 1991.

Parker, Robert, *The Wines of the Rhône Valley and Provence*, Dorling Kindersley, 1990.

Penning-Rowsell, Edmund, *The Wines of Bordeaux*, Penguin, 1989.

Peppercorn, David, *Bordeaux*, Faber, 1991.

Peppercorn, David, *The Wines of Bordeaux*, Mitchell Beazley, 1986.

Poulain, René and Jacquelin, Louis, *Vignes et Vins de France*, ed Flammarion.

Poupon, Pierre and Forgeot, Pierre, *The Wines of Burgundy*, Presses Universitaires de France, 1979.

Ray, Cyril, *Bollinger*, Heinemann, 1971.

Ray, Cyril, *The Wines of France*, Allen Lane, 1976.

Renvoisé, Guy, *Guides des Vins d'Alsace*, Solarama, 1983.

La Revue du Vin de France, ed Leader, Paris.

Robinson, Jancis, *Vines, Grapes and Wines*, Mitchell Beazley, 1986.

Stevenson, Tom, *Sotheby's World Wine Encyclopedia*, Dorling Kindersley, 1988.

Sutcliffe, Serena, *The Wines of Burgundy*, Mitchell Beazley, 1986.

Sutcliffe, Serena, *A Celebration of Champagne*, Mitchell Beazley, 1988.

Vandyke-Price, Pamela, *The Wines of Alsace*, Sotheby Publications, 1984.

Woutaz, Fernand, *Dictionnaire des Appellations*, ed Litec, Paris, 1982.

Glossary

Appellation communale the *appellation* covering a commune, eg Pauillac, where there are different *crus* from specific vineyards.

Appellation contrôlée the system controlling what types of grapes may be planted where, what wine may be made from them and how, and what it will be called.

Appellation régionale the *appellation* covering a sub-region of a main type of wine.

Blanc de Blancs white wine made exclusively from white grapes. This term is most often seen referring to champagne or sparkling wine, where the juice of white and black grapes is usually fermented together.

Blanc de Noirs white wine made exclusively from black grapes. This term is generally reserved for champagne made solely from the Pinot Noir grape.

Botrytis cinerea noble rot or *pourriture noble* (*qv*).

Brut generally the driest version of champagne and other sparkling wines. Wines totally without *dosage* (*qv*) are known as *brut zéro, brut de brut, brut intégral.*

Cépage noble one of the few grape varieties that consistently makes fine wine.

Chambré used of a wine which has taken the temperature of the room after being brought from the cellar.

Champenisé used of wine that has been made sparkling by the *méthode champenoise* (*qv*).

Climat specific vineyard, generally in Burgundy, not classified as Grand or Premier Cru.

En coteaux vines planted on slopes, usually making superior wine.

Crémant sparkling wine that is less sparkling than champagne or *vin mousseux* but more sparkling than a *vin pétillant*. The pressure inside the bottle is between 3 and 4 atmospheres.

Crus vineyards classified geographically or by reputation: Grand Crus (great growths), Premiers Crus (first growths) and so on.

Cuvée a wine from a selected barrel or vat, generally superior to the norm. In Champagne it means the wine from the first pressing.

Cuverie where the wine ferments.

Dégorgement the act of expulsion of sediment formed by the secondary fermentation in bottle to make a sparkling wine.

Demi-muid large oak barrel, generally 600 litres.

Demi-sec between sweet and dry, with the sweetness definitely discernible due either to residual sugar or to *dosage* (*qv*).

Dosage the sweetening of a sparkling wine, especially champagne, to cover natural high acidity. According to the amount of sweetener added, the wine may be *brut, sec, demi-sec* or *doux* (*qv*).

Doux fully sweet. The result of residual sugar in still wines, or *dosage* in sparkling wines.

Elevage the "bringing-up" of a wine, usually in barrel, prior to bottling.

Encépagement the make-up of grapes in a given wine.

En primeur used of a wine that is drunk or sold very young.

En sec style of vinification used to make dry wines from wines that are traditionally sweet.

Flûte either the tall, elegantly shaped bottle used in Alsace and at Château Grillet, or the equally elegant style of glass recommended for champagne.

Foudre large wooden cask, immobile, for fermenting or for storing wine.

Garrigue tough, arid soil in the southern Rhône Valley.

Générique a regional AOC wine without a *cru* or communal *appellation*.

Gouleyant used of a wine that is easy to drink.

Goût de terroir distinctive taste or style imparted by the combination of grape variety and soil.

Gras rich, full-bodied.

Gravier gravelly soil, always found near a river.

Tends to make elegant wines.
Gros rouge dull, heavy, uninteresting wine.

Lieu dit see *Climat*
Liqueur d'expédition the sweetener used in the act of *dosage* (*qv*).
Liqueur de tirage the sugar added to a still wine at the time of bottling, to precipitate and prolong the secondary fermentation necessary to produce the required degree of sparkle.

Macération carbonique a method of vinification in which the grapes are placed whole in the vats to achieve rapid fermentation under pressure from their natural gases. Used to produce fruity red wines for early drinking, typically in the Beaujolais and now in the Loire and Midi.
Marc either the 4,000 kilos of grapes in a champagne press, or an *eau-de-vie* made from macerating spirit with the "cake" of grape skins after pressing.
Mas Vineyard area or *climat* (*qv*) in the northern Rhône.
Méthode champenoise the method used in Champagne to make a still wine sparkle by means of secondary fermentation in bottle rather than in cask or vat. It is a long and expensive process, now used for most good sparkling wines (see page 228).
Méthode dioise *see* Méthode rurale.
Méthode gaillacoise *see* Méthode rurale.
Méthode rurale old-fashioned method of making sparkling wine, still used in Gaillac, Die and Limoux. No *liqueur de tirage* (*qv*) is added, the secondary fermentation taking place with sugar still present in the wine due to retarded alcoholic fermentation.
Moelleux very sweet, luscious white wines, between *doux* (*qv*) and *liquoreux*.

Négociant the middleman between the growers and the retailers.
Noble rot *see* Pouirriture noble.

Oeil de perdrix pale rosé, literally "partridge-eye".

Perlé very slightly sparkling, often discernible only on the palate.
Pétillant semi-sparkling wine with not more than 3 atmospheres of pressure inside the bottle.
Pièce a general word for barrel, but only the small 215 or 225 litre size.
Plafond limité de classement (PLC) quantity of wine allowed to be declared above the permitted yield in a specific *appellation* (see page 11).
Pourriture noble noble rot, or the fungus which attacks white grapes in specific vineyards in the Loire Valley and the South-West, essential to making a great sweet white wine.

Rosé de Noirs rosé made from black grapes only.
Rapé the percentage of wine discarded in Châteauneuf-du-Pape and Gigondas to maintain quality.

Saignée process of drawing off fermenting juice of red grapes to make a rosé.
Sec dry, taken as meaning bone-dry except for sparkling wines, where it means a little less than dry.
Sélection des grains nobles very late picking of selected berries from *botrytis*-affected bunches, specific to Alsace.
Sève sappy, racy, the inherent style and punch of a wine.
Sur lie used of white wine which is bottled from the fine lees from the first (alcoholic) fermentation within the year following the vintage.

Teinturier grapes black grapes with coloured rather than colourless juice whose only positive role is to add colour to certain *vin de pays*.
Tendre delicate, soft, non-acidic wine, light and usually slightly sweet.
Terroir the combination of soil and climate. The main element in the taste of a wine along with the grape variety.
Tête-de-cuvée the finest casks or *cuves* of a particular vintage.
Tonneau a wooden barrel or cask, of any size. This word is also used for the quotation of prices of Bordeaux wines.
 1 tonneau = 4 pièces = 1,200 bottles.
Tout court (eg Beaujolais) the simple *appellation*, as opposed to the Villages *appellation*.

Tries successive picking of a vineyard to harvest only the ripest grapes.

Tuffeau chalky-clay soil in the Saumur and Touraine regions on which some of the best red wines are made.

Vendage tardive late picking of very ripe grapes.

Vin de base used in connection with sparkling wines to denote what the still wine was.

Vin de café red wine light in colour and alcohol.

Vin de carafe pleasant wine for everyday drinking.

Vins de cépage wines where the grape variety takes precedence over the region of origin. Most common in branded wines or for *vin de pays*.

Vin de comptoir generally pleasant wine for everyday drinking served in French cafés.

Vin de garde a wine which should be kept a long time.

Vin de pays everyday wine from a specific region, but less complexly controlled than AOC or VDQS wines.

Vin de presse wine from the grapes pressed after fermentation has finished or, in Champagne, from further pressings.

Vins de terroir wines where the influence of local soil and climate dominates that of the grape variety.

Vin gris very pale rosé wine, almost grey in colour, always light and fresh.

Vin liquoreux very sweet white wine, generally made from grapes affected by *pourriture noble* (*qv*).

Vin mousseux sparkling wine, made either by secondary fermentation in bottle or in tank, or, for inexpensive wines, the addition of carbon dioxide.

Vin ordinaire plain wine with no regional or varietal origin.

Vin tranquille non-sparkling wine.

Chateau Langoa

Index

Acknowledgements

The publishers wish to thank the following organisations and individuals for their kind permission to reproduce the photographs in this book:

J Allan Cash Photolibrary: 128; Nick Barlow: 143; Michael Busselle: 30 top, 149; Cephas Picture Library: Andy Christodolo 121 / Mick Rock 38, 51, 54, 75, 79, 81, 125, 192, 199, 206, 218, 234, 238, 239, 242, 243; Hubrecht Duijker: 96, 135, 165; Patrick Eager: 35, 39, 67, 70, 93, 104, 109, 153, 157, 160, 164, 185, 219, 227, 230; Robert Estall: 116; Susan Griggs Agency: 101, 113, 173, 176, 177 bottom; Robert Harding Picture Library: 134, 215; Denis Hughes-Gilbey: 194, 198; Scope: 47, 97, 100, 169, 211 / Jean Luc Barde 59 / Daniel Faure 30 bottom / Michael Guillard 3, 43 / Jean Daniel Sudres 130; Spectrum Colour Library: 214; Alan Williams: 63; Jon Wyand: 62, 71, 172; Zefa Picture Library: 177 top.